D1338157

DOMINION OF GOD

DOMINION OF GOD

Christendom and Apocalypse in the Middle Ages

BRETT EDWARD WHALEN

HARVARD UNIVERSITY PRESS
Cambridge, Massachusetts, and London, England 2009

Copyright © 2009 by the President and Fellows of Harvard College

ALL RIGHTS RESERVED

Printed in the United States of America

Library of Congress Cataloging-in-Publication Data
Whalen, Brett Edward.
Dominion of God: Christendom and apocalypse in the Middle Ages /
Brett Edward Whalen.
p.   cm.
Includes bibliographical references (p.   ) and index.
ISBN 978-0-674-03629-1 (alk. paper)
1. History—Religious aspects—Christianity—History of doctrines—Middle Ages,
600–1500.   2. Millennialism—History of doctrines—Middle Ages, 600–1500.
3. Popes—Temporal power—History—To 1500.   4. Church history—Middle
Ages, 600–1500.   5. Europe—Church history—600–1500.   I. Title.
BX1069.5.W53   2009
282'.40902—dc22   2009010518

To Lynn, my mother

Contents

Introduction

In the Gospels, Christ predicts to his disciples that the end of days is approaching and will bring about a great tribulation marked by war, pestilence, famine, and the appearance of false prophets.[1] He also declares that his message of salvation will be preached throughout the entire world and will reach all of its peoples before the consummation of history. Although this promised course of events did not come about as quickly as his followers were no doubt expecting, subsequent generations of believers continued to anticipate the eventual fulfillment of their messiah's words. Over the following centuries, a distinctly Christian apocalyptic scenario developed that included the universal spread of the Gospel before the coming of the false messiah, Antichrist, his persecution of the elect, and his ultimate defeat with Christ's victorious return in Final Judgment. The devil, so to speak, was in the details. The earliest Christians vigorously debated the nature of those Last Things, including the question of whether there would be a "millennial" age of peace and prosperity on earth before the end of time. One way or another, Christian believers ever since have had to contend with this dual apocalyptic heritage of hope for the universal realization of their faith and dread of the suffering that awaited the faithful.[2]

During the Middle Ages, the Christian inhabitants of Europe added new layers to this contested vision for the outcome of history. Some of them predicted that the Roman papacy and its followers would reform the Western Church, ridding it of avarice and corruption, restore the wayward Christians of the Eastern Church to the catholic fold, and secure the holy places of Jerusalem from the dominion of the infidels. Coming on the heels of these marvelous changes, pagan peoples would convert and the Jews would finally enter into the Church. This worldwide transformation meant more than the spread of Christianity in fulfillment of Christ's prediction that there would be "one fold" and "one shepherd."[3] Rather, members of the Roman Church envisioned the expansion of a certain kind of Christian religious community—Christendom, the union of right-believing and right-practicing Christians assembled under Christ's deputy shepherds, the popes of Rome. Although the Kingdom of Heaven was declared to be not of this world, Christendom decidedly was. Restricted in the present to the borders of the Western or Latin Church, Christendom was thought by contemporaries to be limitless in its potential. It would, they believed, reach everywhere and everyone before the end of time.

Similar to "empire" and "nation," Christendom is a common term, but difficult to define with complete satisfaction. In reality, regional diversity and political fragmentation characterized the Christian territories of medieval Europe. The self-declared members of Christendom nevertheless viewed themselves as a people unified through their shared faith, their use of Latin as a sacred language, their mutual observance of religious rites, and their obedience to the Roman papacy. Simply put, Christendom formed the "whole society of Latin Christians and the lands they occupied."[4] Scholars of our own time view Christendom as a framework for cultural, religious, and social order. Looking back, they have labeled that union of Christian kingdoms and churches as (among other things) a "cultural community," a "religious community," a "socio-religious unity," and an "international culture."[5] Seen in this perspective, the premodern bonds of Christendom linger beneath the surface of modern Europe like the hidden words on a palimpsest, inspiring and haunting those who seek to understand the role of Christianity in the formation of European, if not Western, civilization.[6]

This book examines Christendom and the promise of its worldwide realization within the historical imagination of the Roman Church from the eleventh through the fourteenth centuries. This period marked the formation, apogee, and decline of the so-called "papal monarchy," an expression that captures the revolutionary claims of the medieval papacy to a position of spiritual and temporal supremacy over Christian society. Historians have generally focused their attention on the resulting clash between popes and emperors—a battle within Europe between the claimants of priestly authority and imperial power.[7] The Roman Church's vision of sacerdotal world order, however, also reshaped Western Christian perspectives on outside peoples and places, above all their Byzantine and Islamic neighbors. The papacy and its clerical supporters, in large part to assert their claims of primacy within Europe, redefined their place in God's plan for salvation, arguing that the Roman Church would assume a role of worldly leadership and pastoral dominion over rulers, churches, and communities everywhere as a prelude to the end of history.

Discussing medieval Christian "concepts of world unity," Ernst Kantorowicz observed that a "united world was indispensable for achieving that state of perfection which, it was generally recognized, would be established just before time ends and doomsday dawns. Thus the medieval Myth of World Unity has a predominantly messianic or eschatological character."[8] Christian eschatology, of course, did not simply relate to the future, but also depended upon a close reading of the past that informed the present and pointed toward events approaching on the horizon.[9] Christ's Second Coming in Final Judgment could not be understood without grasping the reality of his first Incarnation in the flesh. The Incarnation revealed in the Christian New Testament, in turn, led one back into the mysteries of the Jewish scriptures, the Christian Old Testament that "spiritually" contained the promise of Christ's divinity hidden within the "letter" of the Jewish Covenant. Those Hebrew holy writings recorded the course of history from the moment of creation and the lapse of humankind from God's grace that had set the wheel of temporal travails in motion. The unity of the world depended upon the unity of history, as revealed first and foremost through the mysteries of the Bible.[10]

Theology of history—the medieval equivalent to philosophy of history—provided members of the Roman Church with a sacral ideology, a basis for Rome's claims to speak for all believers, as well as peoples that had not yet accepted or heard the news of Christ. In recent years scholars have stressed the importance of historical thinking and writing for the formation of ethnic, national, and imperial identities, but they have yet to apply this insight to the notion of Christendom as an "imagined community" with a "usable" sense of history that determined its membership.[11] In this book I explore how Western Christians invoked historical schemes, narratives, prophecies, and apocalyptic scenarios to theorize the proper ordering of their world. Apocalyptic speculations are particularly instructive in this regard, since their fabricated nature is impossible to miss. Needless to say, history did not lead to the conclusions that Latin prophets, exegetes, and visionaries projected. This does not mean, however, that their interpretation of historical events is any less illuminating for our understanding of contemporary hopes, concerns, and actions. Politics informed the development of prophetic traditions, even as prophetic traditions influenced political realities. In short, politics and prophecy formed part of a "dialectical process."[12] If we overlook their interplay, privileging the former and disregarding the latter, we ignore a critical component of the way medieval Christians viewed themselves and their relationship with the outside world during an expansionary era of Europe's past.

It is widely recognized that the High Middle Ages formed an era of territorial growth and broadening horizons for Christian Europeans through their acts of conquest, crusading, settlement, and missionary activity across all of Europe's frontiers.[13] Leaving aside, for the moment, the Jewish communities that lived squarely within the territories of the Western Church, the borders of Christendom seem easiest to trace when set against the boundaries of lands where the inhabitants did not believe in Christianity (such as the Muslims) or did not practice their Christian faith in the same way as the followers of Rome (such as the Greek Christians of Byzantium). Certainly, the medieval expansion of Europe brought

The Known World. Universal Chronicle, fourteenth century.

Source: Bibliothèque Nationale de France, Paris, lat. 4922.

members of the Roman Church into a more intimate and sometimes violent state of contact with religious "Others," including Muslims and Greek Christians.[14] The crusades provide the best-known and most controversial example of Europe's expansionary capacity during this period, whether the crusaders were seizing Jerusalem from Islamic control in 1099 or Constantinople from Byzantine hands in 1204. There was more to notions of Christendom, however, than the mentality of "us versus them." Ambivalence characterized the idea of Christendom, which formed a limitless community of the faithful, a cosmic congregation, but also an earthly society of believers in the here-and-now. Christendom had borders and was universal. It could be spread by the righteous power of the sword or by the spiritual grace of God. Although contemporaries theorized Christian unity through sanctified violence directed against threatening outsiders, they also dreamed of an eschatological conversion, when the followers of Rome would restore schismatic Christian communities to the harmony of the faith and would spread Christianity among Jews, pagans, and infidels before the end of time. Within this apocalyptic ethnography, both Christian and non-Christian peoples had roles to play in the realization of history. The expectation of Christian world order relied—somewhat paradoxically—on mutually reinforcing languages of exclusion and inclusion, on the identification of God's enemies and the promise of their ultimate redemption, or at least their opportunity to be redeemed.

In his ground-breaking work *The Pursuit of the Millennium*, Norman Cohn highlighted the revolutionary potential of premodern apocalypticism, especially radical millenarianism, which expected a thoroughgoing and often violent transformation of society to pave the way for the coming of God's Kingdom.[15] The pursuit of Christendom, by contrast, engaged the historical and apocalyptic sensibilities of medieval Europe's ecclesiastical elite, sometimes including popes themselves, who anticipated the ultimate triumph of their sacerdotal authority on the grandest of scales. Whatever setbacks they confronted (and there were many), the advocates for a new kind of Christian order in the eleventh, twelfth, and thirteenth centuries asserted their vision of historical reality in some dramatically meaningful ways. In certain cases, such as the crusades, seemingly abstract clerical ideas about God's plan for salvation became a matter of life and death for Christians and non-Christians alike. During the period of their ascendancy, reforming popes and like-minded clergy crafted an imposing and formidable interpretation of history as a sacred process that conferred awesome privileges and responsibilities upon the priestly leadership of the Roman Church.

Even among the clerical elite, however, the eschatological promise of Christian renewal and expansion raised potentially troublesome questions. When exactly would these events happen? How and under whose agency? Just where would the changes in the present order of things stop? By the later thirteenth and fourteenth centuries, some of the most ardent proponents of a world united under the leadership of the Roman Church numbered among the most strident critics of contemporary mores and ecclesiastical institutions, including the papacy itself. Radicals, moderates, and conservatives alike invoked the providential design of history, calling for revolutionary change in current institutions, appealing for their modest reform, or celebrating their power in transcendental terms. In the multivalent symbolism of Latin apocalyptic thought, Rome might be the spiritual shepherd of an eschatological flock, but it could also represent the new "Babylon," a source of greed, corruption, and hypocrisy. It is not a coincidence that one of the final apocalyptic thinkers examined in this book, John of Rupescissa, spent much of his life in a papal prison at Avignon, allowed to record his prophecies but kept on a short leash until he died in 1365.

With the well-known decline of papal prestige in the fourteenth and early fifteenth centuries, accompanied by a temporary halt to Europe's expansionary energies, the impulse of Christians to spread their faith did not disappear. Christian Europeans continued to envision the conversion of the world, including lands that their predecessors never even knew existed. Speculation about the purpose of history, however, began to move in some new directions. For one thing, rising sentiments of national identification relocated the drive to expand the Christian faith. Even popes began to recognize the fact that kings and their servants would assure the promised triumph of Christianity in new lands. Imperial ideologies of history—never absent from the medieval debates between popes and emperors—began to enjoy a new prominence, especially during Europe's global expansion in the early modern era. Indeed, scholars of empire have

long recognized the continuities that bridged medieval and modern notions of imperial power and its universal claims, grounded in a sense of
manifest destiny that stretched from the origins of Roman dominion to
the age of overseas colonialism. What about Christendom and its worldwide realization? Did medieval prophecies of conversion anticipate the
secular "civilizing mission" and other European claims to stand in the
vanguard of historical progress? This is a vast and complex question. We
can begin our search for answers by looking at the historical sensibilities
that medieval Christians brought to bear on their own relationship with
the outside world during an era that is commonly associated with the first
expansion—if not the very making—of Europe.[16]

I

Christendom and the Origins of Papal Monarchy

In 991, a council of Frankish clergymen assembled at the Church of Saint Basle near Reims to resolve a bitter dispute over the city's episcopal see that had begun three years earlier with the death of the previous archbishop, Adalberon. The king of West Francia, Hugh Capet (r. 987–996), had appointed a cleric named Arnulf to replace the deceased prelate.[1] By doing do, Hugh passed over Adalberon's preferred successor, Gerbert of Aurillac, a notable scholar at the cathedral school in Reims. Arnulf, however, was subsequently accused of conspiring with his uncle, Duke Charles of Lorraine, against the king, wrecking havoc in the diocese when he briefly surrendered control of the city to his relation. On these grounds, the assembled churchmen formally deposed Arnulf and elected Gerbert in his place. During the council, the archbishop of Orléans decried an attempt by Arnulf's supporters to appeal the case to Rome. His words were written down (no doubt to a large extent invented) by Gerbert himself when he codified the acts of the council a few years later. The archbishop, also named Arnulf, did not deny the Roman Church's special status as the final court of appeals, but he lamented that the worthy popes of the past had long since vanished, replaced in present times by corrupt and unlearned successors. To whom exactly should one appeal, Arnulf asked, when "Antichrist sits in the temple of God, showing himself as if he were God"?[2] The church of Rome, he continued, had lost its authority over the great churches of Alexandria and Antioch with the "fall of the empire" to the Muslims, not to mention the loss of other churches in Africa, Asia, and Europe. Constantinople had withdrawn from Roman jurisdiction, and much of Spain no longer recognized papal judgments. This state of affairs provided a clear sign that the "falling away" of kingdoms from the Roman Empire, long expected by Christians as a sign of Antichrist's imminence (2 Thess. 2:3), referred "not just to peoples, but also to churches."[3]

By invoking such apocalyptic imagery, Arnulf of Orléans and Gerbert of Aurillac offered a scathing indictment of the current Roman papacy and a grim prognosis for the future. To be sure, the Roman Church had its defenders. A few years later, the papal legate charged with investigating this case, Leo of Saint Boniface, retorted that those who slandered Rome in such a manner represented the real "Antichrists," claiming somewhat weakly that legates from the churches of Egypt, Carthage, and Spain had in fact recently visited the Apostolic See.[4] Indeed, eight years after the council at Saint Basle, Gerbert's own attitude toward the authority of Rome changed considerably when his former student and patron Emperor Otto III (r. 983–1002) appointed him pope. Assuming the name of Sylvester II (r. 999–1003), Gerbert eagerly supported the young imperial ruler's aspirations for a "renovation" of the Christian Roman Empire. Deliberately cultivating the memory of past rulers such as the first Christian emperor, Constantine I (r. 306–337), and the first Carolingian emperor, Charlemagne (r. 768–814), Otto and Sylvester envisioned an age of restoration and expansion for both church and empire under the auspices of Otto's sacral rule.[5] The times were propitious for such an endeavor, or at least they suggested that the approach of the new millennium would bring about a transformation in the existing condition of the faithful. Whether fearful about the rise of Antichrist or hopeful for an era of renewal before the end, contemporaries traded in the language of eschatological expectation with colorful anticipation. In any event, the world did soon end for Otto and Sylvester, who died in 1002 and 1003, respectively, taking their ephemeral vision of glorified Christian Roman Empire to their graves.[6]

Roughly seventy years later, another pope, Gregory VII (r. 1073–1085), formulated his own aspirations for the reform and renewal of Christian churches, peoples, and kingdoms. His ambitions, however, expressed themselves in some radically different ways from those of his papal predecessor around the year 1000. Gregory did not look for the young German emperor, Henry IV (r. 1056–1106), to take the lead in transforming, purifying, and extending the borders of the Christian faith. To the contrary, he believed that it was Henry's place to support the Apostolic See of Rome in those very same endeavors. As Gregory queried on one occasion, "Who doubts that the priests of Christ are to be considered as fathers and masters of kings and princes and of all believers?"[7] Turning his gaze outward, the pope looked upon a world where the might of Christian princes was expanding into territories that had long suffered under the dominion of the infidels, recovering them for the patrimony of Saint Peter. Places such as Spain and Sicily once again recognized the authority and judgments of Rome. Looking eastward, Gregory realized that the ancient concord between the Latin and Greek Churches had faltered, but he confidently asserted that Constantinople would once again return to a state of harmony with Rome, just like a daughter looking to her mother. The pope was painfully aware that unbelievers threatened the Christians of the Greek Empire, doing the Devil's work and slaughtering them "just like cattle."[8] In 1074, he proposed an audacious solution to this sad state of affairs: The pope would lead an expedition of his Western followers to free the Eastern Church from bondage, pressing onward to Jerusalem.[9]

What had transpired between the papacies of Sylvester II and Gregory VII to bring about such a profound change in the papal conception of the Roman Church and its circumstances in the world? Modern historians use the catch-all term "reform" to describe this far-reaching transformation, a label which reflects the self-declared belief of eleventh-century "reformers" that the past provided a model for correcting perceived abuses and shortcomings in the present.[10] As is often the case with those who claim the mantle of reform, their goals involved a great deal of innovation. To secure the "liberty" (libertas) of the Church, that is, its freedom from secular interference, the reformers campaigned against simony and clerical marriage, common practices now redefined as heresies polluting the body of the faithful. Beyond these immediate ends, they eventually set their eyes on a greater prize—nothing less than a reordering of Christian society by fully subordinating the power of temporal rulers to the bearers of priestly authority, with the bishops of Rome standing first and foremost among them. To secure these potentially disruptive goals within medieval Christian society, the papacy and its network of supporters formulated an innovative and provocative concept of Christendom as a universal community united under papal leadership and pastoral guidance. This basic principle revolutionized the way the leadership of the Roman Church viewed the properly ordered, right-believing assembly of peoples, churches, and kingdoms that recognized the papacy as governing the norms and practices of their faith, if not their lives.[11]

Even as the supporters of the papal reform fought to realize their vision of Christendom within the immediate bounds of the Western Church, they projected their dream of world order outward to encompass other Christian communities that were not properly obedient to Rome—at least not yet. Potentially speaking, the entire world formed a part of Christendom and by extension a papal patrimony, delegated by Christ to Saint Peter, and through Peter to his successors, the bishops of Rome. The current reality, of course, looked vastly different. No one was more aware of this uncomfortable disjuncture than the eleventh-century papacy and its partisans. In response, they began the process of trying to reconcile the difference between Christendom's present finitude and its universal potential. Central to that enterprise was a theology of history that projected the boundless authority of the Roman Church into the past, situated it firmly in the present, and hinted at its destiny in the future. God's will was timeless, but the bishops of Rome possessed historical prerogatives and obligations in the fulfillment of the divine plan on earth until its apocalyptic consummation. Indeed, by its very nature, the central question of the reform movement—how to properly order Christendom—was implicitly eschatological. A rightly organized, purified, and global Christian society moved one step closer to the transcendental realization of history. Pushed to extreme conclusions, the political theology of the reform papacy implied a collapsing of the boundary between secular and ecclesiastical governance, leaving the pope as the sole impresario of a unified world that portended the coming Kingdom of God.

To understand what was at stake in this reconfiguration of sacred history, we need to look back before the time of Gregory VII, farther back even than the papacy of Leo IX (r. 1048–1054), the first Roman pontiff who openly pressed for a new kind of papal leadership over Christendom. The diffuse origins of a desire for the renewal of religious life dated back to the later tenth and early eleventh centuries, to the same era when a cleric like Gerbert of Aurillac could lament the historical decline of Roman authority. Above all, we need to consider the preexisting and often contentious parameters of belief in the Latin theological tradition regarding the knowable and unknowable nature of the divine plan for history, especially where imperial power was concerned. Since the patristic era in the fourth and fifth centuries, empire had played a prominent role in shaping the way Christians organized their views of the past, confronted the present, and grappled with the mysteries of the future. By the time of the papal reform, the notion of Christian imperial might possessed a historical pedigree that stretched back centuries, occupying a place of eminence in both legends and prophecies. Emperors embodied a long-standing form of Christian universalism that the nascent papal monarchy had somehow to co-opt or displace. If they were to establish their own historical credentials as providential agents, the popes of Rome had a great deal of catching up to do.

Empire and Antichrist at the Dawn of the New Millennium

In 954, around the time that Gerbert of Aurillac was born, the Frankish Abbot Adso of Montier-en-Der dedicated a tract called *On the Birth and Time of Antichrist* to Gerberga, queen of King Louis IV (r. 936–954) of West Francia.[12] Although conservative in tone, his work suggested a growing concern with the approach of the "apocalyptic year" 1000. Drawing upon a rich if sometimes diffuse tradition of Christian thinking about the eschatological opponent of Christ, Adso crafted a concise and gripping account of the final days. Antichrist, he informed his readers, would be born among the Jews in Babylon, would come to Jerusalem, perform false miracles, and be received by the Jews as the true messiah.[13] Through guile and trickery, he would spread his message across the world, seducing many Christians to his cause, including kings and rulers, while persecuting those who refused to follow him. Adso described the arrival of the "two witnesses," Elijah and Enoch, sent by God to sustain the faithful through their preaching during Antichrist's three-and-a-half-year reign, when Elijah, Enoch, and many others would suffer martyrdom. Around this time, some of the Jews inspired by the two witnesses would finally turn to the Christian faith, fulfilling the promise of Saint Paul (Rom. 9:27; 11:25) that the "remnant of Israel" would convert before the "fullness of the Gentiles" entered into the Church. After Antichrist's defeat with the return of Christ, Final Judgment would not happen immediately. Following earlier exegetes, Adso allowed for a brief space of time before the end of the world, perhaps as a period of "rest" for the faithful or penance for those seduced by Antichrist.[14]

When would all of these things happen? Adso did not exactly say. His work, although compelling, did not imply that he believed himself to be living on the brink of immediate apocalyptic tribulations. Above all, he maintained that the persecution of Antichrist would not happen until the "falling away" of the kingdoms and peoples that lived under the dominion of the Roman Empire, "the restraining force" that held back the end of history. "Granted," Adso observed, "we see that the Roman Empire is for the most part destroyed, nevertheless, as long as the kings of the Franks last, who ought rightfully to hold Roman imperial power, the dignity of Roman rule will not totally perish, since it will stand in their kings."[15] Adso was far from the first Christian thinker to assert that the end of the Roman Empire and its division into a series of petty kingdoms would provide an unerring sign that the final days were drawing near. Before this happened, however, he believed that imperial power under Frankish auspices would in fact enjoy its greatest extent and days of glory. In his tract, Adso predicted the rise of a final emperor, the "greatest of all rulers," who would defeat the infidels, lay down his scepter and crown on the Mount of Olives, and bring about the "end and consummation of the Roman and Christian Empire" before the coming of Antichrist.[16]

Like many historians, exegetes, and theologians before him, Adso of Montier-en-Der exposed a contradiction that lay at the heart of the Christian historical imagination. After all, God's plan is ultimately unfathomable. As Christ remonstrates his followers about the coming of the end, "Of that day and hour no one knows, not the angels of heaven, but the Father alone" (Matt. 24:36), or again, "It is not for you to know the times or moments" (Acts 1:7). At the same time, Christians believed that they needed to pay a great deal of attention to the signs that might offer them a glimpse through the dark glass of God's design for history. In this regard, patristic theologians had left an ambiguous legacy for later medieval thinkers, above all concerning the historical role and destiny of imperial power. For some early Christians, especially those who experienced firsthand the weight of Roman oppression and persecution, the bonds of empire had created an assembly of peoples and nations gathered for a single purpose: the Devil's work of war, in direct contrast to the peaceful effort of the apostles to gather the peoples of the world together in Christ.[17] In the heady days after the conversion of Constantine to Christianity in the fourth century, Eusebius of Caesarea argued by contrast that the Roman Empire had a critical role to play in the triumph and spread of the Church. It was not by coincidence, Eusebius declared, that Christ was born during the reign of Augustus, the first emperor, at a time when the far-reaching embrace of Roman dominion enabled the spread of Christ's message. From this perspective, Constantine's open patronage of the Christian faith and his creation of the imperial church formed a new stage in historical progress. Perhaps such enthusiasm was natural from the emperor's biographer, but Eusebius hardly stood alone in his belief that the Roman Empire had a unique role to play in the fulfillment of history.[18]

Considerable room lay between the poles of demonizing empire and uncritically celebrating its virtues. According to Augustine of Hippo in the fifth century, the link between the fate of the Christian Church and the Roman Empire was far from straightforward. The development of Augustine's "historical agnosticism," his belief that the course of events after Christ could not be known as part of the divine plan, is well known.[19] Needless to say, in the turbulent times after the sack of Rome in the year 410, Augustine felt it safer to sever or qualify any ties that seemed to bind the fortunes of God's eternal City from the mutability of the earthly one. In his mature works, he did everything possible to temper speculation about the providential meaning of observable historical developments. While he did not deny the expectation of Antichrist, Augustine adamantly declared that the future was largely unknowable; he equally insisted that the Book of Revelation should be read in a "spiritual" sense rather than as some sort of historical guidebook. In particular, he tackled the vexed question of whether the "binding" of Satan for "one thousand years" (Rev. 20:2) promised a millennial era of peace and terrestrial prosperity. Such fantasies, he insisted, were fit for carnal-minded heretics. The binding of Satan had begun with Christ, and the thousand years symbolically referred to the remainder of time before the end of the world and the eternal Sabbath.[20]

In Augustine's history of salvation, the destiny of the true Church was not limited to the borders of the Roman Empire or any other terrestrial institution. As Augustine observed on another occasion, the Bible made it clear that the Christian faith would spread among all peoples before the end of time, a process that had begun with the apostles and was still being carried out under the aegis of the Roman Empire. This extension of the Christian faith, he declared in response to a query about the topic, was far from complete. There remained numerous peoples outside the borders of the Roman world, some close to his own home in northern Africa, who had yet to hear the news of Christ; this suggested that the final days were not immediately at hand.[21] One of Augustine's former students, Prosper of Aquitaine, declared in his fifth-century tract *On the Calling of All Peoples* that the grace of Christianity "would not be content" with the borders of the Roman world, adding that many people unconquered by Roman arms were already "subdued to the scepter of Christ."[22] Prosper's view of God's universal fold was ambitious, inclusive, and freighted with eschatological anticipation. Recalling Paul's instructions to pray "for all men" (1 Tim. 2:1), he informed his readers that this call to prayer included supplications:

> . . . not only for the saints and those already reborn in Christ, but also for all the infidels and enemies of Christ's cross, for all the worshippers of idols, for all of those who persecute Christ by attacking his members, for the Jews, whose blindness the light of the Gospel has not dispelled, and for the heretics and schismatics, who are sundered from the unity and love of the faith. Why did he seek this on their behalf, unless, after leaving behind their errors, they shall convert to the Lord, shall receive faith and love, and, freed from the shadows of their ignorance, shall come into the knowledge of truth?[23]

The fact remained, however, that the visible fortunes of imperial power seemed for many Christians to manifest the hidden movements of sacred history. In the Latin tradition, Augustine's contemporary Jerome helped to popularize the scheme of "world empires" based on the Book of Daniel, specifically Nebuchadnezzar's dream of the alloyed statue (Dan. 2: 31–45) and Daniel's dream of the four beasts emerging from the sea (Dan. 7:3–28).[24] The statue's head of gold, chest of silver, thighs of bronze, and legs of iron prophesied the progression of imperial power from the Babylonians to the Persians to the Macedonians and finally to the Romans (as did the four beasts). The "iron" empire of Rome (also represented by the fourth beast) would endure until the end of time, at which point it would be divided up into a series of petty kingdoms symbolized by the statue's mixed feet of iron and clay (as well as by the "ten horns" on the fourth beast). This fragmentation of empire set the stage for the arrival of Antichrist (symbolized by the fourth beast's "little horn" that emerged from the midst of the ten others). Although Jerome, like Augustine, tried to cool chiliastic speculations about the coming of a future Sabbath age, he believed that this process of decline had already begun during the barbarian incursions into the Roman Empire of his own day. On one occasion, Jerome declared that the spread of the Gospel was "already complete or would be completed within a brief time," implying that the end of history must be closer rather than farther away.[25]

Although patristic thinkers generally managed to temper the ardors of those who insisted upon millennial scenarios or a concrete date for the end, Christians continued to search for signs of the divine plan in the course of history. Certain events were far too momentous or calamitous to be ignored. In the famous Syriac work of the so-called Pseudo-Methodius, for example, the author declared that the seventh-century Muslim conquests of the Christian Roman Empire represented a just punishment by God against his sinful people and a harbinger of the apocalypse.[26] Removed from the eschatological coolness of the Latin tradition, this prophecy also promised that the faithful could look forward to the coming of a messiah-like ruler, whose "indignation and fury" would "blaze forth against those who deny the Lord Jesus Christ." This final "king of the Romans" would cast out the infidels, restore the splendor of the Church, convert unbelievers to the faith, and usher in an era of peace before the conclusion of history.[27] From this time forward, the threat of Islam would occupy a prominent place in many Christian scenarios for the end-times.[28] Latin translations of the text were made as early as the eighth century. Although there is no clear evidence that Adso directly knew the Pseudo-Methodian tradition, his appropriation of the "Last World Emperor" role for the rulers of the Franks made perfect sense, given the belief of Frankish historians that the power of empire had been transferred to the Carolingians when Charlemagne assumed the imperial title in the year 800.[29]

Even before they claimed the imperial title, the Carolingians had seized upon the notion that their rule made them the "defenders" of Christ, responsible for the protection and dilatation of the Christian Church. As Charles declared in 796 to Pope Leo III (r. 795–816), it was Charles's role to "defend by arms the holy Church of Christ from the attack of pagans and the devastation of infidels without, and to fortify the confession of the catholic faith within." It was the pope's role to pray for Charles's victory over God's enemies so that "the name of our Lord Jesus Christ might shine forth in the entire world."[30] Acting like good Augustinians, ninth-century Carolingian theologians and exegetes for the most part avoided eschatological speculations about the consummation of history, reading the Book of Revelation in a spiritual rather than literal fashion. Nevertheless, they eagerly fostered a sense of manifest destiny around the role of the Franks in preserving the Church from heretics and spreading Christian imperial power among pagan peoples, both by the sword and by the missionary word.[31]

In the ninth century, the greatest challenge to such claims came from those "other" emperors, the Greek rulers of Constantinople, who possessed a direct claim to Christian imperial authority stretching back to Constantine himself. Carolingian-era thinkers found various ways to deal with this problem. Judging by his subsequent correspondence, Charlemagne was more than willing when it suited him to recognize the equal legitimacy of both the Eastern and Western Empires, which shared a duty to protect the "holy and unblemished catholic Church, spread throughout the world."[32] Some chroniclers did not explicitly mention the Greek rulers when they celebrated Charles's imperial coronation, while others declared that the dignity of empire had ceased among the Greeks because a woman, Empress Irene (r. 797–802), had sat on the throne.[33] Still others associated the Byzantine Empire with the rise of "heresies" like iconoclasm and the rejection of the Roman Church's spiritual authority. Writing around 870, the papal librarian Anastasius Bibliothecarius described the situation this way:

> After the Roman emperors—who are now called Greek—became the promoters and supporters of various errors, not fearing to tear asunder the holy Church of Christ with assorted heresies, God tore asunder their empire and little by little they ceased to rule over the Western parts by the decree of heavenly judgment. They tried to pervert the Roman pontiffs with their wickedness, but did not succeed. On this account, suffering many punishments, they have now lost entirely their power over the West.[34]

Writing to Constantinople around the same time as Anastasius, the Carolingian Emperor Louis II (r. 855–875) made a similar argument that the heterodoxy of the Greeks had resulted in the collapse of their authority over the Western regions and the transferal of their imperial power to the Franks.[35] In the tenth century, much like the Carolingians before them, the Ottonian emperors continued to confront the Byzantine rulers as the principal competitors for their universal claims over the Christian Roman Empire. At times, this competition played into the imagining of future events. In 968, during the reign of Emperor Otto I (r. 936–973), the imperial legate Liudprand of Cremona described his encounter at Constantinople with some Greek prophecies, the so-called "Visions of Daniel." Refuting a Greek prophecy that the "lion and the whelp" (the Byzantine emperor and the Franks) would destroy the "wild ass" (the Saracens), Liudprand offered his own interpretation of the text, namely that Otto I and his son (the lion and the whelp) would destroy the wild ass (the Byzantine emperor)![36]

As we have already seen, Otto's grandson, Otto III, deliberate styled himself the ruler of a renewed Christian Roman Empire. He did so with the eager assistance of Pope Sylvester II, whose name echoed that of the pontiff who—according to an apocryphal tradition—had baptized the first Christian emperor, Constantine. This act was enshrined in the

Donation of Constantine, a famous forgery that had first circulated in the so-called False or Isidorean decretals of the ninth century.[37] According to this tradition, by baptizing Constantine, Pope Sylvester I (r. 314–335) had cured him of leprosy. Out of gratitude, the emperor granted to the pope and his successors authority over Rome and the Western parts of the empire. Constantine also confirmed the Roman Church's primacy over the other major sees of the ancient world, including Alexandria, Antioch, Jerusalem and, anachronistically, Constantinople, while proclaiming that the bishops of Rome stood above earthly judgment. He then proceeded to transfer his imperial power to a new Eastern capital at Byzantium: "For it is not just that an earthly emperor wield power in that same place that the prince of bishops and head of the Christian religion was established by the emperor of heaven."[38] Generations later, Liudprand of Cremona did not hesitate to echo the *Donation of Constantine* when he claimed that Constantine had in fact relinquished imperial power in the West; Otto III, however, was more skeptical about the document, recognizing, no doubt, the untoward power and prerogatives that it apparently bequeathed to the bishops of Rome.[39]

Indeed, although Pope Sylvester II lent his support to the young German emperor, he possessed his own ambitions for the future of the Roman Church and its authority over the Christian world. In spring of the year 1000, for example, Sylvester displayed his vision of papal primacy in a letter addressed to the king of the newly converted Hungarians, Stephen I (r. 997–1038).[40] Opening with an invocation from the Book of Daniel stating that God "changes times and ages, takes away kingdoms and establishes them" (Dan. 2:21), the pontiff gave thanks to the Lord for raising up a king in "our times" like a new David to rule over Israel, the Hungarian people. Sylvester "granted" to Stephen and his heirs not only his crown, but also the blessings and the protection of the Apostolic See of Peter and Paul. In exchange, Stephen promised his obedience and reverence for the Roman Church, "which does not hold subjects as slaves, but receives all as sons."[41] From one perspective, this maneuver complemented the Ottonian drive to expand the borders of the Christian faith into formerly pagan lands. At the same time, the creation of an intimate link between the first Christian ruler of the Hungarians and the spiritual authority of the papacy suggested a different direction: the dilatation of

Christian churches and kingdoms under the pastoral leadership of the pope rather than the emperor.

Sylvester II has been called the "pope of the year 1000."[42] In the view of nineteenth-century historians, the turn of the new millennium inspired terror and despair among Christians, filling them with dread about the approaching apocalypse. Reacting to this overblown picture, subsequent generations of scholars largely downplayed the apocalyptic atmosphere of the era, even to the point of claiming that it did not exist at all. In recent years historians have charted a middle ground between those interpretive extremes, arguing that the muted apocalypticism of the Carolingian period gave way to a new sense of eschatological excitement during the decades surrounding the millennium (evident, for example, in Adso's tract on Antichrist).[43] Contemporaries were far from paralyzed with fear, but they did show a heightened interest in the possibility that history would reach its climax or a new stage during their own times. Moreover, dread could always yield to hope for an age of renewal. According to one tenth-century witness, when the pagan Hungarians had made their first inroads into Christian territories, many believed that they were the apocalyptic peoples of Gog and Magog, predicted in the Book of Revelation.[44] As we just saw, however, within a short amount of time Pope Sylvester II could celebrate their new Christian leader as an obedient son of the Roman Church, whose duty was to assist with the propagation of Christianity.

Observing this change in the Hungarians, the monastic chronicler Rodulfus Glaber proclaimed that "they who formerly pillaged the Christians they came across and bore them off into miserable slavery, now welcome them like brothers and children."[45] Glaber, who lived from 985 to 1047, captured the new mood of the millennium in his well-known chronicle. Although he offered no timetable for the end or concrete apocalyptic predictions, his historical eye fastened upon various signs—famine, plague, comets, war, infidel attacks, and more—to illustrate the eschatological perils and hopes of the time. Heresy in particular concerned him. Reporting on its growth in Italy, he observed that "all this accords with the prophecy of St John, who said that the Devil would be freed after a thousand years."[46] Commenting on the increase of pilgrimages to the holy places of Jerusalem, Glaber opined that this new devotion possibly signaled the approach of the "accused Antichrist who, according to divine testimony, is expected to appear at the end of the world," at which time the faithful would rush to Jerusalem to oppose or serve him.[47] Glaber also hinted at marvelous changes for the better with the arrival of the millennium or again at the thousand-year mark of the Passion in 1033. He famously described the growth of ecclesiastical structures around the turn of the eleventh century, proclaiming that the world was "cladding itself everywhere in a white mantel of churches."[48] At one point, Glaber evinced his belief that the Christian lands where he lived were favored by Christ, who faced west while he hung on the cross, with his right hand outstretched toward the north. The south and east, however, still teemed with infidels and barbarians. "God alone knows," he mused, "why it is that men are more able to receive their own salvation in some parts of the world than in others."[49] Over time, Glaber's successors in the Roman Church would come to feel that they had found convincing answers to precisely that question.

Reform, Orthodoxy, and Heretical Greeks

In 1024, Rodulfus Glaber recorded a particularly disturbing story about the Roman papacy and the Greek patriarch of Constantinople, who had attempted secretly to bribe the pope so that he would acknowledge Constantinople's claims of universal authority over its own territories. This plan, he related, would have succeeded if not for the general outrage that erupted when its terms were finally exposed.[50] The irate Glaber transcribed a letter, attributed to his friend and patron, the monastic reformer William of Dijon, who admonished Pope John XIX (r. 1024–1032) as follows:

> But a rumor has recently arisen concerning you, and the man who is not scandalized by it must know that he is far removed from the divine love. For although the power of the Roman Empire, which once ruled over the whole earth, is now divided in various areas under numerous scepters, the power of binding and loosing in heaven and earth is attached by inviolable gift to the office of St Peter. And we have said this so that you may perceive

that it is from nothing but vain glory that the Greeks have made these demands on you of which we have heard. For the future, we pray that you should behave as behooves a universal bishop, practicing with more ardor the correction and discipline of the holy and apostolic Church so that you may be worthy of eternal happiness in Christ.[51]

Fortunately, wiser counsels prevailed and the ambassadors from Constantinople were sent home without their prize.

This episode illustrated a deep-seated controversy in the eleventh-century Roman Church over the buying and selling of clerical offices and dignities. Even Pope John XIX, Glaber related with disapproval, had reached his own position through bribes. Indeed, the monk held simony largely responsible for the scourges—famine, plague, and war—that God had sent against his sinful people. Toward the close of his chronicle, Glaber praised Emperor Henry III (r. 1028–1056) who had dedicated himself to the eradication of simony, selecting a new pope, Gregory VI (r. 1045–1046), whose "good reputation served to reform the corruption of his predecessor," Pope Benedict IX (r. 1032–1044).[52] Apparently, Glaber died around this time, or perhaps he could not bring himself to record the tangled events that followed, including Gregory VI's forced resignation resulting from charges of simony against him, the short tenure of Pope Clement II (r. 1046–1047), the brief return of the deposed Pope Benedict IX (r. 1047–1048), and the even briefer papacy of Damasus II (r. 1048) before the election of Pope Leo IX in 1048.[53] Leo would prove to be the sort of pontiff that Glaber and others like him had undoubtedly dreamed of for years. Under this pope and his entourage, the somewhat diffuse currents of religious reform—which had originated primarily in monastic centers such as Cluny and Gorze—began to coalesce around the institution of the Roman papacy.[54] Leo's denunciations of simony immediately made their mark among his contemporaries. How could they not, when the pope held a council in Reims in 1049, deposing several bishops for purchasing their offices?[55]

Glaber's story about the ambitions of the Greek patriarch in 1024 foreshadowed another problem facing the "reform" papacy of the mid-eleventh century, namely its status relative to the Eastern Church of Constantinople. During the course of his papacy, Leo showed himself equally ready to engage with challenges from this direction. The circumstances of his crisis with the Greeks are well known. In 1053, the pope's longtime companion Cardinal Bishop Humbert of Silva Candida handed him a letter which had been written by the archbishop of Ochrid in Macedonia. This polemical epistle, which Humbert translated from Greek into Latin, presented a scathing attack on Roman religious rites and habits, above all the Latin use of unleavened bread for the Eucharist, which the Greeks claimed was a form of Judaizing (that is, a literal adherence to the Jewish use of azymes for Passover).[56] Leo and Humbert also learned that the Greek patriarch, Michael Cerularius (r. 1043–1059), had closed a number of churches in Constantinople that worshipped in the Latin rite.[57] Working together, the pope, Humbert, and perhaps a few others drafted a number of letters to the Greek patriarch and Byzantine emperor, Constantine IX Monomachus (r. 1042–1055), refuting the accusations made against the Latin Church. The following summer, the pope dispatched a legation to Constantinople to resolve the dispute, including Humbert, Peter of Amalfi, and Frederick of Lorraine. After a series of bitter debates, Humbert and his companions deposited a bull on the high altar at Hagia Sophia on 16 July 1054, excommunicating Cerularius and his supporters, who followed suit with their own bull that anathematized the Roman legates.[58]

Few events in medieval history have been as misunderstood as the so-called Schism of 1054. Generations of scholars viewed the mutual excommunications of that year as causing the final and lasting breach between the Latin and Greek Churches. Confessional historians on both sides of the conflict continued to perpetuate myths and slanders about its key participants well into the twentieth century, when more even-handed treatments of the topic began to correct the "Black Legend" that surrounded the episode.[59] The interminable debate surrounding the origins of the schism has tended to obscure the meaning that the events of 1054 possessed for contemporaries, who had no idea that their actions would bear the false burden of dividing Christendom. In fact, somewhat ironically, Pope Leo and his cadre of supporters had precisely the opposite intention. Unity was their basic operating premise, albeit on terms that were dictated by Rome. Facing the Greek religious tradition, the reform papacy confronted one of the most serious rivals to its presumed right to speak unilaterally for the universal Church. The Latin response to that challenge formed the first ideological salvo in Rome's newly configured claims to govern the Christians of the world. Decades before the Investiture Controversy, more than forty years before the First Crusade, the crisis of 1054 revealed the papal vision of Christendom in action.[60]

The first letter of response to the Greek patriarch in 1053, drafted by Pope Leo and his circle, plainly captured this assertive posture:

> We are not able to tolerate anyone whosoever, who sets himself out of pride against our Apostolic See and usurps its law, for whoever attempts to diminish or invalidate the privileges and authority of the Roman Church, schemes to overturn and destroy not just that one church, but all of Christendom.[61]

One imagines that this was precisely the sort of response to the Greeks that William of Dijon and others like him had been hoping for in 1024. How did the papacy justify this deliberate conflation of Christendom with the Apostolic See of Rome? The letter included lengthy excerpts from the *Donation of Constantine* to reinforce the idea that Constantine's transferal of empire from Rome to Constantinople was made out of respect for Rome's role in the governance of the universal Church. These selections confirmed that the emperor had set the Roman Church above the other patriarchal sees of the ancient world. In addition, the authors drew attention to the first ecumenical council of Nicaea in 325, when (according to other spurious sources) the emperor had reiterated his surrender of Western imperial power to the bishops of Rome.[62]

In a second letter of complaint about the attack on the Roman rite, this one addressed to Emperor Constantine Monomachus, Leo and his circle stressed the first Constantine's munificence toward the bishops of Rome and pointed to him as the proper model for a pious ruler: "Therefore we exhort you," the epistle called upon the current ruler of Byzantium, "the great successor to the great Constantine by blood, name, and imperial power, also to be the imitator of his devotion toward the Apostolic See."[63] In this letter, the possibilities rather than the dangers of empire for the reform papacy were on display. In 1053, not long before Leo first heard news about the Greek attack on the Latin rite, the pope had led his own troops into battle against the Normans, whose rising power in southern Italy threatened papal holdings and interests. The ensuing battle of Civitate, which resulted in Leo's defeat and capture, hardly favored his ambitions in the region. Smarting from this recent failure, Leo informed Constantine Monomachus that he expected aid from Emperor Henry III against the Normans at any moment, and called upon the Greek ruler to join him. Like the two arms of a body, Henry and Constantine Monomachus would defend the Church of Christ from its enemies and "relieve the shame of Christendom."[64]

Papal authority over Christendom, however, could never rest secure on imperial munificence. After all, what one emperor granted, another could take away. Since at least the fourth century, the popes of Rome had laid claim to their own ideology of universal authority through their apostolic succession from Saint Peter. The logic behind this argument was strikingly simple: Christ had deputized his chief Apostle Peter to establish his terrestrial church (Mt. 16:18), and Peter had deputized the bishops of Rome as his successors, thereby imparting to them a place of supremacy over other churches. Decades earlier, William of Dijon had invoked this very claim when he heard about the Greeks' illicit attempt to solicit from Rome privileges that did not belong to them. From this perspective, the Roman popes did not need Constantine or any other temporal ruler to tell them that they exercised spiritual authority and pastoral leadership over the Christians of the world.[65]

Starting in the 1050s, the advocates of reform made this assertion of apostolic primacy through Peter their mantra. Among other maneuvers, they began to repackage earlier sources of canon law (including forgeries and spurious passages) into easy-to-wield collections supporting their claims that the "sacrosanct and apostolic Roman Church" had obtained its privileges directly from Christ through Peter.[66] At the same time, papal circles reinvented Rome's past in order to distance the Roman Church from the city's pagan greatness and to associate its sanctity firmly with the blood of martyrs spilled in the holy city, above all Peter and Paul, whose remains formed a focal point of Christian devotion there. The martyrdom of those apostles during the persecution of Nero had transformed Rome from the "head of superstition" and ruler of pagan nations into the "head of sanctity" and ruler of Christian peoples—a fit dwelling for the princes of the Church, the bishops of Rome.[67]

Saint Peter and the Apostolic See. Lambert of St. Omer, *Liber Floridus* (ca. 1129), thirteenth century.

Source: Bibliothèque Nationale de France, Paris, lat. 8865.

These "Petrine" claims involved much more than Rome's status of juridical primacy. To refute the Greek charge that the use of unleavened
bread for the Eucharist constituted a form of Judaizing, Pope Leo and his
circle pointed toward Peter rather than Constantine, arguing that the direct line of succession from Peter to the bishops of Rome guaranteed the
orthodoxy of the Roman sacrifice against the heretics who were presently
attacking it. In his life, ministry, and martyrdom, Peter had demonstrated
his role as the foundation of the church. Against Peter, the "gates of hell,"
that is, the arguments of heretics, could not prevail. As the Apostolic See,
it was the role of Rome to defend the faithful and confound the illicit
teachings of all heretics, everywhere they might appear. The defenders of
the Roman rite argued that Peter had played a unique role in revealing the
sacramental mysteries of the faith and removing the "burden of circumcision" and the "yoke" of the Jewish law from the Gentiles. In these terms,
the Greek attack on azymes went much deeper than a point of contention
over a simple difference in sacramental practice. It reached instead
squarely into Christian theology of history, which argued that the Incarnation of Christ marked a transferal from the Old Testament law of the
Jews to the New Covenant of the Christians. With the coming of Christ,
the Jewish use of azymes for Passover had not been abrogated but rather
had been transformed into the Christian sacrifice with unleavened bread.
In contrast to the Latins, described as "Peter's intimate disciples and the
more devout followers of his teaching," the Greeks had failed to understand the fundamental nature of the Christian sacraments.[68]

To make matters worse, the Greek Church had openly attacked the
Latin rite and papal authority. The initial letter of response to the Byzantine patriarch implied that Michael Cerularius and his supporters were
nothing less than "members of Antichrist," some of the "many Antichrists" that the Bible predicted for the "final hour" (1 Jn. 2:18). This statement was not apocalyptic in an immediate sense; the letter cautiously asserted that the "final hour" in fact stretched "from the first coming of
Savior to his Second Coming."[69] This line of attack, however, aligned the
Greek clergy with forces of evil that had opposed the catholic Church
throughout history. The same epistle specifically associated the current
Greek patriarch with infamous ancient heresiarchs of the Eastern Church,
such as Arius, Macedonius, Nestorius, and Eutychius, whose heresies had

been opposed by the first four ecumenical councils at Nicaea, Constantinople (381), Ephesus (431), and Chalcedon (451). Like a daughter who rejected her mother, Constantinople had exhibited a history of rebellion against Rome since the era of peace established by Constantine, when pagan persecutions had yielded to the internal threat of heresy. The current attack on the Latin rite, in this view, fit into a pattern of abuse.[70]

This strident invocation of the past suggested a far more serious problem than a minor point of liturgical difference between the Latin and Greek Churches (as modern scholars often present the azymes controversy).[71] For all of our modern talk of a "schism" between the followers of Rome and Constantinople, the term was not commonly applied to the situation during or immediately after 1054. Pope Leo's biographer referred instead to the "heresy of the Leavenites, who assailed the holy Roman see, nay, the entire Latin and Western Church" for its use of azymes.[72] Another account by Panteleo of Amalfi declared that Michael Cerularius, better known as "a heresiarch rather than a patriarch," had attacked the Roman Church by claiming that "the Greek sacrifice is better than the Latin, since they make an offering of leavened bread, and the Roman Church makes an offering of azymes, as it had learned from the apostles."[73] Yet another anonymous tract composed shortly afterwards declared that the Greek patriarch and his partisans were worse than the Jews; the latter had killed Christ in ignorance about his true nature, while the Greek clergymen involved had attacked the body of Christ willingly.[74] So much for a minor point of liturgical difference!

This language of orthodoxy and heresy points us away from the notion of a long-term Latin-Greek schism toward other debates within the eleventh-century Roman Church over the sacraments and the unique position of Rome as the defender of catholic doctrine and proper religious practice. When the crisis with Constantinople erupted in 1053, the papacy was already involved in a controversy surrounding the Eucharistic teachings of Berengar of Tours. Historians of the schism between the Latins and Greeks rarely point out this simple but important fact.[75] Berengar questioned the still forming doctrine that the sacrificial bread and wine changed "substantially" during consecration while maintaining their outward appearance or "accidents." The details of Berengar's theology do not concern us, but the reaction of Rome to his teaching does. In 1050,

Leo IX condemned Berengar in absentia, an early example of the pope's eagerness to place the Apostolic See on the front lines of determining and defending orthodoxy. Condemned at Tours in 1054 and yet again at Rome in 1059, Berengar was compelled to take an oath rejecting his own teachings and confirming that the Eucharist after consecration was the "true body of Christ." In 1059, Pope Nicholas II (r. 1059–1061) called upon none other than Humbert of Silva Candida to formulate Berengar's self-condemnatory oath.[76]

If the papacy's refutation of Berengar and the Greek patriarch represented two sides of the same coin, the new currency of the land lay in the authority of Rome to monitor the borders of orthodoxy. The Eucharist was not the only sacramental fault-line in this new effort to draw borders around the right and wrong kind of Christians. Before and after Leo's death, the targeting of simony contributed to an unusual amount of concern over the validity of sacraments that were administered by "simoniacal" heretics, above all the rite of baptism. Turning for support to the Bible and the annals of ecclesiastical history, churchmen such as Humbert sought to clarify the boundaries around the catholic community by vociferously identifying its perceived enemies, including pagans, heretics, schismatics, Jews, and, arguably worst of all, "carnal" Christians who pretended to be members of the faith and dissimulated their perversity.[77] They were part of Antichrist's body, rather than the body of Christ, the true Church. A few years after his visit to Constantinople, Humbert of Silva Candida declared in his well-known *Three Books Against the Simoniacs* that clerics guilty of simony were "worse than pagans and Jews." The sacraments administered by them were a source of pollution that lacked the sanctification of the Holy Spirit, the "glue" that bound together the Church, the mystical "body of Christ." In a parody of catholic sacraments, which still shared some of their outer characteristics with the Jewish rites that had prefigured them, the sacraments of Antichrist's servants would continue to look like catholic ones, hiding their inner falsity. Looking into the future, Humbert predicted that the Devil would raise a "profane Trinity" against the faithful at the end of time, consisting of "Satan among the Gentiles, Antichrist among the Jews, and a pseudo-prophet among the heretics." That pseudo-prophet would present the worst threat of all, since he would trick otherwise pious believers into following him.[78]

Humbert, it is worth pointing out, did not harbor an irrational "hatred" of Greeks, as is sometimes supposed. In his books against simony, he was more than willing to praise the Greek Empire for its lack of that particular sin.[79] Rather, his strident rejection of the Greek polemics against Rome years earlier demonstrated a careful project to establish beyond any doubt that the Roman Church embodied the true leadership of the universal Christian community in all matters. Although 1054 did not cause the lasting schism between Latins and Greeks, it remains an important landmark in the papal concept of Christendom, above all the relationship between its Western and Eastern halves.[80] A new terrain had been marked out on the frontiers of belief between Latins and Greeks—an insistence that the doctrines, rites, and habits of the Roman Church were the superior ones, along with the complementary possibility that the leaders of the Greek religious tradition, if not the Greeks as a whole, were at best inferior and at worst heretical. Once exposed, that terrain would never disappear. To the contrary, projecting the proper relationship between Rome and the Eastern Church in the past, present, and future would come to occupy more and more attention from members of the Roman Church over the following decades and beyond.

Imagining the "Gregorian" World Order

Pope Leo IX died before he heard about the results of the legation to Constantinople in 1054, but his ambitious ideology of papal authority persisted more or less unabated after him. Following his papacy, a series of subsequent pontiffs achieved substantial advancements in their cause of ecclesiastical reform, including the establishment of canonical papal elections by an assembly of cardinal bishops in 1059. By all accounts, however, the drive to reshape Christendom assumed a new stridency and pace under Gregory VII, elected pope in 1073. Rome, Gregory declared on more than one occasion, represented the "mother of all Christendom" and the "universal mother of all churches and peoples."[81] These were not exactly new formulations in papal ideology, but he envisioned their significance with an unprecedented insistence on the superiority of priestly authority. The pope was explicit that the "law of the Roman pontiffs" was not limited to the lands formerly or presently commanded by the Roman emperors.[82] Christendom under papal monarchy transcended the borders of empire. One need only glance at the so-called *Dictatus papae* to get a sense of Gregory's audacious and potentially disruptive formulation of papal primacy. Although not disseminated, this point-by-point "manifesto" written in 1075 (perhaps the outline of a never-completed canon law collection) reserved for the papacy the exclusive right to be called apostolic, the right to depose emperors, and absolute freedom from outside judgment. The *Dictatus papae* declared that anyone who did not recognize the authority of the Roman Church was a heretic, cut off from the community of the faithful. This platform did not just seek to elevate Rome's juridical status as the head of Christendom; the papacy stood as the defender and determiner of orthodoxy, deciding and enforcing what was correct in doctrine and liturgical practice.[83]

Whatever the limitations of his abilities to enforce his claims, Gregory demonstrated an unprecedented scope of concern for extending the influence of the Roman Church over alternate Christian traditions. In some instances he directed his attention close to home, investigating news of a supposed Armenian heretic at large in southern Italy, or informing the Greek clergy of Sardinia that they should reestablish the ancient connection between their island and the papacy by observing Roman customs.[84] In other cases, he looked farther afield. The pope saw it as his role to investigate, admonish, and encourage members of the Christian faith everywhere, or (as he put it in a letter to the Catholicus of Armenia) to weep when he heard about those who separated themselves from the body of the faithful and to congratulate those who remained in unity and harmony.[85] Looking toward Byzantium, Gregory kept diplomatic channels open with the Byzantine emperor, Michael VII (r. 1067–1078), communicating with him through his legates and letters about the need to "renew a state of concord" between the church of Rome and its "ancient daughter," Constantinople. Regardless of the precise locale in question, differences of rite and doctrine between Latins and non-Latin communities fell into the widening pastoral matrix of papal authority.[86]

In addition to his claims of leadership over "foreign" Christians, Gregory from the beginning of his papacy envisioned an active role for the see of Saint Peter in the battles taking place on the frontiers between believers and non-Christians. In this case, the pope tapped into another facet of the reform movement that had its origins earlier in the tenth and eleventh centuries, namely a growing clerical comfort with the possibility of justified, if not sanctified, violence against both the internal and external foes of Christendom. Beginning at the Councils of Le Puy in 975 and Charroux in 989, local churchmen and laity in the fragmented kingdom of Francia had begun to respond to the violence of "predatory" lords by delimiting the space and time available for the legitimate use of armed force. Since the ground-breaking study of Carl Erdmann on the origins of the First Crusade, scholars have recognized that this movement—the so-called Peace and Truce of God—contributed to a wider shift in clerical attitudes toward violence.[87] In time, ecclesiastical thinkers began to envision the mirror-opposite of such predatory brigandage, namely, the use of formally sanctioned warfare to protect the Church. The development of this position was protracted and far from systematic, as theologians and canon lawyers drew upon patristic authorities to bolster arguments in favor of those who wielded their arms against the Church's enemies both within, including heretics, schismatics, and violators of the peace, and without, above all pagans and infidels.[88]

By the mid-eleventh century, the papacy began to take a more active hand in directing violence for its own purposes. In 1053, as we have seen, Pope Leo IX displayed this change in attitude when he led his own troops into battle against Norman forces in southern Italy. Some clerics argued that the soldiers who fell there in the service of the pope were martyrs.[89] Just over a decade later, Pope Alexander II (r. 1061–1073) bestowed the papal banner upon Duke William of Normandy, as he prepared for his invasion of England to overthrow the "usurper" Harold Godwinson in 1066. Over the course of his own papacy, Gregory VII conferred the papal banner upon various rulers, including a former papal foe, the Norman leader Robert Guiscard, and Erlembald, a warrior who supported reformist interests in Milan. By fostering the idea that Christian laity could act as "soldiers of Saint Peter" against the enemies of the papacy, Gregory was not so much charting a new direction as channeling the notion that secular fighters had an important duty to fulfill in the service and defense of the Church.[90]

The reform movement also changed the theological significance of violence against the infidel world on Christendom's frontiers. By the later eleventh century, those frontiers were in flux, above all in regions such as Spain where Christendom butted up against Islamic lands. Fueled by sweeping demographic, economic, and political changes, princes such as Alfonso VI of Léon and Castile (r. 1065–1109) and Sancho IV of Navarre (r. 1054–1076) pushed against their southern boundaries in aggressive if somewhat piecemeal campaigns. Medieval contemporaries in the Roman Church framed this expansionary process with their own narratives of conquest. While the reformers struggled to realize their vision of a properly ordered world close to home, they also looked toward places that "properly" belonged to the patrimony of Rome, even if they were currently in the hands of the infidels. Channeling this recovery process, the proponents of papal monarchy crafted some of their most compelling narratives of history as a divinely ordained process that favored Western Christians, even while God laid special obligations on them.

Gregory's predecessor, Pope Alexander II, had already tried his hand at fostering armed Christian action against Islamic Spain by promising the remission of sins for warriors en route to battle against the Saracens there.[91] Although few would now agree with the appraisal of Augustin Fliche that "the crusade started in the West, during the pontificate of Alexander II," that pope's contribution to events like the capture of Barbastro in 1064 spoke of an intensifying papal interest in rolling back the frontiers of belief between Christendom and the infidels.[92] Under Gregory VII, the papacy more forcefully and consistently projected its right to speak for those parts of the Christian world that had until quite recently remained beyond its reach, while encouraging further Christian action against the unbelievers. Gregory's language of expansion was not ours. He did not speak of population growth and economic motivations, but rather of God's plan for history and the destiny of Christendom.[93]

In his epistles to the rulers and churches of Spain, the pope explained both the recent expansion of Christian power in the region and, significantly, the ultimate responsibility of the papacy for these territories that were being "liberated" from the hands of the infidels. As Gregory styled things, the connection between the Apostolic See and Spain had originated in the earliest days of the Church, when Peter and Paul had dispatched their disciples to proselytize in that land, destroying idolatry, planting the seeds of the Christian faith, and eventually sanctifying it with the blood of their martyrdom. From their foundations, the churches of Spain formed part of the "right and property" of the bishops of Rome, while a state of concord had existed between Spain and Rome in the celebration of the liturgy. As time passed, however, the Christians of the region were polluted and cut off from the Roman rite, first by heretical barbarian Goths and next by the invasion of the Saracens.

All of this was again changing, however, in what Gregory called "our times." Through the mercy of God, under rulers like Alfonso and Sancho, the territories of Spain were being returned to Christian power, the infidel yoke cast off, and the liberty of the Spanish churches restored. This expansion of Christian power in Spain opened up a theater of opportunity for the Roman papacy to actualize the principles of the reform program and to demonstrate the exclusive privileges of the Apostolic See as the "universal mother of all churches and peoples." It was the position of Rome to confirm the ancient rights and properties of the defunct churches that were being restored to the Christian faith. Gregory projected an image of the Spanish kings as properly deferential secular rulers who were carrying out God's work, through their battles against the infidels and their role in extending the boundaries of what was, in effect, Saint Peter's parish.[94] This process complemented the papal responsibility for ensuring orthodoxy in the rites and doctrines of non-Western Christian communities. Again following Pope Alexander II's lead, Gregory insisted that the princes and bishops of Spain carry out the process of substituting the proper Roman liturgy for the "superstitious" rites of the "Mozarabes," Christians who had lived under Islamic authority for centuries.[95] In this respect, we find a significant overlap in the papacy's concern with monitoring non-Roman Christian communities and its support for armed aggression in infidel lands.[96] Gregory exhorted Alfonso VI, Sancho IV, the archbishop of Toledo, and others to recognize their lawful mother, the church of Rome, and to receive from Rome the proper forms of worship that should be spread through the recently captured lands of Spain. This was a duty that involved not innovation, but rather the restoration of earlier practices.

At other points, Gregory did not remain content to react to such expansion on the ground, but rather actively attempted to facilitate and direct the energies of those Christians who looked to Rome as the head of their religious community. Addressing a band of Frankish warriors under Count Ebolus of Roucy bound for Spain in 1073, the pope promised special protection for the lands that the warriors seized from the hands of the pagans and reiterated his narrative of conquest and restoration. The kingdom of Spain, he informed them, had belonged since ancient times to the law and right of Rome, before being subject to bondage under the Saracens. Now it was being restored to the special protection of Saint Peter.[97] That process of restoration was not limited to Spain, but extended to other regions recently occupied by infidels that "properly" belonged to the patrimony of the Apostolic See. Writing in 1074 to confirm the rights and privileges of the monastery of Saint Mary on the island of Gorgona, Gregory proclaimed that the religious house there lay under the "special right" and "dominion" of Saint Peter until the island fell under the cruelty of the Saracens, who had banished Christian worship on the island until recent days when God allowed a restoration of their monastic community.[98] Around a decade later in a letter to Alcherius, the archbishop of Palermo, Gregory declared that it was his business to defend and strengthen churches everywhere, to eradicate errors, and to safeguard the Christian religion. This duty included the church of Sicily, formerly noble and famous, lost to the Saracens on account of Christian sins, but now restored to the Christian faith by the arms of the Norman duke, Roger.[99]

Ultimately, the papacy stood at the heart of an expanding Christendom. Fighting to recover Saint Peter's patrimony, rulers in Spain and Sicily were helping the popes in the realization of God's plan for history—not the other way around. Gregory displayed this ambitious view of papal responsibility for Christians everywhere with his "crusade plan" of 1074. The inhabitants of the Eastern Christian Empire, the pope declared to the faithful in the West, were suffering oppression and slaughter by the infidels. In a letter to Duke William of Burgundy, Gregory capitalized on the previous vows of allegiance and fidelity that William and other nobles had taken to Gregory's predecessor, Alexander II, by calling on those "faithful men of Saint Peter" to aid the beleaguered Eastern Christians. In a letter to Henry IV, Gregory claimed that forty thousand troops had already heeded his call and expressed his desire to lead them against the "enemies of God," pushing all the way to the "sepulcher of the Lord" in Jerusalem. Rallying Henry to this cause, the pope revealed another one of his hopes, namely that this effort to aid the "Christian people" and the

"Christian Empire" from the savageness of the pagan would help to re-store the church of Constantinople, the Armenians, and all the Christians of the East to a state of concord with the Apostolic See.[100]

As is well known, this expedition failed to materialize. Soon afterward the entire project was lost in the din of Gregory's developing confron-tation with Henry IV. For something that never actually happened, how-ever, this idea of an armed campaign to liberate the Eastern Church tells us a great deal about the changing papal vision of Christendom. When Gregory called for an expedition to march eastward in defense of the Greek Empire, his first order of business was to pacify the Normans of southern Italy, who were again threatening papal holdings in the area. Un-like Leo IX, Gregory did not style the Normans as "enemies" of Christ's church or a "shame" to Christendom. They were to be shocked into submissiveness, not destroyed. The true enemies of Christendom were the non-believers outside the gates. This was not the last time that the pa-pacy would call upon its nominal defenders within Christendom to take up arms against its external foes. By exhorting Christian soldiers as the sworn faithful of Saint Peter to defend their fellow believers in the East-ern Church, the pope equally demonstrated his belief that such an act of sanctioned violence would help to strengthen the proper bonds of com-munion and obedience between the Roman Church and those "outside" Christian communities.

Through his vision of concerted Christian action on an epic scale, the pope revealed a close linkage between the internal needs of the reform papacy and its broader ambitions in the world, including its relationship with the Eastern Church and a desire to recover the holy places of Jerusa-lem. These three related goals—internal reform, Christian unity, and op-position to the infidels—would inhabit the historical imagination of the Roman Church for centuries to come. For this reason, Gregory's ambi-tions in 1074 stand as a landmark in the papal ideology of Christendom, set against the backdrop of a struggle to protect Christians against the onslaught of the infidels. By the same token, the fact that Gregory's cam-paign failed to happen demonstrated the very real limitations of the pa-pacy in achieving such goals, especially when the popes of Rome were struggling to defend their prerogatives from a more immediate threat, the German empire.

Indeed, by 1075 and 1076, the Gregorian agenda had led to open conflict between Gregory VII and Henry IV, whose clash over the investiture of bishops with the sacred symbols of their office is one of the better-known episodes in medieval European history. The dueling political theologies of the pope and emperor took shape in an outpouring of polemical letters and tracts that supported papal or imperial claims to a position of ultimate superiority in the governance of Christian society.[101] The Roman emperors, though celebrated for their role in the triumph of the Church after Constantine, had never entirely shed their disturbing reputation as a source of oppression against the faithful since the days of Nero (r. 54–68) and his persecution of the fledgling faith. In certain scenarios, Nero and his imperial heirs were themselves seen as a manifestation of Antichrist. From the perspective of the Roman Church, this adversarial relationship had not changed irrevocably with the conversion of Constantine. To be reminded of this uncomfortable fact, the catholic faithful needed only to recall the persecutions of the heretical Arian ruler Constantius (r. 337–361), the pagan Julian the Apostate (r. 361–363), and the iconoclast Constantine V (r. 743–775). Even if they were not the final Antichrist, such rulers manifested his evil and tyranny. When open conflict erupted between Pope Gregory VII and Henry IV, papal partisans positioned the German emperor in a long line of imperial persecutors who had attacked the faithful, in stark contrast with pious rulers of the past such as Constantine and Charlemagne, who had shown the proper deference to the bearers of priestly authority, above all to the bishops of Rome. From the reformers' perspective, one which they did not hesitate to disseminate, the problem was the failure of later imperial rulers to honor those obligations. Instead, the story of empire after the days of Charlemagne and his son Louis the Pious revealed growing abuse and the gradual erosion of the Church's liberty at the hands of temporal princes. It was that former pristine state of liberty that the reform papacy was claiming to restore through the assertion of its "ancient" privileges.

Not surprisingly, in this war of words, the empire struck back. Even pro-imperial polemics did not roundly deny the special privileges of the Apostolic See and its authority over other churches in different parts of the Christian world. In a tract written around 1084 about the current "discord" between the "pope and the king," the anonymous author offered a vision of ecclesiastical history strikingly similar to that of the reformers, citing (spurious) papal epistles that stressed the authority of the Roman

Church, the "head of Christendom," over the Eastern Church. This imperial partisan asserted that Saints Peter and Paul had brought the Christian faith from its roots in the Eastern Church to the Western Church, thereby making Rome the head of the universal Church as Christ himself had intended.[102] Another pro-imperial tract, the *Book on How to Preserve the Unity of the Church,* agreed that Rome was "mother of all churches." After Constantine had transferred his capital to Constantinople, the emperors of that city had fallen into heresy and attacked the catholic faith (presumably a reference to the Byzantine policy of iconoclasm). This onslaught led the bishops of Rome to seek assistance from the Frankish rulers Pepin and Charles, who defended the Roman Church from its enemies and rightfully assumed imperial power.[103] From this perspective, the current conflict between pope and emperor did not stem from imperial arrogance and abuse, but rather from the unprecedented attack by Gregory VII on the rightful privileges of the emperor to protect and adjudicate over the Roman Church in times of crisis.

As Gregory's papacy progressed, his battle with Henry absorbed more and more of his attention, leading him and his supporters to wonder if the current discord in Christendom itself portended the end of history, or at least whether the papal conflict with the emperor manifested a deeper, eschatological battle between good and evil. In his own correspondence, Gregory did not hesitate to label his opponents "members of Antichrist," including simoniacal bishops and the imperially sponsored "anti-pope," Guibert of Ravenna, who claimed papal authority under the name of Clement III from 1084 to 1100. In many ways, this "Antichrist language" was calculated for rhetorical impact, not intended to convince readers that the Last Things were immediately at hand.[104] Nevertheless, Gregory strongly implied that the current struggles between the supporters of the papacy and the empire offered one sign of the apocalyptic troubles foretold by Christ in the Book of Matthew. His tone suggested that those who opposed the papacy were not just opponents of papal policies, but were aligned instead with eschatological forces of evil.[105]

The invocation of the future was not one-sided. Judging by manuscript evidence, there are tantalizing signs that the imperial apocalyptic tradition began to experience a certain amount of revitalization around this same time, above all in the prophecy of the Last World Emperor.[106] In addition to Pseudo-Methodius and Adso, an eleventh-century translation of the so-called Tiburtine Sibyl, a prophetic tradition that originated in the fourth or fifth century, also contributed to this resurgence of interest in the destiny of the Christian Empire. Contemporaries had a variety of reasons to be fascinated by the Tiburtine Sibyl, including the apparent "prediction" of Christ's coming by a pagan seer.[107] Its presentation of imperial power, however, was particularly eye-catching. In various redactions, the prophecy reinforced the promise of a final Roman ruler who would "lay waste to all the islands and cities of the pagans, destroy all their temples with their idols, and summon all of the pagans to baptism, erecting the cross of Christ in every temple." At the same time, the prophecy proclaimed, "the Jews will convert to the Lord, and His tomb will be glorified by all."[108]

Quite a job description. Around the mid-1080s, the imperial supporter Benzo of Alba testified to a contemporary belief that the young Henry IV was fated to recover the Holy Sepulcher and defeat the forces of paganism, a dramatic role that was suggestive of the deeds expected from the messianic Roman ruler.[109] At least one near-contemporary, Bishop Raynier of Florence, took this heightened sense of apocalyptic eschatology one step farther, announcing around the turn of the twelfth century that the historical Antichrist had already been born.[110] The reaction of pro-imperial bishops gathered at Ravenna is telling. In a letter rebuking Raynier, they categorically denied that the current schism in the Roman Church between rival popes was a sign of the end-times, and they reminded Raynier that patristic authorities refused to make clear predictions about the dating of Antichrist's coming. Besides, according to apostolic testimony, the "Son of Perdition" would not appear until the absolute failure of the Roman Empire. Clearly, the assembled bishops asserted, this disintegration of empire had not yet come to pass. Given the apparently radical nature of Raynier's claims, it seems more than likely that even papal supporters would have balked at such a claim that the Antichrist was at hand, even if they remained willing to denounce Henry as part of Antichrist's evil.

In many ways, the edifice of Christendom erected in the eleventh century was a remarkable trompe l'oeil. Gregory VII, namesake of the Gregorian reform, died in exile at Salerno, chased from Rome by imperial forces. The next influential pope to occupy the Apostolic See for any duration, Pope Urban II (r. 1088–1099), continued to be dogged by the anti-pope Guibert of Ravenna, even as the armies of what we now call the First Crusade were assembling. We should never make the mistake of believing that Rome's claims of unity under papal auspices were uncontested or anywhere close to fully realized. To the contrary, the papacy and like-minded clergy in the Western Church insisted upon the existence of Christendom with such creativity and vehemence precisely because of such conflicts, alternatives, and rivalries, not despite them. In large part, Christendom took shape in response to centrifugal forces and arguments, whether they came from Byzantium, the German empire, or others who opposed the reformers' effort to reconfigure the norms of their Christian society.

Although they could not have known it at the time, the advocates of papal monarchy had taken the first steps toward an innovative theology of history that would impact medieval Europe for the following three hundred years. At its opening stages, their effort was largely reactive and defensive, as seen in Pope Leo IX's declaration that whoever attacked the authority of the Roman Church in fact schemed "to destroy all of Christendom." As time passed, the papacy began to envision its role as a more active one, pushing against the frontiers of the infidel world. With the surprising success of the First Crusade under Pope Urban II, that effort to transform the circumstances of the universal Christian community would assume a compelling new dynamic, but the initial steps had already been taken. By placing the papacy at the center of Christendom, the advocates of papal monarchy in the eleventh century equally placed the bishops of Rome at the center of God's ongoing historical design for the Church on earth. A world unified under Rome would be a world that was one step closer to God's kingdom, even if the ultimate realization of that promise would have to wait until the world-to-come.

2

The Chosen People and the Enemies of God

On 15 July 1099, the Christian warrior-pilgrims of the First Crusade captured Jerusalem from its Muslim rulers. By this point, the bulk of the army had spent roughly three years struggling to reach their goal, facing starvation, disease, and the perils of combat. After besieging the holy city without success, the crusaders spent three days fasting, praying, and carrying out a ritual procession around Jerusalem's walls before they renewed their assault. This time, they breached the defenses. Describing the bloody sack of the city, which he witnessed firsthand, Provençal cleric Raymond d'Aguilers declared: "It was truly by the just judgment of God that this place should be filled with the blood of those from whose blasphemies it had suffered for so long . . . that day saw the utter ruin of all paganism, the affirmation of Christendom, and the renewal of our faith."[1] After securing Jerusalem, the crusaders made their way to the Church of the Holy Sepulcher to give prayers of thanks to the Lord for their victory.

More than nine hundred years later, this expression of Christian aggression and piety continues to elicit controversy. In the popular imagination, the crusades represent an infamous symbol of religious zeal coupled

with unfettered violence and are frequently invoked as a premodern ante-
cedent to the "clash of civilizations" between Islam and the West.[2] In
academic settings, historians cannot even agree on what exactly constituted a crusade, when they really began, or the precise mixture of characteristics that distinguished crusaders from other warriors and pilgrims.[3]
One thing is certain: among those who study the crusades and European
history, a widespread sense persists that the First Crusade tells us something crucial about the formation of medieval Christendom and by extension the nature of Europe itself. In the appraisal of various scholars, crusading offered an unprecedented demonstration of Christian unity in
action, realized through a concerted campaign against the Islamic world.
"Christendom," declares Paul Rousset, "found its expression most strongly
in the crusade."[4] According to Denys Hay, the first expedition to liberate
Jerusalem offered a "shared goal for the men of the West," one that created "the consciousness of an identity of Christian society."[5] Tomaž Mastnak likewise insists that the First Crusade represented a "symbolic point
when Christendom became a living reality," thereby forming the "first
Western union."[6] Most recently, Christopher Tyerman has proclaimed
that the "wars of the cross" created "a shared sense of belonging to a
Christian society, *societas christiana,* Christendom, and contributed to
setting its human and geographic frontiers. In these ways, the crusades
helped to define the nature of Europe."[7]

Latin theology of history formed a critical strand in this intensified
sense of common Christian identity. Shortly after the crusaders seized Jerusalem, if they had not already begun to do so, members of the expedition began to reflect on and write about what had just happened to them.[8]
Soon after that, Christians back in the Western Church, who had not participated in the first armed passage to Jerusalem, began to craft their own
histories of the First Crusade, drawing in part upon the oral reports of
crusaders and other written sources. For the most part, it was monastic
and clerical authors who produced this outpouring of literature, steeped
in traditions of biblical exegesis and ecclesiastical history. Whatever the
lived reality may have been of the laity who participated in the expedition
to Jerusalem, the ecclesiastical thinkers who memorialized the capture of
that holy city—both those who went crusading and those who never left
home—created powerful theologies of crusading that explicitly and im-

plicitly continue to shape our own views of the First Crusade. Contemporaries argued that the capture of the Holy Land from Islamic control constituted much more than just a military campaign or a political conquest. Rather, the crusade revealed God's hand in history, an expression of the Lord's immanent justice in the economy of salvation. Framed in this manner, the capture of Jerusalem marked a transformative moment in the collective experience of Christendom, above all for the Western Christian followers of Rome.

In the modern view of the crusades, notions of violence and peace were central to the ideology of crusading. In theory, the papal leadership of the Roman Church reduced the legitimate space for internal violence between fellow Latin Christians and substituted the alternative of sanctified violence against the infidels, who threatened the faithful while unjustly holding their holy places. From this perspective, Islam provided the Christians of medieval Europe with the foil that formed their sense of commonality, a "photo-negative" of their own society, or a "Devil's Mirror" that reflected the image of "right" believers united against "wrong" non-believers.[9] At different points, other peoples, including Jews, pagans, heretics, and Eastern Christians, were caught up in that same reflection, becoming accidental or intentional targets of crusading violence. Turning their gaze toward the "enemies of God," the crusaders stood shoulder-to-shoulder under the guidance of the Roman papacy, forming the bulwark of the Christian West.[10]

This portrait of Christendom united through crusading against the non-Christian world remains compelling, sometimes seductively so. As we saw in the previous chapter, however, theories of Christian unity underwent critical developments during the decades preceding the First Crusade, and not always in reaction to a violent clash between Christians and Muslims. Even during their most triumphant moments, the crusaders themselves (as well as their Islamic opponents) formed groups of sometimes competing interests. In many cases, the reform papacy and its supporters insisted upon their vision of Christendom when confronting not infidels, but rather fellow Christians, either those in the Eastern Church or their imperial competitors within Western Europe. Nevertheless, vivid portraits of Christian unity do emerge from the historical sources for the First Crusade. The chronicles of the expedition, written predominantly but not exclusively by Frankish clerical authors, plainly put on display the cohesion of Christians from the "Western regions" or the "kingdoms of the West," accompanied by the idea that the followers of Rome had a divine destiny to extend their own religious community by combating the enemies of God and liberating churches from bondage under them. The sense of Christendom that modern scholars find in the sources for the crusade was largely a product of this deliberate process, by which educated participants in and observers of the First Crusade attempted to integrate the expedition into the narrative of salvation history.

Historians sometimes argue that this sense of Christian unity turned outward against the non-Christian world played above all into the hands of the "Gregorian" papacy, giving the popes of Rome a means to express their leadership over European society and to harness the energies of their followers. By most definitions of crusading, the legitimate authority to declare a crusade lay squarely with the papacy, as did the right to offer crusaders spiritual benefits (namely, the remission of sins) for their participation in the expeditions.[11] As one scholar puts it: "The pope's desire was, from the First Crusade onwards, to see a gradual expansion of Christianity until it encompassed the whole world."[12] Such a perspective on the crusades captures something authentic about the ambitions of the medieval papacy, but it fails to appreciate the complexity of contemporary attitudes toward crusading, not to mention the limits of papal authority. Certainly, it is difficult to imagine the First Crusade without attributing considerable significance to the role played by Pope Urban II and his "crusade sermon" delivered at Clermont on 27 November 1095. Subsequently, the papacy played a critical role in authorizing and formalizing the circumstances of crusading, including the temporal and spiritual benefits that were bestowed upon crusaders.[13] Directly and indirectly, the papacy contributed to historical interpretations of the First Crusade. In the providentialist packaging of the expedition, one finds threads of continuity with the carefully cultivated ideology of the reform-era Roman Church, including the notion that Christian expansion against the infidels manifested a divinely sanctioned process of restoring and purifying lost Christian communities that had been polluted by unbelievers. Without denying the impact of lay piety on the shape of crusading spirituality, the still forming papal monarchy irrevocably stamped the memory of crusading with its own image.[14]

At the same time, the chroniclers of the First Crusade did not represent instruments of papal propaganda, any more than the crusaders themselves acted as mere agents of papal policy. Upon closer inspection, the image of Christendom found in the historical sources of the First Crusade reveals a variety of hues and tones, the contrast painted between proper Christians and the outside world less stark than we might assume. That the piety of the crusaders led to bloodshed and suffering for members of other faiths is certain. In crusading theology of history, however, one discovers a wide range of reactions to groups that could be seen as falling beyond the borders of Christendom and a variety of ways that clerical authors positioned crusading as a manifestation of God's will toward those peoples. Not to mention the fact that being in the spotlight of salvation history was perilous as well as exhilarating. In the aftermath of the First Crusade, Christians quickly learned that crusading armies would not always be victorious or achieve their goals. Crusader defeat needed explanation as much as crusader victory—perhaps even more so. The example of Israel in the Christian Old Testament provided an inescapable reminder that being God's Chosen People often meant suffering and tribulation more than triumph in the here-and-now.

The Bondage and Liberation of Jerusalem

Well before the era of the crusades, the Islamic possession of Jerusalem posed a problem for Christian thinkers: Why exactly had God allowed non-believers to seize the land of Christ's birth, ministry, death, and resurrection? In a manuscript from the early eleventh century, a self-styled "humble priest" openly wondered about precisely this dilemma in a letter that he addressed to the "prince of the Agarene people, king of Egypt, and emperor of all the Saracens."[15] The answer, he determined, was that God wished the Saracen ruler now in possession of those places to embrace the Christian faith. He pointed to the example of Constantine as a pagan emperor who became a "lover of the Christian religion and faith" through the grace of Peter and Paul, along with the preaching of Pope Sylvester. As a Christian, Constantine became a builder of churches who, along with his mother, Helena, proved worthy to receive the sign of the Lord's passion, the relic of the True Cross. After his conversion, Constantine expanded his realm and enjoyed God's favor. Pointing to this example, the priest exhorted the Saracen ruler:

> Oh good king and most powerful ruler of many provinces and peoples! If you might imitate Constantine, August worshipper of God and most Christian emperor, about whom we are speaking, you shall hold your earthly kingdom for a long while with honor and felicity, and you shall reign in eternity with Christ and his saints.[16]

Since the Islamic conquests of the seventh century, Eastern and Western Christians had commonly argued that their own sins were responsible for the devastating loss of Jerusalem: the Lord was teaching his wayward followers a lesson by allowing non-believers to dominate the holy places. In an interesting twist, the "humble priest" complemented this logic by adding additional pedagogical value to the infidels' reign over the Promised Land—the non-believers themselves would learn about Christ and become Christians.

There are other intriguing signs that the bondage of Jerusalem newly weighed on the minds of Christians in the Western Church around the beginning of the eleventh century. It is perhaps hard for us to appreciate the full importance of the holy places for contemporary chroniclers, exegetes, and theologians. The terrestrial fate of Jerusalem was suffused with transcendental meaning. The Christian Old Testament provided a template for reading providential significance into its military and political fortunes. In a time of sin among the Hebrews, Jerusalem's enemies would be allowed to harass the city or seize it from the Israelites, but when the people walked with God and obeyed his laws, the Lord was merciful, protecting Jerusalem or restoring it to their hands. While these episodes were open to non-historical, allegorical interpretation, they also recorded the literal fate of Jerusalem as an earthly city, whose loss or gain by the sword manifested the hand of God in history. For Christians, Jerusalem's capture by the Roman armies of Titus and Vespasian in 70 C.E. represented an even more significant moment in its history, viewed as a divine punishment against the Jews for their denial of Christ in fulfillment of Jesus' own words (Mt. 23:37–39; Mk. 13:2).[17] The following centuries provided ecclesiastical historians with additional instances where the fate of Jerusalem seemed to manifest the will of God. In the fourth century, the Emperor Constantine claimed Jerusalem for Christianity, proceeding to purify its holy places from pagan defilement and to construct the Church of the Holy Sepulcher. Another popular tradition maintained that the emperor's own mother, Helena, uncovered a portion of the True Cross near the site of Christ's burial and resurrection. In the early seventh century, when King Chosdroe of Persia sacked Jerusalem, he seized the city's relic of the Cross. The tale of his subsequent defeat by the Byzantine emperor, Heraclius, who recovered the holy relic and humbly restored it to Jerusalem, offered another popular episode recorded in chronicles and sermons.[18]

The Saracen invasions, coming on the heels of imperial Christian rule over the holy city, robbed Christ's people of their patrimony and placed much of the Eastern Church under the infidels' dominion—yet another manifestation of God's will.[19] As we saw earlier, from the days of Pseudo-Methodius forward, the Muslim conquests of the seventh century began to assume a place of prominence in Christian historical schemes and eschatology, including the legend of the Last World Emperor, who would recapture Jerusalem as a prelude to the coming of Antichrist. In the tenth and eleventh centuries, Adso's tract on Antichrist and the Tiburtine Sibyl reinforced this association between the Christian possession of the Promised Land and the end of time, when the final bearer of Roman imperial power would once again reclaim the holy places, laying down his scepter and crown on the Mount of Olives. Rodulfus Glaber observed the throngs of pilgrims heading toward Jerusalem in his own time and wondered if this confluence of Christians heading toward the Promised Land somehow indicated that the time of Antichrist was approaching.[20] In another notable portion of his chronicle, he described a Jewish plot to destroy the Church of the Holy Sepulcher in Jerusalem in 1009. According to Glaber, the Jews of Orléans bribed a renegade serf to bear a letter to the Egyptian Caliph al-Hākim, calling upon him to tear down the famous site of Christian devotion before the Christians overran his kingdom. The plot was successful, but the Jews paid a horrible price when their conspiracy was uncovered: they became "objects of universal hatred," subject to the sword and forced conversions. Eventually, Glaber reported, the Christian mother of al-Hākim enabled the reconstruction of the church in Jerusalem, bringing a new round of Christian pilgrims to the site.[21]

Although the details of Glaber's tale are questionable, his chronicle provides evidence of a real growth in mass Christian pilgrimages to the

Holy Land, which would continue for the remainder of the eleventh century.[22] There are tantalizing signs that not all contemporary Christians in the Western Church were entirely willing to accept the fact that their holiest of devotional places remained under the dominion of non-believers. Unlike the "humble" priest described above, some clergymen began to hope that Christian arms might be able to ameliorate the situation or restore Jerusalem to Christian hands, rather than waiting for the conversion of a "Saracen" leader. According to one eleventh-century Latin tradition, Charlemagne himself had already seen fit to journey to Jerusalem and temporarily wrest it from the infidels, returning home with a bounty of sacred relics.[23] Two other sources, attributed to Popes Sylvester II and Sergius IV (r. 1009–1012), captured this changing mood, although it is not entirely clear whether they actually date from the decades around 1000 or instead represent forgeries made closer to 1096, when the armies of the First Crusade were already in motion. The first text, written in the form of a letter from the church of Jerusalem to the universal Church, lamented the fallen state of Christ's tomb and called upon its reader to become a "soldier of Christ," who might use force to render aid and counsel to that holy place.[24] The second text purports to be a papal bull from around the time when the Egyptian caliph destroyed the Church of the Holy Sepulcher. In it, Pope Sergius called for an armed expedition that might free the site from the "Agarene people" with divine aid, promising an "eternal" reward for those who "defended God."[25]

As we have seen, the reform papacy of the later eleventh century made its own contributions to this assertive rather than passive Christian posture vis-à-vis the infidel world.[26] Well before he delivered his famous "crusade sermon" at Clermont in 1095, Pope Urban II explicitly framed the liberation of Christian churches from the Muslims within a theology of history that bore striking continuities with the language of Pope Gregory VII. In his correspondence with rulers and churchmen in Spain and Sicily, Urban offered a familiar narrative that celebrated recent Christian conquests as part of a divine plan. First, he identified the age of the Primitive Church and the holy martyrs, who sanctified places such as the church of Sicily with their blood shed in God's name. Then, because of men's sins, the Saracens conquered those regions, oppressing the worshippers of the Christian religion and reducing the "liberty" of the Christian religion to nothing. Presently, in what Urban referred to as "our times," by the grace of the Lord and the labors of Christian rulers a process of restoration had begun. This recovery was ushering in a renewal of the churches' ancient glory after bondage under non-believers.[27]

As a product and propagator of reform ideology, Urban seized upon the theme of ecclesiastical liberty as a key principle for Christian expansion, thereby revealing a close connection between the papal monarchy's vision of internal order within Christendom and along its expanding frontiers. In a letter to King Alfonso VI of Léon and Castile in 1088, Urban opened with a brief exposition on the basic division between the dignity of the priesthood and royal power, addressing Alfonso as a shepherd speaking to a member of his flock and reminding the Christian king of his obligations to the church of Rome. It was through the power and mercy of God, Urban declared to Alfonso, that the ruler had expelled the Saracens and restored the church of Toledo to its pristine liberty. By addressing Alfonso in these pastoral terms, confirming Toledo's ecclesiastical privileges and sending its archbishop Bernard his *pallium,* the symbol of his episcopal office, Urban demonstrated the reform program in action on the moving borders of Christendom. The pope struck a similar tone when writing to the bishop of Syracuse, declaring that the Norman conquest of the island was a clear sign of God's will to "change the times and transfer kingdoms." Drawing upon the Book of Daniel, famous for its episode about the progression of world empires, Urban declared that the Christian conquests in Spain and Sicily offered a sign of the Lord's will to transfer royal power and to alter historical events. Urban's theology of history, a stage-by-stage progression from ancient glory through former loss to present restoration, formed a dynamic vision of God's hand in shaping what we might now call the geopolitics of the Mediterranean world. Within this framework, the bishops of Rome played a unique role, confirming and protecting the newly won liberty of the churches that were wrested from the pagans. For Urban, the universal parish of Saint Peter was growing by leaps and bounds, with the pope of Rome as an assistant to the Lord in the restoration of Christendom.[28]

In 1095 at Clermont, Urban turned this historical theology of Christian liberation and renewal toward aid for the churches of the East and the recovery of Jerusalem. In this regard, his actions once again bore a striking resemblance to those of Pope Gregory VII, whose "Crusade Plan of 1074" was intended both to assist the Greeks of Constantinople against the Turks and ultimately to reach the Holy Sepulcher. Considering the importance attributed to the pope's words at Clermont for determining the shape of the First Crusade, it is frustrating that we will never know precisely what he said or exactly what he personally intended when he delivered his famous sermon.[29] Although his address was well reported by contemporary chroniclers, some of whom were apparently present at the council, they composed and redacted their accounts years later. The earliest historians of the crusade—including participants in the expedition such as the anonymous author of *The Deeds of the Franks,* Raymond d'Aguilers, Fulcher of Chartres, and Peter Tudebode, as well as those who never left their religious houses and drew upon *The Deeds of the Franks* as a source of information, including Robert the Monk, Baldric of Dol, and Guibert of Nogent—all wrote after the crusaders had seized possession of Jerusalem. When they looked back at the Council of Clermont, they already knew how the expedition had ended. Thus it was inevitable that their knowledge of the crusade's outcome shaped their retrospective presentations of the event that had set the "army of God" in motion toward its triumphant conclusion.[30]

At the same time, the plurality of sources surrounding Clermont provides us with a rich opportunity to explore the meaning of Urban's sermon to different authors and audiences.[31] As Penny Cole puts it, the chroniclers of the crusade interpreted the sermon at Clermont as "an integral part of the history of the expedition that recovered Jerusalem for Christendom, and they undertook to endow it with the dignity and highminded qualities appropriate to the movement it inspired."[32] Various accounts of the council put their own "spin" on the pope's message and intentions, providing us with a fascinating set of contemporary perspectives on the origins and meaning of the crusade. The chroniclers made the exhortation at Clermont their own and appropriated the meaning of the crusade for Christendom in ways that Urban almost certainly would have understood and appreciated, even if they took liberties with his precise words.

Two major themes framed the chroniclers' presentations of the sermon. First, the pope declared that Christian warriors needed to end the "wrong" kind of violence, meaning their brigandage and constant warfare with each other, and to substitute in its place the "right" kind of force to assist the Eastern Christians, who were being assailed by infidels. This campaign meant more than military assistance to the beleaguered Byzantine Empire. Ascribing words to Urban, the chroniclers of the First Crusade made no hard-and-fast distinctions between the "kingdom of the Greeks," "your brothers living in the Eastern land," and those places being defiled in Jerusalem, Antioch, and "other cities of the Eastern regions."[33] As presented by Baldric of Dol, Urban exhorted the knights present at Clermont to end their sinful infighting and to rush instead to the defense of the Eastern Church, the source of the Christian faith: "For She it is from whom the joys of your salvation have come forth," the pope declared, "who poured into your mouths the milk of divine wisdom, who set before you the holy teachings of the Gospel."[34]

There seems little reason to doubt that Urban felt solicitous toward the Byzantine emperor, Alexius I Comnenus (r. 1081–1118), along with the Greek Church as a whole. From start to finish, his papacy was marked by a number of maneuvers to strengthen institutional ties between the two churches, while defusing sources of theological tension between them. In 1089, Urban had successfully negotiated with Alexius to harmonize relations between the churches of Rome and Constantinople, apparently forestalling similar efforts by the anti-pope Clement III in that same direction.[35] It also appears that Alexius played a role—albeit unwittingly—in summoning the First Crusade by asking for military assistance against the Turks earlier in 1095 at the council of Piacenza.[36] Not too long after the crusading armies were set in motion, the pope presided over a council at Bari in 1098, where an assembly of Roman and Greek churchmen debated points of theology and ecclesiastical discipline.[37] Judging by the pope's general tone toward Constantinople, Urban envisioned his authority over the Greeks in pastoral terms. Capturing and crafting the pope's words at Clermont, the chroniclers represented his call for an expedition to liberate the Eastern Church as the act of a shepherd caring for his endangered flock.[38]

Second, beyond aiding members of the Eastern Church, the new expedition had an even greater place in God's design: the liberation of Jerusalem and the holy places from the hands of the infidels. To varying degrees, the reports of Urban's sermon at Clermont drove home the point that the Muslims and their rites formed a source of defilement that needed to be wiped clean; the infidels were accused of everything from pouring blood from their circumcisions into baptismal fonts to sodomizing bishops. This sort of extreme language of pollution was neither unprecedented nor exclusively directed toward Muslims—in many ways, it recalled the denunciations of simoniacal priests and other sources of corruption by earlier generations of reformers. Pointed in the direction of infidels, however, the language of pollution left little room for doubt about the goal of the crusade. Like heretics within the body of the Church, the non-believers in possession of Jerusalem were something to be eradicated or purged.[39] In his own correspondence shortly after Clermont, Urban was clear that he saw the goals of liberating the Eastern Church and the ultimate direction of the crusade toward the recovery of Jerusalem as linked ambitions. The pope exhorted his readers to rush forth for the "liberation of the Eastern churches" and promised spiritual rewards for those "going to Jerusalem," who were "moved not out of earthly greed, but rather only for the salvation of their soul and for the liberation of the Church."[40]

The chroniclers of the First Crusade, writing after the fact and well aware that the crusaders succeeded in conquering the holy city, carefully set the stage for that thunderous event. Both Robert the Monk and Baldric of Dol opened their crusade histories with references to the place of Jerusalem within the biblical and post-biblical past, stretching from the days of the Israelites through the city's sack by the Roman rulers Titus and Vespasian to its conquest by the Muslims. Robert rhetorically asked what could be more miraculous since the dawn of creation than the expedition to Jerusalem "in modern times" (excepting, of course, Christ's sacrifice on the cross).[41] Using an exegetical reference that Pope Urban would have certainly appreciated, assuming that he did not actually use it himself, Baldric opened his chronicle with a reference to the Book of Daniel, proclaiming that God "changes kings and the times." In the present age, Baldric asserted, the Lord had gathered the expedition from the ends of the earth to liberate Jerusalem, "for, so it ought to be believed, it was not without divine inspiration that a great band of soldiers of every means was willing to go from the Western into the Eastern land, and joyfully set out against the barbarous nations, abandoning their estates and homes, sons and wives to fight by hand among innumerable misfortunes."[42]

Framed in these terms, the crusade manifested a common undertaking by all of Christendom, meaning, effectively, Western Christians. Most of the first crusade-historians were French (that is to say, Franco-Norman), and thus it is not surprising that many of the chronicles reserved a special place in the history of the crusade for the "people of the Franks." Robert the Monk was particularly clear in asserting that the crusading Franks were agents of God, following in the footsteps of the illustrious Charlemagne and his (apocryphal) journey to Jerusalem.[43] Throughout their accounts of the crusade, the chroniclers celebrated the regional groups that constituted the crusading armies, above all the Franks, but also Bretons, English, Italians, Scots, and others en route to the Lord's sepulcher, encountering Greeks, Syrians, Jacobites, and Armenians among their Christian brethren, who were being oppressed by Turks, Saracens, Agarenes, and Persians.[44] Beyond these distinct identities, however, one finds a sense of the crusade as the collective effort of Western Christians who were assuming a pivotal role in the history of Christendom by freeing the Eastern Church from the infidels. As Fulcher of Chartres proclaimed in the prologue to his account of the expedition, "The historical words which follow will tell how this work was begun and also how all the people of the West willingly directed their hearts and hands toward the completion of this journey."[45] According to Guibert of Nogent, Urban stressed at Clermont that the Christian armies he was directing toward Jerusalem and the aid of the Eastern Church possessed a common identity as Western Christians. Drawing upon the Book of Isaiah, the pope declared:

> Remember that the voice of the Lord himself said to the Church,, "I will lead your seed from the East, and I will gather you from the West" [Is. 43:5] The Lord has led our seed from the East, since he brought forth for us in a double manner out of that Eastern region the first seeds of the Church. Out of the West, however, he gathered it, for through those who last began the proof of faith, that is the Westerners, lost Jerusalem will be restored—we think that, God willing, this thing will come to pass through your deeds.[46]

Guibert did not develop this exegesis of Isaiah at any length, but his message was clear: the Eastern Church represented the font of the Christian religion, but the younger Western Church, which had received its faith from the East "in a double manner" at the hands of Saints Peter and Paul, was now being called upon to fulfill a preeminent role in the achievement of God's plan.

Guibert's report of the sermon at Clermont is exceptional for its invocation of an apocalyptic impulse behind the calling of the crusade. According to Guibert, Pope Urban himself warned his listeners that the final days were at hand, but that first the Christian rule in the East had to be restored. To fulfill biblical prophecies, the pope declared, Christianity must be thriving in Jerusalem and its environs before Antichrist would arrive on the scene and begin his vicious persecution against the faithful before his final defeat and the end of time. After all, if there were no Christians in the holy places, whom would Antichrist persecute? By setting out on the quest for the Holy Sepulcher, Urban implied, the crusaders were taking the first step toward the eventual realization of this eschatological scenario.[47] Guibert's unique attribution of such a prediction to the pope raises a long-standing debate among modern historians of crusading: Did apocalyptic expectations fuel "popular" eagerness for the First Crusade among the poor and the marginal, who saw the movement as a means to realize the eschatological promise of a millennial Sabbath age?[48] Opinions range from those who believe that apocalyptic eschatology formed the predominant factor in the origin of the First Crusade to those who effectively deny apocalypticism any real role. Some have suggested that Guibert's attribution of such sentiments to the pope reflected a careful channeling of crusade-related millenarian expectations that "respectable" members of the clergy must have found distasteful or dangerous in their more extreme manifestations (expectations, moreover, that did not just appeal to the unlettered, but also to certain clerics who should know better).[49] Certainly, Guibert's own linkage of the crusade to the end of time is explicit but cautious, couched in deferred generalities rather than any immediate sense of eschatological drama.

Regardless of his mixed feelings about the crusade's immediate apocalyptic ramifications, Guibert's chronicle and those of his peers revealed a broader sense of Western Christian manifest destiny. Even crusade-historians who singled out the elusive preacher Peter the Hermit, and not Pope Urban, as the initial source of inspiration for the expedition shared this basic crusading theology. Writing sometime during the decades immediately after the First Crusade, the chronicler Albert of Aachen explained the crusade's origins by describing an encounter between Peter the Hermit and the Greek patriarch of Jerusalem, Simeon II (r. 1084–1106), during Peter's pilgrimage to that city. In response to Simeon's lamentations about the violation of the holy places by the infidels, Peter declared that he would seek out aid from the "Apostolic See" and "Christian lords" for "your liberation and the cleansing of the saints." The Hermit's mission was validated soon afterward by a dream at the Holy Sepulcher, in which God instructed him to search for assistance from his homeland for the purpose of "purging" the holy places and "restoring" the worship of the saints.[50] The Genoese author Caffaro, writing a bit later around 1140, offered yet another variation on the crusade's origins. According to Caffaro, the future crusaders Robert of Flanders and Duke Godfrey of Bouillon devised a plan to liberate the Holy Sepulcher from the "servitude of the Saracens" after returning from their own pilgrimages.[51] Afterwards, they were instructed by an angel to seek out the papal confidant Adhémar of Le Puy, who informed Pope Urban of this plan.[52]

Despite its influential role in shaping the sacred ideology of crusading, the papal monarchy did not "own" the historical memory of the First Crusade in any absolute sense. Chroniclers such as Albert and Caffaro remind us that there was a multiplicity of views on the genesis of the expedition, even among those who shared a belief that the crusade formed a common undertaking for the Western Christian followers of Rome. Indeed, that common sense of Christendom found in various crusading sources demonstrates the wider appeal of such Christian unity for churchmen who fell somewhere outside the immediate orbit of the reform-era papacy, but still shared many of its basic values and aspirations for the liberty, purity, and integrity of the universal Church under Roman leadership. With the genesis of crusading, the theory and anticipation of Christian world order had begun to find a new and powerful form of expression.

Theology of Crusading and the Enemies of God

Following the origins of the First Crusade in 1095–1096, the subsequent course of crusader victories at Nicaea, Antioch, and eventually Jerusalem from 1097 to 1099 seemed to confirm its divine mandate. At least, this was the case after the "first wave" of "unruly" crusaders led by Peter the Hermit was destroyed by the Turks in Anatolia. Although they were sorely tried, the princely warriors of the "second wave" miraculously reached their goal.[53] Both the first-generation chronicles (drafted by participants soon after the capture of Jerusalem) and the second-generation ones (written by non-participants years later) presented the progress of God's army and its triumphant conclusion as signs that the Lord had guided the crusaders. Miracles and divine portents filled the chronicles, ranging from comets to hosts of celestial beings who fought alongside the warrior-pilgrims. Comparisons between the ancient Israelites and the crusaders abounded, along with biblical allusions that framed the deeds of the crusading armies within a broader theology of history. As Robert the Monk declared in the opening to his account, the outcome of the crusade had fulfilled Old Testament prophecies found in Isaiah. Robert reemphasized this theme in the close of his chronicle, declaring that the crusaders had fulfilled in reality *(realiter)* what was promised to Isaiah spiritually *(spiritualiter)*. Biblical prophecy had come to pass before their very eyes.[54]

This providential language of crusading narratives was contingent upon the converse role of non-Christian and non-orthodox peoples as "negative actors" in salvation history. On this point Baldric of Dol was particularly succinct, declaring that the crusaders equally despised "Jews, heretics, and Saracens, all of whom they called the enemies of God."[55] His language of exclusion echoed that of earlier church reformers. There was not, however, one simple answer or clear plan for how the followers of Rome were supposed to deal with those various "enemies." Were they to be converted to the Christian faith? Were they to be ignored, except when they directly opposed Christian plans to liberate the holy places? Were they to be mercilessly wiped out? What about encounters between the crusaders and Eastern Christian communities, fellow believers whose religious beliefs and practices might be suspect? To conceive the place of the crusade in God's historical plan for Christendom, contemporaries were forced to confront anew the sometimes ambiguous status of non-Christian and non-orthodox peoples.

Generally speaking, notions of conversion did not drive the First Crusade.[56] That is, medieval contemporaries did not initially link crusading with an effort to convert Muslims "by the sword" or by the threat of violence. According to the crusade chronicles, individual acts of conversion did happen, but the effort to expand Christendom by "recovering" lands from the infidels did not entail any systematic effort to convert the non-Christian inhabitants of those regions. There was, in fact, little discussion in the Roman Church during the period leading up to the crusade about the necessity or desire for converting infidel societies en masse. The unusual eleventh-century letter mentioned above, written by the "humble priest" who hoped that the "prince of the Agarene people" would follow the example of Constantine and embrace the Christian religion, reads more like a meditation written for internal Christian consumption rather than a genuine plea to an infidel leader for his conversion. A full-fledged theory of mission to the Muslim world would not develop until the thirteenth century, when ideas of crusading and conversion would begin to compete and mutually reinforce each other, both contributing to Christian visions of world order.

In at least one case, however, the First Crusade did initiate an unexpected episode when the conversion of God's enemies to Christianity became linked with the road toward Jerusalem, namely the infamous attacks on the Jewish communities of the Rhineland in 1096. At that time, according to both Hebrew and Latin accounts, bands of crusaders led principally by Count Emicho of Flonheim offered Jews at Speyer, Worms, Mainz, and other cities a choice between conversion to Christianity or death.[57] That such forced conversion flew in the face of official church doctrine is indisputable. Although the Jews were the perennial religious "outsiders" in Christian society, there is evidence that the Jewish inhabitants of German cities were in fact well integrated into the local economic and social fabric. Given these circumstances, the outbreak of violence against them has puzzled modern historians, who also debate about the long-term impact of the crusader pogroms on the status of the Jews in Europe.[58] In the past, responsibility for these acts has been laid at the door of the crusade's "first wave" of less privileged elements, the supposedly rough-and-tumble masses that were expecting the crusade to initiate an eschatological realization of God's kingdom. If such bands of crusaders did anticipate the end of the world, seeking the conversion of the Jews would have made sense, since the "entry" of Israel into the Church formed a standard part of apocalyptic scenarios.[59]

In patristic theology of history, Jews and infidels occupied quite different roles. The Jews (in a formulation made famous by Augustine of Hippo) had a legitimate, if carefully circumscribed and degraded, space in Christian society as "living letters of the Law," unwitting and unwilling witnesses to the Old Testament that prophesied the coming of Christ. In theory, they could be "scattered," but not "destroyed."[60] This "protected status" of the Jews was partially based on the expectation of their ultimate conversion to Christianity at the end of time. In these terms, little theological warrant existed for the attacks in 1096. Indeed, from a papal standpoint, Alexander II had formally declared in Spain decades earlier that military expeditions against the infidels should not molest Jewish communities. As the pope put it, "There is a great deal of difference between the business of dealing with Jews and the Saracens."[61] During the pogroms of 1096, some local bishops took efforts to protect the Jews, although many of the local authorities and Christian townspeople effectively abandoned them to their fate or joined their attackers. Nor, for that matter, can the pogroms be easily blamed on the "unlettered" and "poor" masses of crusaders, who were undoubtedly in the company of "respectable" clerics and members of the lesser nobility. As we have seen, earlier chroniclers like Rodulfus Glaber had already revealed that the protected status of the Jews sometimes competed with a growing sense of antagonism toward them as possible enemies of the Church, much like the heretics and false Christians decried by the reformers. One did not have to be uneducated to believe that the crusaders' swords could have multiple targets among those who threatened the faith.[62]

Without discounting material motives for the attacks, the principal motivation for the pogroms apparently lay in the conviction of some crusaders that the Jews were indeed enemies of Christ, similar to the infidels in Jerusalem, albeit conveniently closer at hand. If some of the crusaders did believe that the expedition would contribute toward the realization of history, they might have seen the conversion of the Jews as an extension of that belief. Unlike the Jews, infidels were accorded no such theoretical protections. Perhaps this helps to explain why the crusade chroniclers openly described without reticence, if not with considerable relish, the slaughter of Muslims in places like Nicaea, Antioch, and Jerusalem. In principle, the liberation, purification, and restoration of those holy places would be achieved by wiping out or pushing out the non-believers who polluted them. By contrast, there was more ambivalence among the chroniclers of the First Crusade toward the pogroms. Some mentioned them only in passing, while others, notably Albert of Aachen, openly criticized the decision to molest the Jewish communities. When the bands of crusaders who committed the pogroms were destroyed in Hungary, Albert attributed their fall to divine punishment for their general rapaciousness and their attack on the Jews, including their acts of forcible conversion.[63] Baldric might have been capturing the genuine sentiments of some crusaders when he wrote that they did not distinguish between "Jews, heretics, and Saracens" as enemies of God, but clearly some crusaders (or at least some chroniclers of the crusade) did make such distinctions.

Moving onward from Western Europe into the Balkans and beyond, the various waves of crusading armies passed by Constantinople, initiating a series of encounters between crusaders and Eastern Christians, including Greeks but also Armenians, Jacobites, Nestorians, and others when the crusading armies reached Syria and Palestine. These interactions raised an even more ambiguous set of relationships for those commemorating the First Crusade than did the status of the Jews. For many modern scholars, it was the crusades and not the Schism of 1054 that caused a lasting breach between the Latin and Greek Churches, as the result of armed clashes between crusaders and Byzantines, mutual hostility over religious differences, and the Latin "colonization" of formerly Greek ecclesiastical sites in the Holy Land. Steven Runciman offers a typical assessment of these developments by declaring that "Urban II's action in launching the Crusade in the East in pious hope that it would rescue the Eastern Churches . . . produced results as far removed as possible from the intentions of the great Pope."[64]

In recent years, however, historians have rightly cautioned that the deleterious impact of the crusades on relations between Rome and Constantinople should not be exaggerated.[65] Certainly, many chronicles of the First Crusade might be described as "anti-Alexian." In the aftermath of the First Crusade, the Norman crusader Bohemond of Taranto, whose ambitions to expand his holdings at the expense of the Byzantine Empire were well known, did everything in his power to foster animosity toward the Greek ruler Alexius, disseminating copies of *The Deeds of the Franks* that portrayed the emperor in an unflattering light and spreading rumors that the Greek ruler had betrayed the crusaders.[66] Bohemond's attacks on Alexius did not fall on deaf ears. *The Deeds of the Franks* provided a source of information and inspiration for subsequent crusade chroniclers, including Guibert of Nogent, Robert the Monk, and Baldric of Dol, who inherited the text's prejudice against the emperor. Guibert also included a well-known and almost certainly spurious letter addressed by Alexius to Count Robert of Flanders, in which the emperor seemed to imply that he would rather see Constantinople in the hands of the "Latins" than the Turks.[67] In general, the chroniclers of the First Crusade fostered a sense that Alexius effectively abandoned the crusaders during their long siege of Antioch in 1098, failing to provide them with reinforcements and supplies as promised. They commonly used words like "fraudulent," "perfidious," and "treacherous" to describe the Greek ruler (although even the chroniclers were not uniformly negative in their depictions of the emperor).[68]

It is misleading, however, to conflate criticisms of the Byzantine ruler with a widespread sense that the Greeks were somehow not proper Christians. One cannot deny that there were signs of a shift for the worse in Western attitudes toward the Eastern Christian communities during the era of the First Crusade. In a famous letter sent by the crusade leaders to the pope after the capture of Antioch in 1098, they called upon Pope Urban to join them and help them in their struggles, "for we have overcome Turks and pagans, but we have not been able to overcome the heretics, Greeks and Armenians, Syrians and Jacobites."[69] More commonly, however, contemporary crusade-histories offered contrary descriptions of the crusaders and native Christians praying together and participating in liturgical processions before battles and sieges.[70] According to some Eastern Christian chronicles, the local Christians in Syria and Palestine greeted the crusaders much as the Western Christians styled themselves—as "liberators" of Christian communities in bondage.[71] Christian harmony and benign neglect, rather than outright antagonism, seem to characterize the sources of the First Crusade.

In fact, one finds only a single explicit condemnation of Greek religious errors in the crusader chronicles, offered by Guibert of Nogent. In the opening of his work, he raised the topic of specific problems with the "faith of the Easterners" that needed correction. This Eastern predilection for deviance stood in stark contrast to the lack of such heresies "in the Latin world." On this account, Guibert proclaimed, God had established a new "lawgiver" (that is, Muhammad) over the Eastern nations, which had formerly observed the Christian faith but had strayed back into paganism. The abbot of Nogent argued that Islam itself represented a product of the Eastern tendency toward heresy, and that the Saracen conquests were a punishment by God against the Eastern Church for its doctrinal and liturgical deviance from the authority of the Church fathers and the Apostolic See of Rome.[72] Guibert's conflation of ancient heresies, Eastern Christians, and infidels into a loose tradition of deviance from the Roman Church was exceptional, but important. In the twelfth and thirteenth centuries, the idea that the rise of Islam was a specific punishment against the Byzantine Empire and Greek Christians for their religious errors would prove to be popular, as would the notion that the Eastern Christians, much like infidels, needed to be "converted" from their heresies to "proper" Roman doctrine and rites.

Beyond sparking straightforward antagonism, the First Crusade created new avenues and opportunities for the followers of Rome to imagine the proper relationship between the Western Church and the Eastern Church, including a belief that members of the Western or Latin community—the younger Christian community—had assumed a place of priority in God's plan for history. As Guibert put it later in his chronicle while celebrating crusader victories in the Promised Land, "It offers no mediocre inspiration to our faith that the Eastern Church is restored by the labor of the Western faithful."[73] Another crusader outside of Antioch in 1097, Anselm of Ribodimonte, proclaimed about the crusaders, "Let the mother church of the East rejoice! For those whom she begot acquire for themselves such glorious renown and miraculously rush to succor the Eastern Church."[74] According to such perspectives, the followers of Rome were responsible for the fate of their fellow Christians (however deviant), the holy places, and, ultimately, all of Christendom.

This mark of divine favor for the Western crusaders was particularly evident in the discovery or acquisition of biblical and other relics.[75] Depending upon their affiliations and loyalties within the crusader camp, chroniclers such as Raymond d'Aguilers and Fulcher of Chartres championed their favorite relics, the possession of which sometimes became a source of contention among various factions of crusaders. Accompanying such factionalism, however, was the belief that the acquisition of such relics formed a blessing for the crusaders as a whole. The discovery of the Holy Lance at Antioch in 1098, described by many chroniclers as a source of inspiration for the entire crusader camp, provides only one well-known example of the central place that relics occupied in the historical memory of the crusade.[76] Equally significant was the acquisition of the True Cross at Jerusalem in 1099 just after the capture of the city. As reported by Raymond, the Jerusalemites who revealed the relic to the crusaders had little doubt about the connection between crusader victories and the restoration of relics at their hands:

> Revelation makes it clear to us that you are the Chosen People of God, freed from trials and given Jerusalem and numerous other cities not by your incredible strength but rather by a vengeful God who blinded the blasphemers. The Lord, your leader, cast open the gates of unconquerable cities and won terrifying battles for you. Since God is on your side, why should we stubbornly hide his relics from you?[77]

During the years following the First Crusade, this theme was adopted and adapted by hagiographers writing for religious communities back in Europe that had acquired Christian relics from the Holy Land and its surroundings. In an immediate sense, hagiographers produced such texts to meet the needs of a given monastery, church, or city, telling the story of the relic's discovery (or theft) followed by its arrival at a new home.[78] In broader terms, however, these sources express the belief that the entire community of the Western Church was benefiting from the blessings of the saints. For example, when crusading Venetians removed relics of Saint Nicholas from a Greek church in Myra in 1100, they expressed their desire with the following words:

> Most holy patron Nicholas! Yield to the prayers of the faithful, deign to visit your Venice and the West. Let it be enough for the East and the Greeks, who regarded you as bishop and doctor, and

after your death kept you nearly seven hundred years. Now, let the West and Latins rejoice, visited by the presence of your body, illuminated with your miracles, prayers, and works sent up to heaven, with the volition and aid of the holy and indivisible Trinity—to which, there is honor and glory, now and forever, through all the ages.[79]

A Venetian cleric named Cerbanus, who described how the participants in a Venetian expedition to the Holy Land around the year 1120 removed the remains of Saint Isidore from Chios, made a similar assertion. According to his account, the Venetians searching for the relics prayed to the saint in the following terms: "Truly, let it be enough already for the East, which has now merited being illuminated by the presence of your body; from this point forward, if heavenly Majesty allows it, do not disdain from coming to and living in the West."[80]

Writing decades after the fact to celebrate the crusaders' discovery of the relics of the biblical patriarchs Abraham, Isaac, and Jacob around the year 1119, an anonymous Latin hagiographer from Hebron presented a theologically laden history of the city from the days of Abraham to the Christian acquisition of the city after the destruction of Jerusalem by Titus and Vespasian.[81] First, the Jews had venerated the site of the patriarchs' burial until they were driven out by the Romans. Centuries later, when the tomb was in Christian hands, envoys from Constantinople tried to uncover the relics and bring them to the imperial capital in the fifth century. Why, the author asked, did God prevent them from doing so by smiting them with blindness and immobility? It was to keep the patriarchs within the land that the Lord had promised to them, reserving the blessing of their patronage for Latin Christians, whom God favored "more than any other people."[82] From the time of the patriarchs to the present, history had led toward the recovery of those holy remains by the new Chosen People, who had taken possession of the very same Promised Land first bestowed upon Abraham by God.

The recovery of such sacred relics formed part of a broader "theology of liberation" that framed contemporary interpretations of the First Crusade.[83] This process of purifying and freeing the Eastern Church and holy sites from the corruption of the infidels meant more than just a military victory over infidel peoples like the Turks, the "enemies of God and holy Christendom."[84] In the chronicles of the First Crusade, one finds little or no talk of converting Muslims, but one certainly discovers what might be called the logic of "liturgical" conversion or colonization, that is, the extension of Christian worship by the crusaders into regions and places that had fallen into disrepute and profanation. This was not simply a question of establishing a Latin ecclesiastical hierarchy in places that were formally part of the Byzantine Church. By reclaiming relics, carrying out ritual processions before battles, and installing their own Christian clergy in sites that were defunct or formerly possessed by Eastern Christians, the crusaders were fulfilling the historical destiny of the expedition through their act of purifying God's community. This presentation of the crusade formed a logical extension of the idea—highlighted in the different versions of the sermon at Clermont—that the infidels represented a source of pollution in the holy places. The capture of cities like Antioch, Bethlehem, and Jerusalem meant that the proper forms of worship were being restored there and the profane rites of non-believers cast out.[85]

As seen with the crusaders' recovery of sacred relics, Latin chroniclers believed that Eastern Christians themselves recognized and celebrated the role of the crusading armies in this act of liberation. According to Albert of Aachen, when Godfrey of Boullion and his forces reached Bethlehem, the Christians living there came forth singing hymns and psalms, proclaiming "Thanks be to God, for in our times, we now are seeing those things come to pass that were always our desire, namely that you Christians, our brothers, are at hand to remove the yoke of our servitude, to restore the holy places of Jerusalem, and to wipe away the stain of the Gentiles' rites from that holy place."[86] In these terms, the recovery and restoration of Christian worship in Jerusalem, including the installment of Latin canons in the Church of the Holy Sepulcher, marked a special triumph for Christendom, one that was quite different from the battles of Christian princes against non-believers in places like Spain, Sicily, and elsewhere.[87]

As we will see in subsequent chapters, for centuries to come the Western possession of the Promised Land would remain the *sine qua non* of Latin apocalyptic schemes that projected the future transformation of all peoples into one "fold" under the authority and pastoral guidance of the

Roman Church. The hazy outlines of an imagined world order were taking shape, one that would include the conversion of the Jews, the reunion
of Eastern Christians with Rome, and the displacement of Islam. In the
heady days after 15 July 1099, the expedition proposed by Pope Urban
must have raised exciting new possibilities in the historical and prophetic
consciousness of Latin Christians. Before long, however, the crusaders
and their compatriots back home would have to confront some unpleas-
ant realities and limitations on their aspirations.

Theodicy and Crusading: Explaining Christian Defeat

In one of the great ironies of crusading history, Pope Urban II died shortly
before news reached Europe about the miraculous outcome of the expedition that he had fostered, followed by the establishment of the "crusader kingdom" of Jerusalem and the city's new Latin patriarchate. In the
immediate aftermath of the crusade, a tone of triumph characterized the
reports of the expedition to the newly elected pope, Paschal II (r. 1099–
1118), along with other churchmen who had remained behind. Not long
after the capture of Jerusalem, the Archbishop Manasses of Reims exulted
that "Jerusalem, the city and glory of our redemption," had been freed
from the "cruelest servitude of the pagans." Paschal agreed with such
sentiments. In one of his earliest letters to the newly established crusader
kingdoms in the Levant, the pope expressed wonder at God's "renewal"
of "ancient miracles" through the defeat of those who oppressed Christians and the liberation of the Eastern Church after a long period of bondage.[88]

Even as the crusaders celebrated the capture of the holy places, however, anxiety did not take long to surface. The archbishop of Reims, in
that same letter, also called upon his fellow Christians to pray that "the
King of kings and Lord of lords shall bestow victory upon the king against
the enemies of the Christians, as well as wisdom and religion upon the patriarch against the sects and deceptions of heretics." The crusaders were
well aware that the infidels would attempt recover their prize. As for the
"sects and deceptions of heretics," this apparently reveals some growing
concern with the non-Latin communities of Christians found in Jerusalem.[89] Signs of trouble did not take long to emerge. In 1101, the Christians

gathered at the Holy Sepulcher waited in vain for the miraculous lighting of the lamps in the tomb on Easter, long known to have happened at the site. When the lamps did not ignite, consternation grew. According to various reports, both the crusaders and Eastern Christians believed that their own sins were responsible for the failure of the annual miracle. The Latin patriarch of Jerusalem, Daimbert, declared that the miraculous sign was no longer needed now that Christians—not infidels—held the holy places, but he prayed that God would nevertheless renew the miracle for the unbelievers and doubters in their midst. The next day, a flurry of prayers and liturgical processions ensued as the patriarch led the crusaders along with Syrians, Armenians, and Greeks into the Holy Sepulcher. To everyone's relief, the lamps miraculously lit up.[90]

In the case of the Easter miracle, the prayer and worship of Western and Eastern Christians together succeeded in averting God's disappointment with their shortcomings. Other disasters proved harder to avoid. Shortly after the capture of Jerusalem, Pope Paschal helped to set in motion the so-called Crusade of 1101.[91] This expedition was composed in part of individuals who had sworn to go on the first armed pilgrimage to the holy places, but had failed to do so. Paschal and in some cases their own family members had berated these reluctant crusaders to fulfill their obligations. The result was a series of military disasters. The expedition floundered in Anatolia and was soundly beaten by Muslim forces, a dramatic reverse for a purported "army of God." Some found a mundane explanation for this failure—the crusaders had been betrayed by the Emperor Alexius. As we saw earlier, many chronicles of the First Crusade (largely written and redacted after the events of 1101) accused the Greek ruler of plotting against the crusaders and abandoning them at Antioch in 1098. Other chroniclers, including a participant in the Crusade of 1101, Ekkehard of Aura, added fuel to the fire by recording that Alexius further conspired with the infidels to destroy this later army of crusaders en route to the Holy Land. As Ekkehard put it, the emperor was "more disposed to favor the part of the Turks than Christians," on account of which everyone called him "a traitor, not an emperor."[92] Still others, however, painted a more complicated picture of the crusade's failure. Reporting the events of 1101, Orderic Vitalis heaped scorn on Alexius, branding him a "perfidious traitor," but he remained equally disappointed by the leaders of the

Christian crusading army, who caused a great deal of disturbance by their hot-headed actions and plundering of Greek territories. After the slaughter of the crusaders, Orderic's admiration was reserved for two groups: the martyrs who had died at the hands of the Turks, and the Syrian and Armenian Christians who tried in a brotherly manner to help the survivors of the slaughter. Albert of Aachen likewise implied that the crusaders of 1101 were themselves responsible for bringing down divine anger against the expedition, by indulging in sinful living and repeatedly violating the Greek emperor's reasonable instructions not to molest his subjects.

The destruction of this crusading army represented the mirror opposite of the success that the First Crusade had enjoyed in achieving God's plan. The election of the Western Church as an agent in salvation history equally meant that the Lord would single out Western Christians for special chastisement when they rejected God's laws.[93] The chronicles of the First Crusade had displayed this same logic in their accounts of the temporary reverses that the crusaders had encountered during the first campaign, for instance during the protracted sieges of Nicaea, Antioch, and Jerusalem itself. To placate God, the crusaders fasted, prayed, performed acts of penance, and even expelled the prostitutes from their camp. In those cases, the ultimate success of the expedition effectively redeemed any momentary setbacks resulting from sinful behavior.[94] After 1101, however, Latin Christians realized that divine forgiveness would sometimes be harder to achieve.

In 1107 a crusading army met an even more shameful end, sputtering out during an assault on the Byzantine empire at Durazzo led by Bohemond, then prince of Antioch.[95] According to various chroniclers, Bohemond returned to Europe in 1105 with the express intent of inciting Western Christians against Alexius. The main charge leveled against the Greek ruler was that he had betrayed the armies of the First Crusade and was assaulting pilgrims bound for the Holy Land.[96] Apparently, Bohemond received some backing for his efforts to raise troops by Pope Paschal, who (according to one report) made Bohemond "the standard-bearer of the army of Christ, and, giving him the banner of Saint Peter, sent him away in peace." The papal legate, Bruno of Segni, accompanied the Norman warlord.[97] Some modern historians have assumed that Paschal, unlike his predecessor Urban II, was not particularly sympathetic toward the Greek Church and agreed to redirect crusading activity against the Eastern Empire, or, alternatively, that Bohemond duped Paschal into supporting a crusade that the Norman warrior redirected toward Byzantium.[98] Neither scenario seems likely. The pope would have had no illusions about Bohemond's intention to attack the Greeks, but he probably saw an opportunity to pursue his goal of supporting the crusader kingdoms by endorsing an attack on Alexius that would have happened with or without his open support.[99]

When Bohemond and Bruno toured around France in 1106, raising support for a new expedition, they did not hide the Norman leader's plan to assault the Greek emperor. Many of the sources reporting their activities, however, make it clear that the warriors who responded to their summons were planning to "hasten to Jerusalem" or "make the journey to the Holy Sepulcher." After the collapse of Bohemond's attack, the chroniclers reported that many of the crusaders indeed pressed onward to the holy places. This sort of testimony implies that the majority of soldier-pilgrims assembled for the siege at Durazzo had every intention of going to Jerusalem in fulfillment of their crusader vows after completing the campaign against Alexius.[100] The campaign of 1107 seems less like a "holy war" against the Greeks than a crusade to Jerusalem that was prepared—if not eager—to attack the tyrant Alexius en route. This was neither the first nor the last time that crusaders planned to "multitask" while fulfilling their vows (after all, as far back as Gregory VII's Crusade Plan of 1074, the pope had intended that his soldiers of Saint Peter would pacify the Normans before pressing onward to the Holy Sepulcher).

In 1107, following the failure of Bohemond's expedition at Durazzo, Western chroniclers were once again confronted with a disastrous outcome for a crusading army. In this case, the "crusaders" were open to the charge that they had in fact gone after the wrong people and violated their spiritual purpose. According to Orderic Vitalis, when it became apparent that Bohemond had lost the battle at Durazzo, the Norman warrior's companions beseeched him to desist, arguing that this attack on the "holy empire" of Byzantium had turned God's ear to the prayers of the "just men who cried out to him against us in Greece."[101] In the still-forming genre of crusade historiography, a sense that the expeditions were righteous and divinely sanctioned formed a critical point of validation for crusading. In 1107, by contrast, we find an express declaration that the expedition against Alexius did not have just cause and was not favored by God. In fact, it could be argued that divine justice was on the side of the Greeks, whom the crusaders had attacked for all the wrong reasons.

Crusader defeat raised uncomfortable questions in Latin theology of history. The same qualities and goals that elevated the expeditions to the Holy Land to sacred status also opened them to criticism when they failed to achieve their purpose or became mired in the carnality of this world. Jerusalem represented a prize and a burden that brought awesome responsibilities. Sin, avarice, and infighting could always undo God's mercy and take away what divine providence had granted. As Pope Paschal wrote around 1107 to feuding churchmen in the crusader kingdom, Jerusalem's position in the middle of "many peoples" made it a prime target for those who tried to cast aspersions on the "Christian faith" and "the purity of Latin worship."[102] In the Holy Land itself, the crusaders experienced their own problems and military reverses during the first two decades after the capture of Jerusalem. In January 1120, a council assembled at Nablus to address sources of discord within the crusader kingdom, including a contentious dispute between King Baldwin II (r. 1118–1131) and the leading bishops of the realm over the collection of tithes. The prologue to the canons declared that the recent plagues, famine, and infidel attacks on the Christians of Jerusalem manifested a just punishment by God resulting from their own sins, intended to correct rather than destroy the Lord's followers.[103] What was needed in this case was not more violence—not the sword wielded against the enemies of Christendom—but rather a transformation within the body of the faithful, a reform of the Church that would encourage the Lord to turn aside his wrath.

The First Crusade did not create the idea of Christendom. The crusades, however, did help to intensify the historical consciousness of the Latin Christian community and its place in the economy of salvation. The expedition that captured Jerusalem in 1099 became a template, a model for subsequent Christian action both at home and abroad when self-proclaimed members of the Western Church confronted heresy and unbelief, saw themselves as threatened, and, in certain circumstances, desired to propagate their faith. There could be no greater sign of God's favor than the possession of the holy places. If anything, this clerical framework for understanding the First Crusade remains among the most powerful aspects of its legacy. Long after the hatred and violence of actual crusaders and their opponents have vanished, this vision of Christendom as a community united in concerted action against the non-Christian world continues to speak to us, in some cases whether we want it to or not.

For centuries before the First Crusade, Jerusalem and its holy places had attracted the imagination and devotion of Western Christians. From 1099 forward, the fate of that holy city—in crusader hands and even more so after it was lost again to Islamic control in 1187—came to occupy a place of immense priority in the historical memory of the Latin Church.[104] Over time, crusading became firmly linked to the ongoing desire for reform within the Western Church and to the establishment of unity between Rome and the Eastern Church. Whatever role apocalyptic expectations might have played in the initial formation of the First Crusade, in the wake of the crusade these three projects—the lasting Christian possession of the holy places, the unification of all Christians, and the internal renewal of the Roman Church—would converge to reshape the world as a prelude to the approaching end of history. After all, how could God's followers hope to extend their faith to all peoples before the end of time, yet fail to achieve the lasting liberation of the sacred city that lay at the world's center?

Even as the crusades intensified the meaning of Christendom, they also opened the door to unsettling critiques of its inhabitants and their own shortcomings. In some cases, contemporaries came to question the utility and very purpose of crusading altogether, precisely because subsequent crusades failed to achieve their stated goals. Invoking divine providence to explain the course of contemporary events such as the capture of Jerusalem came at a price. Theology of history was not just the prerogative of those who favored authority in its present forms; it also belonged to those who were critical of contemporary mores and institutions. In such circumstances, it was not the external enemies of God that threatened Christendom, but the enemy within—the sins of God's own Chosen People.

3

Reformist Apocalypticism and the Battlefield of History

In 1144, Western Christians confronted yet another setback for their crusading fortunes when Islamic forces recaptured the city of Edessa. Responding to this disconcerting turn of events, Pope Eugene III (r. 1145–1153) summoned a new armed expedition to aid the beleaguered crusader principalities of the East. To do so, the pope deliberately invoked the memory of his predecessor Urban II, who had first incited the "sons of the Roman Church from every part of the world" to fight for the liberation of the Holy Land.[1] Echoing the call for the First Crusade, Eugene described the recent tribulations caused by the "enemies of God," who were capturing Christian fortifications, slaughtering the clergy, and scattering sacred relics underfoot. This new crusade, moreover, would not limit its goals to the environs of Jerusalem. More explicitly than Urban, Eugene envisioned concerted crusader action on all of Christendom's frontiers, extending the same privileges and remission of sins granted to Jerusalem-bound warriors to those who were fighting in Iberia and against "the Slavs and pagan peoples living in the north."[2]

Despite these impressive aspirations, however, the resulting Second Crusade proved to be a military debacle, or at least that was how contemporaries viewed the fate of the principal expedition that floundered outside of Damascus.[3]

The Bavarian cleric and exegete Gerhoh of Reichersberg was one such Christian "back home" forced to address the disappointing outcome of the Second Crusade. Around 1150, in his commentary on the Book of Psalms, Gerhoh largely apologized for the crusaders, presenting them as a gathering of the faithful by Pope Eugene and his former abbot, the famous Cistercian mystic Bernard of Clairvaux, whose preaching had been accompanied by signs and miracles. Gerhoh recognized the alloyed nature of the crusaders, some who served the Lord and others just themselves, but he concluded that only God would judge their motives.[4] About fifteen years later, in his tract on Antichrist, Gerhoh left no doubt that God had indeed judged the crusaders and found them wanting. Fault for the disastrous campaign was shared by all God's people, who were stained by the sins of avarice and simony. For Gerhoh, fully committed to the "Gregorian" vision of Christendom, the success of the First Crusade and the failure of the Second fit squarely into his broader theology of history. Looking back at the First Crusade, he presented Urban II as a model of sacerdotal authority when he had sounded the call at Clermont to fight the infidels, summoning the Frankish nobles to march to Jerusalem and liberate the Holy Sepulcher. The successful outcome of the initial expedition provided an unmistakable indication of its sanctified origins. Conversely, the results of the recent expedition represented an exterior marker of Christendom's inner failings and a sign of Antichrist at work.[5]

Gerhoh's appraisal of the crusades, the reform movement, and the evils of Antichrist demonstrated the keen historical sensibilities of his age. As Marie-Dominique Chenu once put it, "It was not the least splendid achievement of Latin Christendom in the twelfth century to awaken in men's minds an active awareness of human history."[6] Others have agreed with Chenu that "no century of medieval historical thought was as productive, as innovative as the twelfth century."[7] In addition to Gerhoh of Reichersberg, scholars commonly associate Rupert of Deutz (a somewhat cantankerous Benedictine monk), Honorius Augustodunensis (an obscure but prolific regular canon), and Anselm of Havelberg (an outspoken member of the Premonstratensian order) with this new spirit of historical inquiry. Taking the Bible as their guide, these monastic and clerical authors scrutinized the divinely ordained patterns of history with a heightened imagination and daring creativity, searching to understand not just the past, but also the tumultuous changes of the present along with the possibility of future changes both for the worse and for the better. Some scholars have even argued that the very idea of progress over time—a hallmark of modern European culture, if not modernity itself—originated from within this twelfth-century milieu.[8]

A variety of terms have been used to describe this cluster of thinkers and their style of theology, including "symbolic," "speculative," "poetic," and "contemplative." Such labels, while apt in many ways, imply a dreamlike quality in those monks and clerics, immured in the abstract figurative landscape of their minds. Nothing could be farther from the truth. For all their hermeneutical genius, such twelfth-century theologians directly and indirectly tackled the most heated political, religious, and social issues of their day. After all, a properly ordered Christian world required a properly ordered sense of history, stretching from the beginning of God's plan for salvation until its consummation. In recent years scholars have begun to use the term "reformist apocalypticism" to capture the mood of exegetes that include Rupert, Honorius, Anselm, and Gerhoh, describing their view of clerical reform as "an unprecedented crisis of truly apocalyptic significance with God's forces massed against those of Satan."[9] As the name indicates, reformist apocalyptic writers drew their basic inspiration from the ideology of the eleventh-century reformers and their drive to create a purified Christian community. During the twelfth century, that Gregorian impulse was further complicated by the well-known "reformation" of Europe's religious landscape. Channeling a desire to recreate the evangelic fervor of the apostolic age, new monastic and clerical groups such as the Cistercians and Premonstratensians emerged alongside the traditional forms of Benedictine life. In many ways, this development drew upon the same creative tensions that fueled the earlier ecclesiastical reform movement, marked by a desire to renew not just the institutional Church, but rather Christian society as a whole. A source of inspiration to some, such innovation posed a threat to others, who decried the illicit changes that were sweeping like a storm through the Roman Church.[10]

Witnessing and participating in this fight for proper order within Christendom, reformist thinkers stressed three themes in their analysis of history: first, that the past was a record of conflict between the forces of evil and the elect; second, that the turmoil of their own days represented a new stage in that unfolding drama; and third, that history's consummation was closer than many suspected. This was not history for history's sake. The struggles of the present formed another stage in the unfolding conflict between the forces of evil and righteousness. Battle lines were being drawn between faithful Christians, on the one side, and the enemies of God on the other, the latter including heretics, schismatics, pagans, Jews, and other opponents of Christendom. In addition, there were increasing complaints about Greek Christians as a source of heresy and schism because of their divergence from Rome. The ultimate enemy of Christendom, however, still lay in the future. Inevitably, theological schemes of history pointed toward the coming of Antichrist, who would be served by still more Jews, heretics, pagans, and infidels. By speculating about the insidious activities of such "outsiders," reformist apocalyptic thinkers implicated themselves in another characteristic of the twelfth century—a hardening in Christian attitudes toward groups targeted as deviant or threatening.

The reformist apocalyptic view of the world, however, did not simply entail a stark condemnation of non-Christians and the non-orthodox. First of all, this strident tone toward the outside enemies of Christendom accompanied open criticism of corruption and avarice in present-day ecclesiastical institutions. All was not right with the Roman Church. False and hypocritical Christians were as bad (if not worse) than Jews, heretics, and other servants of Antichrist. In this sense, the reformist expectations of the later eleventh century, never completely realized, had set the stage for major disappointments. Moreover, Latin theologians of history commonly shared a hope that a time of true reform, renewal, and peace awaited Christendom under the spiritual guidance of the Roman papacy either before or after the apocalyptic struggle that would precede Final Judgment. Exegetes hinted about a future terrestrial transformation that would see the universal spread of the Gospel, the conversion of pagans and the Jews, and harmony among all true believers. In the works of Abbot Joachim of Fiore, who can be thought of as the latest and greatest reformist apocalyptic thinker of the twelfth century, those hints became full-blown predictions that Jews, schismatic Eastern Christians, pagans, and perhaps even Muslims would gather as an eschatological fold under the Roman Church before the end of time. Joachim will be discussed in detail in the following chapter, but many of the developments examined here shed light on intellectual trends that anticipated the abbot's writings.[11]

Scripture, Liturgy, and the Patterns of History

At the opening of the twelfth century, there was nothing new or unusual about the belief that observable historical events formed only surface movements, betraying deeper currents and eddies that moved in accordance with the will of God. Both the eleventh-century reform movement and the outcome of the First Crusade revitalized the historical imagination of the Latin Church. Up until that time, a relatively stable consensus had persisted in the Latin intellectual tradition regarding people's abilities to discern that providential design, built around the authority of patristic authors, above all Augustine of Hippo. It was one thing, Augustine had asserted, to see the hand of the Lord in biblical history, but another thing entirely to find points of coordination between historical events occurring after the New Testament and that divine plan. In his own works, the bishop of Hippo had disseminated two "safe" templates for Christian theology of history: first, the division of time into seven ages based on the seven days of creation, and second, time's division into three stages characterized by an era "before" the written Jewish law, "under the law," and "under Christian grace."[12] In both arrangements, the incarnation of Christ formed the hinge of history, marking the transition into the sixth and final age that would be followed by the eternal and ahistorical Sabbath. Both schemes remained deliberately vague about the course of events after the time of Christ. Augustine vehemently denied that there was any meaningful way to subdivide or periodize the sixth age of history, leaving little formal room in the Latin tradition to speculate about the ever-increasing stretch of time between Christ and the end of the world.[13]

Although Augustine managed to set some effective limits on how far

the majority of educated churchmen would go in their formal explora-
tion of "historical theory," his stultifying effect on Latin theology of history was far from absolute. History was not static. Within a Christian
theological framework, it seemed hard to imagine that God had completely withdrawn his hand from crafting or coordinating momentous
events after the time of the Bible. For example, in Augustine's own lifetime, his former student Orosius had claimed that there had been "ten
persecutions" of the Church before Constantine, matching the ten plagues
of Egypt in the Book of Exodus. This notion remained highly popular
despite the fact that Augustine himself had belittled it.[14] The patristic
model of progressive "world empires" remained equally well known, subsequently used by Carolingian-era thinkers to explain the reconstitution
of empire under the Franks along with the attendant decline of imperial
dignity among the Greek rulers of Constantinople. The "translation of
empire" remained a prominent feature in the imperial ideology of the
twelfth century, above all in the universal chronicles of churchmen with
pro-imperial sympathies such as Sigebert of Gembloux and Otto of Freising. Both authors structured their histories around the divinely ordained
movement of empire or royal power from people to people until the imperial dignity of the Romans came to rest among the Franks and their
German successors.[15]

Another scheme, newly popular in the late-eleventh century, divided
the history of the Church into a series of persecutions, based on the
"seven seals" found in the Apocalypse (Rev. 6–8): the first seal and the
white horse represented the age of the Primitive Church and its oppression by the Jews; the second seal and the red horse, the Church of the
martyrs and its bloody persecution by pagans; the third seal and the black
horse, the Church after Constantine and its struggle with the internal
threat of heresy; the fourth seal and the pale horse, the contemporary
Church and the problem posed "hypocritical" Christians. The remaining
seals indicated the future trials under Antichrist and the triumph of the
saints.[16] This exegesis was codified in the *Ordinary Gloss,* fast on its way in
the early-twelfth century to becoming the standard work of biblical commentary in the Roman Church. The gloss reinforced the interpretation
of the seven seals as a loosely chronological scheme for the history of
the faithful. It also disseminated Augustine's adamant belief that the

The Four Horsemen of the Apocalypse (Rev. 6:2–8). Apocalypse Commentary, thirteenth century.

Source: Bibliothèque Nationale de France, Paris, nouv. acq. lat. 2290.

thousand-year binding of the Devil referred to "the time from Christ until Antichrist," not any sort of millennial period after Antichrist. Although the glossators allowed that "there will be peace in the Church after the death of Antichrist," they stressed that "judgment will come quickly" after his three-and-a-half-year persecution.[17]

In the twelfth century, reformist exegetes and apocalyptic thinkers began to push beyond this normative theology of history. Rupert of Deutz stands as an early innovator in this regard. Rupert, who lived from around 1075 to 1129, was in many ways a conservative figure who railed against contemporary logicians in the nascent cathedral schools and against the newly emerging forms of monastic life in his day. He was also a creative exegete who avidly supported the goals of the ecclesiastical reform movement. In 1095 Rupert encountered the dangers of the era personally, when he was forced to flee from his monastery at Liège after supporters of the German emperor attacked it—an event that he interpreted as an apocalyptic sign.[18] About a decade later, the rhythms of the liturgy inspired Rupert to speculate about the ordering of history in one of his first major works, his *Book on the Divine Offices*. This detailed liturgical commentary, written around 1111, was the first of its kind since the Carolingian period. In this work Rupert reused a number of traditional patristic schemes to organize the history of the Church, including a standard reading of the liturgical cycle that connected the seven weeks before Easter with the seven ages of the world.[19] He further aligned those seven ages with the "seven gifts" of the Holy Spirit (Isa. 11:2), linking each gift in turn with the liturgical offices for the seven days after Pentecost. Following this logic, Rupert posited a basic scheme for the experience of the Church after Christ: the gifts of "wisdom" and "understanding" were given to the Apostolic Church, manifest in the sacraments and reading of Scripture; "counsel" brought the Gentiles to God; "strength" supported the martyrs against pagan persecution; "knowledge" sustained the Church Fathers against heretics; "piety" would convert the Jews before the end of time; and finally, "fear" of God would prepare the faithful for Final Judgment.[20]

While Rupert's scheme is hardly a detailed guide to post-biblical history, it marked his willingness to go beyond Augustine and speculate about patterns of historical order after Christ. Toward the close of his commentary on the liturgy, Rupert offered another loosely chronological scheme for the history of the Church based on the nightly readings during the weeks after Pentecost. These readings started with the first two Books of Kings, which recorded the rejection of Saul and the elevation of David. According to Rupert, these books also marked the rejection of idolatry and the elevation of the Christian faith throughout the Roman Empire. The following two Books of Kings recorded the schism between Judah and the ten tribes of Israel, followed by the establishment of the two golden calves at Bethel. These books designated the time after Constantine, when heretics attempted to tear apart the faith through their false teachings.[21] This basic sense of progression from the early Church to the martyrs to the attack of heretics after Constantine was hardly unusual, but it hinted at a growing preoccupation among "Gregorian" exegetes, namely how to unlock the providential patterns of history from the time of Christ until the tumultuous events of their own present and beyond.

Rupert further displayed his view of history as a battlefield in his *Commentary on the Apocalypse,* written around 1120, and his tract *On the Victory of God's Word,* composed around 1124. In the latter text, the struggle of the Devil against the followers of God from the moment of creation until the end-time formed the ordering principle of the entire work. To illustrate that stage-by-stage combat, Rupert revisited several sections of Scripture that were commonly read for their apocalyptic portents: the great red dragon with seven heads (Rev. 12:3) and Daniel's dream of the four beasts along with the "beast from the sea" possessing seven heads and ten horns (Rev. 13:1). According to Rupert, the first head of the dragon symbolized the kingdom of Egypt; the second, the schismatic kingdom of Israel; the third, the kingdom of Babylon, which destroyed the Jewish Temple; the fourth, the Persians and Medes, who menaced the Jews with destruction; the fifth, the pagan Greeks, including King Antiochius who profaned the rebuilt Temple; and the sixth, the kingdom of the Romans, who crucified Christ and persecuted the martyrs. The seventh head of the dragon, Rupert declared, "will be the kingdom of Antichrist."[22] Following this same logic, Rupert aligned the four beasts from the Book of Daniel with the third through the sixth heads of the dragon (the lioness symbolized Babylon, the bear the Medes and Persians, the leopard the Greeks, and the final beast with ten horns the Romans). He also associated the seven heads of the "beast from the sea" with the series of empires leading to Antichrist, whose power, servants, and preachers would extend "throughout the entire world," from "sea to sea, east to west, and north to south."[23]

Rupert of Deutz was not alone in his willingness to take a fresh look at the providential pattern of history that pointed toward the coming of Antichrist. The sprawling works of his contemporary Honorius Augustodunensis displayed a similar ambition. There has been a great deal of mystery about the life of this regular canon, who spent parts of his ecclesiastical career in England and Germany before he died around 1135.[24] The details of his activities remain hazy, but Honorius became a popular author, whose creative historical thinking informed his sermons, his world chronicle, his liturgical commentary *The Jewel of the Soul*, and his works of exegesis, above all, his *Exposition on the Song of Songs*.[25] Judging by his writings, much like Rupert, Honorius stood as a committed Gregorian reformer, who did not shy away from expressing his opinions about the proper subordination of secular power to priestly authority. In his tract *The Highest Glory*, he paid particular attention to the reign of Constantine, when "royal power" was humbled before Christ and pagan rule was transferred to the "Christian kingdom." Figures like Constantine, who defended the Church from "pagans, Jews, and heretics," and Charlemagne represented models of imperial deference toward the papacy, in contrast to heretical rulers who persecuted the faithful.[26]

This struggle for proper order in Christendom colored Honorius's perspective on the patterns of history. In his *Exposition on the Song of Songs*, for example, he subdivided history into a series of battles fought "before Christ" *(ante Christum)*, starting with God and the Devil, and "after Christ" *(post Christum)*, starting with Christ and the Devil, followed by Christian struggles against pagans, heretics, "false brothers," and the anticipated struggle against Antichrist. This scheme offered another variation on the exegesis of the "seven seals" that organized post-biblical history into a series of persecutions against the Church.[27] This basic model of history also drew attention to the groups and orders among the faithful that fought to secure the triumph of the Church and to defend it from persecution, including the apostles, the martyrs who suffered open persecution, the confessors who battled insidious heresy, and the monks of Honorius's own day who vied against false Christians. Following a similar logic, Honorius also divided the history of the Church into ten stages that reflected its development from the time before the Jewish law to the anticipated trial of Antichrist. Through such schemes, Honorius demonstrated a notable characteristic of twelfth-century theology of history, namely its search for greater detail and coherence in historical theorizing. Reformist apocalyptic thinkers pushed beyond allegorical readings of the Old Testament as foreshadowing New Testament truths, searching for more explicit connections between recorded events in the time of Israel and the divine pattern of God's dispensation after Christ.

This drive for clarification can be seen in the remarkable fourth book of *The Jewel of the Soul,* in which Honorius used the calendar of scriptural readings on the Sundays after Pentecost to align historical events "under the law" with those "under grace."[28] Of course, such a basic distinction between the era of the Jewish law and the era of Christian grace was by itself unremarkable. The amount of detail in Honorius's "liturgical map" for history, however, showed a striking departure from traditional exegesis, connecting the coronation of Solomon to the conversion of Constantine; the consecration of the Jewish Temple to the Council of Nicaea; the biblical reign of King Josiah to that of the pious emperor Theodosius II; the Babylonian sack of Jerusalem to Alaric's sack of Rome in 410; and so forth. Honorius followed this logic through the age of Charlemagne until present times, beyond which he projected the coming of Antichrist, whose persecutions would match the trials of the Jews under Holofernes and Antiochus. In this scheme we see not only the successive persecutions of the faithful, but also the lost "golden age," when the bearers of imperial power protected rather than preyed upon the Church. Honorius's liturgical model for history remained vague about actual historical events stretching from Charlemagne's "restoration of empire" up until the present. In the early-twelfth century, this lack of specificity persisted as the safe Augustinian position to take, rather than making potentially troublesome connections between current events and apocalyptic timetables. One suspects, however, that Honorius's contemporaries could read between the lines. All of his schemes finished with the climactic struggle between Antichrist and the faithful, providing a clear mark of his reformist sensibilities. Sympathetic observers knew that the German Empire was currently disturbing the Roman Church, foreshadowing the final showdown between good and evil. Without predicting any precise date for the end of the world, exegetes such as Honorius were bringing a new sense of polemical urgency to their theology of history.

Heresy, the Holy Spirit, and the Division of Christendom

In casting a familiar set of foes arrayed against the faithful throughout consecutive historical eras, including Jews, pagans, and heretics, reformist thinkers clearly echoed the sentiments of earlier Gregorian reformers. Since the earliest stages of the reform movement, however, Rome and its supporters had faced another potential source of subversion represented by the Greek Church of Constantinople. This did not change in the twelfth century. In fact, the problematic status of "the Greeks" began to consume more and more attention from members of the Latin clergy. Bernard of Clairvaux captured this mood in his tract *On Consideration*, written for Pope Eugene III on the responsibilities of the papal office during the aftermath of the Second Crusade. Addressing the need for the conversion of Jews, pagans, and heretics, Bernard specifically added some comments about the "obstinacy of the Greeks, who are with us and yet not with us. Although joined with us in faith, they are separated from us in peace, and even in faith they have strayed from the proper paths."[29] Those proper paths, of course, lay with the orthodox teachings and guidance of the Roman papacy. The question that weighed on people's minds was what to do about the undeniable divergence between the Western and Eastern Churches.

This growing "Greek problem" revealed itself in a variety of ways. As we saw earlier, the crusade-chronicler Guibert of Nogent opened his history of the First Crusade with a denunciation of Greek religious errors, linked to the origins of Islam. Around the same time, the famous theologian Anselm of Canterbury tackled both the lingering dispute over azymes and the *filioque* controversy.[30] He might have been inspired to do so after his encounter with Greek Christians at the council of Bari in 1098, but his works "against the Greeks" equally reflected his wider concern with sources of unbelief and heterodoxy.[31] Generally speaking, Anselm struck a moderate tone in his refutations of Greek errors, using the cutting-edge tools of logic and reason to demonstrate the superiority of

Roman doctrines and practices. Not everyone was so circumspect. A few decades later, the failure of the Second Crusade, attributed by some to Greek treachery, did little to improve relations between the two peoples. The French chronicler and crusader Odo of Deuil did little to hide his displeasure with the Greek Christians of Constantinople. In contrast to the *ad hominem* attacks against Emperor Alexius a generation earlier, Odo gives us a glimpse of a broader antagonism toward the Greeks, including the accusation that they were less-than-perfect Christians. In particular, besides being too cozy with the infidels, the Greek Church erred in its doctrine and rites, including its slanders against azymes, denial of *filioque*, and refusal to recognize Roman authority. Some of the crusaders passing by Constantinople en route to the Holy Land even advocated an attack on the city, although in this case, cooler heads prevailed and the crusaders eventually moved onward.[32]

During these same decades, the continuing aspirations and anxieties of the Gregorian reformers drew further attention to the problem of Greek religious difference. Largely overlooked by scholars of the Latin-Greek schism, the reformist preoccupation with the proper ordering of Christendom in many cases contributed to a hardening in attitudes toward the Greek Church. In his *Book on the Divine Offices,* for example, Rupert of Deutz's dismay over the problem of heresy within Christendom extended to a denunciation of Greek Christians for their rejection of Rome's teachings. Discussing the Eucharistic sacrifice, Rupert addressed the decades-old controversy over azymes. Familiar with the events of 1054, he did not find it surprising that Greece, "leavened with many heresies," sacrificed with leavened bread nor that a heresy-ridden Constantinople refused to concede to Roman authority on this issue. By contrast, Rupert stressed the special place of Rome in defending orthodox belief and practice: "The Roman Church," he noted, "founded high atop the rock of apostolic faith, has stood firmly and has always confounded the heretics of both Greece and the entire world, passing a sentence of judgment handed down from the loftiest court of the faith."[33] He did not specifically state that the Greek use of leavened bread was improper, but their attack on the Roman rite placed them in the ranks of heretics who were a threat to the orthodox faith.

Rupert was also aware of the *filioque* controversy, which assumed a distinctive significance in his theology of history. In his massive treatise *On the Holy Trinity and Its Works,* Rupert based his entire interpretation of Scripture on the premise that each person of the Trinity formed an active agent throughout the course of salvation history, starting with an age of "creation" linked to the Father, an age of "redemption" linked to the Son, and an age of "renewal" linked to the Holy Spirit.[34] In his exegesis, he repeatedly stressed the double procession of the Holy Spirit from the Father "and from the Son" *(filioque)* as a way to integrate more fully the three persons of the Godhead, which acted together to shape the course of history. This being the case, Rupert consistently denounced past heresiarchs, such as Arius and Macedonius, who detracted from the full divinity of the Holy Spirit by arguing that it was a created entity or somehow a lesser person of the Trinity. In his commentary on the Gospel of John and his work *On the Glorification of the Trinity,* Rupert likewise inveighed against "certain heretics among the Greeks" who denied that the Holy Spirit proceeded from the Father and the Son. Considering *filioque*'s importance in Rupert's theology of history, this must have seemed a particularly damnable sin.[35]

Decades later, Gerhoh of Reichersberg drew some similar conclusions about the Greek denial of the Holy Spirit's double procession. Gerhoh displayed his views of history among other writings in his *Minor Work on the Edifice of God,* his *Little Book on the Order of the Holy Spirit's Gifts,* his sprawling tract *On the Investigation of Antichrist,* and his final composition, *On the Fourth Watch of the Night.*[36] Familiar with Rupert's writings, the Bavarian cleric was clearly indebted to his emphasis on the work of the Trinity in history. In his *Little Book on the Order of the Holy Spirit's Gifts,* Gerhoh loosely mapped out the course of Church history before and after the Incarnation according to the seven gifts of the Holy Spirit.[37] He employed a similar Trinitarian model in his tract *On the Investigation of Antichrist.* Following from Christ's statement "I am the way, truth, and life" (Jn. 14:6), Gerhoh read everything in threes: the three general disciplines (moral, natural, inspective), the three virtues for battle against the Devil (humility, wisdom, strength), and the three orders of men within the Church (active, contemplative, theorists, also described as married, continent, and rectors). According to Gerhoh, the threefold nature of salvation history was particularly evident in the judgments of the Trinity against men who, like the Devil, sinned through their pride, vanity, and impurity. In the Old Testament, these three judgments were the flood, the division of languages, and the destruction of Sodom. Gerhoh paid particular attention to the division of languages, a punishment for the presumptuous building of the Tower of Babel that symbolized heresies against the Godhead.[38] This train of thought led him to refute various heretical attacks on the Trinity, including the Greek denial that the Holy Spirit proceeds from the Son. Setting his comments in the form of a disputation between a "Latin" and a "Greek," Gerhoh claimed that ancient Greek authorities had themselves supported the doctrine of the double procession, in stark contrast with the "modern Greeks." After the close of this mock debate, Gerhoh reviewed the arguments of his tract on Antichrist, placing this modern Greek deviation from Roman doctrine into his broader narrative that had progressed from the "fall of the Tower of Babylon, in which heretical perversity exhaled its primordial audacity," to the "error of the Greeks, who stubbornly deny that the Holy Spirit proceeds from the Son."[39]

By clarifying the boundaries between orthodoxy and heterodoxy, schemes of providential history raised the possibility that the contemporary Greek Church fell on the wrong side of that border. Such a determination, however, was not inevitable. One of the more remarkable historical thinkers of the twelfth century, Anselm of Havelberg, took a quite different stance toward the "Greek question." The bishop of Havelberg, who died in 1158, was active during his ecclesiastical career both as an imperial legate to Constantinople and a crusade-preacher for the Second Crusade. He grappled with the patterns of salvation history in his tract the *Antikeimenon*, sometimes called the *Dialogues*.[40] Addressed to Pope Eugene III, this work consisted of three books: the first book, often referred to as *On the One Form of Believing*, tackled the issue of religious diversity within the Roman Church, while the second and third books dealt with differences between Latin and Greek Christians. Largely on the basis of the first book, scholars frequently associate Anselm with Rupert of Deutz because of his creative theology of history that viewed the Holy Spirit as the prime mover of religious life in the Church after Christ. This modern affiliation between Rupert and Anselm would have struck the two as ironic, since they stood on opposite sides of the period's debates over monasticism: Rupert defended traditional Benedictine life, while Anselm celebrated the Premonstratensian order (not to mention the fact that Anselm elsewhere took a jab at Rupert's "fat belly"). It was in large part to defend the Premonstratensians and their founder, Norbert of Xanten, that Anselm composed the first book of the *Antikeimenon*.[41]

In the first book of this tract, Anselm justified innovation in religious life by appealing to the constantly evolving forms of God's dispensation. While there was only one true community of believers, he explained, variation and mutation in the forms of worship had been the rule rather than the exception since the days of Abel and would persist until the end of time. Interweaving the patristic scheme of natural law, written law, and grace, along with the division of history into seven ages, Anselm charted the transformations of rites through Noah, Moses, David, and Christ. This process included two major "transpositions" or "mutations," first from idolatry to law, and then from law to Gospel.[42] Building on traditional apocalyptic exegesis, Anselm employed the seven seals of Revelation to organize the history of the Church after Christ, including the first era of the Primitive Church, the second era of the martyrs, and the third era marked by the challenge of heresy. What the ancient enemy, the Great Dragon of the Apocalypse, had not managed to do through persecution during the days of the martyrs, he attempted to do through the wiles of heretics such as Arius, Sabellius, Nestorius, Eutychius, and Macedonius. This heretical attack was met by the ecumenical councils of the Church, including Nicaea, Constantinople, Ephesus, and Chalcedon, just as the threat of the fourth era, the pale horse of hypocrites and "false brothers," was opposed by the learning of the Church Fathers and diverse orders of religious men, ranging from the monks of Saint Benedict and Norbert of Xanten to the Cistercians and the Templars. The age of the present, Anselm declared, was influenced by this ongoing agency of the Holy Spirit, the driving force of beneficial changes in rites, habits, laws, and sacraments.[43] In this context, Anselm first noted the "diverse kinds of religious men among the Greeks, Armenians, and Syrians, who agree in one catholic faith, yet nevertheless differ considerably amongst themselves in customs, in rank, in habit, in victuals, and in the office of chanting the psalms."[44] Toward the close of book one, he briefly related to his readers his own experience as a traveler in Constantinople, where he saw "many orders of the Christian religion" that included monks living under the

rule of Anthony, Pachomus, and Basil. Here we see a fascinating convergence of Anselm's lived experiences and his theological-historical sense
of the Holy Spirit's ongoing activity in the diverse forms of religious life
within the Christian community.

This same convergence of experience and theological speculation
shaped his attitudes toward the Greek Church in the second and third
books of the *Dialogues,* which presented a stylized "report" of a series of
debates held between Anselm and Archbishop Nicetas of Nicomedia,
while Anselm was residing at Constantinople as an imperial legate in the
year 1136. Typically, scholars interested in apocalypticism tend to high-
light book one of the *Dialogues,* while historians of the ecclesiastical
schism between Rome and Constantinople focus on the remaining two
books. As Jay T. Lees argues, however, the three books are best thought of
as an integrated whole. Anselm's treatise on the problem of religious difference within the Roman Church carefully set the stage for his discussion of divergences between the Latins and Greeks. By the same token,
the "debates" between Anselm and Nicetas reflected back on the current
controversy within the Roman Church over innovation in religious life,
providing an example of how churchmen could and should debate issues
of religious difference and innovation.[45] At once a tract on the *filioque,* a
commentary on azymes, and a treatise on Roman apostolic authority,
Anselm's work represented the first comprehensive Latin attempt to ana-
lyze the theological, liturgical, and ecclesiological divisions that had developed between the two halves of Christendom by setting them within a
broader theology of history.

In the opening to the second book of the *Dialogues,* Anselm segued
from the apparent scandal of religious variety within the Roman Church
to another source of potential scandal: the Greek divergence from the
Latins over *filioque* and azymes. How could there be such discrepancies,
he queried, when there were so many Greek saints honored in the Roman
Church and when past Greek prelates had sat on the see of Saint Peter?
This question set the stage for his presentation of the debates at Constantinople. Through this format, Anselm exposed a broad and sometimes
contradictory range of arguments about the religious divergences between the two Christian peoples by attributing words both to himself and
to his opponent, Nicetas. Within the text, Anselm "the debater" employed

standard scriptural and patristic sources to defend the Latin doctrine of the Holy Spirit's double procession and the use of azymes for the Eucharist. Both in doctrine and in rite, he argued, the Roman Church stood as the defender of orthodoxy. By contrast, the Eastern Church of Constantinople was a seedbed of heresies. The transfer of imperial power to Constantinople—a human and not a divine act—had meant nothing for the city's ecclesiastical privileges. If it were otherwise, any city with a claim to royal or imperial power could call itself the head of the universal Church. The ancient Greeks had respected the primacy of the Roman papacy: "Would that modern Greeks," Anselm "the debater" lamented, "were as humble and obedient to the Roman Church as they were!"[46]

Through the person of Nicetas, Anselm the "author" presented counter-arguments against this association of the Greeks with infamous heresies. Point by point, Nicetas proclaimed the Trinitarian orthodoxy of the Greek Church and refuted any connection with the false teachings of Arius, Sabellius, Macedonius, and others. Regardless of what Nicetas actually said at Constantinople in 1136, Anselm's composition presented to Western readers an effective disassociation of the Greeks from the very same heresies to which authors such as Rupert, Gerhoh, and even Anselm (as a character in his own text) were linking them. The figure of Nicetas also offered a counter-narrative of the division between the Eastern and Western Churches. Without rejecting Roman primacy, his character defended Constantinople's ecclesiastical privileges and position second only to Rome, which dated back to the first council of Constantinople. Heresies had arisen in the Eastern Church, he noted, but they had been quashed by Eastern councils and churchmen. The followers of the Roman Church, not the Greeks, had caused the division of the Eastern and Western Churches. According to Nicetas, the modern temerity of the Latins had begun in the days of Charlemagne, who had violently seized imperial power, initiating a dispute between the Greeks and Latins over their rites and ecclesiastical discipline.[47]

Who was correct about the division of Christendom? The *Dialogues* made no effort to answer this question absolutely. Through its disputation format, the text presented the reader with the first comprehensive guide to the major points of divergence between the followers of Rome and Constantinople, both past and present. Neither the arguments of

Anselm nor those of Nicetas held absolute sway. Both "modern Greeks" and "modern Latins" appeared to have deviated from their ancient harmony. At the end of the second and third books, the two clerics agreed that a general council should be called to address these points of difference between the churches. Only then, Nicetas noted, would the Greek Church be convinced to adopt the *filioque* and to use azymes for the Eucharist.

Anselm's portrayal of the disputes ends on a harmonious note. According to the text, Anselm gave thanks to God for removing his suspicions of the Greeks, while Nicetas looked forward to a general council that would "make both Greeks and Latins one people under one Lord, Jesus Christ, in one faith, one baptism, and one sacramental rite."[48] While not framed in explicitly eschatological terms, Anselm's powerful ecumenical vision of future Christian unity anticipated a common theme of subsequent Latin apocalypticism—the notion that all Christian peoples, East and West, would be joined together into "one fold" before the consummation of time.

Antichrist and the "Refreshment of the Saints"

For all of their skills and desire to uncover the patterns of the past leading up to the present, twelfth-century theologians of history reserved much of their acumen for imagining the future. Of course, speculation about the course of future events brought Latin exegetes up against the most strident prohibitions of patristic theologians, who had canonized a conservative distaste for scenarios of radical eschatological change. Reformist apocalyptic thinkers did not reject the normative Augustinian position on millennial theorizing, but they did began to play around its edges, opening the door to a veritable "paradigm shift" in Latin clerical apocalyptic culture during the later twelfth and thirteenth centuries. In time, this willingness to innovate would contribute to some of the most radical formulations of Christendom imagined as world order.

To be sure, relatively conservative voices continued to set the tone for mainstream Latin apocalypticism during the twelfth century. The early scholastic thinker Hugh of Saint Victor, for example, clearly appreciated the nature of history as a temporal process of salvation that stretched from Creation to the coming of Antichrist and Final Judgment. In his tract *On the Sacraments of the Christian Faith,* however, Hugh did not go into any of the gruesome details about the Antichrist's birth and activities before that final struggle.[49] Well aware of the current controversies that surrounded innovation in religious life, Hugh emphasized that although the true faith of God had grown over time and changed its external forms, faith itself was unchanging. In his work, he charted some of those transformations in the sacraments from the period before the written law to the time under the law and then under grace, always progressing toward "more dignified" spiritual forms. God had instituted the sacraments for human salvation and, as time moved forward toward its conclusion, the Lord ameliorated and expanded their function. This progression of history inevitably led toward the coming of Antichrist, but Hugh's treatment of his persecutions and related eschatological events did not seem likely to inspire much hope or terror.[50] His apocalyptic scenario sounded rather clinical—an unavoidable coda to the history of salvation. Hugh dwelt at greater length on the resurrection of the body and Final Judgment. This "coolness" toward Antichrist is exactly what one would expect from early scholastic circles, concerned with the systematic analysis of theology rather than dramatic theories about history.

To take another example, Hugh's contemporary Otto of Freising, writing about universal history rather than sacramental theology, capped his chronicle with a relatively standard presentation of Antichrist, including the rise of his followers among the Jews, his seduction of many Christians, and his killing of the two witnesses during his three-and-a-half-year reign of terror.[51] In his *History of the Two Cities,* Otto declared that those events would not happen until the expiration of the Roman Empire, although he noted that the predicted removal of the "restraining force" before Antichrist's arrival might also refer to "the priesthood and the Roman see." Otto, who represented the continuing vitality of imperial theology of history and apocalypticism, was not unsympathetic to the goals of the Gregorian reformers, which perhaps explains his intriguing suggestion that the Roman Church, rather than the Roman Empire, was slated to endure until the coming of Antichrist. Otto had studied in Paris during his younger days, and might have adopted this idea from Hugh of Saint Victor, who noted in his commentary on Second Thessalonians that the "restraining force" might refer to either the "terrestrial Roman Empire" or the "spiritual empire of the Roman Church" (indeed, Gerbert of Aurillac had hinted at this possibility toward the close of the tenth century).[52]

This coolness toward the Son of Perdition, however, was not shared by everyone. As evident in *The Play of Antichrist,* imperial circles showed their own growing interest in the false messiah of history's end.[53] Written around 1160, most likely at the court of Emperor Frederick I (r. 1152–1190), this remarkable piece stages the coming of Antichrist after the final ruler of the Romans has subdued the kings of France, Greece, and Jerusalem before laying down his crown on the Mount of Olives. Long associated with the legend of the Last World Emperor, this surrender of imperial power leads to the emergence and crowning of Antichrist, who is greeted as the son of God by heretics and hypocrites (the latter denoting the "Gregorian" reformers). In many ways, this eschatological drama provided an antidote to the ideological claims of the reform papacy, assigning the pope little role in the eschatological drama. Even the emperor's role in the end-times, however, hardly ends on a triumphal note. Ultimately, the imperial ruler himself is seduced by Antichrist, whose false reign of "universal peace and security" is abruptly overturned at the play's end by a thunderbolt from heaven.[54]

Another arresting account of Antichrist was offered at this time by Hildegard of Bingen, a conservative Benedictine abbess, who nevertheless rebuked the highest ecclesiastical and imperial authorities of her day for their laxity toward the reform of the Roman Church and the rooting out of abuses.[55] Hildegard's visions, which lasted over many years until her death in 1179, brought her considerable fame within her lifetime (both Bernard of Clairvaux and Pope Eugene III openly praised her). Such visions included her prediction of five forthcoming "epochs of temporal rule" symbolized by five beasts: the fiery dog (the present times of corruption and abuse), the yellow lion (a time of war), the pale horse (an era when the Church and earthly kingdoms would fail), the black pig (a time of renewal in prophecy), and finally the gray wolf. The wolf symbolized the reign of Antichrist, an era of great tribulation for the faithful, who would be strengthened by the coming of Elijah and Enoch before the Second Coming of Christ. In one of the more vivid descriptions of Antichrist, Hildegard also related the vision of a woman (symbolizing the corrupt

Church) with a "black and monstrous head" in the "place where a female is recognized." This head with "fiery eyes" and "iron-colored teeth" would try to "seduce people by evil deceptions, and at first speak to them flatteringly and gently, but then trying cruelly to pervert them by force."[56]

These visions of the end-time found in *The Play of Antichrist* and Hildegard's prophetic works shared a grim pessimism about the future persecutions of the faithful, whose redemption from suffering would be secured only with the Second Coming of Christ and Final Judgment. The consummation of history, however, did not necessarily promise unmitigated gloom and doom. Hildegard of Bingen herself believed that there would come a time of renewal for the Church after Antichrist. For that matter, even the most conservative of patristic and medieval authorities, ranging from Jerome to Bede to the *Ordinary Gloss,* allowed for a period of terrestrial "refreshment" that would see the conversion of the Jews and pagans to the Christian faith.[57] For example, one twelfth-century gloss on the Book of Revelation by an anonymous French cleric emphasized that the text offered useful signs about past persecutions, as well as those of the "present church and the future in the time of Antichrist." In particular, this author stressed the role played by "orders of preachers" throughout the "seven seals" of history, including the final tribulations when preaching would be needed "lest the Church fail in so great a tribulation." A seventh and final order of preachers, symbolized by the angel bearing the "eternal gospel" (Rev. 14:6), would go forth to preach the Trinity in the four corners of the world among the Jews and Gentiles, bringing about the conversion of both peoples.[58]

Reformist apocalyptic thinkers—including Rupert of Deutz, Honorius Augustodunensis, and Gerhoh of Reichersberg—eagerly embraced this notion of a future era that would include the conversion of the Jews and pagans before the end of time. In Rupert's case, his vision of change was closely tied to his theology of the Holy Spirit and its role in history. In his work *On the Holy Trinity,* for example, he stressed the Holy Spirit's role in the destruction of Jerusalem by Titus and Vespasian, an event commonly associated with God's vengeful punishment of the Jews for their rejection of Christ.[59] For Rupert, this divinely ordained event confirmed that the "spirit of counsel" had removed the yoke of the ancient Jewish law from the Gentiles. In the "age of renewal," however, the Holy Spirit would play a role in the Jews' penultimate redemption when the "spirit of piety" would turn them to the true faith. Through such exegesis, Rupert demonstrated the characteristic hardening in twelfth-century Christian attitudes toward the Jews as religious outsiders, while suggesting a new interest in their final salvation (albeit as Christians) rather than their outright destruction.[60]

Honorius Augustodunensis pursued some similar themes in his own writings, including his commentary *The Jewel of the Soul*. At various points in the liturgical calendar, he commented on the future trials under Antichrist, whose assault would encompass the three portions of the world (that is, Europe, Africa, and Asia). After the time of Antichrist, however, much like the rebuilding of the Jewish Temple after the Babylonian Captivity, the Church would be rebuilt: Jews, pagans, and Christians would come together to form a single faith and religion.[61] In his commentary *On the Song of Songs*, he offered a particularly dramatic scenario for the future, centered on the relationship between the Synagogue and the Church. According to Honorius, among the four brides who approach the king (that is, Christ), the bride from the East symbolized the "multitude of the elect before the law in the faith of the patriarchs"; the bride from the South, the "crowd of people collected under the law in the faith of the prophets"; the bride from the West, the "multitude of Gentiles under grace attracted to the faith of Christ through the apostles"; and the bride from the North, "the crowd of infidels under Antichrist converting to the faith" (these brides were also represented by the daughter of the Pharaoh, the daughter of the king of Babylon, the Sunamite, and the Mandragon). Honorius stressed that there was, in effect, one Church with a twofold nature: the "church of the Synagogue," visited by the prophets, and the "church of the Gentiles," visited by the apostles. He did not hesitate to remind his readers that the first members of the Primitive Church were, of course, Jews themselves. According to Honorius, the church of the Gentiles wept and prayed for the Jews, who had deviated from the Lord, to rejoin them in faith. This joining would come about in the future, when the queen of the South (also symbolizing the church that emerged from the pagan Gentiles) would lead the Sunamite (the "enslaved" synagogue) to God through the "voice of preaching" toward the end of time. Adding a twist to the standard claim that the Jews would serve Antichrist, Honorius declared that the members of this converted synagogue would in fact battle against him.[62]

Ultimately, after great tribulations, Antichrist would be destroyed. Like the dawn coming after the darkness, there would be a time of peace after the persecution when the bride and the groom would go forth together in the field (Cant. 4:11–12), allowing time for lapsed Christians to perform penance, for multitudes of infidels to receive the faith, and for unconverted Jews to join the fold of the faithful. At one point, Honorius declared that the church of the Gentiles would greatly admire the converted Synagogue, which would itself attract numerous infidels to the faith through its preaching and deeds during and after the tribulations under Antichrist.[63] In his insightful analysis of Honorius's eschatology of conversion, Jeremy Cohen has commented that Honorius found in the Jews "the shock troops of the church in her final struggle against Antichrist, those who will serve as leaders and provide inspiration for all the faithful."[64] Cohen observes that this proposition places Honorius outside the general trajectory of an increasingly acrid anti-Judaism in the twelfth-century Roman Church. In a period when Christian scholastic thinkers—committed to the use of reason for the explication of their faith—identified Jews as "irrational," when Christian mystics began to associate the "murderous" Jews with the human suffering of the crucified Christ, Honorius's vision of the future struck a different chord.[65] "Let there be no mistake," Cohen adds, "Honorius offers no anachronistically ecumenical blueprint for religious pluralism at the end of days; the only Jews to be saved will be baptized Jews." The fact remains, however, that Honorius's glorification of the Synagogue demonstrates how reformist apocalypticism—even as it drew a line in the sand between the elect and the forces of evil—opened the door to a future transformation that could change the very nature of the elect.[66]

Much like Rupert and Honorius, Gerhoh of Reichersberg offered his readers an explicit interpretation of present-day problems as a sign of apocalyptic dangers, while holding out the hope for a future renewal in the status of Christendom. As we saw earlier, in the wake of the Second Crusade, the Bavarian canon came to see the crusaders' failure in the Holy Land as a divine scourge, visited upon Christians as a result of rampant avarice and other sins among God's followers. More openly than Rupert or Honorius, Gerhoh offered scathing criticisms of simony and other persistent abuses within the Roman Church. He was particularly outspoken during the papal schism between Pope Innocent II (r. 1130–1143) and the antipope, Anacletus II, and also when open conflict broke out between Pope Alexander III (r. 1159–1181) and the German emperor, Frederick Barbarossa. Gerhoh remained an impassioned supporter of the Roman papacy until his death in 1169, although he grew increasingly pessimistic about the abilities of the current Roman Church to withstand its present and imminent trials.

In his commentary on the sixty-fourth psalm, written around 1152, Gerhoh offered a typical reformer's view of the relationship between royal power and priestly authority, set within an exegetical framework of history that compared the fortunes of Israel after the Babylonian Captivity with the Christian Church after Constantine.[67] Similar to Cyrus, who freed the Hebrews and enabled the rebuilding of the Jewish Temple in Jerusalem, Constantine had liberated God's Church from the tribulation of pagan persecution and endowed it with many riches. This proper secular deference continued until the time of Charlemagne and Louis the Pious. With the passage of time, however, "heretical kings" had begun to attack the liberty of the Church, including those in the "modern age" who sold "spiritual gifts" which they did not truly own.[68] Like the Jews, who subsequently faced persecution by Antiochus (commonly considered to be a symbol or foreshadowing of Antichrist), Christians faced their own tribulations in the gathering apocalyptic gloom.

By placing the struggles of the reform papacy within such a framework, Gerhoh demonstrated a distinctly "Gregorian" apocalyptic sensibility. Certainly, we can imagine that earlier generations of clerical reformers would have sympathized with the overall trajectory of his narrative for Christendom, presented as an ongoing battle between the faithful and the forces of evil that included Jews, heretics, and, in Gerhoh's own day, false and avaricious Christians. He revisited these themes throughout his major and minor works.[69] For Gerhoh, moreover, the figure of Antichrist was not restricted to the future: there had been many lesser Antichrists in the past, and there were "new and modern" Antichrists in the present. The arrival of the final Antichrist was not far off. As he put it on another occasion, anyone who opposed the efforts of the papacy to stamp out simony thereby opposed the "rock" of the Church founded by Christ. In this sense, they were opposing Christ, making them by definition members of Antichrist.

Like his fellow reformist apocalyptic thinkers, Gerhoh also anticipated a time of eschatological peace for Christendom after its trials, an era which would bring converted Jews and infidels into the gathering of Christ's fold.[70] In his last known work, *On the Fourth Watch of the Night,* Gerhoh organized the history of the Church according to the story of Christ appearing to the apostles at sea during a storm (Mt. 14:22–27): the first watch signified the struggle of martyrs against pagan tyranny; the second, that of confessors against heretics; the third, that of saintly men against corrupt prelates and clergy; and, in Gerhoh's own present, the watch of the papacy against simony and other abuses of the church during the struggle between the bearers of priestly authority and royal power.[71] In recent times, zealous popes such as Gregory VII and Urban II had struggled to defend the liberty of the Roman Church from heretical rulers such as Henry IV, who tried to rob Christ of his patrimony. These events preceded the approaching watch against the forces of an "avaricious" Antichrist, manifesting the evils of simony. Gerhoh went so far as to criticize the papacy of his present day as being corrupted by the stain of simony. Like Peter, who began to sink beneath the waves when he attempted to walk on water beside Christ, the church of Rome was sinking and unready to fight the Antichrist of the fourth watch.

Just as he had done with Peter, however, Christ would stretch out his hand to the Apostolic See, rescuing the papacy before it was completely submerged. A newly spiritualized papacy would take up the fight against Antichrist, resuming and consummating the reform of the Church before the end of time. This vision of a renewed and purified papacy anticipated one of the more popular apocalyptic ideas of the thirteenth and fourteenth centuries: the hope for a future "angelic" pope, who would rid the Church of corruption and unify the peoples of the world under the Christian faith. In his tract on Antichrist, Gerhoh had offered a similar vision of history and hints about the coming of "spiritual men" who would reform the Roman Church.[72] Despite his criticisms of Rome, Gerhoh of Reichersberg seemed to believe that Christendom's best days were still ahead, even if things were going to get much worse before they got better. In such predictions of spiritual renewal, we find the critical eye of reformist apocalyptic thinkers toward the present state of Christendom along with the promise of better things on the horizon—the hope that God's plan for history would miraculously bring about what his flawed followers had failed to achieve.

Since the earliest days of their faith, the followers of Christ had thought about their messiah's particular place in history, as both the present fulfillment of past prophecies and the announcement of God's Heavenly Kingdom that would arrive after the apocalyptic clash between good and evil. In subsequent epochs, later generations placed their own distinct stamp on this basic historical view, elaborating upon its details, often arguing about its true meaning. In the Latin tradition of the twelfth century, Christian theology of history assumed an unprecedented coherence, framed by the schematic and symbolic exegesis of the Bible. Perhaps this development should not surprise us. In the appraisal of modern scholars, the twelfth century stands as one of the most dynamic and expansive periods in Europe's medieval past, when the Roman Church and Latin clerical culture succeeded—to an often remarkable extent—in realizing the Gregorian notion of Christendom as an assembly of orthodox believers that followed the Latin rite, adhered to Latin patristic doctrines, and recognized the primacy of Rome. In order to exist in the present, Christendom needed both a past and the promise of a future. The reformist exegetes of the era provided just such a history, one that privileged the teachings, practices, and authority of their own religious community.

Reformist apocalyptic thinkers envisioned the triumph of Christendom, somewhat paradoxically, as both an inevitable part of God's plan and something that was desperately imperiled. Jews and pagans, Muslims and heretics, and even non-Latin Christians posed a persistent challenge to the Church. Would such enemies be defeated and destroyed? Or turned to the Christian faith under the authority of the Roman Church? Even more disturbing were the inner failings of the Christian community. The papacy itself, the head of Christendom, was not above criticism by the most devoted of Gregorian reformers. Certainly, the final victory of God's people at the end of history was assured, but the precise script of that eschatological drama was not always clear to the faithful acting in it. In the later twelfth century, the hopes and fears of the reformist apocalyptic tradition would find their greatest expression in the works of Joachim of Fiore, who displayed both the appeal and the potential dangers of such historical scenarios for the mainstream Roman Church.

4

Joachim of Fiore and the Sabbath Age

Inspired visionary, dangerous heretic, social revolutionary—Abbot Joachim of Fiore has been many things to many people.[1] Joachim is best known for his division of history into three stages that were modeled after the Trinity: the age of the Father, from Adam until Christ; the age of the Son, from Christ until around the abbot's own time; and the future age of the Holy Spirit, an earthly Sabbath that would transform the world into an irenic kingdom for the faithful followers of the Lord. This final historical era, the abbot proclaimed, would be "without war, without scandal, without worry or terror, since God shall bless it and he shall sanctify it, because in it, he shall cease from all of his labor that he has accomplished."[2] Joachim's anticipation of such millennial transformations, taken to radical extremes by some of his devotees, gained him his lasting fame, if not notoriety. His eschatology, however, depended on a sometimes bewildering tradition of biblical exegesis and historical schemes that placed him squarely in the "reformist" intellectual climate of the twelfth century. Joachim was a remarkable innovator, but he was hardly a quixotic figure on the margins. Within his own lifetime, the abbot developed a far-flung reputation as a prophet and interpreter of Scripture whose predictions and opinions were admired and sought after by popes and kings. After his death, his writings had an unrivaled impact on the medieval European apocalyptic imagination that would continue into the modern era.[3]

Joachim was born in Celico in the region of Calabria around the year 1135.[4] While on a pilgrimage to the Holy Land as a young man, he experienced two spiritual revelations about the inner meaning of the Bible. Returning to Calabria by way of Sicily, he wandered as a preacher and settled briefly at the Cistercian house of Sambucina before next moving on to the Benedictine monastery at Corazzo. Around 1171 Joachim took orders at Corazzo, where he was soon elected abbot. His efforts at reforming the monastery met with mixed success, as did his effort to incorporate Corazzo into the Cistercian order. Around 1183 he experienced another revelation while visiting the Cistercian house at Casamari, where he began his efforts at writing in earnest.[5] Perhaps not surprisingly, his claim to have privileged insights into the Bible and the meaning of history attracted attention. At about this time, the abbot had an interview with Pope Lucius III (r. 1181–1185) at Veroli, where he sought and acquired papal permission to record his revelatory readings of Scripture.[6] Dissatisfied with the state of reform at Corazzo, Joachim increasingly turned his attention to his own works. Formal permission to write was reiterated by Pope Urban III (r. 1185–1187) and by Pope Clement III (r. 1187–1191); the latter formally relieved Joachim of his abbatial duties. Around the year 1188, Joachim withdrew to the Sila Plateau and founded the monastery of San Giovanni in Fiore. Despite removal to his new monastic house, Joachim maintained a high profile during the following years, meeting with Emperor Henry VI during his siege of Naples and King Richard I of England during his journey to the Holy Land on the Third Crusade. Joachim continued to write until his death in 1202.[7]

Among his innumerable interests in the shape of history, Joachim devoted a great deal of attention to the future union of both non-Christian and non-orthodox peoples with the Roman Church. As part of his eschatological vision, the abbot declared that the Jewish people would finally recognize Christ and join harmoniously with their Christian brethren before the end of time. In this case, he was building upon the long-standing tradition that the "remnant" of Israel would join the Church preceding the end of time. Joachim, however, was not content with the stock and somewhat colorless descriptions of this future event, which he turned into a vivid component of his schemes.[8] In addition, the abbot took the unprecedented step of linking this Jewish conversion to the restoration of communion between the schismatic Greek Church and the church of Rome. Preceding the conversion of the Jews, the Greeks, who had fallen into heresy through their rejection of Roman doctrine and authority, would undergo their own form of conversion to the more spiritual faith of Rome, the "new Jerusalem." As a result, according to Joachim, there would come into being "one fold" under "one shepherd," an assembly of God's people gathered together by members of the Western Church around the time of the struggle against Antichrist and the dawn of the new Sabbath age.[9]

It is no exaggeration to say that Joachim of Fiore was one of the most innovative and important historical thinkers of the Middle Ages. His writings, peerless for their creativity, stand out as a turning point in medieval theology of history because of their theoretical sophistication and their unflinching willingness to see the hand of God in the pattern of historical developments after Christ.[10] Judging by their reception, his words carried considerable weight among his contemporaries and were even more influential among subsequent generations. Without detracting from his undeniable creativity, however, it is equally important to appreciate the apparent continuities between Joachim and immediately preceding generations of monastic and clerical authors. For all of his ingenuity, the abbot read the Bible with the same restless energy that was demonstrated by earlier "Gregorian" exegetes, including Rupert of Deutz, Honorius Augustodunensis, Anselm of Havelberg, and Gerhoh of Reichersberg. Although there is no evidence of direct connections with them, in many ways Joachim represented another reformist apocalyptic thinker, an intellectual product of the reform movement that had started in the Roman Church during the century before his birth.[11] The theme of conflict between secular power and priestly authority permeated Joachim's writings, as did the problem of corruption and abuse within the ecclesiastical institutions. His concerns—with the true spiritual liberty of the Church, with history as a conflict between good and evil, with the ordering of religious life, with the relationship between the Trinity and history—were shared by many of his monastic and clerical contemporaries, even if Joachim outdid them all by his innovation and departure from traditional constraints.

The abbot's categorization of the Jews and the Greeks as peoples that had successively enjoyed and lost divine favor points us toward a broader field of historical theorizing, one that assigned Rome and its Western followers a place of priority in the realization of God's earthly plan for salvation. More than any of his reformist predecessors, Joachim believed in the fulfillment of Christ's promises that there would be "one fold" and "one shepherd" before the end of days, a redemptive process that would restore the "lost sheep" of the Greeks and finally the Jews to the true faith under the auspices of the Roman Church. Given such views, it is hardly surprising that a series of popes, including one of the most powerful popes of the High Middle Ages, Innocent III (r. 1198–1216), found inspiration in his schemes. At the same time, the abbot's writings remind us that reformist end-of-world scenarios did not always sit comfortably in the institutional Roman Church. Joachim's predictions about the conversion of Jews and Greeks may have been attractive to Latin Christians for obvious reasons, but his schemes left a legacy of criticism for voices of dissent within their ranks. Before the coming of the Sabbath age, the corruption and decadence of Rome would be exposed for all to see before the horrible persecutions of Antichrist purged the Western Church of its sins and shortcomings. These were hardly the sort of messages that would appeal uncritically to those heavily invested in the present-day ecclesiastical hierarchy.

The Principle of Concordance and the Three *Status*

Because of their sheer bulk and sometimes frustrating intricacy, Joachim's writings defy any neat and tidy summarization. He began his three principal works, the *Book of Concordance of the New and Old Testament,* the *Exposition on the Apocalypse,* and the *Psaltery of Ten Chords,* at Casamari in the early 1180s, revising them over the following two decades.[12] Around the time that he died, the abbot was composing a fourth major commentary, the *Tract on the Four Gospels.* Other well-known works include his *Exhortation to the Jews* and his commentary *On the Life of Saint Benedict.*[13] Joachim also produced a number of illustrations and diagrams to accompany his works, subsequently compiled in the so-called *Book of Figures*.[14] As a result of the persistent labors of scholars interested in the abbot, an increasing number of his minor writings are available for consultation in modern editions, including his *Genealogy* (his earliest extant work), his commentary *On an Unknown Prophecy*, his short tract *On the Seven Seals*, and a collection of his sermons.[15]

Joachim remains best known for his division of time into three stages, based on the idea of the Trinity. The abbot, however, did not develop this idea in isolation from the basic principles of Christian exegesis. Rather, he continued to interpret God's historical plan for salvation through the successive development of the Old and New Testaments. For all his bewildering hermeneutics, he never abandoned this basic foundation, reading the "letter" of Scripture for allegories that revealed hidden "spiritual" meanings. Joachim boldly diverged from the patristic tradition in his belief that the historical events recorded in the "time of the Old Testament" provided a detailed set of coordinates for understanding the course of events in the "time of the New Testament." The abbot argued that all of history was divided into these two time periods: the first from Adam until the arrival of Christ, and the second from Christ until the end of time. Important figures, groups, wars, and other developments that occurred in the time of the Old Testament directly corresponded to figures, groups, wars, and developments in the time of the New Testament. Like a strand of DNA, history ran on these two parallel but interlinked tracks.

The basis for this "principle of concordance" can be discerned in one of Joachim's earliest tracts, *On an Unknown Prophecy*. This text offered a commentary on some Sibylline verses circulating at the papal curia during the abbot's audience with Pope Lucius III, when he sought permission to write about his spiritual insights. This work apparently records statements that the abbot made openly at the curia. The fact that Joachim was asked to interpret the prophecy seems to indicate that he was already acquiring a reputation as someone with appropriate skills for such a task. At the beginning of his exposition, Joachim presented a simple but powerful scheme that would underpin virtually all of his subsequent writings:

> It ought to be remembered by us that the Hebrew people endured
> seven particular persecutions, which beyond any doubt signify

the seven particular oppressions of the Christians, as the Apostle makes evident, when he said "all those things happened to them in figure." For, as the Savior came into the world for the redemption of humankind when the seven tribulations of the Old Testament were finished, so the Judge of this world will likewise come for the purpose of punishment when the persecutions against the Church are complete.[16]

First, the Egyptians persecuted the Hebrews; second, the Midianites persecuted them; third, other Gentiles; fourth, the Assyrians; fifth, the Chaldeans; sixth, the Medes and Persians; and seventh, the pagan Greeks. According to Joachim, this series of persecutions corresponded with the following attacks on the Church: the first by the Jews; the second by the pagans; the third by Arian heretics (including the barbarian Goths, Vandals, Alemanni, and Lombards); and the fourth by the Saracens. The fifth and remaining tribulations, Joachim warned, were now at hand and would form a new "Babylonian Captivity" culminating in the persecution wrought by Antichrist and his servants.[17]

Joachim did not invent this scheme on the spot. He had already put forth the premise that history consisted of two sets of persecutions, one against the Hebrews and the other against the Church, in his first extant work, the *Genealogy*, written in 1176.[18] In part, this concept built on the long-standing interpretation of the seven seals of the Apocalypse as revealing the persecutions of the Christian Church by Jews, pagans, heretics, and false brothers in the past, followed by the forces of Antichrist in the future. As we saw in the previous chapters, such a view of history as a record of battles between the forces of good and evil became newly popular in the late eleventh and twelfth centuries as a result of the polemical clashes occasioned by the ecclesiastical reform movement. When Joachim composed the *Genealogy* and *On an Unknown Prophecy*, political tensions between the papacy and the German empire were running particularly high after decades of conflict between Pope Alexander III and Frederick I Barbarossa. In the second of these works, Joachim made an explicit reference to this struggle between the pope and emperor as part of the contemporary Roman Church's troubles under the fifth seal.[19] Joachim took this insight in dramatic new directions, however, by explicitly aligning the

seven "seals" or "persecutions" of the Hebrews in the time of the Old
Testament with the seven seals and battles against the Church in the time
of the New Testament. The abbot had discovered a basic grid for map-
ping history.

In his subsequent writings, Joachim pushed this pattern even farther.
Although the details changed from text to text, the principle remained the
same: history was divided into two sets of seven seals marked by a persecution, trial, or battle for God's people.[20] It should be added that Joachim
did not abandon the traditional Augustinian principle that history was divided into seven ages matching the seven days of creation. Departing
from Augustine, however, he insisted that the sixth age of the world was
itself divided into "sub-ages" marked by the seven seals. In the *Book of
Concordance* the abbot went even farther, claiming that the times of the
Old Testament and the New Testament directly corresponded by numbers of generations: there were forty-two generations from Jacob until
Christ, and a matching forty-two generations from Christ until the end-
times. This division of biblical and post-biblical history (requiring some
mathematical gymnastics) enabled Joachim to be uncannily specific in his
alignment of events that happened during corresponding generations
before and after Christ.[21] This principle of concordance, moreover, led
Joachim beyond observations about the past into speculations about the
future. In his own day, he believed—the fortieth generation after Christ—
the opening of the sixth seal was imminent. Although the exact number
of years could not be determined, there were only two generations remaining before the end of the sixth age. This point in time would bring
about two successive persecutions (the sixth and seventh, respectively),
followed by the opening of the seventh seal.[22] Unlike Augustine and other
patristic authorities, Joachim viewed the subsequent seventh age of history as just that—a part of history, not an eternal Sabbath that would follow the Last Judgment.

For all of his skills as an exegete and historian, it was Joachim's vision
of the future that would bring him his greatest fame and infamy. Without
abandoning his earlier insights into the nature of history's two basic divisions, those of the Old and New Testaments, in his major works that were
begun at Casamari, Joachim articulated a model of history divided into
three stages *(status):* the *status* of the Father, the *status* of the Son, and the

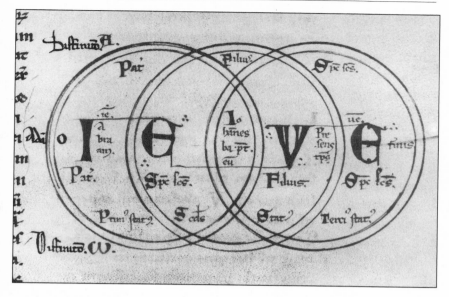

Joachim of Fiore's three *status* of the Father, Son, and Holy Spirit. *Exposition on the Apocalypse,* thirteenth century.
Source: Bibliothèque Nationale de France, Paris, lat. 427.

status of the Holy Spirit, a terrestrial era of spiritual perfection that would bloom after the imminent completion of the second *status.* The first *status* originated with Adam, came to fruition with Abraham, and ended with Christ. The second *status* began with Uzziah, came to fruition with Zachary (father of John the Baptist), and was drawing to a close in Joachim's own lifetime. The third *status* had begun with Saint Benedict of Nursia, was coming to fruition twenty-two generations later (again, around the abbot's own day) and would end with the conclusion of history.[23] This Trinitarian model can be seen in Joachim's famous figure of the three interlocking rings that represent the *status* of the Father, Son, and Holy Spirit, respectively.[24]

The *status* of the Father, the abbot declared, represented an age when men lived a life that followed the "way of the flesh," while men lived during the *status* of Son by a "mixture of both the flesh and the spirit." The *status* of the Holy Spirit would form an age when men lived "by the spirit" alone. In another variation on patristic models, the abbot described the three stages of time as "under the Law," "under grace," and "more fully under grace." In these terms, the predicted Sabbath age of the Holy Spirit marked an evolution rather than an abrupt rupture in God's plan for salvation. Nowhere was this integration of the three *status* more evident than in the origins and progression of monastic life. The abbot grouped religious life into three principal orders, corresponding to the three stages of history: those who were married in the *status* of the Father, the celibate clergy in the *status* of the Son, and the order of monks in the *status* of the Holy Spirit. The monastic order, Joachim believed, had originated both in the *status* of the Father with prophets such as Elijah and Elisha, and also in the *status* of the Son with Benedict of Nursia. From the perspective of Latin theology, this "double" origin of the monastic order from the *status* of the Father and the Son made perfect sense, because the Holy Spirit itself proceeds from the Father "and from the Son."

With the coming of the third *status,* the order of monks would give rise to a new kind of "spiritual men" *(viri spirituales),* who would play a crucial role in the initiation and realization of the earthly Sabbath.[25] Matching the Jews in the *status* of the Father, and the Gentiles in the *status* of the Son, in the *status* of the Holy Spirit the spiritual men from the Latin Church would form a vanguard for the realization of God's divine plan.[26] One of the most important duties that awaited them was their role in the conversion of the non-believing Jews to Christianity and the restoration of the heretical Greeks to the unity of the Roman Church. Perhaps not surprisingly, given his tendency to view history through the prism of the Trinity, Joachim also divided God's followers into three peoples: Jews, Greeks, and Latins. Over time, divine grace had abandoned the Jews for the Greeks, and then abandoned the Greeks for the Latins. Among Latin Christians, the monastic order would come to its spiritual fruition, leading to the ultimate redemption of all God's peoples.

The Synagogue of the Jews, the Greek Church, and the New Judah

Joachim believed that the Jews represented the elect people of God during the time of the Old Testament. Under the Old Testament's first seal, the twelve tribes of the Hebrews had endured oppression by the Egyptians, fled from bondage under them, and received the written Law. Under the second seal, they had battled against the people of Canaan and established both their royal power and their priesthood in the land of Jerusalem. After the death of Solomon, during the third seal, the kingdom of the Jews was divided between Judah's two tribes and Israel's ten tribes, with the latter lapsing into idolatry. Under the fourth seal, Israel had paid a heavy price for its sins, being conquered and deported by the Assyrians. Judah was protected until the fifth seal, when the Chaldeans overran Jerusalem. Under the sixth seal, the Jews had suffered captivity in Babylon until they were permitted to return to Jerusalem. Finally, under the seventh seal, the Temple was rebuilt and the Jews enjoyed a time of peace until their final persecution by the pagan Greeks. This brought both the time of the Old Testament and the *status* of the Father to an end with the dawning of the New Testament and *status* of the Son.

The coming of Christ formed a critical juncture for the Hebrews that resulted in their displacement as God's Chosen People—a common enough theme in Christian thought. Joachim explored this development through his exegesis, including the story of Tobit (Tob. 2:7–10), whose blindness represented the blindness of the Jews. Despite their past piety, the Jews were wearied by their "carnal" observation of the law and lacked the inner sight to see the "true light of Christ, the savior of the world."[27] Joachim read the story of Zachary and Elizabeth (Lk. 1:5–7), the mother of John the Baptist, in a similar fashion. Zachary signified the prelates of the Jews and Elizabeth the "church of the Levites." Elizabeth's pregnancy revealed that the Synagogue would give birth to Christ. Zachary, however, did not initially believe the angel Gabriel's proclamation that Elizabeth would conceive a child and was struck mute, representing the incredulity of the Jewish priesthood.[28] As Joachim declared in the *Book of Concordance,* Tobit and Zachary were both pious men, but they were deprived of their sight and speech, respectively, by the just judgment of God.[29] The Synagogue had likewise erred by denying the Trinity and the "spiritual intelligence" that revealed the true meaning of their own holy writings. As a result, the Jews had lost both their priesthood and their royal power, both of which were transferred to the Gentiles.

In the time of the New Testament and the *status* of the Son, God's favor came to lie instead with the Church, consisting of the few Jews who had recognized Christ and the Gentiles. Like Israel, however, this new Christian community faced its own series of persecutions and trials. Under the first seal, the "carnal" Jews persecuted the new Church when the earliest Christians separated themselves from the Synagogue and preached their new faith to the Gentiles.[30] Through the mission of Paul and Barnabas, the followers of Christ began their spiritual conquest of the Roman Empire, when the Church suffered its second persecution by the pagans. This time of suffering ended with the conversion of the Roman emperor Constantine. Joachim, like previous generations of clerical authors who both supported and opposed the Roman reform movement, viewed Constantine as a historical figure of the utmost importance. The peace established by the emperor brought about a radical transformation in the status of the Church by uniting Christianity with imperial power throughout the entire world.

This point in history formed a moment of particular significance for the Roman Church. Familiar with the basic principles of Roman primacy, Joachim believed that Peter (like Caleb, who led the Jews into Canaan after the Exodus from Egypt) had led his faithful followers away from the Synagogue, establishing Rome for them as the "new Jerusalem" in the tribe of Judah. Baptized by Pope Sylvester, Emperor Constantine later confirmed the prerogatives of this "royal priesthood" for the pontiffs of Rome.[31] In addition, Constantine founded a glorious new capital for the Roman Empire. As the "new Rome," Constantinople became one of the five patriarchates of the ancient church, like a bride for the church of Rome. In this act, however, lay the seeds of future tribulation for God's people. Under the third seal, Joachim drew a remarkable conclusion from his model of concordance, aligning the schism that developed between the biblical kingdoms of Israel and Judah (1 Kgs. 12:20) in the Old Testament with the division between the Greek and Latin Churches in the New Testament. In the traditional seven seals of the Apocalypse scheme, the third seal and the "black horse" commonly represented the internal assault of heresy during the Constantinian peace. Joachim redirected this well-known exegesis specifically toward the "heretical" church of Constantinople, which had sundered itself from Rome and began to tyrannize the Eastern Church. From this point forward, the Greek emperors acted like "pharaohs" of Egypt rather than "spiritual kings" of Jerusalem.[32]

The schism between the Latins and Greeks, Joachim realized, was just as much a part of God's plan as the division between the Synagogue and the Church. Much like the Jews before them, the Greeks had failed to transcend fully their carnal understandings of God's word. They had rejected the decrees and guidance of the Roman Church, refusing to acknowledge the apostolic authority granted to the papacy by Peter. Their priests took wives, not realizing that the Church was a cleric's true bride. They believed that Latins hated them, as much as they hated Latins. The abbot was well aware that the Greeks were the first Gentiles to receive the divine law through the Septuagint and were the first ones to receive the Gospel of Christ.[33] Just as the Jews had preceded the Gentiles, however, but lost their place of priority in God's plan to them, the Greeks had come before the Latins in the faith, but had ceded to them their birthright of spiritual grace. In his commentary on the Gospels, Joachim used the example of Phares and Zaram, the twin sons of Thamar, who signified "the two people, namely the Greek and Latin, whom Peter along with the other apostles begat through his Gospel."[34] Zaram emerged first from his mother's womb, sticking out his hand, which the nurse marked by tying a piece of string around it. This symbolized the Greeks, who had first committed themselves to the Christian faith. Zaram, however, withdrew his hand and Phares was born first, revealing how the Greeks had ceded their place to the younger Latin Church.[35]

The Greek rejection of Roman doctrine and authority brought disastrous consequences. Under the fourth seal, matching the Assyrian conquest of Israel, the Saracen invasions devastated the Eastern Church. Joachim drew this connection between the rise of Islam and Greek religious error in some of his earliest writings.[36] If he expressed these sentiments directly to the papal curia at Veroli, one can imagine that they would have fallen on receptive ears. Once again, Joachim brings us into some familiar territory, but from his own unique perspective. From the prophecies of Pseudo-Methodius to Guibert of Nogent's crusade chronicle, Christian authors viewed the Saracens as a scourge sent by God against his sinful people. As we saw earlier, Guibert linked the rise of the Saracens to the deviant nature of the Eastern Church. Through his model of concordance, Joachim creatively tied the Saracen conquests of the Eastern Roman Empire to the Greek rejection of Rome and its teachings. In the same way that God had allowed the Assyrians to conquer Israel because of their idolatry, the Lord permitted the Saracens to overrun the majority of Greek lands because the Greeks chose "to obey exalted secular power, rather than the vicar of Christ, and to submit to their heretical bishops, rather than to catholic ones."[37] In one favorite piece of imagery, the abbot associated the devastation of the Greeks with God's instructions in the Book of Revelation, 11:2: "Exclude the court outside of the Temple, and do not measure it, for it has been given over to the Gentiles." The Greek Church was "the court" outside "the living Temple" established at Rome, given over to the Saracens for "trampling."[38]

From that point forward, God's favor lay with the Latins. Continuing onward, the principle of concordance allowed Joachim to make sense out of a tumultuous period in the history of the Western Church that modern historians inescapably think of as the "decline and fall of the Roman Empire." Under the third seal of the Old Testament, the kingdom of Judah had suffered its own share of troubles, including attacks by foreign peoples and by the ten tribes of Israel. At other points, the kings of Judah made alliances with the wicked rulers of Israel, infecting Judah with the sin of their idolatry. Joachim applied this biblical framework to the period of the barbarian invasions of the Latin Church during the third seal of the New Testament. Servants of the Greek emperors, the Goths, and other heretical peoples plagued the Western regions, above all Italy, infecting them with their heresies. This devastation revealed something important about Joachim's alignment of the kingdom of Judah with the Roman Church: one had to take the bad with the good.[39]

This same era of tribulation in the Western Church, however, formed a crucial moment for the progress of the three *status* and the fruition of the monastic order among the Latins. As we have seen, Joachim believed that the order of monks had a double origin in the *status* of the Father and the *status* of the Son. Its first origin was in the days of Elijah, Elisha, and the "seven thousand men" in the idolatrous kingdom of Israel who had refused to worship Baal (2 Kgs. 19:18). Through the principle of concordance, the Old Testament prophets who had remained among the wicked men of Israel corresponded to a remnant of the Greeks, "hermits and abbots with many disciples in monastic perfection," who had continued to be faithful to the Roman Church despite the persecution they suffered from their own Arian bishops.[40] Joachim was well aware that the fathers of the Greek Church were first in "monastic discipline" and that the monastic way of life had reached the West from its origins in the Eastern Church during a time when "the perfection of religion, and spiritual life and doctrine, newly flowed from the Greek people to the Latins, as there was still then peace and concord between each church."[41]

Echoing Rupert of Deutz and Gerhoh of Reichersberg, Joachim identified the Greeks' rejection of the *filioque* as one prominent example of their heretical divergence from Rome. By misunderstanding the "double procession" of the Holy Spirit from the Father and from the Son, the Greeks did not simply err over Trinitarian doctrine; they also failed to recognize the place of the monastic order in salvation history.[42] The second origin of the monastic order in the *status* of the Son occurred during the days of Benedict of Nursia, who stood as a "mediator" between Greek and Latin monasticism. From the time of Benedict forward, Joachim declared, the zeal for perfect monastic living had been transferred to the followers of the Roman Church, thriving in Italy, Gaul, and Germany. The abbot did not invent the notion that there had been a "translation of religious life" from the East to the West (a concept also found in Otto of Freising's universal chronicle). Set within Joachim's elaborate theology of history, however, this idea took on new significance. The Holy Spirit and monastic life had come to rest in the Latin Church, where they would germinate and flourish with the coming of the third *status*.[43]

To clarify these developments, the abbot borrowed another popular concept from Latin theology of history, arguing that the "transferal of empire" offered yet another marker for the divine ordering of events. The westward movement of imperial power from Constantinople to the Franks in the time of Charlemagne's grandfather, Charles Martel, confirmed the movement of grace from the Greeks to the Latins. The abbot placed this event under the fourth seal, from Emperor Justinian to Popes Gregory III (r. 731–741) and Zachary (r. 741–752), when "the patronage of the Roman Church was removed from the emperors at Constantinople and bestowed upon Charles, ruler of the Franks, and his successors."[44] In Joachim's generational concordance, the twelve generations of the New Testament that started with King Charles of the Franks aligned with the twelve generations of the Old Testament that had begun with King Hezekiah. The Lord added fifteen years to Hezekiah's life and promised him protection for Jerusalem (2 Kgs. 20:6). According to Joachim, this paralleled God's protection of the Latin Church under the Franks from the Muslims after the Greek Empire was effectively destroyed. This basic picture appeared early in Joachim's writings, including the *Genealogy* and his commentary *On an Unknown Prophecy,* where he specified that God had granted this respite because of the prayers of the Roman Church.[45]

The rise of the Franks and their union with the papacy fascinated Joachim, as it did other reformist thinkers. First, that event demonstrated that the power of the Byzantine Empire had effectively lapsed, even if the rulers of Constantinople still sat on their thrones. Second, it inaugurated the fifth seal, an era of peace and stability for the Latin Church, just like the "fifteen years" that God granted to Hezekiah, marked by the establishment of proper relations between secular and ecclesiastical powers. In this case, Joachim echoed reform-minded writers ranging from Humbert of Silva Candida to Gerhoh of Reichersberg, looking back from the tumultuous clashes of the reform church with the German emperors to a time of supposed harmony between priestly authorities and temporal powers. The political message of such historical observations was clear. In contrast with contemporary emperors, the early Frankish rulers had shown proper deference for the Roman Church. The logic of Joachim's concordance, however, dictated that such a period of peace would not—could not—last. Despite Judah's reprieve when Israel was destroyed by the Assyrians, under the fifth seal of the Old Testament, Judah was carried into captivity at Babylon. In a sense, time was not on the side of the Western Church. The abbot's historical schemes led him inexorably to the present era of the reform papacy and the "new Babylonian Captivity," the papal struggle with the German emperors at the close of the New Testament's fifth seal.

In a short commentary entitled *An Understanding of the Fig-Baskets,* written around 1186, Joachim took the "liberty" of the Church as his theme.[46] Reviewing his basic model of concordance, the abbot divided the history of the church into three stages: the time of "Israel," from Christ to Constantine; the time of "Egypt," from Constantine until Charles, king of the Franks; and the time of "Babylon," from Charles until the present. In the time of spiritual Israel, the Church was "despised by carnal people" but enjoyed a time of freedom while isolated from the power of earthly rulers. With the coming of Constantine, the church of Rome openly assumed its status as the new Judah, enjoying the royal priesthood. The emperors and prelates of Constantinople, however, ushered in the time of Egypt through their heretical rejection of Roman doctrine and authority. This period lasted until the Franks assumed Roman imperial power. Although at first they showed their devotion to Rome, the Franks later became "in spirit" like the kings of Babylon, "reducing the liberty of the Church nearly to nothing."[47]

Through such observations, Joachim responded to the political, social, and cultural forces that characterized the reform-era Roman Church, including the tumultuous conflict between priestly authority and royal power that had disrupted medieval European society. His concern over the current state of ecclesiastical affairs reminds us of the double-edged nature of apocalyptic scenarios, which testify to the ultimate triumph of good but also bring dire warnings of present and impending tribulations. For the writers of prophecy and apocalyptic commentaries, there was always a potential slippage between the true community of the "spiritual" elect and contemporary ecclesiastical institutions, often revealed to be flawed and corrupt. Looking around him, Joachim saw clear signs that the Latin Church had entered into those days of lamentation predicted by the prophet Jeremiah. The time was rapidly approaching, the abbot warned, when God would separate the "good and bad" baskets of figs.

An informed historian, Joachim knew that the effort of the Roman Church to rid itself of simony and other forms of corruption had begun in earnest with the papacy of Leo IX. In his tract *An Understanding of the Fig-Baskets* and in the *Book of Concordance,* Joachim aligned Pope Leo with King Josiah of Judah, who had reformed religious life in his kingdom, but was still destroyed by the Pharaoh Neco (2 Kgs. 22:1–2). Like Josiah, Leo was a just man, who sought to reform the Roman Church. The pope did not understand, however, that the Lord's anger had been kindled against his people, something made clear when Leo was defeated and captured by the Normans at the battle of Civitate in 1053. Joachim declared that Leo had erred by placing his faith in "material arms" rather than "spiritual ones." The key to the true liberty of the Church lay in humility. When liberty turned to pride, it became the "wicked" kind of liberty, forcing God to cast down the faithful so that they might recall through their servitude the true nature of their spiritual freedom.[48]

Joachim's message was hard to miss. The Roman Church had no business taking up arms to protect its temporalities from the unavoidable scourge of the "New Babylon," the German emperors. Since the time of Henry IV and Pope Pascal II, there had been great confusion among the faithful during times of subsequent conflict between the papacy and the German empire. The abbot offered a grim prognosis for the faithful on the edge of the sixth seal. From Joachim's perspective, the principle of concordance made these tribulations of the "New Judah" inevitable. Even with the most pious of intentions, efforts at reform were not enough to save the Roman Church, just as the last kings of Judah were unable to prevent the Babylonian Captivity by their own efforts at purifying the cult of God.

Joachim's attitude toward the crusades reveals a similar ambivalence about the use of force to achieve supposedly spiritual goals. Indeed, scholars have seen the abbot as both a supporter and a critic of the crusading movement.[49] He never addressed the capture of Jerusalem by the crusaders or its aftermath at great length. In the *Book of Concordance,* he made no mention of the First Crusade or of Pope Urban's role in calling for the expedition. This omission is hardly surprising, since the dramatic capture of Jerusalem did not fit neatly into his principle of concordance. After all, there was no equivalent event in the time of the Old Testament during the waning days of Judah to match the conquest of the holy city by Latin Christians in the time of the New Testament. A great deal can be gleaned, however, from Joachim's comments about the crusades that are scattered throughout his works. Much like Pope Leo's expedition against the Normans, the effort to liberate Jerusalem was misguided, however pious its intentions. The Saracens, who had plagued the faithful in the past, would not be overcome, since they had a future role to play in the chastisement of God's people.

Toward the close of the *Book of Concordance,* Joachim turned his attention to the well-known scheme of "world empires," revealed through Nebuchadnezzar's dream of the statue made from gold, silver, bronze, and iron, with feet of iron and clay. The ancient Christian fathers, the abbot acknowledged, had interpreted the "iron" portion of the statue as symbolizing the Roman Empire, which would endure until the end of time. Unlike them, Joachim knew about the subsequent rise of the Saracens. Armed with this knowledge, the abbot declared that the bronze portion of the statue represented Rome, which had suffered but endured the invasions of the Goths, Vandals, and others until the rise of the Saracens, represented by the iron portion of the statue, who violently occupied the "the borders of the Romans." The feet of the statue, made of both iron and clay, represented the Saracens mixed in with other "diverse nations" that would assail the faithful in the days of Antichrist.[50] Both Daniel's dream of the four beasts that emerged from the sea to destroy the kingdoms of the world, and the seven-headed dragon from the Book of Revelation, cast further light on the role of the Saracens in history.[51] In the abbot's *Book of Figures,* Joachim associated the fourth, fifth, and sixth heads of the dragon with Muhammad, a Muslim figure named Mesemothus, and Saladin, the conqueror of Jerusalem in 1187.[52] The abbot expressed particular interest in John's statement that one of the heads looked "as if it were dead," which the abbot associated with the temporary lapse of infidel power during the First Crusade: "For so it was in the days of Pope Urban," the abbot noted in his commentary on the life of Saint Benedict, "that there was a great movement of Christians from every part of the Western Church heading across the sea to liberate holy Jerusalem."[53] The head, however, was not truly dead. On account of Christian sins, the Saracens arose again to slaughter the faithful under Saladin, recapturing Jerusalem and the holy places. Joachim could not ignore the crusades, but he could and did make it clear that they were an abortive attempt to accomplish things that ran contrary to the will of God. It was through humility, rather than the sword, that the true liberty of the Church would be achieved in the future Sabbath age.

This ambivalence was evident when the crusading movement came knocking on the abbot's door, so to speak, during his meeting with King Richard I. The English monarch was en route to the Holy Land during the Third Crusade (1189–1192), called after the Islamic leader Saladin had destroyed crusader forces at the battle of Hattin before recapturing Jerusalem in 1187. According to chroniclers who reported this meeting, Joachim's reputation had preceded him as someone endowed with the "prophetic spirit" or "spiritual intelligence." Richard requested the interview and eagerly attended to the abbot's words, as did the learned churchmen accompanying the English king. Among other things, the abbot explained to his listeners his interpretation of the seven-headed dragon from Revelation: five heads were past, and Saladin, the sixth head, currently raged against Christians. After the demise of Saladin, there would remain the seventh head, Antichrist, who would usher in a final persecution against the faithful.[54]

As presented by the English chroniclers, however, Joachim's prophetic opinions were certainly not above question. When he stated that Antichrist had already been born in Rome, the clergymen accompanying Richard insisted to the contrary that Antichrist would be born in the East from the tribe of Dan, the traditional scenario found in Adso of Montier-en-Der and elsewhere.[55] In addition, there was some uncertainty about the abbot's forecast for the success of Richard's crusade. According to the earliest report of the meeting (written, perhaps, by the English chronicler Roger of Hovedon), Joachim declared that Christians would return to their lost pastures and that God would give Richard victory, although the trial of Antichrist was still to come. In Roger of Hovedon's longer, redacted version of that same chronicle, the abbot proclaimed that Saladin would not be defeated until seven years after his capture of Jerusalem in 1187 (writing around the mid-1190s, Roger would have known that Saladin had in fact died in 1193). When Richard inquired further about the role he would play in this prolonged drama, Joachim still insisted that the king's expedition was necessary and that God would "exalt his name over all the princes of Earth," but this did not change the fact that Richard's expedition was arriving too early.[56] According to the laconic report of the Premonstratensian chronicler Robert of Auxerre, likewise writing in the aftermath of the lackluster Third Crusade, Joachim asserted that both Richard and the French King Philip Augustus (r. 1180–1223) "would accomplish nothing or very little," since the time for Jerusalem's liberation was not at hand.[57] Whatever Joachim actually said to Richard, such reports echoed the abbot's own prophetic insights. The restoration of the earthly Jerusalem did not comport with the general trend of history toward the imminent opening of the sixth seal and the coming of the "great Antichrist," followed by an era of spiritual renewal.

The Sabbath Age and the Unity of God's Fold

Despite his predictions of future tribulations, Joachim's view of the future was far from pessimistic. Years earlier in his work *On an Unknown Proph-*

ecy, he had observed that the Jews would convert to Christianity some-time after the apocalyptic struggle of the sixth seal.[58] Taken alone, this was an unremarkable prediction that certainly would not have raised any eyebrows at the papal curia. It was common for Christians to assign the Jews some role in their eschatological drama, both as servants of Anti-christ and as converts to the Christian faith. This theme, barely mentioned in the abbot's early writings, came to assume a prominent place in Joachim's major works and later tracts. The abbot's vision of a Jewish conversion was particularly well developed in his final and unfinished composition, his *Tract on the Four Gospels.* In addition, Joachim explicitly linked the future conversion of the Jews to the restoration of unity be-tween the Greek and Latin Churches. By adding this theme of a Greek "conversion," he broke new ground in Latin apocalyptic eschatology. The Greeks, and then the Jews, would both be saved through the agency of the "spiritual men" that would arise from within that incubator for the full flowering of the Holy Spirit, the Latin Church.[59]

Similar to Anselm of Havelberg a generation earlier, Joachim inter-preted the recent changes in religious life as a sign of the Holy Spirit at work. The abbot reserved particular admiration for Bernard of Clairvaux and drew upon the Cistercian order as a model for his own efforts at mo-nastic reform, although there are signs that he later grew somewhat disil-lusioned with the Cistercians, which perhaps encouraged him to found his own monastic order. Indeed, Joachim's enthusiasm for the future role of monks (symbolized by the apostle John) led him to claim that they would rebuke and effectively transcend the more "carnal" order of the clergy (symbolized by the apostle Peter).[60] In his *Tract on the Four Gospels,* the abbot seemed to flirt with the idea that the Roman papacy would somehow pass away when the monastic order assumed a place of priority over the clerical order. For the most part, however, Joachim appeared to envision a continued role for the "spiritualized" papacy in the coming Sabbath age. In one notable passage of the *Book of Concordance,* he hinted at a connection between the future papacy and the coming of a "new leader," the "universal pontiff of the New Jerusalem" who would renew the Christian faith throughout the world. Given the fact that Joachim met with three popes, all of whom approved of his writings, it seems hard to imagine that the abbot harbored notions of a future era that had no special place for the bishops of Rome, even if he did believe that the Roman papacy of the spiritual age might look quite different from that of the current era, "mixed" between flesh and spirit.[61]

The monastic order of the Latin Church, under the leadership of a purified papacy, would provide the impetus for the salvation of both the heretical Greeks and non-believing Jews. Joachim gave one of his earliest expositions on this process in the fifth book of the *Book of Concordance* through his exegesis of Tobit, interpreting Tobit's blindness as a symbol for the blindness of the carnal Jews, who had failed to recognize Christ, the Trinity, and the spiritual intelligence. In this biblical story, Tobit sends his son, Tobias, to reclaim ten talents of silver which he had left with a man named Gabael in the city of Rages. Accompanied by the archangel Raphael, Tobias meets and is betrothed to Sarah, daughter of Raguel, whom Raphael cures of her demonic possession. Looking to the future, Joachim foresaw marvelous developments revealed through this story. Preachers from the Latin Church would bring the "spiritual intelligence" to the Greek people, inviting them to Sarah and Tobias's wedding, that is, "the unity of the Roman Church." Both Latins and Greeks, Joachim predicted, would thereby share "one peace and joy in the Church of Christ."[62]

This spiritual conversion of the Greeks, contingent upon their obedience to Rome, would be followed by the conversion of the Jews to the Christian faith, symbolized by the eventual restoration of the elder Tobit's sight. Joachim developed this notion with even more detail in his *Exhortation to the Jews*. Tobias's journey to the Medes with the angel Raphael represented the journey of the apostles to the Gentiles, first to the Greeks, and then to the Latins, among whom Tobias and Sarah celebrated their "spiritual marriage" that had endured from the time of Saint Peter up until Joachim's present day. After the nuptials, Tobias returned to his blind father and restored his sight, which symbolized that the successors of the apostles—the "spiritual men" of Joachim's schemes—would preach among the Jews. In his exegesis of Zachary, the abbot explained that Zachary's voice was restored when his son, John the Baptist, was born, thereby revealing that the "people of the Jews" would at last turn to the Lord after the conversion of the Gentiles. Through this act, the Jews would finally come to enjoy their spiritual patrimony with the Gentiles.[63]

At various points the abbot expressed a basic sense of geographical purpose in this process, observing that God's grace had moved from the East to the West, and in the future would move from the West back to the East.[64] Joachim frequently reiterated this theme of a Greek and Jewish union with the Latin Christian faith. In his commentary on the Apocalypse, he offered an interpretation of the Gospel of John, which records the discovery of Christ's tomb by Mary Magdalene, who runs to tell Peter and John (Jn. 20:1–18). John arrives first at the tomb, but enters after Peter. After the two disciples depart, Christ appears to Mary. According to the abbot, Peter represented the Latins, the first to "enter" into the more spiritual understanding of Scripture; John represented the Greeks, who would ultimately follow the Latins into their mystical doctrine; and Mary represented the Jews, who would finally recognize Christ. This same process was foreshadowed by Christ's healing of the blind man at Jericho (that is, the Greeks) followed by the ill tax-collector Zacchaeus (that is, the Jews), and also in the passage when Christ passed through Samaria, conversing with the Samaritan women at the well (Jn. 4:3–26), indicating the future passage of the spiritual men to the Eastern Church and the Jews.[65]

It should be noted that this process of redemption was predicated upon the Greek and Jewish recognition of their failure to transcend their literal understandings of God's dispensation for salvation. The Greeks would acknowledge Roman doctrine and authority, and the Jews would turn to Christ. In a particularly ironic twist for the Greeks, who denied the double procession of the Holy Spirit from the Father "and from the Son," they would be saved by the "spiritual men" of the monastic order, which itself originated from the *status* of the Father and from the *status* of the Son. These are crucial qualifications; we should not see in Joachim some sort of modern "multiculturalism." At various points, the abbot expressed his belief that all converted peoples would be included in God's eschatological fold. In his *Exhortation to the Jews,* Joachim informed his putative Jewish readers that they had misread Ezekiel's proclamation of God's intention to "gather you from all the countries and bring you into your own land" (Ez. 36:24):

> It does not behoove you to understand carnally that "nations" in
> this passage refers to people of faith, but more so to infidels, such

as pagans and Saracens, nor ought you to reckon that the "land" refers to that arid province of Canaan which God gave to your fathers, but more so to the universal Church of the Christians.[66]

When exactly would these marvelous conversions happen? There has been some debate over this question, due in large part to the complicated nature of Joachim's schemes when they reach the traumatic events that would accompany the sixth and seventh tribulations. In the *Book of Concordance,* the abbot predicted that a "considerable multitude" of both Jews and Greeks would join the "unity of the Church" before the great persecution under Antichrist, although some Jews would continue to harass and insult Rome and the pope until the final defeat of Antichrist's evil forces.[67] One gets the overall impression that Joachim saw the conversion of the Greeks and Jews as a protracted development which would begin before the opening of the sixth seal, continue during the persecutions under Antichrist, and achieve its fulfillment with the beginning of the Sabbath age (which would itself be short). At various points, Joachim hinted that the time for the beginning of this process was quite near at hand or had perhaps already started. One reason he composed his exhortation to the Jews, the abbot declared, was because he believed that "the time of mercy for them, a time of consolation and their conversion" was close at hand. Elsewhere, Joachim noted that he had seen the recent visit of an Armenian delegation to Pope Urban III, which he interpreted as one more step toward the forthcoming reconciliation between the Eastern Christians and the Latins. For those who knew how to read the signs, the message was clear. The world was poised on the edge of terrors and marvelous transformations.[68]

In some ways, Joachim of Fiore fully realized the Gregorian reformist vision of history that had begun in the eleventh century. Every historical theory seemed to have its place in the scope of his imagination—the notion of Christian unity under the Apostolic See of Rome, the transferal of religious life, grace, and empire from East to West, the sense of progression in God's favor until it settled among the Latins, the schism between the Latin and Greek Churches, the brief triumph and disillusionment of the crusades, and so forth leading up to the time of Antichrist and beyond. Through his vision of millennial conversions, Joachim offered his readers a glimpse of Christendom realized on a worldwide scale, the penultimate union of all peoples in fulfillment of Christ's promises. Jews, Greeks, pagans, and perhaps even Saracens would be led to salvation by the spiritual men of the Latin Church and assembled under a purified Roman Church. Never before had any Christian thinker dared to imagine such a process of historical transformation with this sort of audacious precision and boldness.

In other ways, however, Joachim's vision of history could be provocative and potentially disturbing. His tone of optimism about the future was leavened by a deeply felt sense of worry about the present state of his own religious community. During his meeting with King Richard of England, Joachim supposedly reported that Antichrist had already been born in Rome—and would one day become pope. Another English chronicler, Ralph of Coggeshall, recorded some similar sentiments when describing yet another interview of the abbot in 1198 by the Cistercian monk Adam of Persigne. Much like King Richard and his entourage, when Adam heard Joachim's claim that Antichrist was already alive and would someday sit on the see of Saint Peter, he protested that Antichrist would be born in Babylon. Rome, Joachim replied, represented Babylon "mystically."[69] In light of such comments, together with his cryptic statements about the future "new leader" that would emerge from the Roman Church, the "universal pontiff of the New Jerusalem," Joachim left an ambiguous legacy about the future of the institutional papacy, associated both with absolute evil and with angelic good.

In Ralph of Coggeshall's report of the meeting between Joachim and Adam of Persigne, the abbot denied any privileged status as a prophet in the traditional sense of the word, declaring that he was first and foremost an exegete, albeit one who was gifted with special spiritual insights. His protests would do little good. In the generations after his death, more and more members of the Roman Church would be captivated (or repelled) by Joachim's vision of the future Sabbath age, "in which the spirit of God will pour forth more abundantly upon the elect from on high, and there will be peace and truth in every land."[70] It is no exaggeration to say that the self-proclaimed inhabitants of Christendom would never look at history or their place in the world in quite the same way after Joachim. Indeed, during the decades following his death, surprising historical developments would give Western Christians ample reasons to revisit Joachim's schemes and to push them in controversial new directions.

The Shepherd of the World

In a sermon commemorating the life of Pope Innocent III not long after the pontiff had died on 16 July 1216, the English Cistercian monk Matthew of Rievaulx opened his paean by declaring that this "vicar of Christ, by God's favor, completely restored the schismatic Eastern Church—namely Constantinople with its territories, which comprised the greatest part of Christendom and had been blinded by the shadows of its errors for three hundred years—to the bosom of the universal Church, bringing it to obey the highest pontiff."[1] Matthew was referring here to the unexpected outcome of the Fourth Crusade, which had captured the Byzantine capital in 1204. He proceeded to list Innocent's other accomplishments "in our days," including the pope's struggles against pagans in the Baltic region and against Cathar heretics in southern France. Matthew implied that through the work which Innocent had begun, it seemed certain that Jerusalem would soon be restored to Christian hands. Considering his optimistic tone, it is likely that the Cistercian monk was writing before the disappointing outcome of Innocent's final and posthumous crusading expedition, the Fifth Crusade, which collapsed in Egypt in 1221. Even if Matthew had known about that crusade's failure, however, it seems more than likely, given the general tenor of his sermon, that his opinion of Innocent's legacy would have remained undiminished.[2]

Over the last fifty years or more, portraits of Pope Innocent III have shifted away from a somewhat restricted view of the pontiff as a hard-headed realist, consummate politician, and calculating canon lawyer to a more nuanced image of Innocent as a theologian and spiritual leader with deep-seated convictions and a genuine sense of his pastoral responsibilities.[3] This change in emphasis, however, does not alter the fact that Innocent was one of the most powerful popes of the Middle Ages, a figure who might be described as the epitome of the papal monarchy. In the person of Innocent III, one finds a savvy administrator with boundless ambition to maximize the institutional authority of the papacy. To realize his goals, the pope vigorously marshaled well-known sources of theoretical support for the primacy of the Roman Church and, more broadly, the ultimate preeminence of priestly authority over the Christian faithful. In his position as the successor to Saint Peter, Innocent's authority and pastoral responsibilities knew no bounds. "For thus each magnate holds his own province, and every king his own kingdom," Innocent declared on one occasion, "but Peter presides over all places in fullness as much as extent, for he is the vicar of the One to whom belongs the earth and its fullness, the entirety of the world and all those who live within it."[4] Particularly in the early stages of his papacy (perhaps before the actual limitations of his office had truly set in), Innocent celebrated the prerogatives of the papacy in the most grandiose of terms.

Whatever setbacks he later faced, the pope never abandoned his drive to defend Christendom from its enemies, both within and without, and to expand its frontiers under the auspices of the Roman Church. Throughout his papacy, from the planning stages of the Fourth Crusade until the Fourth Lateran Council (1215) and the declaration of the Fifth Crusade, Innocent III framed his universalizing vision of Christian order around three interrelated goals: the reform of the Western Church; unity with the Eastern Church; and the drive to recover the holy places. The fact that the Fourth Crusade resulted in the violent seizure of a fellow Christian city did little to deter the pope's plans. Quite the opposite. Although the sack of Constantinople evoked criticism from some Latin clergy, many contemporaries insisted that the capture of the Byzantine capital was a divinely ordained event intended by God to achieve the unification of the Western and Eastern Churches. First and foremost among those who interpreted the crusade in this way stood Pope Innocent, who had set the crusade in motion, attempted unsuccessfully to keep it on track, and, when confronted with its unexpected outcome, decided it was yet another example of God's will to order historical events and transfer imperial power to his more obedient followers. Innocent, who had made his de-sires for Christian unity with the Eastern Church quite plain before the Fourth Crusade, interpreted the capture of Constantinople within a broader theology of history that pointed toward the conversion of Jews and pagans along with the recovery of the Holy Land from the infidels. The pope was not naïve about the tool that God had used to bring about this miraculous unification of Christendom. After the sack, reports that the crusaders had plundered Constantinople's ecclesiastical treasures and had violently abused its citizens dismayed him. Nevertheless, he judged that the crusaders had made a virtue out of necessity through their sei-zure of the Greek Empire, and he decided to follow suit, interpreting the outcome of the crusade as one manifestation of Christ's promise that there would be "one fold" under "one shepherd" before the end of time.[5]

This sort of reaction was not confined to the pope or the immediacy of the papal curia. Contemporaries of the Fourth Crusade frequently offered positive evaluations of the expedition that had resulted in the triumph of Latin Christians over the "schismatic city" of Constantinople, which had arrogantly strayed into heresy and schism from the Roman Church.[6] In particular, clerical and monastic authors chronicled one of the greatest benefits bestowed upon the faithful by the seizure of Con-stantinople, namely the transfer of sacred relics from the Eastern Church to their new homes in the West.[7] Whatever the grim reality of 1204 may have been, some members of the Roman Church openly declared that the "great betrayal," "unholy crusade," and "ungodly war" (as some mod-ern historians have labeled it) represented a just judgment of God and another sign of the favor he showed toward Western Christians—perhaps the most remarkable revelation of divine purpose in history since the capture of Jerusalem by an earlier generation of crusaders.[8] For years af-terward, clerics such as Matthew of Rievaulx celebrated the capture of Constantinople as a first step toward the recovery of Jerusalem, perhaps leading to a far-reaching transformation in the status of Christendom and its place in the world. From this perspective, the period of Innocent III's papacy demonstrated Latin theology of history at its most sophisticated and elastic, when notions of universal Christian unity could be used to justify even the shedding of Christian blood.

Reform, Christian Unity, and Crusade under Innocent III

In a number of sermons during the opening years of his papacy, some delivered shortly after his consecration, Innocent confidently expounded on his papal duties and prerogatives. In particular, he emphasized the centrality of Christ's pastoral commission to Peter, and by extension to his successors sitting on the Apostolic See, "which possessed and possesses primacy and principality over the entire world."[9] Echoing the earliest generation of papal reformers and their supporters, Innocent stressed the marvelous transformation of Rome through Peter, whereby its former imperial dominion became the superior, spiritual authority of the apostolic pontiffs. To illustrate this idea, the pope repeated a favorite biblical episode from the Gospel of Luke (Lk. 5:3–11), in which Peter casts his nets at Christ's command to yield a burgeoning catch of fish. For Innocent, these passages plainly revealed the role of Peter and his successors in converting the city of Rome and spreading the word of God among all peoples.[10]

As was the case for his papal predecessors since the days of Pope Gregory VII, Innocent faced the German emperors as the principal rivals for this theoretical position of Christian universal leadership. The pope, however, was afforded an auspicious opportunity to assert his authority when a struggle broke out between two claimants to the imperial throne, Philip of Swabia and Otto of Brunswick, following the death of Emperor Henry VI (r. 1190–1197). Innocent, who initially threw his support behind Otto, seized this chance to proclaim the principal and ultimate prerogative of the papacy to delegate the imperial office. First, he observed, the power of empire had been transferred under papal auspices from Greece to the West in the days of the Frankish ruler Charlemagne, for the purpose of making the Western emperors the protectors of the papacy.[11] Second, he stressed, popes ceremonially bestowed the imperial crown.

Drawing heavily upon scriptural imagery in a letter to the secular and ecclesiastical leaders of Germany in May 1199, Innocent reminded his readers that Christ, both the "king of kings" and the "priest for eternity after the order of Melchisedek," stood as a model for the concord that ought to exist between royal power and priestly authority. When that relationship existed in harmony (that is, when emperors acknowledged papal supremacy), the faith was expanded, heresies confounded, justice served, peace established, and, among other things, the "barbarity of pagans" subdued. By contrast, the current division in the empire encouraged heretics and emboldened the pagans, who were "glorying" in their possession of the holy places. To resolve this infelicitous state of affairs, Innocent arrogated for himself the privilege to settle the Roman Empire's current state of discord, which jeopardized all of Christendom. His goal, he stressed, was the "conservation and exaltation," not the "destruction," of the empire, for although some emperors had persecuted the Church in the past, others had served it honorably.[12]

In turn, Innocent linked this notion of Christian order to a goal that had lost none of its immediacy since Saladin's capture of Jerusalem in 1187, namely the recovery of the holy places for Christianity. After nearly ninety years of emotional and ideological investment in the Latin possession of Jerusalem, the destruction of crusader forces at the battle of Hattin and the subsequent loss of Jerusalem represented a devastating reminder of the potential for Christian sins to evoke God's wrath. Summoning a new crusade in the immediate aftermath of Jerusalem's fall, Pope Gregory VIII (r. 1187) had called upon all believers—not just crusaders—to do penance and perform works of piety in response to this divine punishment.[13] Contemporaries were particularly unsettled by the loss of the True Cross, the prized relic of the crusader kingdom of Jerusalem that had been seized by the Muslims at Hattin. As one anonymous English author bemoaned, this "worthy thing was borne away unworthily by the unworthy, oh alas!" For about eighty-nine years, he lamented, the city of Jerusalem had been in the possession of "our people," but it was lost in a brief amount of time and the "law of Mahumet" extended over it.[14]

Pope Innocent hoped to reverse this state of misfortune through the internal reform of the Roman Church, along with a call for Christians to take up arms in the proper spirit of piety. He first declared his desire for the recovery of the holy places in a letter to the titular Latin patriarch of Jerusalem in February 1198. Echoing Pope Gregory VIII, Innocent expressed his belief that Christian fasting, prayer, and works of piety offered the initial step toward regaining their inheritance.[15] Over the following two years of his papacy, the pope repeatedly expressed his hope to liberate Jerusalem, issuing a number of crusading bulls that called upon the faithful to contribute—both militarily and financially—toward a task that had been shamefully left undone by the Third Crusade. As early as June 1198, he assigned Laurence of Syracuse and Luke of Sambucina as legates to oversee the newly forming expedition, which would "walk in the law of the Lord."[16] Luke, it is worth noting, had formerly worked at Casamari as a scribe for none other than Joachim of Fiore. Around the same time, in fact, Innocent also called upon Joachim to act as one of his crusade-preachers in Sicily. Given his ambivalent attitude toward crusading, Joachim would have made an interesting crusade-preacher, although there is no sign that he ever heeded the pope's call.[17] Looking toward France, Innocent later supported the charismatic French preacher Fulk of Neuilly, who called upon his listeners to reform their wicked ways and free the holy places from the infidels.[18] In his crusading bull *Post miserabile,* issued in August 1198, Innocent declared that the infidels' possession of the land where Christ had assumed the flesh and died for human redemption was a source of shame for the entire Western Church. In this bull and the subsequent calls for a new crusade, Innocent clarified crusading privileges and made careful financial arrangements for the new expedition, while calling upon his audience to realize that their own moral reform was the key to restoring the holy places.[19]

At the same time, Innocent pursued support for his new crusade from a different direction, calling upon the Byzantine Emperor Alexius III Angelus (r. 1195–1203) to take an active role in the effort to recover Jerusalem.[20] In a letter written to Alexius in late August 1198, Innocent implicitly tied the need for Christian concord to the success of a new expedition. The loss of Jerusalem and the withdrawal of the Greek people from the unity of the Apostolic See, he declared, formed a double source of shame for both the pope and the emperor. Innocent therefore called upon Alexius to exert himself for the unity of the two churches and to assist in the liberation of the Holy Land "from the hands of the pagans."[21] Although this letter was measured and cautious in the demands it made on the Greek ruler, Innocent left absolutely no doubt about the fundamental basis for the unity of Christendom. It lay in submission to the Roman Church and its bishop, commissioned by Christ through Peter to be the "mother and instructor of all churches." In another address to Emperor Alexius written around this time, the well-known papal decretal *Solitae,* the pope hammered home his view that the wielders of the imperial dignity were ultimately subject to the bearers of priestly authority, the former represented by the lesser light of the moon, and the latter by the greater light of the sun.[22]

In an accompanying letter sent to the Greek patriarch Georgius II Xiphilinus (r. 1191–1198) or to his successor John X Camaterus (r. 1198–1206), the newly elected pope took a similar stance, emphasizing the need for Christian concord through the recognition of the Apostolic See as the rightful head of the universal Church.[23] Innocent exhorted the patriarch to return the "commonality of the Greeks" to the unity of the Church under the guidance of the Roman papacy so that there might be "one fold and one shepherd." By that "shepherd," the pope did not simply mean Christ himself—Innocent was clear that he meant Christ's delegate here on earth, the "vicar of Christ," the bishop of Rome.[24] Innocent repeated these themes in yet another epistle to John X Camaterus, responding to the latter's polite skepticism about papal claims to universal primacy.[25] In an equally polite but firmly worded response to Camaterus, Innocent approached the problem of papal primacy less like a canon lawyer and more like a preacher, expositing upon biblical episodes that illustrated Peter's special status. Indeed, portions of this letter read much like Innocent's sermons on Saint Peter. According to the pope, the fact that Peter was the first to recognize Christ as the Lord and swam alone to him (Jn. 21:7–8) symbolized Peter's privilege to "govern the entire world," while the other apostles remained in their boat, indicating that they were not deputized with any sort of universal mission, but rather each with his own province or church. When Christ instructed Peter to join him in walking over the waters (Mt. 14: 22–33), this prefigured Peter's status as the Vicar of Christ and his power over all peoples.[26] Likewise, when Peter lowered the "nets of preaching" at Christ's command and captured a multitude of fish, this revealed that apostle's role in the conversion of both the Jews and Gentiles. The universality of Peter's commission was reinforced by the location of his ecclesiastical dominion in Rome, the seat of imperial monarchy and the ruler of nations. Because of the Roman Church's divinely ordained and canonical position as the mother of all churches, Innocent declared, the Greek patriarch rightly owed obedience to the Apostolic See regardless of any "disparity of rites" or "diversity of doctrine."[27]

In terms of their concrete outcome, this exchange of letters and legates in the opening years of Innocent's papacy accomplished little, despite calls on both sides for a general council to meet in order to resolve some of the ongoing tensions between the Latin and Greek Churches. Of course, even in this case, both sides had different ideas about the nature of such an ecumenical gathering. For the Greeks, it would be an assembly of episcopal equals, but for the Roman Church, it would represent a meeting of bishops subordinate to papal authority. This lack of tangible results, however, does not indicate that Innocent viewed his role as the vicar of Christ with anything less than the utmost conviction. His language was unflinching, as was his insistence that papal authority was divinely ordained and limitless in terms of its scope.

Innocent's overtures to the Byzantine emperor and patriarchs represented only part of his broader aspirations toward the wider world during the early stages of his papacy. In letters to Kalojan, king of Bulgaria, Innocent praised the ancient veneration of the Bulgarians toward the see of Saint Peter and their recognition of papal primacy before they were corrupted by the gifts and promises of the Greeks.[28] In his correspondence with the ruler of Cicilian Armenia, Leo II, and the Armenian patriarch, Gregory VI, Innocent drew upon a tradition of warmer Armenian respect for the prerogatives and reputation of the Apostolic See.[29] King Leo, threatened by Turkish forces and entangled in a dispute over control of Antioch with the crusader Count Bohemond IV of Tripoli, needed all the friends he could get. For Innocent, this situation provided him with another opportunity to assert the primacy of the Roman Church over all other Christian communities and to link Christian unity with the longed-for recovery of the Holy Land. Crowned by the papal legate Conrad of Wittelsbach in 1199, Leo was expected to bring concord between the Armenian Church and Rome, while devoting his energies to the struggle for Jerusalem.[30] In December 1199, the pope sent to King Leo the "banner of

Saint Peter," appropriate for a ruler who "devoutly receives the mandates and faithfully observes the commands of the Apostolic See," while taking up arms against "the enemies of the Cross" in order to free Christ's patrimony from their hands.[31]

In the words of John Gilchrist, for Pope Innocent III, fighting "the Lord's war" became for Christians "a testing ground of their faith, a faith solidly embedded in obedience to Rome."[32] Whether addressing Western prelates and princes or Eastern rulers and patriarchs, Innocent conjoined moral reform, Christian unity, and the struggle against the infidels more explicitly and forcefully than any pope before him. During the years 1202 and 1203, he must have been gratified to see the organization and departure of a new expedition to liberate the Holy Land, but it was far from the crusade that he had anticipated. The pope, who had invested himself in the mutually reinforcing goals of Christian unity and the recovery of Jerusalem, soon confronted a scenario that seemed to promise the realization of his most audacious hopes, while highlighting the persistent problem of Christian sins that threatened once again to call down God's wrath.

The Fourth Crusade and Capture of Constantinople

The contentious events that led the Fourth Crusade to Constantinople and its ultimate sack of the Byzantine capital have been treated by scholars elsewhere and can be summarized briefly.[33] In 1202, the predominantly French warriors of the new expedition assembled at Venice. Strapped for cash and heavily in debt to Venice for the ships that the city had provided them, the crusaders agreed to attack nearby Zadar at the Venetians' behest in November 1202. Pope Innocent anathematized them for assaulting that Christian city, although his interest in preserving his longed-for crusade led him to lift the ban against the non-Venetian members of the army. Disregarding or oblivious to papal instructions to the contrary, members of the crusade next sailed to Constantinople with the goal of elevating the young prince-in-exile, Alexius, to the Byzantine throne. Innocent, who had been visited by Alexius in 1202, was generally unsupportive of the young man's plight, despite Alexius's declaration that he would show proper veneration to the Apostolic See should he be restored to his rightful place as the son of the deposed and imprisoned Byzantine ruler, Isaac II (r. 1185–1195, 1203–1204).[34] Alexius had better luck enlisting notable members of the crusader army to his cause, although not everyone was happy with this unexpected detour.[35]

In July 1203, the army of the Fourth Crusade succeeded in driving Alexius III out of Constantinople and installing the young Alexius IV as co-emperor along with his father, Isaac. Even as Innocent reacted to these rapidly unfolding events, over the winter the Latin armies at Constantinople found themselves increasingly at odds with their erstwhile Greek allies. Isaac died, and Alexius was deposed by a member of the Byzantine court, Mourtzuphlus, who was crowned as Alexius V Dukas. Alexius IV died not long afterward, apparently at Mourtzuphlus's hands. Any Byzantine obligations toward the crusader army died with him. After months of growing antagonism and sporadic hostilities, on 8 April 1204 the crusaders assaulted Constantinople without success. Four days later they attacked the city a second time, seizing it for themselves.[36]

Innocent's complex and shifting reaction to these developments reveals a great deal about his conception of papal authority, his view of the Greek Church, and his theological reading of historical events.[37] When the first crusader assault had resulted in Alexius IV's elevation to the throne in August 1203, Innocent had no illusions about the motivations behind this coup d'état. In an earlier letter to the crusaders, Innocent had cautioned the leaders of the army that the pretense of restoring Constantinople to Roman ecclesiastical authority would not serve to justify an attack on the city.[38] Confronted with the initial capture of the city, Innocent continued to insist that the ends did not justify the means: the Greek failure to obey the Roman Church did not make them legitimate targets for such an attack. At the same time, the pope had no qualms about trying to hold the leaders of the crusade and the new emperor to a prominently stated reason for their alliance, namely the restoration of communion between the Eastern and Western Churches.[39] As he wrote in February 1204 to the crusading bishops of Soissons and Troyes, he was certain they shared his desire that there "might be one fold and one shepherd, nor will there be any more a distinction between Latins and Greeks, but they shall both be joined together in the catholic faith and in ecclesiastical unity."[40]

Even as Innocent foresaw the resolution of the division between the two churches, the situation on the ground at Constantinople was deteriorating. According to eyewitness accounts, when the second siege of the city stalled and morale was low, the leading clergy of the army openly preached that the Greeks were legitimate targets for crusading violence because of their betrayal of their rightful lord, Alexius IV, their refusal to submit to Roman authority, and their deviant religious practices.[41] For the first time, the state of religious divergence between the Latin and Greek Churches was expressly and undeniably held up by members of the Latin clergy as a reason for crusaders to take up arms against the Eastern Roman Empire, not simply as part of a "just war" to restore a Byzantine prince, but as part of a "holy war" to humble the schismatic and heretical Greeks. According to one later chronicler of the siege, the bishops of Soissons, Troyes, Halberstadt, and Bethlehem had declared to the crusaders that an attack against Constantinople was "acceptable to God, just as if the holy city of Jerusalem had been captured."[42] After the sack of the city, the newly elected Latin emperor of Constantinople, Baldwin of Flanders, sent a widely disseminated letter to the pope and other notables in the Western Church explaining what had happened as a result of the "perfidy" of the Greeks, who had scorned the Apostolic See and included the rebaptism of Latin Christians among their "vile rites." Never before had the refusal of the Greeks to obey Rome, along with issues of doctrinal or ritual contention between the two churches, been so plainly invoked to justify sanctified violence against Eastern Christians.[43] Baldwin knew his audience and emphasized reasons for the attack that he hoped would appeal not just to Pope Innocent, but to other Western Christians who received his letter. Perhaps not surprisingly, his epistle suggested that the capture of Constantinople would not have been possible without the approval of divine providence.

Pope Innocent stood first and foremost among those who greeted the capture of the Greek empire as a miraculous event. On 13 November 1204, the pope issued a remarkable letter addressed to the Latin clergy in the recently conquered city. Invoking the Book of Daniel, he declared that the Lord had "transferred the empire of Constantinople from the proud to the humble, from the disobedient to the obedient, from schismatics to catholics, namely from the Greeks to the Latins."[44] To explain this event, Innocent borrowed (without attribution) from Joachim of Fiore's *Exposi-*

tion on the Apocalypse, specifically, the abbot's commentary on the discovery of Christ's empty tomb by Mary Magdalene. Mary rushes to tell the disciples, Peter and John. According to Innocent—following Joachim— Mary Magdalene represented the Synagogue of the Jews, while Peter represented the Latin people and John the Greek people. The Greeks had been the first Gentiles to receive God's word after the Jews, but (like John, who arrived first at the tomb and did not enter) they had failed to penetrate its deeper mysteries. Like Peter, who reached the tomb after John but entered first, the Latins had received God's word after the Greeks, yet it was the Latin people who were the first to enter fully into the interior mysteries of the Christian faith.[45]

Innocent declared that the Greeks were now poised to learn proper doctrine from the Latins. In the near future, according to the pope, a remnant of the Greeks would be converted to the Roman faith. "Soon they will know, so we believe and hope, they will know, certainly they will know and there will be converted a remnant from among them in their entire heart," Innocent again quoted Joachim, "and they will come to Zion seeking the Lord and David, their king, and they will worship on the altar that was erected in Rome as an everlasting pledge, and from then on the hand of the Lord will be upon them."[46] Like John, entering at last into Christ's tomb, the Greeks "will believe what the Latin Church believes, so that, from now on, they might walk together in harmony in the house of the Lord."[47] Following Joachim's lead, Innocent turned next to Mary Magdalene, who represented the Synagogue of the Jews. Looking within the tomb, Mary saw two angels dressed in white, symbolizing the Old and New Testaments. Christ then appeared to Mary and revealed himself as arisen from the dead. According to the pope, this demonstrated that God would ultimately call the Jews back to himself, saving the remnant of Israel after the restoration of unity between the two churches.[48]

It is worth pausing here to consider the fact that Innocent turned to Joachim of Fiore's apocalyptic eschatology in the wake of the Fourth Crusade. In later years Joachim and his writings would generate a great deal of excitement and controversy among members of the Western Church; eventually, he would fall out of favor among conservative members of the clergy. In 1204, however, there was nothing to prevent Innocent from enlisting Joachim's compelling exegesis to make sense out of recent events. As we have already seen, crusading kings and popes were not unfamiliar with Joachim and his apocalyptic predictions. On several occasions, the abbot had submitted his writings to the Apostolic See for papal approval. Innocent's positive evaluation of the Calabrian abbot followed in the footsteps of other notables and intellectuals, including his immediate predecessors on the see of Saint Peter. The pope, moreover, shared a connection to the Italian apocalyptic thinker through his own confessor, Rainer of Ponza, who had been one of Joachim's close companions.[49] Moreover, Innocent had chosen the abbot's former scribe and biographer, Luke of Sambucina, to act as one of his crusade-organizers, and had even called upon Joachim himself to preach in support of the newly forming crusade in 1198.

In April 1204, two years after Joachim had died, Innocent confronted a much different situation than previous popes when he embraced the abbot's scriptural exegesis and eschatology. Constantinople, the heart of the wayward Greek Church, had fallen into Latin hands. The reunion of the Latin and Greek Churches formed a prominent strand of Joachim's thought, linked to the conversion of the Jews and the worldwide realization of God's fold during the future Sabbath age. There are no signs in Innocent's own correspondence that he understood—or, if he did understand, that he was willing to accept—the full implications of Joachim's complicated schemes, including the notion of a transformative third *status* and the birth of a new monastic order that would largely supplant the clerical order of the second *status*. Either the pope only knew portions of Joachim's works, or he invoked them selectively. Either way, in Innocent's apocalyptic turn of mind after the capture of Constantinople, we see a fascinating convergence between Latin theology of history and the Fourth Crusade, one of the most dramatic—for many, the most infamous—examples of medieval European expansion.

The significance of this moment was not lost on Innocent, who revisited his theological-historical reading of Constantinople's sack in a subsequent letter issued on 21 January 1205. In this epistle he returned yet again to the Gospel of Luke and the "catch of fishes," when Peter casts his nets at Christ's command and is joined by another boat that comes to assist him when his nets are full.[50] According to Innocent, Peter's boat represented the church of Rome, which had "filled its nets" with a multitude of pagan converts in places like Livonia and also with errant Eastern Christians who were being led back to the Roman faith.[51] The "other boat" that came to aid the apostle signified the Greek Church, which had alienated itself in the past from the authority of the Roman Church. Now, however, thanks to the divinely ordained capture of Constantinople, the Greeks were on their way to help Rome in the task of spreading the faith.[52] After the transferal of empire from Constantinople to Latin hands, Greeks and Latins, working together in an "undivided fellowship," would bring about the conversion of numerous Jews and pagans to the Christian faith. In the future, the sees of Alexandria and Antioch would be recovered from the infidels. The pieces of the apocalyptic puzzle, the pope seemed confident, were falling into place.[53]

After his initial surprise at the capture of Constantinople, it must have seemed quite appropriate to Innocent that the army of the Fourth Crusade—despite its spotty track record of obedience to the Apostolic See— had provided such an opportunity for the unification of the Latins and the Greeks. In his theology of crusading, the pope consistently packaged the moral reform of the Roman Church, hope for Christian unity with the Greek Church, and the recapture of the Holy Land as separate but connected components of Christendom's renewal. In this regard, Innocent pursued a trajectory that had its origins all the way back in the time of Pope Urban II, if not earlier under Pope Gregory VII. Although it was unexpected, Innocent saw that a crusading army had enabled the union of the two churches under papal authority and secured Constantinople as a strategic base for the capture of the Holy Land.[54] While he was torn by a continued desire for the crusade to pursue its ultimate goal, Jerusalem, the pope quickly devoted his attention toward the health of the Latin Church and the new polity planted in Byzantium. In the aftermath of Constantinople's fall, he took concrete steps to defend papal interests in that city (he was particularly anxious about limiting the influence of the Venetians, who had installed one of their own citizens, Thomas Morosini, as the new Latin patriarch of the city). In April 1205, for example, Innocent dispatched a new legate, Benedict of Suzanne, with an explicit mandate to represent the Apostolic See in the new Latin Empire.[55]

Throughout his correspondence, even while dealing with pragmatic concerns, Innocent never abandoned his belief that the sack of the city manifested the divine plan for history, encompassing not just the fate of empire, but of Christendom as a whole. As he declared to the new Latin emperor in May 1205, Innocent remained convinced that God himself had ordained the "translation of empire" in order to effect a "translation of the priesthood" from the Greeks, who had rejected Roman authority and angered God, to the more deserving Latins.[56] He explored these same ideas in his letters to Christians back in Western Europe. Shortly after the capture of Constantinople, in a letter to Archbishop Guido of Reims and a number of other prelates, the pope offered yet another typological reading of the crusade's outcome that is reminiscent of Joachim's exegesis. In the opening to this letter, Innocent described how the two wives of Elcana, Anna and Phenenna (1 Sam. 1:1), foreshadowed the Latins and Greeks. "The Mediator of God and man, Jesus Christ," Innocent wrote, "calling to himself the Gentiles, namely the Greek people and the Latin, joined both to himself through the sacraments of the faith."[57] The Greeks, however, had broken away from that unity (in this case, Innocent pointed specifically to their denial of the Holy Spirit's double procession as an example of their error), thereby leading God to transfer the "empire of the Greeks" from the "disobedient to the devout."[58] The work of truly uniting the churches, however, had just begun. Innocent called upon Guido and others to support the Latin inhabitants of the newly captured empire. In a similar letter addressed to the clergy and monks of France on behalf of the Emperor Baldwin, the pope exhorted the prelates of France to send Cluniacs, Cistericans, and regular canons to Constantinople, where they might sustain the catholic faith implanted there by bringing with them missals, breviaries, and other sacred books. Through the harmony achieved by those books, Innocent proclaimed, the "Eastern Church shall not be discordant from the Western Church, but, just as there is one faith, so both East and West will praise and glorify him with one voice."[59]

Without being cynical about Innocent's motives, his vested interest in justifying the outcome of the Fourth Crusade is not hard to understand. The pope was not alone, however, in his insistence that God had used the crusaders to arrange the transferal of empire from the Greeks to the Latins for a divine purpose. After more than a century of speculation about the meaning of the crusades, contemporaries in the Roman Church were well supplied with the intellectual tools to interpret Constantinople's fall in 1204. Few members of the Western Church would have had any reason to reject outright the argument that crusading violence had been used to chasten heretical or schismatic Christians. Although the precise status of the Greeks remained open to debate, previous generations of Latin Christians, in canon law, in scholastic theology, in liturgical commentaries, and in hagiographies and histories, had repeatedly voiced their concern that all was not right with the Byzantine Church. Although the Fourth Crusade had not set out to punish the wayward Greeks, Western contemporaries quickly adjusted their notions of what the crusaders accomplished at Constantinople in light of the Greeks' doctrinal errors, liturgical deviance, and refusal to recognize Roman primacy. Safely distant from the brutal realities of Byzantium's fall, members of the Latin Church "back home" came to view the outcome of the crusade as yet another step toward the proper ordering of Christendom.

To be sure, the diversion to Constantinople had its open critics, such as Peter of Vaux-de-Cernay, who had abandoned the crusader army at Zadar and accompanied his lord, Simon of Montfort, to the Holy Land.[60] Another eyewitness chronicler, whose report of the crusade is known as the *Devastation of Constantinople,* offered the subtle criticism that the leaders of the crusading army had betrayed its rank-and-file members by diverting the crusade to Zara and Constantinople, while withholding the spoils from the poor and humble (the author, it is worth noting, apparently had little problem with violence against Greek Christians).[61] The majority of commentators, however, described the crusade either in guardedly neutral terms or with the explicit declaration that the transferal of empire from the Greeks to the Latins was divinely ordained. The capture of Constantinople made a strong impression on monastic authors of universal chronicles, many of whom openly celebrated the "deeds of the Latins" at the schismatic Greek city.[62] They justified the unexpected sack of Constantinople as yet another example of God's will to arrange earthly events, including the rise and fall of kingdoms. Some chroniclers evinced their belief that the capture of the city had indeed resulted in the restoration of the Greek Church to a state of communion with Rome. Although they offered little overt discussion of Greek religious errors, the chronicles persisted in their sense that the Greek Church had cut itself off from rightful papal authority. Informed by correspondence from the crusader

army, some monastic authors knew that Alexius had promised to reunite the Greeks with the Roman Church. By a divinely ordained turn of
events, that union was accomplished "in those days, when the schismatic
city of Constantinople was captured, and passed over to the power and
dominion of the Latins."[63] Robert of Auxerre, for example, highlighted
the facts that Alexius had promised the submission of the Greeks to Roman authority and that God had arranged the transferal of the "Eastern
Empire" from the Greeks to the Latins. From this perspective, the capture
of the Greek empire signaled an end to the division between Rome and
Constantinople.[64]

Members of the Cistercian order, heavily invested in the Fourth Crusade from its beginnings, paid particular attention to the outcome of the
crusade. After resolving a dispute with Pope Innocent over his expectations for the Cistercians' financial contribution to the new expedition, a
number of the order's prominent abbots had joined the crusaders after
Fulk of Neuilly delivered a rousing crusade sermon at the Cistercian General Chapter in September 1202. Later chroniclers, including Alberic of
Trois-Fontaines and Ralph of Coggeshall, avidly followed the adventures
of the crusaders from their order.[65] For Alberic, writing decades after
the events, the history of the crusade inspired by Fulk *was* the history of
what happened at Constantinople—his chronicle gave no sense that the
crusade had been diverted at all. Describing the situation after the capture
of the city, when the Greeks under Theodore Lascaris and other claimants to the Byzantine throne continued to plague the crusaders, Alberic
made the telling comment that "these were men whom the Lord left in
the land, so that he might make a trial through them of Israel, that is, the
Latin people."[66]

Hagiographical texts that commemorated the transferal of Constantinople's plundered relics to Western religious communities provide further insights into the meaning of the Fourth Crusade for Latin contemporaries. Although there is no evidence that the city's sacred wealth acted
as an inducement for the diversion of the crusade, afterwards the victorious crusaders did not hesitate to help themselves to Constantinople's
legendary religious treasures. The resulting accounts of "holy theft" demonstrated striking continuities with twelfth-century hagiographies that
celebrated the crusaders' acquisition of biblical and other Eastern relics

during and after the First Crusade, revealing how contemporaries could graft the historical memory of the Fourth Crusade onto an existing set of beliefs about relics, crusading, and the holy places of the East. Some Latins, such as the author of *The Deeds of the Bishops of Halberstadt,* celebrated their protagonist's participation in the crusade while glossing over the exact circumstances in which he obtained his relics.[67] Others, however, including Rostang of Cluny, Gunther of Pairis, and the Anonymous of Soissons, placed the conquest of Constantinople into a framework of crusading history directly linked to the fortunes of the Holy Land from the time of the Old Testament to the crusaders' capture of Jerusalem, followed by the city's loss to Saladin.[68] At Soissons, much like other houses, the arrival of the relics from Constantinople was made part of the liturgical calendar, a celebrated part of the church's historical memory.[69] At Cluny, Rostang wrote that the sinful mixing of Jerusalem's Christian inhabitants with peoples of "diverse languages and customs" had angered the Lord, much like the Israelites mixing with the Canaanites in the Christian Old Testament, leading God to take back the gift which he had given to his people. Because of this sad state of affairs, however, Innocent III had summoned a new crusading expedition that captured Constantinople and eventually resulted in the relics of Saint Clement coming to Cluny.[70]

From this perspective, by the hidden judgment of God, the followers of Rome once again strode on the stage of salvation history by capturing the schismatic capital of the Eastern empire and transferring its sacred wealth to a more deserving home among the Latins. Despite the moral quandary posed by the crusaders' victory over Eastern Christians rather than infidels, for many observers in the Roman Church, the Fourth Crusade's conquest of Constantinople assumed its place alongside the First Crusade's capture of Jerusalem as an event of providential magnitude. Yet another hagiographical account, this one written to celebrate the arrival of Paul the Martyr's relics at Venice in 1222, declared of the Fourth Crusade that "God wanted more to punish the pride of the Greeks" than to "vindicate the injury caused by the Saracens and barbarians."[71] Despite such sanguine appraisals of the expedition, no one could ignore the simple fact that the Fourth Crusade had failed to achieve the ultimate goal of crusading, the recovery of the holy places. During the decade after 1204, however, hope persisted that the Latin control of the Greek empire constituted the first step toward the liberation of the Promised Land. After that, anything might be possible.

The Fourth Lateran Council and the Origins of the Fifth Crusade

It goes without saying that Greek Christians did not share such Latin readings of salvation history and the plunder of their cherished relics.[72] All the theological sophistication in the world could not change the fact that the Latin capture and subsequent occupation of Constantinople was an act of violence between fellow Christians. During the years after the Fourth Crusade, Pope Innocent became increasingly aware of crusader misdeeds during the sack of the Greek capital and the severe problems that still faced the Roman Church in the newly established Latin empire. As he observed in July 1205 to Boniface of Montferrat, the looting of churches and ecclesiastical treasures made it likely that "the Greek Church, however much afflicted by persecutions, might scornfully refuse to return to ecclesiastical unity and the devotion of the Apostolic See, since it has seen in the Latins nothing but an example of perdition and hellish works, so that now it justly detests them more than dogs."[73] As the immediate sense of triumph from 1204 faded, the pope had to confront the darker side of crusading theology—a sense that the moral failings and sins of God's Chosen People could bring down divine wrath and undo what the Lord had mercifully bestowed upon them.

Despite growing misgivings, Innocent never abandoned the most powerful and persuasive point of justification for the outcome of the crusade. Through the capture of Constantinople, he had declared, God was giving his devout followers an opportunity to accomplish great things, including the recovery of the holy places. The question remained whether they would squander it. Not content to rely upon the workings of divine providence, Innocent clearly believed that action was required to seize the moment. For the remainder of his papacy, he alternately pushed for the Latinization of the Greek rite and increasingly made compromises in order to accommodate the messy reality of worsening tensions between Latins and Greeks in crusader Greece.[74] His letters during the years after the capture of Constantinople were filled with exhortations to his own legates, the Venetians, and the new Frankish rulers of the city, declaring that they all shared a duty to stabilize the Latin Empire and to implant the Latin rite. The pope did not shy away from proclaiming his view of the crusade's outcome to the Greeks themselves, even when he recognized the misdeeds of the warriors who had captured the Byzantine Empire. In April 1208, responding to accusations against the Latins made by Theodore Lascaris, Innocent declared that while the crusaders remained far from guiltless, "nevertheless, we believe that the Greeks, who tried to tear asunder the seamless garment of Christ, were punished through them by the just judgment of God."[75] In spite of his reservations about the violence occasioned by the Fourth Crusade, the pope came to believe that the ends did ultimately justify the means.

Innocent's hopes for unity between the Western and Eastern Churches, in turn, remained linked to his persistent ambitions regarding the holy places of Jerusalem, along with his broader view of crusading as a means both to defend Christendom and to expand its borders. To call the pope's crusading ideology and activities wide-ranging is an understatement. During the years following the Fourth Crusade, Innocent turned his attention toward the problem of heresy in southern France, calling upon the French king to extirpate the Cathar communities in the region. In 1207 the pope encouraged the first in this series of campaigns, known as the Albigensian Crusade, formally extending the same privileges and spiritual benefits to those fighting the "perfidious" heretics as given to those "who labor for the succor of the Holy Land."[76] Looking toward the northern frontiers of Christendom, the pope intensified the fitful support of the papacy for the so-called Baltic Crusades that sought to conquer and Christianize the pagan peoples of Livonia and Estonia. Initially, Innocent called upon the faithful to defend the Christians living in the region from pagan attacks, placing those who fought in such a manner under the "special protection" of Saint Peter; eventually, he extended the same benefits to those fighting in the Baltics as he did to those struggling to restore Jerusalem.[77]

Facing the Islamic world, Innocent did not neglect the ongoing effort of Spanish kings to overcome the infidels and continue the "recovery" of Christian lands in Iberia. During the months leading up to the battle of Las Navas de Tolosa (1212), he called upon Christians everywhere to support Alfonso VIII of Castile (r. 1158–1214) in his confrontation with the infidels. The pope himself staged a liturgical procession of men and women in Rome for "the peace of the universal Church and Christian people, especially so that God might look propitiously upon those committed to fighting the war between themselves and the Saracens."[78] When he received a report from Alfonso about the overwhelming Christian victory on 16 July 1212, Innocent responded with a letter of praise for the Christian king, couched in biblical language that celebrated the power of God to humble the proud and elevate his favored people.[79]

Whatever successes the crusading forces might have had in Greece, Spain, the Baltics, and southern France, the recovery of the Holy Land remained paramount in Innocent's crusading ideology and theology. Toward the closing years of his papacy, the pope invested his energy in formulating yet another major expedition for that purpose. In his bull *Quia maior,* summoning what became known as the Fifth Crusade in April 1213, the pontiff once again expressed a view of crusading activity that was freighted with apocalyptic significance. The provinces of the East, he declared, had been a dwelling place for Christians up to the time of Pope Gregory I, but had then fallen under the domination of the Saracens with the coming of the "pseudo-prophet" Muhammad. In the Book of Revelation, the pope pointed out, the number of the beast was 666—and nearly six hundred and sixty-six years had passed since the infidels first seized control of Christ's birthright, a sign that the dominion of the Saracens was about to come to an end.[80]

Innocent's willingness to be so specific about the chronology of the end-times was striking and somewhat unusual for an ecclesiastical figure of his stature. He was no doubt well aware, however, that this sort of "apocalyptic pitch" for the crusade was bound to appeal to contemporary sensibilities. Chroniclers with an interest in crusading activities during Innocent's papacy, such as the English cleric Ralph of Coggeshall, shared a fascination with schemes that linked the power of the Saracens to the coming of Antichrist. Ralph showed a general interest in prophecies about the infidels and their ever-increasing occupation of "Christian lands," including predictions attributed to Joachim of Fiore that "the Gospel of Christ will be preached everywhere and the Church of the faithful will be extended among all peoples" before Antichrist's persecutions.[81] In the present age, however, Islam was on the rise. Echoing Guibert of Nogent,

Ralph linked the growth of Islam to the earlier spread of Arianism throughout the Roman Empire. Arius, in turn, was followed by Muhammad, the "king of Mecca," whose foul teachings and sect were now extending bit by bit into every land. The Saracens, "precursors of Antichrist," thereby set the stage for Antichrist's arrival.[82] Another chronicler who described the call for a crusade in 1213 wrote that Innocent was "persuaded by the king of Greece and instructed by the authority of divine books, especially the Book of the Apocalypse," to summon a new expedition for the rescue of the Eastern Church, which "still remained under the power of the Saracens."[83]

Not long after he issued *Quia maior*, Innocent added further exhortations and instructions for his new crusade in the bull *Vineam Domini*. In this address, he spelled out the two great desires of his heart: the "recovery of the Holy Land" and the "reform of the universal Church." Innocent explicitly linked crusading to a broader program of ecclesiastical "reformation" by announcing his intention to celebrate a new general council that would, among other things, devote itself to "reforming morals, wiping out heresy, and strengthening the faith," while "inducing Christian princes and peoples to the succor and aid of the Holy Land."[84] In that same month, Innocent even warned Sultan al-ʿĀdil of Damascus and Cairo about the forthcoming expedition, calling upon him to surrender the holy places and thereby avoid bloodshed. As the prophet Daniel testified, the pope explained, it was God's will to "change the times and transfer kingdoms."[85] Christians had lost Jerusalem because of their own sins, provoking God's wrath, but now they had turned once again to the Lord. Their time of victory was clearly at hand.

Innocent's aspirations to reform the Roman Church, to direct the redemptive process of the crusades, and to act as a shepherd for all the Christian peoples of the world reached their crescendo at the Fourth Lateran Council in 1215. The council's sweeping legislation demonstrated the papal monarchy in action, determined to bring proper order to Christendom, among both catholic believers and groups that fell outside the proper bounds of the faithful. The implications of Fourth Lateran are far too numerous to discuss here in detail, but the sixty-eighth canon—decreeing that Jews and Saracens must wear distinguishing marks on their clothing to tell them apart from Christians—provides one example of the council's ambitions to monitor Christian society and its limits. The council's legislation took equally strong measures for the extirpation of heresy. In addition to dealing with Jews, Saracens, and heretics, the assembly also addressed religious disagreements between Latins and Greeks. Declaring that the Greeks had returned to the catholic fold, the fourth canon targeted two of their lingering practices for elimination: the rebaptizing of Latins and the washing of altars that had been used by Latin priests. "Desirous of removing such scandal from the Church of God," the canon declared, "and advised by this holy council, we strictly command that they do not presume to do such things in the future, but conform themselves as obedient children to the Holy Roman Church, their mother, so that there might be 'one fold and one shepherd.'"[86] Unity did not necessitate absolute uniformity. Taking a moderate stance, the canon acknowledged the legitimacy of Greek forms of worship in general. The acknowledgment of papal authority, however, remained as critical as ever for the realization of God's Christian community under the auspices of the Roman Church.

In a sermon delivered at the council, speaking about the "reform of the universal Church" and the "most important liberation of the Holy Land," Innocent reminded his listeners about the efforts of King Josiah to reform the Jewish temple in the eighteenth year of his reign (2 Kgs. 23:1–14). It was now the eighteenth year of Innocent's papacy, and he likewise hoped to reform the Church.[87] In anticipation of the new crusade taking shape, the final mass celebrated at the Fourth Lateran Council included a procession with a relic of the True Cross, specifically, a fragment of the Cross that had come to Rome from Constantinople after the sack of the city. Perhaps, as Jane Sayer suggests, this relic brought to the Latin West after the Fourth Crusade was meant to remind the participants about the relic of the True Cross lost to Saladin in 1187.[88] Such symmetry, implying that the capture of Constantinople and its relics in 1204 would eventually lead to the recovery of the holy places and its relics from the Muslims, certainly would have appealed to Pope Innocent and others in his orbit. Whatever disappointments they encountered, the pope and his supporters never seemed to waver in their belief that history was leading toward the reform of the Western Church, unity with the Christians of the East, and the triumph of Christendom over its enemies—in short, toward the realization of a world order imagined since the first decades of the reform papacy.

Innocent died before witnessing what became of his new crusade, which might have been a mercy for him, given the fact that the Fifth Crusade ultimately floundered in Egypt. During the years immediately after his death, when the expedition was still taking shape, the pope's memory remained indelibly linked with his past crusading activities and aspirations. Much like the Cistercian monk Matthew of Rievaulx, one of Innocent's own preachers for the Fifth Crusade, Oliver of Paderborn, would later celebrate Pope Innocent's defense of Christendom on all sides by spreading the faith among the pagan peoples of the Baltics, capturing the schismatic city of Constantinople, and combating heretics in southern France.[89] Starting in 1217, Oliver had found himself personally involved in this broader struggle against the enemies of Christendom when he took part in the new crusade that had attacked Egypt as a first step toward liberating Jerusalem.

At the close of Innocent's papacy, churchmen such as Matthew and Oliver had little idea that they stood on the cusp of a new era in medieval Europe's awareness of the outside world, a far larger place than Latin Christians had ever imagined, inhabited by previously unknown or barely glimpsed Christian peoples, infidels, and pagans. Likewise, the participants at the Fourth Lateran Council had no inkling that Latin missionaries would soon be traveling as far afield as China, or that two of the new religious orders formally acknowledged by Pope Innocent III, the Franciscans and Dominicans, would bring about a drastic transformation in the missionary ideology and practice of the Roman Church. Among certain Franciscan circles, in particular, the goal of realizing universal Christian unity, converting unbelievers, and recapturing the holy places would find fertile ground, expressing itself in an outburst of eschatological speculation about the unification of the Latins and Greeks, the conversion of the Jews and other peoples, and the final defeat, if not conversion, of the Muslims as a prelude to the universal spread of Christendom before the end of time.

6

Crusaders, Missionaries, and Prophets

While campaigning in Egypt during the Fifth Crusade, James of Vitry believed that he was witnessing the fulfillment of ancient prophecies. Writing in 1221 to Pope Innocent III's successor, Honorius III (r. 1216–1227), the newly elected bishop of Acre described several marvelous works that were circulating in the crusader camp during and after the siege of Damietta two years earlier. In his correspondence with the pope, he included lengthy excerpts from letters that described the recent conquests of "David, the king of the Indians, who is popularly called Prester John."[1] Rumors of King David's recent victories against infidel peoples clearly impressed James, who styled that legendary Christian ruler of the East the "hammer of pagans" and "the destroyer of perfidious Machomet's vile tradition and execrable law." Next, he described a prophetic work, this one attributed to a Muslim seer who had foreseen the rise of Islam and its ultimate destruction. This ancient vision "predicted" the victories of Saladin followed by the improvement of crusader fortunes with the capture of Damietta and other events that, as James put it, "we saw before our very eyes." Toward the close of his letter, he remarked upon yet another book brought to the crusaders' attention by some Syrian Christians, the *Revelations of Saint Peter the Apostle*. This apocalypse related the state of the Church from its origins until the time of Antichrist. Among other things, it predicted that two kings would come to aid the crusaders at Damietta: one from the West, the much-awaited crusading emperor, Frederick II (r. 1212–1250), and one from the East, the aforementioned Prester John. Acting together, these Christian kings would smash the power of the infidels, killing some and converting others. As a result, the "fullness of the Gentiles" would enter into the faith and "all of Israel would be saved," followed by the coming of Antichrist and Final Judgment.[2]

James of Vitry's fascination with prophecies that spoke of crusaders, faraway Christian peoples, and the triumph of Christendom over the infidels marked a deepening European engagement with the wider world during the thirteenth century. Western Christians had many reasons to pay closer attention to lands beyond their ken, including a persistent occupation with crusading, despite or perhaps because of the continued failure of the crusades to recover the Holy Land. In the wake of the Fourth Crusade, the establishment of the Latin Empire in Greece had opened a new theater of crusade-related expectations and obligations. As various Byzantine claimants to the throne grew in strength, hope that the Latin control of Constantinople would bring the crusaders one step closer to the capture of Jerusalem gave way to a pressing need to defend Constantinople itself. At the same time, the Roman papacy continued to pursue an institutional reconciliation between the Latin and Greek Churches, alternately threatening and negotiating with the Byzantine rulers and patriarchs-in-exile at Nicaea. Unity with the Greeks, in turn, formed one front in a broader effort to harmonize the sundered Eastern and Western halves of the Christian world. Increasingly, the papacy and its supporters sought to secure the acknowledgment of Roman authority by other Christians of the East, including some who had taken steps in that direction (such as the Maronites) and others who were coming to the notice of the Roman Church for the first time.[3]

During this same era, the unanticipated rise of the Mongols created an entirely unexpected opportunity for medieval Europeans to broaden their horizons. Starting in the 1230s, the "Tartars" (that is, the people from Hell) quickly emerged as public enemy number one for the kingdoms of the Christian West, including regions ravaged by their swords such as Poland and Hungary. In immediate response to the Mongols' depredations, contemporaries called for armed, unified Christian action against the invaders—a crusade to defend Christendom against this new menace. Just as quickly, however, members of the Roman Church began to project some of their most ambitious dreams of world union onto the Mongols, whose anticipated conversion to Christianity would result in the recovery of Jerusalem and the final defeat of Islam. Although the results of the European encounter with the Mongols were for the most part ephemeral, the so-called *pax mongolica* opened a new chapter in the Western historical imagination.[4]

Such dreams of world conversion moved alongside concrete attempts at action to further that goal. The thirteenth century signaled an unprecedented era of development in both the theory and practice of mission, not just to pagan peoples like the Mongols, but also to Muslims and Eastern Christian communities that the Roman Church deemed schismatic or heretical. With the oversight of two energetic popes, Gregory IX (r. 1227–1241) and Innocent IV (r. 1243–1254), the European ambition to realize Christendom flourished as never before. One can track the aspirations of the papal monarchy to create a single "fold" from pagans, Jews, infidels, and Eastern Christians in papal bulls and correspondence, canon law and legal commentaries, and crusading and missionary projects. Two new religious orders of the era, the Dominicans and above all the Franciscans, eagerly advanced themselves as the primary agents for this innovative missionary impetus.[5] Indeed, one could argue that the papacies of Gregory IX and Innocent IV, followed by the temporary eclipse of imperial power after the death of Frederick II in 1250, brought the realities of the papal monarchy and the theories of its universal dominion into their closest proximity.[6]

In this heady if sometimes anxious period of Western Christian expansion, theology of history provided Latin contemporaries with an adaptable set of narratives, prophecies, and apocalyptic scenarios for making sense out of their widening world. Picking up where Innocent III had left off, his papal successors brought the language of historical providence to bear on their crusading and missionary endeavors, two means to achieve the divinely ordained spread of Christendom. The papacy, however, did not hold a monopoly on the interpretation of history. Inspired largely by Joachim of Fiore, a new generation of exegetes and apocalyptic thinkers generated a flood of new prophetic works, many of which were ascribed to the Calabrian abbot. In general, such "Joachites" were less than comfortable with the current state of affairs in the Roman Church and Christian society. Increasingly ardent in their criticisms, these figures did not abandon the notion of a worldwide union between Christian and non-Christian peoples; instead, they brought this vision to bear upon their wider critiques of contemporary mores and corrupt ecclesiastical institutions. After a series of apocalyptic tribulations, Joachite thinkers declared, a purified and "spiritualized" Christendom would welcome the Jews, Greeks, and infidels into its ranks, resulting in a new era of peace under the guidance of a spiritually transformed papacy. The death of Pope Innocent IV in the year 1254 set the stage for an increasingly bitter conflict between mainstream members of the Roman Church and these unconventional voices of prophecy.

Spreading the Faith by the Sword and the Word

Oliver of Paderborn, another participant in the Fifth Crusade, shared James of Vitry's fascination with history, prophecy, and mission. The two men had a great deal in common: both were educated at Paris in theology and were committed to preaching proper doctrine to "unlettered" Christians with a less-than-perfect understanding of their own faith. In this sense, they shared the yearning for apostolic renewal and ecclesiastical reform that was characteristic of their age. Their support for the internal reform of the Roman Church fueled their enthusiasm for crusading on various fronts. Pope Innocent III had engaged both James and Oliver as crusade-preachers for the Albigensian Crusade and the Fifth Crusade. During the course of the latter expedition, they met for the first time. As reformers and crusaders, they produced a prodigious body of writings. In addition to his letters, James of Vitry wrote his popular *History of the East,* a wide-ranging account of the Holy Land running from the Bible until the era of the crusader kingdoms, along with a complementary volume, the *History of the West,* a moralizing treatise on the sins and shortcomings of the Western Church.[7] Picking up where James left off, Oliver composed a descriptive account of the holy places, two histories of crusader Jerusalem, and a detailed account of the Fifth Crusade, the *Damietta History*.[8]

These works exposed the contours of a persistent fascination with the place of crusading in salvation history, as well as an innovative spirit of universal mission that transcended the traditional purview of crusading ideology. Fascinated with the Holy Land as the birthplace of Christianity, James and Oliver believed that the initial flowering of the faith there had fallen into ruin when the infidels conquered the region. In his *History of the East*, James included a lengthy and vituperative "anti-hagiography" of Muhammad to make his point that the Islamic faith was perverted and ruinous. When the infidels seized the holy places, the glory of the Eastern Church had been transferred to the Western Church. The Western Church, in turn, acted as a source of renewal and redemption for Jerusalem by liberating the city from its bondage during the First Crusade. Religious life subsequently flourished there with the rise of various orders. Pilgrims flooded the holy places from every part of the world, speaking every language. James, who had read widely from earlier crusade histories and used them as sources for his own work, offered a now-familiar message that the First Crusade represented a moment of liberation for the East, one that had been prophesied in the books of the Old Testament.[9]

The persistence of sin, however, posed a disastrous problem for both the Eastern and Western Churches. As a result of Christian sins, Eastern Christians had lost the holy places to the infidels; for the same reason, the Lord had allowed Saladin to recapture Jerusalem from the Western Christian crusaders. This notion, of course, was far from new, but the commitment of both James and Oliver to the goal of evangelical renewal imparted a heightened urgency and sophistication to their theodicy. Much like Innocent III, both men placed a fervor for the internal reform of the Roman Church at the center of their crusading theology. As James observed in the opening to the *History of the West*, God was punishing his wayward people on all fronts through the scourge of the "Moors" in Spain, Cathar heretics in Italy and Provence, "schismatics" in Greece, and "false brothers" living everywhere.[10] Echoing these sentiments in his *History of the Kings of the Holy Land*, Oliver celebrated Pope Innocent's defense of Christendom on all sides in the pagan Baltics, schismatic Greece, and heretical southern France.[11] In this multi-front battle against the enemies of God, the reform of the Roman Church represented the first step toward the ultimate triumph of Christendom.

The persistent domination of the holy places by infidels drew the particular attention of both men in their capacity as historians, preachers, crusaders, and missionaries. James of Vitry and Oliver of Paderborn demonstrated what we would now call an ethnographic interest in the peoples of the region, above all, the Eastern Christians, including Syrians, Jacobites, Armenians, Georgians, and others. The two clerics' wide-ranging observations noted those peoples' languages, alphabets, dress, marriage customs, and other habits. Their primary concern, however, remained the religious rites of such Easterners, ranging from the Jacobite practice of circumcision to the Armenian use of unleavened bread for the Eucharist. The rituals and teachings of the Roman Church provided James and Oliver with a yardstick to measure their fellow Christians, leading them to the not surprising conclusion that the practices and doctrine of these Eastern peoples had deteriorated badly as a result of their long servitude under the power of pagans and infidels. As he reported in a letter to Paris, James was shocked and disgruntled by the open diversity of religious traditions that he encountered at Acre when he arrived there as the city's new bishop late in 1216.[12] Although some of these groups, such as the Armenians and Maronites, had taken steps in the right direction by acknowledging the authority of the Roman papacy, the state of the Eastern Churches was described as heretical and deviant.

Yet there was hope for the future. Similar to James of Vitry, Oliver believed that he was living through the realization of ancient prophecies while participating in the Fifth Crusade. As a preacher for the expedition and its chronicler, he was heavily invested in its fate. Oliver recorded that a collection of texts written in Arabic by a pagan prophet turned up in the crusader camp shortly before the crusaders captured Damietta in November 1219. In addition, he described another prophetic tradition by an anonymous infidel author who promised that a Christian king from Nubia would capture the city of Mecca and scatter the bones of the "pseudo-prophet" Muhammad. This dramatic occurrence would start a chain of events that would bring about the "exaltation of Christendom and the shame of the Agarenes."[13] When the crusaders captured Damietta shortly afterwards, he continued, another foreign Christian king, the ruler of

Georgia, sent letters to the crusader camp expressing his amazement that the Franks from across the sea had taken the initiative in seizing the city from the infidels, putting him to shame. The Georgians' lands, Oliver added, extended to the Caspian mountains where the ten tribes of Israel were enclosed, awaiting the time of Antichrist when they would burst forth and cause a great slaughter.[14]

As both James and Oliver knew, this cluster of prophecies about an Eastern ruler who would come to assist the crusaders in their struggle against the Islamic world pointed toward a figure known as "Prester John," the priest-king of a wealthy and powerful Christian land in India or elsewhere in the East.[15] Although the details of its origin are hazy, this Western expectation—one is tempted to say obsession—for knowledge of Prester John stretched back roughly a century before the Fifth Crusade. Inspiration for this tradition might have begun with a purported visit from the "patriarch of the Indians" to Rome in 1122 during the papacy of Calixtus II. When the Indian prelate had traveled to Constantinople to confirm his election, legates from Rome who happened to be on hand informed him that the Roman Church—not the Byzantine—was the true "head of the world." Armed with this information, the patriarch proceeded to Rome, where he regaled the papal curia with tales of his kingdom that had been converted to Christianity by the apostle Thomas.[16]

Not long afterward, in 1145, Otto of Freising described "a certain John, priest and king, living with his people in the extreme East beyond Persia and Armenia, who was a Christian, although a Nestorian."[17] A few decades later, around the year 1165, a letter began to circulate that described Prester John's kingdom, ostensibly the Latin translation of an epistle from Prester John to the Byzantine emperor, Manuel Comnenus. In it, the potentate inquired about the Christian faith of the Greek ruler and informed him about the wonders of his own kingdom. Enough interest was generated in this elusive figure that Pope Alexander III drafted his own letter to "John, king of the Indians," around 1177. He opened this epistle with a declaration of papal primacy based on the Apostolic See's foundation by Peter and encouraged John's burning desire to learn about the catholic faith from its source, the Roman Church.[18] For someone who never existed, Prester John came to occupy a prominent place in the imagination of Christian Europe throughout the later Middle Ages and into the early modern period. Precisely how much James of Vitry, Oliver of Paderborn, and their companions knew about these various traditions is uncertain. From what both James and Oliver tell us, the crusaders greeted rumors that Prester John was coming to assist them in Egypt with considerable enthusiasm. Clearly, members of the army had heard of Prester John and were intrigued by the idea that the defeat of the Muslims and recovery of the Holy Land would open the door to a much wider Christian world. For those who did not know about such prophecies, James of Vitry helpfully arranged for the prophetic texts to be translated into the vernacular, so that they might be disseminated around the crusader camp.[19]

Belief in the imminent arrival of Prester John did not preclude concrete action on the part of Western Christians toward the expansion of Christendom. To the contrary, James and Oliver complemented their dreams of a world conversion with practical efforts at missionary work among both infidels and Eastern Christians. As soon as he reached Acre, before heading onward to Egypt, James had begun to preach through interpreters to local Jacobites, exhorting them to abandon their improper practices. On another occasion, he left Acre to preach furtively by night to communities of indigenous Christians living under Islamic political authority. The new bishop of the city specifically connected the liberation of the Holy Land to the potential for converts among the Saracens, who, he believed, would be all the more willing to embrace Christianity if they were brought under the power of Christian princes. This would be especially true, he declared, if the crusaders could conquer Egypt and establish a link with Prester John, bringing about a new world order. As James put it on one occasion,

> Further beyond toward the East all the way until the end of the earth, there are Christians everywhere. Whereupon, if we are able by the mercy of God to take possession of this land, we might join together the Christian religion in a continuous succession from the West to the East.[20]

Much like his interpretation of crusading, James couched his sense of mission in a providential sense of geography. In one of his letters, he specifically linked the conversion of the Egyptian infidels after the fall of Damietta with the "light of truth" returning "from the West to the East."

The bishop even tried his own hand at spreading Christianity among the Egyptians by baptizing some Muslim children.[21]

This connection between crusading and mission began to form an innovative strand of religious thought in the Roman Church. Through their preaching, missionaries would tackle the infidel challenge much as the Christian clergy sermonized among the "unlettered" laity, inculcating them with the proper beliefs and apostolic values.[22] In some cases, an emphasis on the power of preaching accompanied rumblings of criticism against crusading as a violent act that drove non-believers away from the Christian faith. More commonly, however, contemporaries viewed mission less as an alternative to crusading and more as a peaceful adjunct to it—preferable to the naked sword, but more effective when backed up by armed force. In a letter to the Egyptian sultan, al-Kāmil, Oliver of Paderborn made this connection clear, declaring that the Church of God would freely and joyfully invite people to the fellowship of the catholic faith, if only the infidels would publicly admit Christ's teaching and preachers. Since they did not, however, the "law of catholic princes" allowed them to "use the material arm for the defense of Christendom," thereby countering "force with force."[23] This projected role of crusading as a means to open up missionary territory had implications not just for the conversion of pagans and infidels, but equally for Christian communities living under the power of those non-believers. In the developing missionary language of the era, the border between acts of "conversion" and the "restoration" of schismatic Christians to the Roman Church was quickly eroding. As James of Vitry put it, "There are many heretics dwelling in the Eastern regions, as well as Saracens, who, so I believe, would easily convert to the Lord if they hear proper doctrine."[24] Crusading would provide access to both infidels and non-catholic Christians, who needed to hear the word of God as taught by Rome.

During the course of the Fifth Crusade, James and Oliver witnessed one of the most famous missionary encounters between medieval Christianity and Islam, the attempt by Francis of Assisi to convert the Egyptian sultan. The details of Francis's religious vocation and broader commitment to the evangelic renewal of his own Christian society form a remarkable subject in their own right.[25] From the beginning of his internal conversion to a life of poverty and preaching, Francis viewed missionary work among Muslims as one of his callings. Simply put, preaching the

Christian faith to the infidels with the possibility of martyrdom was an important part of how he envisioned his new ministry. As is well known, Francis attempted twice without success to preach among the Saracens before his journey to Acre and Egypt in 1219. That same year, he exhorted some of his followers to undertake a voyage to Morocco to "preach among the infidels" (five friars were subsequently martyred there in 1220). Shortly after Francis returned to Italy from Egypt following the Fifth Crusade, he codified these sentiments in the Franciscan Rule, which included specific guidelines for those friars who desired to "go among the Saracens and other infidels" just like "sheep going into the middle of wolves."[26]

Contemporaries quickly seized upon Francis as a model for the new missionary spirit. In both his letters and the *History of the West,* James described Francis's inspirational act of crossing enemy lines to preach the Christian faith openly at the court of al-Kāmil.[27] In the latter work, James praised the friars as a "fourth order" added to the traditional religious ways of life found among hermits, monks, and canons. He declared that even the Saracens and other non-Christians "living in the shadows" admired the Franciscans' "humility and perfection." According to James, the sultan himself was so impressed by Francis that he allowed him to preach openly against the law of the infidels. Although he did not in fact convert, the Muslim ruler guaranteed Francis's safety and reverently restored him to the crusader camp. This episode would prove to be of lasting fame, due in large part to Thomas Celano, who described it in his hagiography of the saint. In both the initial version of the *vita,* written around 1228, and the later revision drafted around 1244, Thomas emphasized Francis's desire for martyrdom as one motivating factor in his efforts to preach among the infidels. He also stressed that Francis was filled with a prophetic spirit at the time, as evident in his accurate prediction to the crusader army outside Damietta that they would be humbled by soundly losing an upcoming battle—one more example that prophecies were in the air during the crusade, or at least in the memory of the expedition.[28]

Francis did not achieve either his martyrdom or the conversion of the Egyptian sultan. In the short term, James, Oliver, and Francis must have been extremely disappointed with the outcome of their efforts in Egypt. As a military venture, the Fifth Crusade notoriously collapsed in the summer of 1221. Among numerous other problems, Frederick II had never arrived on the scene to aid the crusading army nor, needless to say, did Prester John. Contemporaries were not oblivious to the dissonance between their prophetic hopes and harder realities. Writing about the crusade roughly a decade later, the Cistercian chronicler Alberic of Trois-Fontaines informed his readers about a "certain prophecy," written in the script of the Saracens, which the papal legate on the Fifth Crusade Pelagius had translated into Latin and sent to the pope. This text (apparently the same one described by James of Vitry) accurately predicted many recent happenings in the Holy Land, Alberic related, including the crusaders' capture of Damietta. "Yet this prophecy," he noted, "although it spoke the truth in some things, nevertheless deceived in many others."[29] He went on to explain how the prophecy also promised the arrival of a king named David, along with another ruler from the West, who would destroy the lands of the Saracens before freeing Jerusalem. In this case, the actual course of events trumped prophecy. When King David heard about the Christian defeat, Alberic related, he returned with his armies back to his own kingdom in the East.[30]

These immediate results, however dismaying to contemporaries, revealed an important shift in the Roman Church's perspective on the outside world. Despite yet another crusading failure, the promise of Christendom as world order not only persisted, but began to express itself in new ways. Thirteenth-century Europeans would continue to call for crusades, but, perhaps because of the crusading movement's increasingly evident limits of effectiveness, they also began to envision a sustained missionary project to both infidels and schismatic Christian communities, bringing about the single "fold" promised by Christ before the end of time. Crusade, mission, and prophecy would be bundled together with increasing frequency. In this sense, Francis, James, and Oliver stood as harbingers of innovative directions in crusading, missionary activity, and historical speculation about the future spread of their Christian faith and society.

Mendicants and Missionary Eschatology

The long careers of two successive popes are emblematic of this remarkable widening in imaginative capacity of Christian Europe when facing the outside world: first, Ugolino dei Conti, elected Pope Gregory IX; and second, Sinibaldo dei Fieschi, who took the name Pope Innocent IV about a year and half after Gregory's death. The tenure of these two pontiffs on the Apostolic See, spanning close to thirty years, shared a number of common challenges and opportunities. Both popes struggled against Emperor Frederick II, whose revitalized imperial ambitions presented the papal monarchy with its greatest challenge since the twelfth century. Both popes demonstrated a relentless drive to protect the catholic community of the Roman Church from perceived sources of heresy and deviance. Gregory initiated the first formal procedures of inquisitorial activity directly overseen by the papacy. In particular, both he and Innocent extended their reach to determine what was orthodox beyond the bounds of the Christian faith, targeting the Talmud for confiscation and burning as a "Jewish heresy" that blasphemed against the Christian faith. Taken together, their papacies marked a new phase in the efforts of Rome to ensure conformity and order within Christendom.[31]

At the same time, Gregory and Innocent oversaw a similar expansion of the papal commitment to converting non-Christian and non-Western Christian communities that lay outside the borders of Christendom proper. The two popes drew considerable support from the Dominicans and the Franciscans in their capacity as combaters of heresy, crusade-preachers, envoys to foreign powers, and missionaries. Starting in the late 1220s and 1230s, the mendicants began to leave their fingerprints on every aspect of papal "foreign policy." For some of them and their supporters, these activities quickly assumed an eschatological air. Drawing upon a sense that Dominic, Francis, and their religious rules represented a source of renewal for the Church, contemporaries viewed their preaching to both Christians and non-Christians as part of an ongoing historical drama that was drawing to an end sooner or later (probably sooner).[32] In a letter sent around 1234 to James of Vitry, one Spanish admirer of the mendicants, Lucas of Tuy, made the special destiny of the two orders abundantly clear in his explanation of a prophecy attributed to an Austurian hermit named John.[33] As interpreted by Lucas, John's vision foretold apocalyptic tribulations symbolized by various beasts that ravaged a procession of apostles and holy saints led by Francis and Dominic. After defeating a first wave of attackers, the saints praised the Lord in Latin and

Greek; after defeating a second wave, the multitude offered thanks to God in Hebrew, Greek, and Latin. The inference from these passages seemed clear, Luke proclaimed, namely that the future would see a reunion with the Greeks and then the conversion of the Jews during a time of peace and order in the Church, when "the Roman pontiff will be exalted as the vicar of Christ over every nation."[34]

As implied by Lucas's letter, the "rump" Greek Church and Empire at Nicaea numbered prominently among the many groups that needed to be reconciled with the Roman Church. The mendicants took a hand in bringing this reconciliation about.[35] In 1232, a band of Franciscans returning from captivity among the Muslims met with the Greek patriarch, Germanus II, before returning to the papal curia with letters from Germanus that broached the subject of restoring communion between the two churches. Responding to this overture, Pope Gregory IX dispatched two Dominicans, Hugh and Peter of Sézanne, and two Franciscans, Haymo of Faversham and Rodulph of Reims, as his legates to the Greeks. The envoys bore two papal letters to the patriarch. In 1234, they debated about possible terms for ecclesiastical reunion with their Greek counterparts, first when they arrived at Nicaea, and then during a second convocation at Nympha in Bythinia.[36] In his first letter to the patriarch, Gregory stressed that the Greeks' rejection of the Apostolic See and its Petrine authority associated them with the "court" outside the Temple of God, given over to the Gentiles for trampling. This scourging of the Greeks, Gregory added, was "already visibly fulfilled." Later in that same letter, he prayed that God would illuminate the hearts of the Greeks, as he had restored sight to Tobit, thereby leading them back to the "one fold" under "one shepherd." In the second letter to Germanus, Gregory declared that the schism of the ten tribes under Jeroboam signaled the "schism of the Greeks," just as the pagan practices of Samaria represented the heresies of the Greek Church that had strayed from Rome. Toward the close of this epistle, the pope defended the Latin use of unleavened bread for the Eucharist by claiming that the Greeks sacrificed with leaven to symbolize Christ before his resurrection, and the Latins with azymes to symbolize the purity of the Lord after he was raised from the dead. To drive this point home, Gregory compared the Greek and Latin peoples to John and Peter when they reached Christ's tomb. John arrived before Peter, but Peter entered first, symbolizing the Latin entry into the superior "spiritual sense."[37]

The association of the Greeks with the "court" outside the temple, trampled and "not measured"; the use of Tobit as a figure that symbolized the future return of the Greeks to the catholic faith of Rome; the linking of the Greeks with the ten tribes of Israel; the reading of Peter and John at Christ's tomb as a type for the Latins and Greeks—all of these exegetical references bore a striking resemblance to passages found in Pope Innocent III's letters and, looking even further back, to the works of Joachim of Fiore.[38] From this perspective, the schism with the Greeks was an established fact, visible in present events and revealed through the mysteries of Scripture. The Greeks, of course, did not share this view. At Nympha, in fact, the final section of Gregory's letter which interpreted Peter and John as types for the Latins and Greeks caused trouble for his own legates. During one of their disputations, the Greeks asked if the pope intended to imply that there were two separate Eucharistic sacraments, one for the Latins and one for the Greeks. The papal envoys replied (one imagines nervously) that it was not their business to interpret the pope's words. If the Greeks wanted to know exactly what Gregory meant, they would have to ask him for themselves.[39]

From the perspective of Rome, the meeting at Nympha yielded disappointing results. More often than not, the disputes degenerated into mutual accusations and interminable disagreements about deeply ingrained divergences between the two churches, including azymes, *filioque,* and papal primacy. Over the following years, recognizing the growing threat that Byzantine forces posed to the Latin Empire of Constantinople, Gregory IX attempted to divert enthusiasm for a new crusade toward the defense of the Latin Empire.[40] Once again, he drew support for this effort from the mendicants, above all the Franciscans. The interest of the papacy and the mendicants, however, increasingly extended well beyond the recalcitrant Greek Empire and Church. The Greeks, after all, were just one Christian community among many who believed the wrong things, practiced the wrong rites, and failed to obey Rome. In the year 1237, for example, Philip, the Dominican prior of the Holy Land, announced that he had convinced the patriarch of the Jacobite Church to abjure his heretical beliefs and recognize Roman primacy. As Philip informed Pope Gregory:

> Blessed be God, the Father of our Lord, Jesus Christ, who in our times, holy father, by his clemency, restores to their shepherd his sheep that have strayed for so long. For in our days, he reveals to us the season of his goodness and begins to fill his fields with fruit, as he recalls to your obedience and to the unity of the holy mother Church those nations which have wandered from the unity of the Church for many an age.[41]

Declarations such as these captured the growing energy and aspirations of Western Christians to extend the "proper" form of Christianity to all such errant Christian communities under the guidance of the Roman papacy, God's "shepherd" for the remaining duration of history. Increasingly, the Franciscans and Dominicans placed themselves on the front lines of this drive for unity between Western and Eastern Christian peoples. For our purposes, the reality of Philip's claims is less important than the illusion they fostered—that God's fold of catholic believers was growing in leaps and bounds through the work of the Roman Church and its servants.

Back in Western Europe, monastic chroniclers such as Alberic of Trois-Fontaines and the English Benedictine monk Matthew Paris reported these happenings in distant lands with as much avidity as they showed for local events. Excerpting papal, Franciscan, and Dominican letters, both chroniclers created a portrait of a foreign world filled with familiar menaces, such as the "law of the Saracens," persistent problems, such as the Greek rejection of Roman authority, and marvelous new opportunities, such as the return of aberrant Eastern Christians to the catholic fold. Despite his criticisms of both the contemporary papacy and the mendicant orders as corrupt and avaricious, Matthew Paris enthusiastically reported the Dominican prior Philip's efforts to convert the Jacobites and other Eastern Christians. In his entries for the year 1234, Alberic recorded that "nine special orders of Christendom" would assemble at the Holy Sepulcher before the coming of Final Judgment: first, "our order of Christians, namely the Latins, that is, the Romans"; and second, the Greeks along with the Russians, followed by the Syrians, Armenians, Georgians, Jacobites, Nubians, the Christian followers of Prester John, and the Maronites. His list was an apocalyptic roll call of Christians, with the followers of Rome first and foremost on the list.[42]

When Latin Christians thought about mission, eschatological expectations were never far behind. In 1233, around the same time as the legation to Nympha, Gregory IX had issued the remarkable bull *Cum hora undecima*. This papal pronouncement confirmed special privileges—such as the right to hear confessions or absolve excommunicates—for Franciscan friars who were active as missionaries in the "lands of the pagans and infidels." The bull presented an explicit apocalyptic framing in its opening lines, which declared that the "eleventh hour" was at hand when "men with the purity of the spiritual life and the gift of intelligence" should go forth to "prophesy among all men and all peoples, speaking every tongue and in every kingdom."[43] It was only after this "fullness of the Gentiles" had entered into the Church that the remnant of Israel would be saved before the final days. In these terms, *Cum hora undecima* represented a landmark in the development of what E. Randolph Daniel has called an "apocalyptic" approach to mission based on the premise that history "would climax with the miraculous conversion of non-Christians."[44]

This belief, in turn, fit into a broader matrix of missionary theory taking shape during the thirteenth century. For some proponents of mission, the key to winning the hearts and minds of Jews, heretics, pagans, and infidels ultimately lay with their minds—that is, by convincing them through reason and logic that Christianity was the superior faith. This "intellectual" approach to mission required the learning of foreign languages (principally Hebrew, Greek, and Arabic) along with other preparatory actions before embarking on missionary endeavors or disputing with non-catholic Christians.[45] At their inception, apocalyptic expectation and rational argumentation formed distinct but not mutually exclusive strands of missionary theory. Beginning in the 1230s, both approaches to mission began to flourish together in papal and associated mendicant circles. Franciscans and Dominicans quickly put themselves at the forefront of this new impetus for spreading the Christian faith of the Roman Church around the world, whether it was through training in foreign languages or speculating about the approaching end of time.

Toward the closing years of Gregory's papacy, the advent of the Mongols radically transformed the playing field for both the theory and practice of a worldwide mission. In 1238, Matthew Paris reported that Muslim emissaries had informed French King Louis IX that a "monstrous and inhuman race of men" had exploded from the mountainous lands to the north. The Saracens, who sought aid against the furor of the "Tartars," also dispatched an envoy to the English court. According to Matthew, when Bishop Peter of Winchester heard the report of the devastation caused among the Saracens by the Tartars, he declared blackly:

> We should permit these dogs to devour each other, so that consumed they shall perish. At that point, we will descend upon those enemies of Christ who remain left over, slaughtering them and wiping them off the face of the earth. As a result, the entire world will be brought under the one catholic Church, and *there shall be one shepherd and one fold.*[46]

Although no one could have known it at the time, the raids of those "Devil's horsemen" formed the vanguard of a new Mongol dominion that would eventually stretch from the eastern edges of Europe to China during the thirteenth and fourteenth centuries. More bloody-minded than most, the bishop of Winchester was far from the only one who hoped that the arrival of the Mongols would somehow transform the existing political and religious landscape between Christendom, Islam, and the wider world.

In immediate reaction to the Mongols, Pope Gregory authorized a crusade against them in 1241. The mendicants supplied him with support for this venture, but this campaign against the Mongols never materialized. Gregory died later that year. In addition to inheriting Gregory's conflict with Frederick II, his successor, Innocent IV, eagerly projected himself into a panorama of interests that included continued crusading activity, persistent negotiations with the Greek Church, and dealing with the Mongols. With respect to the latter, Innocent's initial reaction was one that he shared with many of his contemporaries: trepidation. The Tartars, as Matthew Paris described them, "struck considerable fear and horror into all of Christendom."[47] Matthew also recorded a rumor that Jews living within Europe had been conspiring with the Tartars, planning to sell them weapons until their plot was foiled by an alert bridge-guard in Germany. Whatever wild stories may have circulated at this time, the military threat was indisputably real to Western Europe. As news of the Mongols' devastation in regions such as Poland and Hungary spread throughout neighboring lands, even enemies like the pope and emperor agreed that the Tartars must be stopped for the "common utility and need of all Christendom," even if they disagreed about whether papal or imperial power was ultimately responsible for defending the Christian peoples of the West.[48]

In 1243 Pope Innocent IV authorized a formal crusade against the "messengers of Satan and ministers of hell," echoing earlier calls for concerted action against the invaders.[49] Two years later, the pope presided over the First Council of Lyons. At the opening of the synod, the pope listed what he saw as the five great "wounds" plaguing Christendom. First, he noted the laxity and corruption of prelates within the Roman Church, a common enough complaint of the period. Second, he listed the "insolence of the Saracens." Innocent was particularly concerned by the violent conquest of Jerusalem not long before by the Khawarizmian Turks in 1244. Third, the pope called attention to the schismatic Greeks, who were threatening the Latin control of Constantinople. Thus the problem of internal reform, the challenge represented by Muslims in the Holy Land, and the division between the Latin and Greek Churches continued to form a mainstay of papal policy toward the internal and external ordering of Christendom. Fourth, Innocent spoke about a new threat, the Tartars, who had "invaded the land of the Christians" and occupied Hungary, killing their victims indiscriminately without regard to age or sex. Finally, he addressed Emperor Frederick's persecution of the Roman Church.[50]

Out of these five concerns, the battle with the emperor admittedly represented the most pressing problem for the pope, who (like Gregory IX before him) associated the German ruler with Antichrist. On 17 July 1245, the pope formally anathematized Frederick for heresy and failing to honor his oaths taken as a papal vassal. He also excoriated Frederick for his alliances with "infidel" princes (ironically, while on crusade in 1228, Frederick had negotiated with the Egyptian sultan to restore Jerusalem to Christian hands, nominally recovering the holy places).[51] Under Innocent's leadership, the council issued a number of canons about the additional threats facing Christendom, starting with the need for a crusading expedition to bring aid to the Latin Empire of Constantinople and the Holy Land. Following the lead of Pope Innocent III, Innocent IV viewed these crusading goals as mutually reinforcing. The council also addressed the menace of the Tartars, seen as an impediment to the extension of the Christian religion "far and wide throughout the world." The pope exhorted Christians everywhere to gird themselves for battle against the invaders, who had already destroyed the "Christian regions" of Russia, Poland, and Hungary.[52]

Within a short time, however, Innocent IV began to contemplate an alternative approach to the "Mongol problem." As described by James Muldoon, Innocent devoted considerable and innovative attention over the course of his papacy to the legal status of infidel societies.[53] Neither the *Decretum* (the standard collection of canon law in the twelfth century) nor the *Decretals* (the compendium of canon law assembled under Pope Gregory IX) had addressed this particular problem in any great detail. Instead, previous generations of ecclesiastical lawyers had reserved their legal scrutiny for the Jews and heretics, non-Christian and non-orthodox communities that existed within the bounds of Christendom.[54] Under Innocent IV, this lack of codification began to change. In his own legal commentary on the *Decretals,* the pope pointed to the Greek Church as a textbook example of schism. Turning his eye toward infidels, he charted what was, in many respects, a moderate position toward papal authority over non-Christian societies. While affirming the traditional justifications for declaring crusades, he did not deny the right of non-Christians to wield their own dominion under natural law (that is, simply being an infidel did not mean that infidels were legitimate targets for armed Christian conquest). As heir to Saint Peter, however, Innocent arrogated for his office the ultimate responsibility for the salvation of all peoples. Christ's commission to Peter to "feed" his sheep knew no bounds. Accordingly, Innocent reserved the right to judge infidel peoples and to declare armed action against them when they violated natural law or prevented peaceful Christian missionaries from entering their lands.[55]

Innocent stood as a ground-breaker in theoretical justifications of papal dominion over the non-Christian world. Like Gregory IX, he also supported Christian missionary work on many fronts to make that vision a reality. By 1244, the pope had already shown his support for Dominican preachers living among Eastern Christians such as Jacobites, Nestorians, and Armenians, granting them special dispensations to restore such Easterners to communion with the catholic community, if and when they recognized papal authority.[56] In March 1245 he confirmed similar privileges for the Franciscan order, reissuing *Cum hora undecima*. At the opening of the bull, Innocent added a far more specific list of target-communities for the friars' missionary activities among the "nations of the East." The bull explicitly set into an apocalyptic context missions that were directed both to pagans and infidels, the "peoples that do not recognize the Lord, Jesus Christ," and also to non-Western Christians, the "withdrawn sons, who do not obey the sacrosanct Roman Church."[57] With this repeated public statement in *Cum hora undecima*, the Roman papacy demonstrated two things: that there was little difference between the conversion of non-Christians and heretical Christians, and that a sense of apocalyptic expectation continued to frame its missionary ideology.

Confronting the new threat posed by the Tartars, Pope Innocent turned to the friars, dispatching the famous embassy to the Mongols under the Franciscan John of Plano Carpini in 1245.[58] The arduous journey of John and his companions to the Mongols does not concern us here, although it is important to note that his expedition first raised the possibility that the incursion of the Mongols might be turned aside by their conversion to the Christian faith. If Innocent's accompanying letter sent to the "king and people of the Tartars" revealed the audacity of papal hopes for the worldwide spread of Christendom, the response of the Mongol khan, Göjük, conversely illustrated the limits of the papacy to convince or constrain others by its vision. Drawing on his authority as the heir of Saint Peter, Innocent called upon the khan to renounce his errors and embrace the Christian religion. Unimpressed, Göjük replied with the alternate projection of a world ordered under the power of the Mongols. The khan, styled in the Latin translation of his letter as the "emperor of all men," declared that God was clearly on the side of his people, as evident in their recent conquests. He equally questioned the claims made by the "men of the West" that they alone were truly Christian and the bearers of God's grace. If the pope and his followers refused to submit to his authority, the khan informed them, "then we shall know for certain that you desire to wage war with us."[59]

Despite this inauspicious beginning, Innocent's papacy marked the beginning of a remarkable effort by the Roman Church to maintain diplomatic ties with the Mongols, partly in hopes of their conversion to Christianity. The Franciscan order was central to this outreach, although the Dominicans also provided papal missionaries to the Tartars as early as 1247.[60] To be sure, the papacy did not have a monopoly on such aspirations. More than a decade earlier, around 1235, King Bela IV of Hungary had dispatched several Dominican missionaries into the pagan regions of the Urals, making them among the first Western Christians ever to encounter and write about the newly arrived Mongols.[61] Even in this case, however, the figure of the pope possessed a special significance. During their travels, one of the Dominicans named Richard heard the tale of a pagan people who had been told by their own prophets that they ought to convert to Christianity. They dispatched envoys to a neighboring Christian ruler, who sent them a priest, but the priest refused to baptize them on his own authority: "It is not for me to do this, but for the Roman pope," he declared, "for the time is near when we all ought to receive the faith of the Roman Church and be subject to its obedience."[62]

Several years after John of Plano Carpini's embassy, while crusading in Egypt and the Levant, the French King Louis IX expressed his own interest in converting the "Tartars." In 1248, according to Louis's biographer Joinville, Mongol emissaries approached the king at Cyprus about the possibility of an alliance against the Muslims, perhaps even leading to the recovery of Jerusalem. Intrigued, Louis sent the Dominican Andrew of Longjumeau and a companion to the khan, equipping them with a tent "made in manner of a chapel," decorated with biblical scenes to help his envoys instruct the Mongols in the Christian faith. He also sent along liturgical vessels and books so the Dominicans could celebrate mass before them.[63] In 1253, the French ruler dispatched the Franciscan William of

Rubruck on another mission to the Mongols; William composed a gripping account of his travels and considerable time spent in their camps. Little came of these efforts, however. William, in particular, experienced mostly frustration when he attempted to proselytize (his intoxicated interpreter did not make matters any easier).[64]

Nevertheless, over the following decades, the dream of converting the Mongols, collaborating with the elusive Prester John, and forging a coalition that would smash the Islamic grip on the Holy Land came to form a persistent theme in the Western Christian view of the outside world. Given the rich tradition of Latin eschatological thought about the future spread of Christianity to all peoples of the earth, it was almost inevitable that some members of the Roman Church would interpret this worldwide projection of papal authority and Christian mission in apocalyptic terms.[65] There are no explicit signs that missionaries like John of Plano Carpini or William of Rubruck viewed their activities as bearing some sort of apocalyptic significance. At least, in the histories of their missions to the Tartars, they made no such claims (although William did relate the story of his encounter with an Armenian who prophesied that the Franks in the Holy Land, allied with the Armenians, would defeat the Saracens and convert the Mongols as a prelude to universal peace in the world).[66] Soon enough, however, their fellow friars and other interested parties back home would make that connection for them.

Apocalyptic Conversion and the Joachite Tradition

When John of Plano Carpini returned to Lyons in 1248, he was greeted with considerable fanfare. The Franciscan friar and chronicler Salimbene of Adam numbered among those who avidly listened to the tales of his travels. Writing his chronicle decades later, Salimbene recounted the excitement that had surrounded John's news of the menace posed by the Tartars. He transcribed Göjük's scathing reply to Innocent IV's letter of greeting to the khan, and described a round-table reading of John's history of the Mongols with the author on hand to field questions and offer additional comments. According to Salimbene, the threat that the Tartars posed to Italy was not happenstance, but rather represented the conclusion to a series of preordained invasions. First, he wrote, the Vandals had invaded Italy; second, the Huns during the time of Pope Leo I in the fifth century; third, the Goths under their Arian ruler, Theodoric; and fourth, the Lombards in the time of Pope Gregory I. The Tartars, he claimed, were the fifth and final invaders who were poised to occupy the peninsula. When Salimbene described the invasion of Italy by the Huns, he included the observation that this had happened under "Leo the First, who, according to Abbot Joachim, holds a place of concordance with King Josaphath of Judah. Look in Joachim's *Book of Figures* and in his *Book of Concordance,* and you will see how they correspond to each other."[67]

This was not a casual aside. Like many of his Franciscan peers, Salimbene was highly interested in Joachim of Fiore's interpretation of history, above all where it seemed to touch upon the role of the Franciscan order.[68] As we have already seen, the Calabrian abbot had begun to achieve a certain amount of prophetic fame well before the mid-thirteenth century. In his own lifetime, Joachim was consulted by popes and rulers. Rumors of his spiritual insights into Scripture and his ability to predict future tribulations caught the attention of chroniclers as far away as England, while scholastic masters in Paris were at least aware of his innovative exegesis by the close of the twelfth century.[69] During the papacy of Innocent III, Joachim's ideas had helped the pope to explain the unexpected crusader sack of Constantinople in 1204. Not all of this attention was positive, however. At the Fourth Lateran Council in 1215, the assembled clergy addressed a controversy over the differing Trinitarian theologies of Joachim and the Parisian scholastic master Peter Lombard. The details of this debate do not concern us, but the outcome does: the council's second canon condemned Joachim's suspect views on the Trinity, although the canon also emphasized that Joachim was otherwise orthodox, recognizing the Apostolic See as the "mother and instructor of all the faithful."[70]

The middle decades of the thirteenth century marked a new phase in the spread of Joachim's theology of history, due largely to his adherents among the Franciscans, who played an important role in spreading Joachim's works.[71] Salimbene provides a crucial source of information about the abbot's devotees, thinkers whom Salimbene himself labeled "Joachites." In his chronicle, he described the Joachite intellectual circles that had formed among members of the Franciscan order at places such as Pisa, Naples, Provins, and Hyères. These networks did not consist of obscure friars. John of Parma (minister general of the Franciscan order from 1247 to 1257), Hugh of Digne (a well- known preacher), Rudolph of Saxony (a master at Pisa), and Bartholomew Guiscolus (a prolific intellectual from Parma) were among those described as "the greatest Joachites" or "completely Joachite."[72] While earlier churchmen had shown a limited interest in the abbot's predictions about the successive persecutions of the faith, the coming of Antichrist, and the final apocalyptic battle at the end of history, these Joachite thinkers dug more deeply into Joachim's exegesis and theology of history. In particular, they were attuned to his model of the three *status* and his argument that a transformative age of the Holy Spirit would soon dawn on earth.

During this same period, "pseudo-Joachite" tracts began to surface in those same intellectual circles. Contemporaries assumed that these anonymous texts, most of them produced or redacted by Franciscan authors, represented genuine works by the Calabrian abbot. The so-called *Commentary on Jeremiah* was the most popular among them, followed by the *Commentary on Isaiah,* written in the early 1240s and early 1260s, respectively.[73] A host of additional prophecies cropped up around this time, including the *Commentary on Ezekiel, On the Three Stages of the Church, On the Burden of the Prophets, On the Burden of the Provinces,* and *On the Ten Plagues.*[74] Often these texts circulated with other prophetic works, including the so-called Erythrean Sybil, prophecies attributed to Merlin, and Joachim's supposed commentary on those two texts.[75] This Joachite tradition had a number of characteristic features. First, these prophecies showed considerable concern with the current depredations caused by Frederick II or (after the emperor died) by his Hohenstaufen heirs. This internal conflict seemed to be tearing the Western Church apart at its seams. In general, Joachite authors were far from friendly toward Frederick, declaring the emperor to be Antichrist and associating him with the final head of the apocalyptic seven-headed dragon. Second, the texts took an almost equally critical stance against current ecclesiastical institutions within the Roman Church, sometimes including the papacy itself. Intensifying a long-standing tradition of reformist apocalypticism, the Joachite authors excoriated the abuses and sins found in contemporary religious life. In the future, they predicted, the followers of the Roman Church would be scourged by persecutions from within as well as infidel invasions from without. Third, these works directed attention toward the coming of Joachim's "third age" of the Holy Spirit, typically targeting the year 1260 as the point of origin for that new era. Unlike the first generation of Joachim's admirers, who largely focused on his predictions of Antichrist, his readers in the mid-thirteenth century were well attuned to the dramatic implications of his Trinitarian model of history and notion of a forthcoming spiritual era.

Finally, and understandably given the Franciscan involvement in its creation, this collection of texts assigned a conspicuous role in the development of the third *status* to the mendicant orders, especially the Franciscans.[76] The notion that Dominic, Francis, and their rules marked a new stage in God's eschatological plan for the Church was not confined to the Joachite tradition. Thirteenth-century Joachites, however, more fully developed the idea that the coming of the mendicants had been predicted by the abbot and foreshadowed in both the Old and New Testaments. The two orders, they believed, represented the "spiritual men" of the abbot's schemes, and their emergence was one sign of the approaching era of the Holy Spirit. Before that time, however, the faithful would face the persecutions of Antichrist, the conclusion to a series of such attacks on the Church throughout its history. In that imminent struggle, the spiritual men of the two mendicant orders would form the shock troops for the succor of the faithful in their time of need. After the final tribulations, moreover, they would help to usher in a new era of peace and perfection before the end of time.[77]

This fixation on the spiritual transformations of the future led Joachite authors to make dramatic predictions about the future of the papacy, its schism with the Greeks, its struggle with the infidels, and the penultimate union of all the world's peoples as "one fold" gathered under "one shepherd," namely the guidance of the "new Judah," the church of Rome. The popular commentary on Jeremiah, for example, presented the division of Christendom as the result of God's plan for history, foretold and inevitable since the days of the biblical prophets. The commentary reinforced Joachim's idea that Scripture could be read in a detailed manner to reveal the mysteries of biblical and post-biblical history. By this logic, Jeremiah's prophecies about the fate of Judah and Israel in the Old Testament equally applied to the future of the Latin Church and the Greek Church. Similar to Joachim's authentic writings, this text excoriated the Greeks for their tendency toward heresy in both the past and the present, along with their rejection of Roman authority.[78] The *Commentary on Isaiah* likewise viewed that prophet's statements about the fate of Judah and Israel as equally applying to the Latin and Greek Churches. The commentary reinforced the basic idea that the Greeks were in a state of schism from Rome, infected by religious errors such as Arianism and punished by the successive invasions of the Persians and the Saracens.[79]

Joachim's vision of the third *status,* however, promised an end to the schism, the future conversion of non-Christian peoples, and the renewal of the faith in the Western Church. When the Book of Jeremiah proclaimed that the kingdom of Israel would return to the Lord and to the house of Judah (Jer. 3:12–14), this passage indicated that the Greeks, punished for their sin of heresy and rejection of Rome, would finally end their schism from the Latins: "So it is now and will be that the Greek Church shall return to the faith of the Church," the commentary proclaimed, "and there will be one pastor and vicar of Christ, of both the Eastern Church as well as the Western Church. He will sit in Zion, that is, in Rome, where the universal bishop chose his see."[80] The *Commentary on Isaiah* likewise promised that the two churches would be reunited under a common faith and leadership at some point in the future. The Latins and Greeks might currently be in a state of schism, but in the future, they would suffer together and be reborn together before the coming of the new apostles during the age of spiritual regeneration.[81]

Although Rome remained the "new Zion," the "new Judah," and the "new Jerusalem," the two orders prophesied by Joachim would take the lead in reforming the Western Church before preaching the "law of the lamb" in response to the ravages of the infidels and would spread the spiritual faith among the Greeks and other Eastern peoples. The Western Church sorely needed such renewal. Criticism of corruption in current ecclesiastical institutions was a prominent theme in the Joachite tradition, which built upon and intensified the themes of self-criticism found in the reformist apocalypticism of the previous century. Spiritually speaking, Rome might be the new Zion, but as an earthly institution it was stained by simony and fornication. The Greeks, noted the Jeremiah commentary, were not the only ones to err. So had the Latins—in particular, those who fell into the heresy of the Cathars, which polluted the Latin Church much as Arianism had polluted the Greek Church earlier in history. The abbot's devotees were well aware of the dangers awaiting them at the hands of tyrants, lax prelates, and servants of Antichrist, enemies from both inside and outside of Christendom; vigilance and fear, along with guarded optimism about the future Sabbath age, were the order of the day.[82]

In 1255 John of Parma and Humbert of Romans, master general of the Dominican order, issued a remarkable joint encyclical.[83] In its opening lines, they declared that God had raised their two orders "in those final days at the end of the world" to aid in the salvation of men. Echoing the Joachite tradition, the encyclical invoked a number of scriptural types that prefigured the coming of Dominicans and Franciscans, including the two great lights of the heaven, the sun and the moon, and the two cherubim on the Ark of the Covenant. Although they did not quote Joachim directly, John and Humbert clearly drew upon the spirit of his works, both genuine and spurious. Reminiscent of *Cum hora undecima,* this encyclical demonstrated the interest of the mendicants' highest circles in theology of history, including their sense of mission as part of the providential plan. Indeed, by the 1250s, a basic Joachite scenario for the future of Christendom had emerged. After the persecutions of Antichrist, a new age of peace would dawn. The "spiritual gospel" of the third *status* would be preached throughout the entire world, leading to the reunion of sundered Christian peoples followed by the conversion of Jews and pagans under the guidance of the Roman Church.

The commitment of the papacy and its mendicant supporters to the universal spread of Roman Christianity drew upon and fostered this missionary eschatology. Despite the struggles between the papacy and the empire, the initial fear of the Mongols, and the anticipation of apocalyptic sufferings under Antichrist, a sense of optimism pervaded the Western Christian view of the outside world during this period. More vividly than ever before, contemporaries could imagine a global Christian order under the authority of the Roman Church in realization of Christ's promise that the gospel would reach all the nations. During the middle of the thirteenth century, however, even as apocalyptic eschatology enjoyed this golden age, signs of trouble were brewing. Pope Innocent IV had died in 1254, not long before John and Humbert issued their joint encyclical. During the following decades, speculations about the world's end would be caught up in greater stresses and strains that were erupting in the Western Church, especially over the question of apostolic poverty. Joachite schemes possessed a latent radicalism, particularly when they assigned a role of spiritual preeminence to the mendicant orders and criticized the regular clergy. The future transformations of the Church during the age of the Holy Spirit sounded promising but equally disturbing. What would be the extent of that change? What would happen to the existing structures of religious life? Increasingly ardent in their criticisms of the contemporary Roman papacy, prophets and exegetes did not abandon the notion of a worldwide union between Christian and non-Christian peoples. Instead, they incorporated those ideas into their wider critiques of present-day institutions. In the future, after a series of trials and tribulations, Christendom would be transformed both within and without. The truly "spiritual men" of Joachite schemes would take the lead in renovating the Roman Church and extending the word of Christ to the peoples of the world under the auspices of a purified papacy. The subversive implications of this apocalyptic eschatology were not lost on popes and their supporters, particularly university theologians. Like the Talmud and other sources of perceived deviance, errant Christian beliefs about the end of the world would be subject to increasing scrutiny and even outright condemnation by threatened ecclesiastical authorities.

7

Contesting the End of Days

During his frequent travels, the Franciscan chronicler Salimbene of Adam crossed paths more than once with Gerard of Borgo San Donnino, a fervent believer in Joachim of Fiore's apocalyptic schemes. The first occasion was at Provins in 1248, not long after King Louis IX had embarked for Acre while on his crusading expedition to Egypt. According to Salimbene, Gerard and another Franciscan friar named Bartholomew, both of whom Salimbene described as "totally Joachite," possessed the *Commentary on Jeremiah* among other books. Their reading of these prophetic works led them to the conclusion that Louis's crusade would utterly fail. Subsequent events, Salimbene noted, including Louis's capture by the Muslims and the death of many French warriors, proved them correct. Another time, in a religious house at Modena about six years later, Salimbene and Gerard secretly discussed Joachim under the grapevines in a meadow behind the dormitory, where Salimbene plied Gerard for information about the coming of Antichrist. By the time he wrote his chronicle decades later, however, Salimbene was well aware that Gerard's devotion to Joachim had led the good-natured friar into horrible errors of judgment. Later in his life at a convent in Imole, Salimbene instructed another Franciscan named Arnulf to burn his copy of Gerard's *Introductory Book to the Eternal Gospel*, a guide to Joachim's three major works, the *Book of Concordance of the New and Old Testament*, the *Exposition on the Apocalypse*, and the *Psaltery of Ten Chords*.[1]

Gerard's beliefs about the future of Christendom and the coming of a transformative Sabbath age, commonly referred to as the "Scandal of the Eternal Gospel," marked a new stage in medieval Europe's apocalyptic hopes and anxieties. More directly than ever before, contemporaries inspired by Joachim of Fiore or Joachite literature brought their theories about the direction of history to bear on questions of wider social and political significance both inside and outside of the Western Church. The Franciscan order played a particularly important role in this intensification of apocalyptic eschatology. By the middle of the thirteenth century, the Franciscans' seemingly limitless growth in the life of the Roman Church, ranging from their role in erudite theological circles at the University of Paris to the carrying out of common pastoral tasks, had begun to elicit loud complaints from the secular clergy. Deliberately or unwittingly, Gerard of Borgo San Donnino walked into the cross fire of this bitter dispute between Franciscans and secular masters, who seized upon Gerard's "heretical" beliefs as a sign that the Franciscans were themselves servants of Antichrist.

In the light of this controversy, Joachim's notions of a future spiritual age performed a double duty, predicting horrible tribulations for the faithful followers of the Lord—a group that was apparently getting smaller and smaller—followed by their ultimate blessing in a new era of the Holy Spirit. Apocalyptic thinkers grew less and less reticent about directing their criticisms specifically against the Roman papacy, envisioning a future when Antichrist would sit on the see of Saint Peter. Conversely, they hoped for the coming of an "angelic" pope, a saintly figure who would help to succor the faithful and lead them into the Sabbath age.[2] The shortcomings of the present-day papacy implied by this yearning for a purified Roman Church were hard to miss. This is not to say that every apocalyptic commentator became directly involved in the debates over radical Joachite scenarios. "Respectable" apocalypticism, as David Burr calls it, persisted in the circles and workshops of intellectuals like the Dominican master Hugh of Saint Cher or the Franciscan theologian Alexander of

Hales. Increasingly, however, theorizing about the future transformation of Christendom represented a potentially subversive business.[3]

The Joachite expectation for the conversion of the world's peoples to the Christian faith of the Western Church formed an important strand of this dynamic and increasingly contentious apocalyptic imagination. As they had for roughly two hundred years, prophets sometimes had to scramble to keep pace with the changing political realities of the papal monarchy and its relationship to the outside world. During the mid-thirteenth century, a series of popes from Alexander IV (r. 1254–1261) to Pope Gregory X (r. 1271–1276) continued to push their crusading plans, missionary activities, and negotiations with "schismatic" Eastern Christians. These efforts culminated with the Second Council of Lyons in 1274. In the flurry of activity leading up to the council, the mendicant orders provided the papacy with its primary agents for proselytizing among non-Christians and restoring schismatic communities to the catholic fold. In the period before the council, churchmen from both the Franciscan and Dominican orders dedicated their attention to the three major problems facing Christendom: the need for internal reform within the Roman Church; the unfulfilled desire to restore communion between the Latin and Greek peoples; and the persistent failure to recover the Holy Land from the infidels. At Lyons, a Greek legation formally recognized the authority of the Roman Church and submitted to its doctrinal norms. For some Latin contemporaries, this union achieved with the Greeks seemed to furnish a clear sign that the conversion of schismatic and non-Christian peoples had begun, setting the stage for the recovery of the Holy Land and the creation of a single fold under the authority of the Roman Church.[4]

In the aftermath of Lyons, such optimistic views soon confronted the limitations of what had actually been achieved during the council's deliberations. The internal reform of ecclesiastical institutions fell far short of contemporary hopes; plans for a new crusade were scrapped; and the union secured with the Greeks proved to be illusory. Theories about the meaning of history responded to those changing historical circumstances, including what many critics saw as a growing failure of the Roman papacy to provide proper spiritual leadership for the faithful in the Western Church. During the closing decades of the thirteenth century, one sees the signs of a new pessimism in Latin theology of history. Even though they would continue to plan crusading expeditions and missionary activities, Western Christians would find the realization of Christian unity on a worldwide scale under the auspices of the Roman papacy harder to imagine without expecting radical changes, eschatological or otherwise. The gap between the imagined Christendom and the circumscribed reality of the Roman Church's position in the world was starting to widen rather than close.

The Scandal of the Eternal Gospel

What did Gerard of Borgo San Donnino write in his *Introductory Book to the Eternal Gospel* that so fascinated some of his contemporaries and outraged others? As is often the case with works condemned by ecclesiastical authorities, our principal source of information about Gerard's heretical teaching comes from the records of its condemnation. No complete copy of his work remains. Allowing for the fact that his enemies might have misrepresented his claims, official summaries and refutations of his ideas give us some sense of his eschatological beliefs. As we have seen, Salimbene declared that Gerard was a decent and well-meaning friar who had unfortunately fallen into a deep obsession with errant Joachite beliefs about the anticipated transformations of a coming spiritual age. Salimbene reported that Pope Alexander IV had rightly condemned Gerard's introductory volume, which contained "many falsities contrary to the teaching of Abbot Joachim, which the abbot had not written, namely that the Gospel of Christ and doctrine of the New Testament lead nobody to perfection and were to pass away in the year 1260."[5] Throughout his reporting of these events, Salimbene stressed two points: first, that Joachim's writings were not heretical in and of themselves; and second, that Franciscan authorities, not just the papacy, had investigated, judged, and punished Gerard. The order, he eagerly pointed out, had been more than capable of policing itself.[6]

Gerard's work first circulated in Paris in 1254. His timing and location could not have been more provocative. Around the middle of the thirteenth century, the Franciscans were locked in an increasingly bitter struggle with the secular clergy and masters at the University of Paris over everything from their right to teach as members of the faculty to their expanding performance of pastoral duties such as preaching and hearing confessions.[7] In 1248, the minister general John of Parma had spoken out vigorously in defense of the friars against the Paris masters, including one of the most vehement critics of the order, William of Saint Amour, but tensions between the secular clergy and the mendicants persisted.[8] With his *Introductory Book*, Gerard handed the order's detractors a powerful weapon to use against it. In the spring of 1254, when William of Saint Amour journeyed to the Roman curia to present another round of complaints about the mendicants, he brought with him a compilation of thirty-two extracts from Gerard's work. Pope Innocent IV arranged for a commission of cardinal bishops at Anagni to investigate this "Eternal Gospel." The cardinals completed their work under Innocent's successor, Alexander IV, and condemned Gerard's writings on 23 November 1255.[9]

Gerard identified the era of the Eternal Gospel with the coming of Joachim's third *status,* a new spiritual age of transformation on earth. Apparently abandoning Joachim's cautions about the persistence of Christ's dispensation until the end of time, Gerard declared that the New Testament would come to an end upon the full realization of this spiritual Gospel, which had begun with the composition of Joachim's major works. The Paris masters summarized these points in their list of Gerard's errors:

I. That the Eternal Gospel, which is the teaching of Joachim, excels the teaching of Christ and therefore both the New and Old Testament.

II. That the Gospel of Christ is not the Gospel of the kingdom, nor is it the foundation of the Church.

III. That the New Testament will be rendered null and void, just as the Old Testament was rendered null and void.

IV. That the New Testament will only endure in its strength for six more years to come, namely, until the year of the Lord's incarnation 1260.[10]

The list continued at some length. Much like the Synagogue of the Jews in the Old Testament, the "carnal" Church of the New Testament would be superseded with the coming of a more spiritual age. Adopting Joachim's notion that there were three primary orders in history, match-

Angel with the sign of the living God (Rev. 7:2). Apocalypse Commentary, thirteenth century.

Source: Bibliothèque Nationale de France, Paris, lat. 10474.

ing the Trinity, the Eternal Gospel additionally taught that the sterile clerical order would yield to the monastic order and its more spiritual form of living—specifically, in this case, the "bare-foot" order of mendicants, the Franciscan friars. Francis, symbolized by the angel that bore the "sign of the living God" (Rev. 7:2), had initiated this new form of religious life. The spiritual preachers at the beginning of the third age would form a "new priesthood," outstripping the deeds of the apostles and their own mission at the beginning of the second age.[11]

In addition to leveling general criticisms at the clerical order, the Eternal Gospel opened the door to a more direct eschatological attack than ever before on the authority of the Roman papacy. By its very nature reformist apocalypticism involved a critical attitude toward contemporary problems and sources of corruption in ecclesiastical institutions, including the bishops of Rome. Within the frame of Gerard's radical Joachite views, such criticisms intensified. The Eternal Gospel openly predicted the rise of a "pseudo-pope" around the time of Antichrist and linked the dominion of the current Roman Church with the "whore of Babylon" (Rev. 17:3–18). Following Joachim's lead, Gerard also anticipated the rise of a "new leader," a universal pontiff of the "New Jerusalem," most likely a Roman pope who would preside over a spiritualized Church of the future age.[12] Turning the typical view of the schism with the Greek Church on its head, Gerard claimed that the division of the Greeks from Rome manifested the workings of the Holy Spirit and provided a justification for the "spiritual men" of the third age to reject papal authority. In fact, he said, the Holy Spirit favored the Greek Church, which was more in a "state of grace" than the "carnal" Roman Church, just as God the Father had favored the Jews in the past. Although the Lord had punished the Jews "in this world," at the end of time he would bless some of them and free them from oppression, even though they would remain "in their Judaism."[13]

From the perspective of mainstream ecclesiastical authorities, the Eternal Gospel represented a heady and subversive interpretation of the imminent future (the date for the coming of this new age was fixed at the year 1260).[14] For the first time, a critic of the mainstream Roman Church had turned a sophisticated theology of history and a set of apocalyptic expectations directly against the sacraments, doctrines, and papal authority. In reaction, the Franciscan order imprisoned Gerard, who remained incarcerated for the rest of his life. Although Pope Alexander continued to support the mendicant orders, he did not hesitate to enforce the condemnation of the Eternal Gospel by the commission at Anagni, which he saw as a necessary move to protect the "good name" of the Franciscans. In October and November 1255 the pope directed letters to Paris, ordering that copies of Gerard's work should be burned and that anyone who harbored them should be excommunicated. The proponents of radical eschatological change had been put on notice.[15]

For the university masters at Paris, this condemnation of the Eternal Gospel must have seemed like a broader blow against the mendicants—or at least, it had dragged the friars' good name through the mud despite what Pope Alexander had said. Eager to drive home a devastating critique of the Eternal Gospel and its supporters, William of Saint-Amour had written his own tract, *On the Dangers of the End Times,* around 1255.[16] This apocalyptic treatise attacked the Franciscan order by associating it with the "false prophets" and "false preachers" which Christ himself had predicated would accompany the final days. By infringing upon the proper pastoral duties of bishops and the secular clergy, William claimed, the mendicants had revealed themselves to be servants of Antichrist, a clear indication that the end of history was near at hand. William offered a number of signs that this was indeed the case, including the fallacious claim by some people that a new Eternal Gospel was replacing the Gospel of Christ. His readers should not be fooled: the Eternal Gospel manifested the false law of Antichrist.[17] By contrast, William stressed that the end of time would be an era of mercifully brief tribulation (three and a half years), rather than one of spiritual blessings before Final Judgment. In short, he completely repudiated the Eternal Gospel's transformative vision.

Another tract on Antichrist, produced by William or with his oversight, offered a traditional view of the apocalypse from the *Ordinary Gloss,* Augustine, and other patristic sources as an antidote to the heretical promises of a future Sabbath age.[18] This text also highlighted signs that the end was fast approaching. First, the Roman Empire seemed to have expired with the death of Frederick II. Second, the Gospel had apparently been preached to all the peoples of the world (though the author qualified this by saying that the Gospel would be heard by all peoples, but not all of them would in fact convert, something evident in the fact that the infidels still possessed the holy places despite their exposure to the news of Christ). In addition, the false prophets and preachers promised by Christ had appeared on the scene—none other than the Franciscan friars.[19] The tract took aim specifically at Joachim's *Book of Concordance, Exposition on the Apocalypse,* and the *Psaltery of the Ten Chords,* decrying the abbot's "frivolous concordances" and "inane genealogies."[20] The coming of the Holy Spirit had been fulfilled in the New Testament during the days of the apostles—there would be no more "transferal" of the priesthood or new law. It had been more than sixty years since Joachim predicted the coming of a "new leader," a universal pontiff of the "New Jerusalem," and that figure had not materialized. Clearly, the abbot himself was a false prophet. This tract also reasserted the standard view of the Jews as servants of Antichrist. After the coming of the two witnesses, Elijah and Enoch, the Jews would convert following Antichrist's three-and-a-half-year persecution of the faithful, leaving little room afterwards for a worldwide conversion of peoples to the Lord.[21]

For William of Saint Amour, this victory over the mendicants was a pyrrhic one. In 1256, Pope Alexander IV subjected William's own tract to a similar process of investigation and condemnation. The pope sent another round of letters to Paris and to the French king, Louis IX, denouncing William for his attacks on the mendicants, his questioning of papal judgments in support of the friars, and his views of Antichrist. Moreover, William had supposedly complained that Joachim's works would never be properly condemned at the papal curia because the abbot had so many defenders there.[22] Eventually, William was forbidden to teach on the faculty at Paris and banned from the kingdom of France.[23] About a year later, his former opponent John of Parma was forced from his position as minister general in 1257 and replaced by Saint Bonaventure. The exact circumstances of John's deposition are not entirely clear. According to Salimbene of Adam, however, John's unseemly enthusiasm for Joachim's historical ideas was one of the main reasons for his fall.[24] Three years later the anticipated *annus horribilis et mirabilis*, 1260, came and went. Some admirers of Joachim, including Salimbene of Adam, later expressed their disappointment that this much-vaunted point in history passed without any sort of apocalyptic transformations.[25] Others, however, remained undaunted. In 1263, a council of churchmen at Arles felt it necessary to again condemn troublesome "Joachite works" on familiar grounds, including their claim that the sacraments of the New Testament would come to an end and that the Holy Spirit had yet to be fully revealed.[26]

The double condemnations of Gerard and William, along with John of Parma's removal from office and the condemnations at Arles, indeed represented a sign of things to come—not the arrival of Antichrist, but rather a changing ecclesiastical climate in which apocalypticism largely assumed "hot" and "cool" forms. In the hands of religious critics, the former would take on an increasingly radical tone and demonstrate sometimes wild leaps of creativity. In the hands of clerical authorities, the latter would be invoked to reject and contain such disturbing expectations of Christendom's eschatological transformation.

Searching for an Apocalyptic Middle Ground

Perhaps not surprisingly, during the years after the Scandal of the Eternal Gospel, relatively conservative voices succeeded in setting the tone of apocalyptic eschatology within both the Dominican and Franciscan orders. Two well-known figures, Thomas Aquinas and Bonaventure, are emblematic of this development in their own distinct ways. Both men, made masters at the University of Paris in 1257, must have been painfully familiar with the crisis over the Eternal Gospel and the damage it had done to the prestige of the mendicants. Rejecting the extreme positions taken both by Gerard of Borgo San Donnino and by his critics (principally William of Saint Amour), Aquinas strongly reasserted a traditional timetable for the end of days. Bonaventure, by contrast, cautiously continued to draw inspiration from Joachim, taking great pains to chart a distinctly Franciscan eschatology that incorporated popular Joachite ideas while firmly refuting their more radical implications. Still others, such as the English Franciscan Roger Bacon, largely avoided this problem altogether, projecting their own enthusiasm for the future union of the world under the authority of the Roman Church in equally creative but less controversial directions. This wide range of attitudes demonstrated how important the apocalyptic question remained during the aftermath of the Eternal Gospel.[27]

Aquinas developed his views of the end-times over a number of years, stretching from his early career in Paris in 1256 until his return there in 1269 after time spent in Italy.[28] His refutation of apocalyptic speculation rested on the traditional position that anyone claiming specific and privileged knowledge of future events acted contrary to biblical authorities. People had been wrong before in their projections of historical patterns, he pointed out, as evident in Orosius's belief that there were ten major persecutions of the Church before the Constantinian Peace, matching the ten plagues of Egypt. Clearly, as Saint Augustine had pointed out long ago, there had been many more such assaults before and after the time of Emperor Constantine. As for the notion that the apocalyptic number "1260" indicated the entire duration of the Church from Christ until the dawn of a new Sabbath age, Aquinas reasserted that this figure referred to the time of Antichrist's "forty-two-month" persecution and nothing else.[29]

Taking aim at the misleading conjectures made by Abbot Joachim, the Dominican master acknowledged that the Old Testament generally prefigured the New, but denied Joachim's "principle of concordance" that specific events in the Old Testament corresponded to specific events during the centuries after Christ, "especially since all the figures of the Old Testament were fulfilled in Christ."[30] For Aquinas, the Old Testament offered a predicative source of realized eschatology in the New Testament rather than serving as a basis for eschatological speculation about the future of the Church. In his effort to restore a safer sensibility to apocalypticism, he devoted particular attention to the Joachite claim that the Eternal Gospel—not the superseded Gospel of the second age—would be preached everywhere and to all peoples before the end of time. Aquinas argued against those who claimed that the law of the New Testament would not endure until the consummation of history, based on the belief that the Gospel had already been preached throughout the entire world, and yet time had still not ended. On this account, they reasoned, the "Gospel of the kingdom" referred to by Christ (Mt. 24:14) must be "another future Gospel of the Holy Spirit, just like another law." Invoking the *Ordinary Gloss* and other authorities, Aquinas denied this proposition. First of all, nothing was superior to the law of the New Testament. Moreover, the Holy Spirit had already been bestowed upon the apostles in the age of the Primitive Church. Not to mention the fact, Aquinas observed, that the full spread of the Gospel had not in fact been achieved throughout the entire world.[31]

Aquinas also scrutinized the counter-claim that the Eternal Gospel represented the false law of Antichrist and therefore offered a sign that the consummation of history was drawing near. Rather, he argued, this heretical doctrine represented merely one more heresy in a long line of heresies since the earliest days of the Church and was hardly a sign of Antichrist's imminent arrival. He also refuted the claim that the spread of the Eternal Gospel was fulfilling Christ's predictions that the Gospel would be preached everywhere before the end of time, thereby signaling the imminent conclusion of history. As Aquinas put it in his work *Against Those Attacking the Rite and Religion of God:* "When the Lord says 'the Gospel of the kingdom will be preached,' this does not refer to the preaching of those empty signs, but rather to the preaching of the Christian faith, which ought to be announced throughout the entire world before the coming of Christ."[32] By downplaying the Eternal Gospel, demoting it to the status of a pedestrian heresy rather than a sign of the apocalypse, Aquinas tried to rob the mendicants' critics of their chief weapon against the orders and their way of life, above all the accusation made by William of Saint Amour that the friars were "pseudo-preachers" or "pseudo-prophets" of Antichrist.

Beyond his interest in defending the mendicant orders, Aquinas attempted to defuse any and all types of apocalyptic expectation and eschatological speculation beyond the careful boundaries imposed by traditional authorities. According to his interpretation, there would be no transformative spiritual age and no new law of the Holy Spirit. The basic structures of salvation, including the sacraments and priesthood, had been unchanged since the coming of the New Dispensation with Christ and would remain so until the end of time. The details and precise dating of that end were unknowable, and there was no sign that the apocalypse was imminent. Among other indicators that this was the case, Aquinas reminded his readers about Augustine's cautionary words to Heyschius in the fifth century, namely, that the Gospel had not yet reached all the peoples of the world, and therefore, history would endure.[33] The Dominican master could not have done much more to throw cold water on the torrid hopes of Joachite thinkers for the final conversion of the world during a new Sabbath age, while also dousing the heated accusations made against the mendicants by their enemies.

Even among those who rejected the more radical implications of Joachite apocalypticism, not everyone was as ready as Aquinas to completely abandon the Calabrian abbot's inspired reading of history. This was particularly the case among members of the Franciscan order, who had eagerly borrowed from Joachim's predictions about the coming of the "spiritual men" to celebrate their place in salvation history. In the aftermath of the Eternal Gospel, the new Franciscan minister general,

Bonaventure, offered a distinctly Franciscan eschatology that did not completely reject Joachim, but avoided the pitfalls of taking his historical speculations too far.[34] Earlier in his theological writings, Bonaventure himself had associated Francis with the angel that bore the "living seal of God," hinting at the notion that the Franciscans marked a new and perhaps final stage in the renewal of the Church through their commitment to the apostolic life. At the same time, he denounced the stances championed by both Gerard of Borgo San Donnino and William of Saint Amour, taking pains to emphasize the centrality of Christ in salvation history while denying any future dispensation of the Holy Spirit.

In 1273 Bonaventure laid out his theology of history in a series of sermons at Paris, recorded by his listeners as the *Collationes in Hexameron*.[35] In this commentary on creation, Bonaventure incorporated traditional historical schemes, such as the division of time into seven ages and the three stages from natural law to Christian grace. He made his rejection of the Eternal Gospel clear—there would not be any "new law" following the New Testament. He did claim, however, that the future would bring about an era of spiritual renewal and regeneration. Shying away from Joachim's model of the three *status,* he drew instead from the abbot's "principle of concordance" between the time periods of the Old Testament and the New Testament. Following Joachim, Bonaventure divided the history of the Church after Christ into seven "little ages": the first was marked by the bestowal of grace that lasted from Christ to Pope Clement I; the second, by baptism in blood from Clement to Pope Sylvester; the third, by the establishment of catholic norms from Sylvester to Pope Leo I; the fourth, by the justice of law from Leo to Pope Gregory I; the fifth, by the sublimity of the Apostolic See from Gregory to Pope Hadrian I; and the sixth, by the clarity of doctrine from Hadrian until the present.[36] Among other implications, Bonaventure's use of Joachim led him to identify the Greek Church as heretical since the days of Pope Gregory I, when the bishop of Constantinople illicitly claimed the title of "universal patriarch." During the fourth age, he observed, there had been an "expansion of the Church in the West" through the conversion of Gaul, Britain, and Germany to the faith, a growth of the faith "in the Promised Land, not in Egypt—not among the Greeks—but among the Latins."[37] During the fifth age, the Greeks had paid the price for their deviance when the Saracens laid waste to their church and empire, just as the Assyrians had overrun the ten tribes of Israel.

Such interpretations borrowed directly from Joachim, without raising any of the dangers that accompanied his speculations about the coming of a Sabbath age. As for the future, Bonaventure declared, the seventh age would bring peace and renewal after the trials under Antichrist. "In the seventh time," Bonaventure observed, speaking about the Old Testament, "we know that these things happened: the rebuilding of the Temple, the restoration of the City, and the bestowal of peace. Likewise, in the future seventh time, there will be a restoration of divine worship and a rebuilding of the City." The Franciscan master, however, did not say much more about this future era of renewal, nor did he belabor its characteristics except to note that "how long that peace will endure, God knows."[38] In the twenty-second book of the *Collationes,* Bonaventure compared the "Church militant" to the celestial hierarchy of angels, claiming that the "Thrones" symbolized the monastic orders; the "Cherubim," the Dominicans and Franciscans; and the "Seraphim," Francis himself. In addition, he observed that the Seraphim might symbolize a new order of Francis's spiritual followers, stating that this order might already exist or would exist sometime in the future. Clearly, Bonaventure wished to preserve a place for the Franciscans in the realization of the Lord's plan for the reform and regeneration of the Roman Church, but he also wished to defuse any hint of heresy or danger from such "spiritualized" speculations.[39]

In this fashion, Bonaventure drew inspiration from Joachim's general eschatology of renewal while containing the subversive potential found in Joachite schemes. Still other Franciscans effectively steered clear of this controversy, finding alternative outlets for their historical theorizing. The works of Roger Bacon provide a case in point. Starting his ecclesiastical career as a master at Oxford and Paris during the 1230s and 1240s, Bacon joined the Franciscan order around the year 1257. Both before and after his entry into the order, Bacon participated in a broader network of Franciscan intellectuals in England, including Adam Marsh and Robert Grosseteste, both of whom had shown some interest in Joachite writings. Although Bacon knew about Joachim and had resided in Paris just a few years after the Scandal of the Eternal Gospel, his writings and apocalyptic speculations showed no discernible influence from Joachim's ideas.[40] To describe Bacon's own interests as wide-ranging is an understatement, roaming as they did through the study of grammar, philosophy, geography, mathematics, and optics, to name a few of his pursuits. Starting in the mid-1260s, he produced a series of works that brought his extensive knowledge to bear on what he believed to be the pressing problem of corruption in the present-day Roman Church. Learning in its many forms, the English Franciscan believed, would enable the proper governance of the Roman Church and unlock the door to the restructuring of Christendom. He addressed his early calls for such reform to Cardinal Guy Foulques, later elected Pope Clement IV (r. 1265–1268). In his capacity as pope, Clement encouraged Bacon to continue his labors, which culminated in three related works: the *Major Work, Minor Work,* and *Tertiary Work.* Shortly after Clement died, Bacon produced his *Compendium of Philosophical Study.*[41]

In addition to his program for the internal renewal of Christian society, Bacon showed keen interest in the problematic relationship between Christendom and the lands outside of its borders—problematic, since Bacon believed that the right-believing Christian followers of Rome formed a small and endangered minority among the various peoples of the world. He variously divided humankind into a number of principal "sects" or "laws" that included Saracens, Tartars, pagans, idolaters, schismatics, Jews, and catholic or Latin Christians. He identified these groups by their languages, religious rites and laws, beliefs about the afterlife, and other characteristics, including their planetary alignments.[42] Through his observations, Bacon revealed himself to be a sophisticated proponent of missionary activity to convert non-believers to the catholic Christian faith. Although not uniformly against the use of force in the defense or expansion of the faith, Bacon believed that peaceful means for converting infidels were preferable to the use of arms against them. "For thus they are not converted," he observed about such violence, "but instead they are killed and sent to hell."[43] Bacon's commitment to the programmatic reform of learning informed his missionary theory. For example, he declared that knowledge of geography was critical "for carrying out the business of Christians among the nations of the infidels, especially the business of the Church, above all for the conversion of infidels."[44] He also emphasized the need to learn foreign languages, including Hebrew, Arabic, and Greek, to debate with potential converts through rational argumentation. Even astrology became a critical tool in the missionary's toolkit. While in Paris, Bacon had read his fellow Franciscan William of Rubruck's account of his travels among the Mongols at the behest of the French king. Had Rubruck known more about astrology, Bacon reported, he would have been better able to make his case for Christianity before the Tartars, who numbered astrologers among their great men.[45]

Although such attitudes placed Bacon among those who advocated an "intellectual" approach to mission, he layered his writings with a sense of apocalyptic expectation for future changes in the status of Christendom. In his works, he reinforced the value of prophecies and other forms of revelation, mentioning Joachim of Fiore by name.[46] In this regard, education offered yet another utility to Christians, namely to help them prepare for the coming of Antichrist, an event that was not that far away according to the opinions of learned men.[47] Citing the work of an Islamic astrologer named "Albumazar," Bacon declared that the "law of Muhammad" would only last for 693 years. According to the Arabic calendar, the present time marked the year 665, meaning that the infidels' law would be "destroyed quickly through the grace of God, which ought to be a great consolation to Christians." The Mongol sack of Baghdad in 1258, Bacon noted, provided one sign that this failure of their law might come even sooner than predicted.[48] After the law of Muhammad, the "law" or "sect" of Antichrist would sweep away other laws and threaten the elect in the Christian Church, found among the Latin faithful, rather than schismatics and heretics.[49] Borrowing again from William of Rubruck, Bacon hinted that the rise of the Tartars might offer one sign that these days were drawing near, although he qualified this by saying that the Tartars might represent just one more barbarian invader from eastern lands.[50]

Roger Bacon's apocalyptic eschatology was undeniably restrained, lacking the immediacy and radical implications found in the Eternal Gospel. By the time he wrote in the 1260s, a general sense of caution pervaded Franciscan ranks in regard to eschatological speculation and the production of any new works, which were carefully monitored by the order.[51] Although the exact circumstances are not clear, even Bacon himself had experienced some difficulties with his superiors, perhaps linked to his interest in Joachim. One of his most intriguing predictions involved the coming of a wondrous pope, who would oversee the conversion of the world's peoples into a single community of believers following the internal reform of the Roman Church.[52] As he declared to Pope Clement IV in the *Tertiary Work:*

> There will be one pope in those times, who will purify canon law and the Church from the quibbles and deceits of lawyers. There shall come to pass justice everywhere without the uproar of litigation. On account of the goodness of this pope, there will come to be truth and justice, so that the Greeks will return to the obedience of the Roman Church, the greater part of the Tartars will convert to the faith, and the Saracens will be wiped out. And there will be one fold and one shepherd, as thus the word of the prophet rang out to those listening.[53]

If God willed it, Bacon added, these things might come to pass "in our times." In general, he assumed an exhortatory tone with Clement, implying perhaps that Clement himself might prove to be this prophesied leader. After the pope died in 1268, Bacon reiterated this vision in his *Compendium of Philosophical Study,* where he foretold the coming of a "most blessed pope" who would "wipe away every corruption" in the Church and "renew the world," so that the fullness of the Gentiles and the Jews would enter into the faith.[54] In this vision of the "blessed pope," Bacon also reserved room for a "greatest prince" who would assist the pope, joining the material sword with the spiritual one for the purpose of purging the Church—the emperor and the pope, no longer at odds, would work together for the renewal and expansion of Christendom.[55]

The Second Council of Lyons

Under Pope Clement IV's successor, Gregory X, such dreams of reordering the Christian world found new sources of inspiration in unfolding events. On 25 July 1261, the Greek ruler Michael Palaeologus had recaptured Constantinople from Latin hands. Pope Urban IV (r. 1261–1264) duly responded by issuing the call for a new crusade to restore the Latin empire. In a letter to the Franciscan provincial minister of France, he lamented the Roman Church's recent loss of Constantinople, recalling "the breathless effort and labor by which our predecessor, Pope Innocent III of blessed memory, conquered that imperial city for catholic unity."[56] The illusory dream that crusader control of Greece would somehow unite the Latin and Greek Churches was over, but papal efforts to secure a formal Byzantine recognition of Roman ecclesiastical authority were just beginning. In fact, Urban was somewhat lackluster in his efforts to raise support for a new crusade to regain Constantinople. Years earlier, Pope Alexander IV had already begun to negotiate directly with the Greeks about the possible terms for a formal reconciliation between the two churches. A now familiar set of doctrinal and liturgical disputes was on the table for resolution, including the *filioque* controversy and azymes, along with the Greek refusal to accept the Latin doctrine of purgatory. Calling upon the Byzantine ruler to return to the "maternal embrace" of the Roman Church, Alexander promised in return to pray that God would protect and strengthen his imperial throne.[57]

A delicate diplomatic dance had begun. Greek rulers indicated their willingness to recognize Roman primacy and make concessions in religious disputes, while a series of popes offered in return to deter, discourage, or deflect military and political ambitions of Western rulers toward Byzantine lands, above all, Constantinople. Members of the mendicant orders played a key role in this effort as ambassadors, complementing their sustained commitment to missionary work in the Eastern Mediterranean and beyond.[58] In addition to pressing for a Greek capitulation on specific religious issues, these negotiations provided the papacy with an opportunity to articulate its finely honed vision of proper order through a constant emphasis on the authority of Rome. Despite flattering appeals to the Greek emperor as a righteous son of God and Christian ruler, the insistence remained that there was one faith, one "heart and spirit," one baptism, and one head of the universal Church, namely the Apostolic See. Whatever give-and-take was expected on a pragmatic level, in theory the papal conception of Christendom provided an all-encompassing frame for the Western hopes to end the schism with the Greeks.[59]

In 1274, these ambitions culminated in the Second Council of Lyons. The assembly was a long time in the making. A decade earlier, Pope Clement IV had indicated to Michael Palaeologus his intention to summon a general council that would formalize and strengthen the bonds of unity between the Latin and Greek Churches. His successor, Pope Gregory X, deliberately followed suit upon his election in 1272. A flurry of complicated negotiations ensued, with the Franciscans front and center as papal legates to the Greek emperor and patriarch.[60] Inviting the Byzantine ruler to the general council later that same year, Gregory set the restoration of the bond between Latins and Greeks within a broader call of the "mother Church" to all its sons and daughters, scattered throughout every land, thereby hinting at the eschatological promise of their union as foreshadowed by Old Testament prophecy. He indicated as well the need for this synod to deliberate about "providing usefully and efficiently for the necessary succor of the Holy Land" and about the "general reformation of morals."[61]

In addition to these practical diplomatic efforts, Pope Gregory demonstrated his interest in the theoretical architecture of the council and what might be achieved through its deliberations. During the two previous years, churchmen including Gilbert of Tournai, William of Tripoli, and Humbert of Romans had produced tracts about the goals of the council in direct response to papal appeals for such literature. In his tract *On the Scandals of the Church,* Gilbert chose to focus his attention on the internal problems that beset the Roman faithful.[62] Without stepping into overt or extreme criticism of the papacy, Gilbert offered a reformer's critique of present laxity and avarice among the clergy and prelates. It was because of sins within the church of Rome, he said, that God had punished his people with the loss of the Holy Land. Gilbert also took note of the fact that the Greeks along with other schismatics and heretics were evading the "net" of ecclesiastical authority and continuing to abuse and mistreat the Roman Church.[63] William of Tripoli, on the other hand, devoted his work to the pressing need of Rome and its followers to confront the external threat of Islam. His tract *On the State of the Saracens* offered a lengthy and detailed exposition on the history and errant beliefs of the infidels following their "pseudo-prophet" Muhammad.[64] Toward the close of his composition, echoing to a certain extent Roger Bacon, William claimed that Islamic prophets had revealed the imminent failure of their own power and religious tradition. According to his report, the infidels realized that the Mongol sack of Baghdad in 1258 was a portent of their own doom and that their own law, just like "the law of the Jews," was finite and would not last. By contrast, they foresaw that the "status of the Christians" would endure until the end of history. To capitalize on this situation, William saw the need for Christian action to convert the infidels, something that would happen not through violence or even rational argumentation, but rather through simple sermons and evangelical inspiration.[65]

Humbert of Romans offered the most comprehensive analysis of Gregory's stated aims to execute a new crusade, reunite the Greeks with Rome, and reform the Roman Church. His modestly titled *Minor Work in Three Parts* offered something like an official program for the Second Council of Lyons.[66] The course of salvation history made the linkage between crusade, ecclesiastical unity, and reform plain to see, as Humbert noted by comparing the three great trials of the Israelites to those of the Christian people:

> First, the people of Israel from the time of Abraham until the end were assailed by infidels almost continually. Second, they were divided all about under Roboam and Jeroboam. Third, that part which honored the forms of worship to the true God ensnared itself with greater crimes. So the Christian people have always endured and will endure the persecution of infidels from without. Second, it suffered the division between Greeks and Latins, who wrestled in the womb of Rebecca (that is, of the Church), on account of which the kingdom of the Church, divided within itself, shall wretchedly be laid to waste. Third, the church of the Latins, having kept the faith, as far as practices are concerned, is caught up in great foulness.[67]

Humbert was not a Joachite thinker, in the sense that he did not draw upon Joachim's notion of the third *status*. As we saw above, however, as early as the joint encyclical issued with John of Parma in 1255, the Dominican master had been willing to present his order in eschatological terms that invoked Joachim's "spiritual men." This portion of his *Minor Work in Three Parts* clearly echoed the Calabrian abbot's "principle of concordance," aligning the struggles of Israel with the trials of the Church, including the schism between the Latins and the Greeks. In fact, the exegesis of Jacob and Esau fighting in Rebecca's womb as a type for the Latins and Greeks featured in the *Commentary on Jeremiah*.[68] In a different section of his work, Humbert employed another popular Joachite scheme, aligning the historical persecutions of the Church after Christ with the seven heads of the Dragon from the Book of Revelation.[69]

By 1274, despite the dangers posed by Joachite thinkers who had taken their speculations too far, such "safe" apocalyptic imagery had become part of the common language for discussing the historical fortunes of Christendom. Against this backdrop, Humbert addressed the three pressing concerns for the approaching council, starting with the projected crusade to the Holy Land. Out of the different peoples who had menaced Christendom, he identified the Muslims as the longest-lasting and most pernicious threat, above all because they seemed impervious to Christian efforts at converting them. This portion of the tract formed an apology for crusading against those who questioned its utility or justifiable purposes. Through Humbert's response to those critics, one can get a sense of the complaints that were being levied against the crusades, including the claim that they roused Saracens' hatred toward the Christian faith and led to the shedding of infidel blood rather than to their conversion (a point made by Roger Bacon).[70] One by one, Humbert refuted these arguments and defended crusading. In particular, he highlighted three reasons why the armed expeditions to recover the Holy Land should not be abandoned: because they offered a path to salvation for Christians; because they helped to suppress the power of the Saracens who plagued Christendom; and finally, because there was hope for an ultimate triumph in this cause. Humbert took special pains to emphasize the unique authority of the papacy over crusading expeditions, as evident in previous examples including Popes Urban II and Innocent III.[71]

In the second portion of his tract Humbert addressed the schism between the Latins and Greeks, the resolution of which would aid the recovery of the Holy Land. In the opening of this section, he stressed the unity of the Church by describing the many different churches in the world as being like the "many stones in a single structure." It was naturally appropriate that the one Church should have one shepherd and leader: "Therefore," he concluded, "all of Christendom, since it is one Church, has one highest pontiff," meaning the pope of Rome. Although he recognized the role of Latin misdeeds in antagonizing the Greeks, Humbert held the latter responsible for the existing schism, since they had cut themselves off from the rightful head of the universal Church. In particular, he identified three sources of historical discord between the churches: first, the division of empire in the time of Charlemagne, which led the papacy to turn its back on the Greek emperor; second, their disputes over articles of faith such as *filioque;* and third, the Greek rejection of Roman primacy, accompanied by their attempt to elevate Constantinople's ecclesiastical privileges.[72] Humbert offered a decidedly pragmatic plan for reconciling the churches. Responsibility for ending the schism, he believed, lay with the Latin Church, above all the pope, who should visit Greece in person. He proposed a series of practical measures that fit well with the contemporary missionary spirit of the Dominican order. Latin scholars needed to learn Greek in order to read their books and to preach in their language. Legates should be exchanged frequently between the churches. By intermarriage, Greek magnates should be drawn into closer affinity with the Latins, while Latin rulers should cease their oppression of the Greeks. Thus would the sundered halves of the Christian world be rejoined.[73]

Finally, Humbert addressed the call for the internal reform of the Roman Church. Much like Gilbert of Tournai, he avoided any extreme criticism of the papacy, tackling the need to reform the secular clergy and to limit the admittedly burgeoning population of new religious orders, including women who traveled about freely and shamefully begged for resources. Taken together with the tracts by Gilbert and William, Humbert's work offered an ambitious program for transforming the internal workings of Latin Christian society, while reconfiguring its relationship with the outside world by restoring the Greeks to the Roman Church and finally ridding the Christian holy places of Islamic dominance. Although Humbert did not present his goals within an apocalyptic framework, there was no mistaking the eschatological import of his plan for Christendom. After all, the renewal of the Western Church, reunion with the Eastern Church, and the defeat of the infidels fueled many popular prophetic scenarios.

With such high expectations, Gregory X convoked the Second Council of Lyons on 7 May 1274, addressing some two hundred churchmen about the triple goals of the assembly, namely "aid to the Holy Land, union with the Greeks, and the reformation of morals."[74] In immediate terms, the results of the council seemed impressive. About a month after the deliberations began, a delegation of Greeks arrived, and during subsequent sessions they promised obedience to the faith of the Roman Church and recognized its primacy. A joint liturgy was celebrated, including a recitation of the creed complete with the contentious phrase *filioque*. A Mongol legation was also on hand, sent to explore the possibility of a military alliance with the Christian powers of the Western Church against the sultanate of Egypt. According to contemporary reports, during the course of the council several of the "Tartar" envoys were baptized.[75] Whatever this ceremonial act may have meant to the legates themselves, one can imagine just how exciting this event must have been for those Christians observing it. With the achievement of this ecclesiastical union between the Latins and the Greeks, as well as the promise of their common cause with the soon-to-be-converted Mongols, the future prospects for the recovery of the Holy Land and the extension of Christendom must have seemed exceedingly bright.

In the period immediately following the council, reactions to its results were marked by a sense of optimism, or at least the expectation that its achievements fit into widely anticipated eschatological developments. For years afterward, chroniclers of universal histories describing the results of the council shared the impression that Pope Gregory X had truly succeeded in restoring the Greeks to the catholic fold and in securing an alliance with the Tartars. Even though they did not make any explicit apocalyptic claims, a dramatic sense of destiny hovered over such reports of the council and its outcome.[76] One prophecy supposedly delivered at Lyons declared that the stage was set for the end of the Saracens' power in the Holy Land "by divine, not human operation." The Tartars would recapture Jerusalem before their power finally began to wane. Alexandria would be restored to the Christians and the land of Armenia would be subjected to the power of the Franks, while the Greeks would again lose Constantinople to them.[77] Another short prophecy from around this time predicted a period of tribulations for the Roman Church, followed by the return of the Greeks to unity with Rome before the coming of "Antichrist's preachers."[78]

Even the somewhat disillusioned Joachite, Salimbene of Adam, testified to the expectations raised by the events at Lyons. Recording the death of Gregory X in 1276, Salimbene commented on some prophetic verses that he had seen shortly before the pope's election around five years earlier.[79] He was above all interested in the prophecy's closing lines, which referred to the recovery of Christ's tomb from the Muslims and the conversion of the "Archivi" (that is, the Greeks). According to Salimbene, Gregory's plans for a crusade had made him a likely candidate for the fulfillment of the former prediction, although the failure of the pope's expedition to materialize demonstrated that the time was not right for the liberation of Jerusalem. Clearly, for his own inscrutable reasons, God desired the holy places to remain in infidel hands.[80] The Second Council of Lyons, however, had fulfilled the latter prediction about the return of the Greeks, an outcome predicted by Joachim of Fiore. Citing Scripture, Joachim's commentary on the Gospels, and the *Commentary on Jeremiah,* Salimbene proclaimed that the abbot had rightly foreseen the "conversion" of the Greeks at Lyons, a development that would be followed by the conversion of the Jews and the remainder of the Gentiles before the end of time.[81]

Subsequent events, however, would again reveal that prophecies could deceive as much as enlighten. Richard Southern once called 1274 "the last hopeful year in the Middle Ages."[82] There are a number of symbolic reasons to mark 1274 as a high point for medieval Europe, followed by a turn for the worse in its fortunes. Two prominent figures died that year: Thomas Aquinas, en route to the Second Council of Lyons, and Bonaventure, who passed away while participating in its deliberations. Pope Gregory X died two years after the council was completed. Despite the efforts of subsequent popes to follow through on their new relationship with the Greek Church, a lasting reconciliation between Rome and Constantinople proved elusive. Over the following years, members of the Latin Church confronted the fact that the reunion achieved at Lyons was fleeting and repudiated by many of the Greeks, who labeled their own emperor a heretic for making such concessions to Rome. In 1282, at the behest of Charles of Anjou, who had political designs on the Greek empire, Pope

Martin IV (r. 1281–1285) excommunicated the Greek emperor and his followers, souring whatever goodwill remained between the two churches.

Immediate hopes for a new crusade also faded with the passing of Gregory X. The following period witnessed a flourishing of so-called "crusade proposals" after the fall of crusader Acre in 1291.[83] These tracts, which one scholar has described as more "strategic" than "theological" or "ideological," marked out the best routes for armies, the superior way to organize finances, and the most effective means to structure military expeditions; they only implied or left unsaid just how those goals fit into the broader design of God's plan for history.[84] Even the Mongols continued to play a role in such projects. When confronted with the fall of Acre, Pope Nicholas IV (r. 1288–1292) had appealed to Arghun, Il-Khan of Persia, for his assistance in smashing the power of the infidels and freeing Jerusalem. Nicholas hoped that the khan would fulfill his desire to "expand the borders of Christendom" and adopt Christianity himself, perhaps receiving baptism in a newly liberated Jerusalem.[85] The papacy, however, would not follow through on any of its major crusading projects, while the dream of a Christian-Mongol alliance seemed increasingly unlikely with each passing year.[86]

Apocalyptic thinkers took note of this changing climate. In his work *Knowledge of the Age*, for example, the German cleric Alexander of Roes's coverage of history, geography, and eschatology demonstrated a new sense of pessimism about the present and future.[87] Writing in Cologne around 1288, Alexander looked back at the Second Council of Lyons as a remarkable moment when "not only the Christian people and ecclesiastical prelates, but also the kings of the world, the Jews, the Greeks, and the Tartars coming together recognized the Roman bishop as the monarch of the world."[88] This historical high point in the fortunes of priestly authority, however, matching a corresponding low point for the empire, left the authority of the pope nowhere to go but down, and the power of the emperor nowhere to go but up. Alexander excoriated Martin IV for disturbing the Church of God by inordinately favoring his own French people. During Martin's watch, Michael Palaeologus had withdrawn the Greeks from unity with Rome, the Tartars had renewed their attacks in Eastern Europe, the Saracens had grown restless in Africa, and internal wars had erupted among Christians. Cautious about claiming any specific knowledge of future events, Alexander saw signs of apocalyptic gloom on the near horizon, perhaps within a few decades. As the thirteenth century drew to a close, this sense of disquiet would grow rather than diminish.[89]

Insecurity and anxiety did not mean that contemporaries in the Roman Church lost hope for the expansion of their faith. Even Alexander of Roes predicted (albeit in a somewhat perfunctory manner) positive changes after the tribulations under Antichrist, including the recovery of the Holy Land, the conversion of the world's peoples, and an age of peace for the Church. Other contemporaries, such as the Catalan philosopher Raymund Llull, continued to speculate about the possibility of transforming the world through crusade and mission. Llull, born in Majorca around 1232, experienced a series of visions when he was about thirty years old, resulting in his conviction that he should devote his life to the service of God, particularly as a missionary. In 1292 he addressed two treatises, *How to Recover the Holy Land* and *How to Covert the Infidels,* to Nicholas IV and the cardinal bishops of the papal curia.[90] Over the following years, he penned further letters and tracts that called upon the leadership of the Roman Church to take the lead in organizing missionary programs and crusades.[91] Much like Roger Bacon before him, Llull called for programs to teach missionary languages and advised that monasteries should be founded for this purpose.[92] At the same time, he left room for armed force in protecting the Roman Church and opening up missionary territories. The Catalan theorist believed that the papacy possessed both "temporal" and "spiritual" authority, not to mention temporal and spiritual treasures. Where spiritual authority and treasures did not suffice, the pope was required to delegate temporal means to secular powers. People like the schismatic Greeks, the Saracens, and pagans should have the chance to listen to peaceful preaching and argumentation. If they did not respond, then they would face coercive action.[93]

Nevertheless, for all his planning, Raymund Llull displayed his own concerns for the status and safety of the Christian faith in a much wider world. On one occasion, he noted that there were one hundred infidels for every catholic Christian—hardly favorable odds. At other times, he expressed a particular fear that if the followers of Rome failed to secure the conversion of the Tartars, they might become Muslims, a situation that would create a dramatic threat to Christendom (indeed, the ruling khans of Persia did convert to Islam).[94] This sense of pessimism was not entirely new. After all, Roger Bacon had expressed some similar fears decades earlier. Nevertheless, events had conspired against the earlier enthusiasm of crusaders, missionaries, and those who planned their efforts. As the years passed, increasing tensions and conflicts within the Roman Church, especially over the Franciscan commitment to apostolic poverty, would do little to mitigate these growing uncertainties. With the waning of papal power, a rise in religious dissent, and a creative outburst of eschatological theorizing, the notion of universal Christendom would achieve its most fantastic formulations, even as the papacy and its supporters decried such visions of a world transformed.

8

The New Jerusalem and the
Transfiguration of Christendom

Five years after the Second Council of Lyons, the Franciscan exegete and theologian Peter John Olivi tackled a source of growing contention within his order, namely, the role of poverty in Franciscan life. Olivi, who had trained at the University of Paris before returning to his native Provence, approached this problem with scholastic rigor and remarkable imagination about the role of the Franciscans in history. In his tract *On the Poor Use,* he insisted that the restricted usage—as opposed to outright ownership—of goods formed an integral part of the Franciscan vow. Saint Francis, Olivi declared, had come toward the final days of the world as the "renovator" of the evangelical poverty observed by Christ and the apostles.[1] By contrast, those who attacked or blasphemed evangelical poverty paved the way for Antichrist. Toward the end of his life, Olivi revisited this eschatological concept of Franciscan renewal when he composed his *Lesson on the Apocalypse.* Inspired in part by Joachim of Fiore, Olivi offered a sophisticated theology of history that scathingly criticized the present-day Roman Church, viewed by the friar as a corrupt entity perched on the edge of apocalyptic tribulations. After a time of persecution by Antichrist, however, Olivi believed that the rigorist members of his order, those committed to apostolic living, would inaugurate a Sabbath age of peace and renewal for the faithful before the end of time.[2]

Before he died in 1298, Olivi had become a controversial figure for holding suspect views that had little or nothing to do with his apocalypticism.[3] Although Pope Nicholas III (r. 1277–1280) had formally defended the Franciscan "poor use" in 1279, the issue remained far from settled during the following decades.[4] Olivi emerged as an outspoken champion of evangelical poverty along with a number of other "questionable" theological stances. From 1283 to 1285, Franciscan authorities investigated and censured a number of his teachings, although he successfully avoided outright condemnation as a heretic. In 1299, however, shortly after Olivi's death, the Franciscan General Chapter of Lyons burned his writings.[5] Posthumously, the growing crisis between the so-called "Spiritual" and "Conventual" Franciscans thrust his radical apocalypticism into the center of an acrimonious debate over poverty and papal authority. At the opening of the fourteenth century, Olivi's writings on the apocalypse joined a flood of increasingly subversive prophetic literature, much of which favored the Spiritual position and condemned their opponents, including the current popes of Rome.[6]

The institutional papacy of the era had particular reasons to be sensitive to complaints that it had strayed from true apostolic values. In 1294 the papal election of Pietro Angelerio, a hermit known for his saintly behavior and extreme piety, had elated the rigorist circles of the Franciscan order. Taking the name Celestine V, the new pope openly favored the Spiritual Franciscans, going so far as to recognize the leading Italian circle of rigorists as a new order, the "Poor Hermits of Pope Celestine."[7] When Celestine resigned less than a year later, some disaffected Franciscans rejected his successor, Pope Boniface VIII (r. 1294–1303), who proved far less sympathetic to the Spiritual cause. In this case, Peter Olivi assumed a moderate stance. When Celestine abdicated the papal see, Olivi spoke out against those who denied the legitimacy of his resignation and the consequent election of Pope Boniface. He vigorously defended the "most universal power" of the Roman papacy and the right of any pope to resign his office. Even when he defended papal prerogatives, however, Olivi did so with a certain twist. Addressing the related question of whether the pope had the right to relieve someone of the evangelical vows that they had taken, Olivi defended the right of the papacy to do almost anything, but added that a true pope would never attempt to commute vows of poverty. Such an act would in fact reveal that pope to be heretical and "like a devil" rather than a "vicar of Christ," especially if he did anything to oppose the rule of Saint Francis.[8]

Boniface's tenure on the Apostolic See illustrated the paradox of papal monarchy at the dawn of the fourteenth century. From a certain perspective, the leadership of the Roman Church seemed poised to wield the same influence and enjoy the same prerogatives that it had for generations past. In 1300, the pope declared what became known as the first "Jubilee" year, promising the same remission of sins and indulgences enjoyed by crusaders to pilgrims visiting Rome. By all accounts, the promise of such spiritual rewards brought floods of pious travelers from all over the Western Church to the holy places of the city.[9] Two years later, Boniface issued the famous bull *Unam sanctam,* the most uncompromising statement of papal supremacy on the books, which flatly stated that "it is absolutely necessary for salvation that every human creature be subject to the Roman Pontiff."[10] With hindsight, however, his papacy marked a watershed in the fortunes of papal authority, especially relative to the power of secular monarchies. In large part, Boniface issued *Unam sanctam* as a broadside against King Philip IV (r. 1285–1314), whose encroachment upon ecclesiastical privileges and properties had led to outright conflict between the French crown and Rome. The fact that brigands led by Philip's agents briefly seized the pope at Anagni in 1303, contributing to his demise shortly afterwards, exposed the weakness behind the grandiose claims of *Unam sanctam.*

After the brief papacy of Benedict XI (r. 1303–1304), the move of the papal curia to southern France under the pro-Capetian Pope Clement V (r. 1304–1314) set the stage for still more controversy surrounding the papal office, inaugurating the so-called Avignon papacy, known by its critics as the new "Babylonian captivity." At the same time, the ongoing and intensifying conflict over apostolic poverty continued to plague the papacy and the Franciscans. At the Council of Vienne (1311–1312), Pope Clement made a final effort to resolve the debates that were tearing the Franciscan order apart, acknowledging many of the rigorists' complaints, but ultimately settling upon the need for their obedience to their superiors. As often seems to be the case with such compromises, this "Clementine settlement" satisfied neither the Spirituals nor the Conventuals.[11] Starting in 1317, Clement's successor, Pope John XXII (r. 1316–1334), gave Franciscan authorities free reign to move aggressively against the rigorist friars. The burning of four recalcitrant Spirituals from Narbonne in May 1318 illustrated the rapidly diminishing space for dissent by the proponents of apostolic living.[12]

Debate over the worldwide realization of Christendom assumed a high profile in this changing and turbulent climate. As Peter John Olivi foresaw in his *Lesson on the Apocalypse,* the coming "spiritual men" from the Franciscan order would be persecuted horribly by members of the "carnal Latin Church," but they would go forth and prosper among the "Greeks, Saracens, Tartars and finally the Jews."[13] Christ's promise about the spread of the Gospel, Olivi believed, would be fulfilled, although the dissemination of God's word would happen despite—not because of—the current institutions and practices of the mainstream Roman Church. This is not to say that the fourteenth-century papacy turned its back on the outside world—far from it. The Avignon popes continued to dispatch envoys and missionaries to the Mongols, Muslims, and schismatic Christians.[14] A widening dissonance, however, had begun to emerge between the current realities of the papal monarchy and the prophetic formulations of universal Christian order. Apocalyptic thinkers after Olivi continued to dream about the recovery of the holy places, union with the Greeks, and the eschatological assembly of "one fold" under an "angelic" pope or even a holy Roman emperor working together with the Church. Ecclesiastical authorities did not fail to recognize the subversive nature of such claims about the future spread of the Christian faith. As the fourteenth century progressed, holding the "wrong" beliefs about the future of Christendom and the conversion of the world came to result in censure, imprisonment, or even death.

Peter John Olivi and the Evangelization of the World

Before he wrote his commentary on the Apocalypse, in his *Exposition on the Rule of the Friars Minor,* Olivi revealed his perspective on Francis's sense of mission.[15] In his commentary on the twelfth chapter of the rule, he compared the preaching of the apostles, first to the faithful among the Jews and then among the Gentiles, with the preaching of Franciscans, first to the "Latin" faithful and next among the "nations of the infidels." By going forth to those non-believers, the Franciscan order would thereby save the "fullness of the Gentiles" followed by "all of Israel." Olivi associated these events with the sixth seal of the Apocalypse, the sixth angel with its trumpet, and the sixth angel bearing the "sign of the living God." This latter angel represented Francis himself, who, in the sixth year after his spiritual awakening, had crossed over to the Saracens to seek their conversion.[16] In the conclusion to his commentary, Olivi divided history into six ages—the standard Augustinian notion—and further subdivided the time of the Church after Christ into six stages: first, a period of evangelical light; second, that of the martyrs; third, the flourishing of ecclesiastical worship after Constantine; fourth, the thriving of anchorites; and fifth, the period of cenobitic monastic life. "In the sixth stage," according to Olivi, "under Francis, the mendicancy of Christ entered the world." Looking ahead, he predicted that "under the more complete opening of the sixth seal, we can expect the conversion of infidel nations and also the Jews with the renewal of the solemn martyrs."[17] For Olivi, the Franciscan commitment to poverty and the spiritual renewal of the Western Church under the rule of their founder shaped the order's universal sense of mission. The evangelical life would transform Christendom both within and without.

Olivi's commentary on the Franciscan rule offered just a taste of what was to come in his *Lesson on the Apocalypse,* completed not long before he died. This vast work is difficult to summarize. Grappling with the meaning of the Apocalypse, Olivi borrowed and modified a number of basic schemes that were found in the works of Joachim of Fiore, including the division of history after Christ into a series of six sub-ages along with the more detailed "principle of concordance" between the time of the Old and New Testaments. In addition, Olivi organized history according to Joachim's scheme of the three *status,* including his controversial Sabbath of the Holy Spirit.[18] Plumbing the exegetical depths of the ever-cryptic Book of Revelation, Olivi touched upon all manner of issues relating to contemporary ecclesiastical life, politics, and society. In particular, he criticized the Roman or Latin Church of his day as being "carnal" and corrupt, showing a vehemence that went far beyond the typical complaints of previous reformist writers. Olivi also assigned Francis and his spiritual followers a critical role to play in the renewal of religious life during the sixth and seventh ages. Finally, as part of his eschatological predictions, Olivi imagined a worldwide transformation among the schismatic, pagan, and infidels peoples of the world, followed by the conversion of the Jews into one assembly of the Christian faithful.[19]

Much of what Olivi had to say about the basic patterns of history would have looked familiar to anyone with a passing knowledge of Joachim's major works or the popular pseudo-Joachite writings that passed under his name. The experience of the Church was divided into seven seals or stages, each marked by a struggle or conflict. The imminent opening of the sixth seal would bring the "sect of Antichrist" and horrid tribulations, followed by a period of peace and restoration on earth before the ultimate persecution of the faithful by Gog and Magog.[20] Olivi spent considerable time discussing the threats of the fourth seal—the Saracens—and the fifth seal—corrupt, carnal Christians. During the fourth seal, beginning with Saint Anthony or the Byzantine Emperor Justinian, the followers of Muhammad had overrun the schismatic Eastern Church and other lands. The "sect of the Saracens" had reduced "true Christendom," which formerly extended throughout the entire world, to the territories of the Latin or Roman Church.[21] The Lord had specially protected the followers of Rome from their depredations, although the infidels continued to plague the Latins and would do so into the future. In this regard, Olivi followed Joachim's insights about the special destiny of the Western Church, which was spared the full brunt of the Islamic invasions that overran the "heretical" Eastern Church and Empire.[22]

The fifth seal had begun with Charles the Great, when the power of empire was transferred from Constantinople to the Franks. Much like Joachim, Olivi viewed the subsequent era as one of peace and prosperity in the Roman Church characterized by deferential secular rulers, but later degenerating into simony, greed, and the abuse of ecclesiastical offices.[23] These were typical complaints of reform-era ecclesiastical critics. Olivi, however, was unusually severe in his attacks on the carnal Latin Church. As he understood it, with the waning of the fifth age and beginning of the sixth era, present-day ecclesiastical institutions, worship, and ways of life would be superseded, similar to the carnal Synagogue of the Old Testament which had been passed over with the coming of Christ at the dawn of the New Testament. Olivi believed that he was living in a transitional era between the lingering fifth seal and full realization of the sixth age, which had begun with Saint Francis. With the initiation of this "more perfect" spiritual era, the corrupt Roman or Latin Church—like the old Israel of the Jews—would be left behind as the faithful entered a new stage in salvation.[24]

Not surprisingly, Olivi believed that the persecution of the Spiritual Franciscans by carnal Christians formed part of God's plan. He viewed the struggles of his own day between the secular clergy and the mendicants, as well as within his own order, through this apocalyptic lens. Ultimately, he predicted, the carnal Latin Church would be destroyed by internal strife and outside forces, including an invasion by infidels and the rise of the "ten kings" who would precede the coming of the great Antichrist.[25] In an innovative move, Olivi posited that there would in fact be two Antichrists associated with the sixth seal: first a "mystical" Antichrist, and then the "proper" or "great" Antichrist. The mystical Antichrist, he believed, would be a "pseudo-pope," a corrupt prelate who would occupy the see of Saint Peter.[26] After the defeat of the mystical and great Antichrists, however, the new era of the Holy Spirit introduced by Saint Francis would begin in earnest.[27] In his anticipation of a coming Sabbath age, Olivi was careful not to displace Christ or somehow detract from the Incarnation as a pivotal point in salvation history. In another daring move, he argued that there would in fact be three advents of Christ: the first, when he founded his Church; the second, when he came to reform his Church with evangelical living; and the third, in Final Judgment.[28] Francis and the new age of the Holy Spirit did not displace Christ's dispensation; rather, they fulfilled it.

While he focused increasing attention on these internal conflicts within the Roman Church, Olivi did not shrink from speculating about the future of the pagans, infidels, and Jews, who still remained outside of the Christian faith and beyond the borders of the Western Church.[29] Much like the first Christians who had fled from the Synagogue in the first age of the Church, the spiritual men of the new sixth era would be forced to flee from the false Christians of the corrupt Roman Church, the new "whore of Babylon."[30] Olivi explicitly stated that the Spiritual Franciscans would not initially prosper in the carnal Latin Church, and would therefore go forth among non-orthodox and non-Christian peoples to spread their message. With the coming of the sixth seal, he foresaw a miraculous "time of renovation for the world," a process of evangelical conversion that would mirror the first age of apostolic mission among the Gentiles, but more perfectly, more completely, and more spiritually.[31] He highlighted one passage of the Apocalypse's instructions to "prophesy again to many nations, and peoples, and tongues, and kings" (Rev. 10:11). Why did this passage say "again"? Olivi asked. The answer, he believed, was that the spread of the Gospel would be completed in three stages. First, the apostles had preached to the Jews and then the Gentiles. Second, starting with Saint Francis's mission to the Saracens, the members of the Franciscan order had begun to preach far and wide during the time before the mystical Antichrist. Finally, between the mystical and the great Antichrist, the Spiritual Franciscans would again preach the message of Christ in every land.[32]

After the defeat of the great Antichrist, the "light of God" would be fully revealed in the world during the Sabbath age, a time without war or spiritual struggles.[33] Pagans and infidels would convert, followed by the Jews. Olivi was particularly adamant that the Jews would ultimately be restored to the Lord.[34] In some passages, he declared that Rome—ravaged by apocalyptic tribulations—would be restored as the "principal see of Christ" during the future, but in other places he suggested that perhaps the center of Christendom would move back to Jerusalem:

> We ought not wonder that the place of our redemption shall then be exalted over all the places of the earth, especially since that place will be more suitable to the highest priests of the world for the conversion of the world and for governing of all those who are already converted, for it lies dead-center in the middle of the habitable earth.[35]

Olivi offered a powerful vision of the world transformed—precisely the sort of eschatological scenario that Thomas Aquinas and other authorities had forcefully dismissed decades earlier. For mainstream church-

The whore of Babylon (Rev. 17:3–5). Apocalypse Commentary, thirteenth century.
Source: Bibliothèque Nationale de France, Paris, nouv. acq. lat. 1366.

men, Olivi's vision would raise the specter of the Church changed beyond recognition, as previously found in the Eternal Gospel. According to patristic sources, when the unchanging Gospel of Christ had reached all peoples, it would signal the coming of Antichrist and his three-and-a-half-year persecution of the faithful, followed quickly by the conversion of the Jews, the end of time, and Christ's return in Final Judgment. Such a conservative scenario left little room for the sorts of marvelous but disruptive events that Olivi proposed. Indeed, considering the contested status of Pope Boniface VIII and the ever-widening gap between the conventional and rigorist branches of the Franciscan order, ecclesiastical authorities viewed all but the most staid apocalyptic scenarios with growing suspicion. The stage was set for another round of contention over the shape of things to come.

Eschatology Unleashed

The years after Olivi's demise witnessed the emergence of yet another famous "apocalyptic personality," Arnold of Villanova.[36] An educated layman from the region of Valencia, Arnold became a well-traveled poly-math and prominent physician, spending much of his career as an adviser and doctor at the royal court in Aragon. He also believed that he had spe-cial insights into the coming of Antichrist and the end of the world. In 1300, Arnold presented his tract *On the Time of the Antichrist* to the mas-ters of theology at the University of Paris, hoping for their approval of his breakthrough in calculating the dating of Antichrist's appearance.[37] Ac-cording to his figures based on the Book of Daniel, the "Son of Perdition" would arrive 1290 years after the destruction of the Temple by the Ro-mans and the subsequent cessation of the Jewish rites. This meant that Antichrist could confidently be expected around the year 1366 or 1376, depending on exactly when one reckoned the end of the Jewish worship in Jerusalem.[38] Arnold also predicted a time of tranquility for the Church after the defeat of Antichrist, when the world's peoples would join to-gether in one fold, fulfilling Christ's promise in the Gospel. Hardly an iconoclast, Arnold reserved a unique place for the papacy in this process of conversion, at one point describing the Roman pontiff as a "Christ on earth" who would spread salvation everywhere.[39]

The masters at Paris, however, were far from impressed with this layman who claimed privileged information about the end of days. They not only dashed Arnold's hopes for approval; they also arrested him and tried him for heresy, forcing him to recant several of his statements and burning his book on Antichrist. Undeterred, Arnold appealed his case to Rome in 1301, only to face another trial and yet another burning of his apocalyptic volume. Around this same time, Arnold produced another tract to clarify and defend his positions, *On the Mystery of the Bells of the Church*—that is, the "ringing" sound of the Old Testament prophets who announced the Incarnation of Christ. The book also included present-day prophecies that foretold Christ's Second Coming.[40] Fortunately for him, Pope Boniface VIII fell ill after the second trial. When Arnold managed to cure the ailing pontiff, he acquired a powerful patron who protected him from his detractors until Boniface died in 1303.[41] Arnold's enemies once again leapt into action against him, forcing him to defend himself before Pope Benedict XI at Perugia in 1304. Benedict showed himself less favor-ably disposed toward the physician turned prophet. Before Arnold's status was settled, however, Benedict himself died. Heading to Sicily, Arnold spent a brief time at the court of King Frederick III before returning to the papal curia to seek the support of Clement V in 1305. Clement showed little enthusiasm for Arnold but refused to condemn him, leaving him free to write until his death around 1313.[42]

Arnold of Villanova's roller-coaster experience revealed the increasingly thin line between someone who was respected, or at least tolerated for his spiritual insights into the meaning of history, and someone who was targeted for condemnation as a heretic. It was also clear that such prophets were increasingly willing to provide concrete dates for apocalyptic events. In Paris around 1305, for example, the so-called "Columbinus prophecy" foretold the revelation of Antichrist at Jerusalem in 1316, and a time after his defeat when "every creature shall come to know the power of our lord, Jesus Christ, and shall convert to him."[43] The Columbinus prophecy may very well have been written by a Spiritual Franciscan. In Arnold's case, his advocacy for the Spirituals no doubt contributed to his questionable reputation.[44] Even worse, he was a layman rather than a cleric. By 1300, ecclesiastical authorities shared a growing concern over the fact that apocalypticism with a subversive edge was spilling over into lay communities, such as the Beguines, voluntary associations of women living together for the purposes of prayer and other pious activities. Among the Beguines of southern France, for example, Peter John Olivi had quickly assumed the status of a true prophet and spiritual voice following his death in 1298. Indeed, the devotion of such "unlettered" groups, accused of anti-sacerdotal attitudes and the unsupervised reading of the Bible, contributed to the posthumous decline in Olivi's reputation. For the Beguines, who read apocalyptic literature in vernacular translations, current events seemed to confirm Olivi's pessimistic vision of the corrupt Roman Church persecuting the spiritual elect.[45]

From 1300 to 1307, one Italian prophet known as Fra Dolcino and his band of "Apostolics" took expectations for radical apocalyptic change even further.[46] Although Dolcino lacked any clear connection to Joachite or Spiritual Franciscan circles, he clearly tapped into similar currents of eschatological excitement. According to the complaints of his detractors, Dolcino taught among other things that the Roman Church represented the "whore of Babylon" from the Book of Revelation, arguing that papal leadership had degenerated from the time of Pope Sylvester up to the present (with the notable exception of Celestine V). The true "spiritual power" given by Christ to the Church now lay among the men and women of the Apostolics, the elect of God.[47] In the near future, Dolcino declared, King Frederick of Sicily would be crowned Roman emperor and would appoint nine kings in Italy, who would despoil ecclesiastical property and "kill the lord pope, whoever he might be at that time." Afterwards, Dolcino himself would become a new "holy pope." In a sort of medieval "Rapture" scenario, the Italian prophet and his followers would be elevated into Paradise during the persecutions under Antichrist, returning after his defeat to "preach the correct faith of Christ to everyone, converting all those living then to the true faith of Jesus Christ."[48] Not content to wait for these events, Dolcino and his Apostolics embarked on a violent campaign of plunder and protest in the countryside of northwestern Italy, establishing an armed camp on Mount Rubello before ecclesiastical authorities wiped them out and burned Dolcino at the stake.

Although Dolcino represented an extreme case, prophecy-minded churchmen commonly anticipated the coming of a new "holy" or "angelic" pope, a scenario found, among other places, in the so-called *Prophecies about the Supreme Pontiffs*. There has been considerable debate about the origins of these "pope prophecies," but scholars agree that the first version of the text, known as the *Genus nequam* group, drew inspiration from the "Leo oracles," a set of Greek predictions about a line of messianic Byzantine emperors.[49] The pope prophecies, which circulated with a series of fifteen images by 1304 at the latest, presented a series of historical pontiffs starting with Pope Nicholas III and ending with Boniface VIII or Benedict XI. With the exception of the fifth pope listed, commonly identified as Pope Celestine V, the prophecies portrayed the bishops of Rome as increasingly sinful and corrupt. The final pope, however, would be a saintly and pious pontiff, who would end simony and begin an era of spiritual regeneration in the Roman Church before the coming of Antichrist.[50] Perhaps not surprisingly, contemporaries often attributed the text and illustrations to Joachim of Fiore. Whoever created it, this popular tradition clearly favored the Spiritual Franciscans' criticisms of the papacy and hopes for the renewal of apostolic living.

Spiritual circles produced and circulated two other works around this time, the *Angelic Oracle of Saint Cyril* and the *Book of Fiore*. Written during the late 1290s, the *Angelic Oracle* purported to be a prophecy sent from an Eastern monk, "Cyril the Carmelite," to Joachim of Fiore so that the abbot might read and comment upon it. The text included both the original prophecy and Joachim's supposed gloss. Among notable passages, the commentary declared that the prophecy's lines about a "snake reentering the cavern" foretold the return of the kingdom of the Greeks to the "unity of the Church," although the snake would only pretend to "rest" inside the cave, that is, the Greeks would not remain in that state of harmony. Clearly, this "prediction" referred to the temporary union achieved at the Second Council of Lyons.[51] The prophecy paid even more attention, however, to the internal troubles of the Roman Church. Commenting on the divide between the biblical rulers Roboam and Jeroboam, the *Angelic Oracle* predicted a schism between an "orthodox pontiff" and a "pseudo-pontiff." Ultimately, however, a saintly pope would resolve this crisis, inaugurating an era of spiritual renewal.[52] Written around 1303–1305, the *Book of Fiore* offered a similar picture of papal decline from Pope Gregory IX until the arrival of "angelic" popes who would renew the Roman Church. This book also described an "order of the dove" that would suffer internal divisions and persecution, a clear reference to the Spiritual Franciscans.[53]

One Franciscan proponent of apostolic poverty, Angelo Clareno, wrote an entire history to describe the oppression of the Spirituals.[54] Clareno, who joined the Franciscan order in 1270, became an active figure in the rigorist network around the region of Ancona. Imprisoned by his superiors following the Second Council of Lyons, he spent time after his release in 1289 with a party of like-minded friars in Armenia. In 1294 Clareno returned to Italy to enjoy the brief patronage of Celestine V, followed by a less favorable climate under Boniface VIII and Clement V.[55] Under the subsequent pope, John XXII, the tide began to turn strongly against the proponents of apostolic poverty. Clareno, investigated once for heresy under Pope Clement, knew the dangers of this period quite intimately. In 1317 Pope John questioned Clareno in person about his beliefs, asking whether he claimed that papal authority had ceased with Boniface VIII, and also whether he considered the Eastern, Greek Church superior to the Western Church. In a lengthy written response, Clareno denied these and other charges, adroitly professing his obedience to the Roman papacy and also to his vows of poverty. The friar escaped outright condemnation, but remained under suspicion until he died in 1337.[56]

In his *History of the Seven Tribulations,* written between 1323 and 1326, Clareno reflected on the past and present vicissitudes of the Spiritual Franciscans, setting their experiences into an apocalyptic framework. From the beginning of the Franciscan order, the rigorist mendicant argued, the true champions of poverty and apostolic living had suffered oppression, starting with Francis himself and continuing through the rapid expansion of the order under his successors. Clareno showed particular sympathy for John of Parma, targeted by his enemies for his devotion to poverty and his enthusiasm for Joachim of Fiore.[57] He identified a series of tribulations leading to the fifth persecution, against Peter John Olivi; the sixth persecution, starting with the resignation of Celestine V; and the incipient seventh persecution, beginning under John XXII around 1319. The Italian Spiritual greatly admired Peter Olivi, believing that his coming had been prophesied by Joachim of Fiore and others.[58] Drawing upon his personal experiences, Clareno also detailed the fortunes of the Spirituals in missionary territories such as Armenia and Greece, where they won the admiration of local Eastern Christians but also attracted the envy and malice of conservative Franciscans.[59]

For those who had read Olivi, current events seemed to confirm his predictions of a mystical papal Antichrist, along with his claim that the "spiritual men," hounded by the "carnal" Latin Church, would prosper among schismatics and infidels. Ecclesiastical authorities were not slow to recognize the importance of Olivi's apocalypticism for such Franciscan dissidents, not to mention the Beguines and other groups.[60] Both Boniface VIII and Clement V had already taken some steps toward investigating Olivi's *Lesson on the Apocalypse.* In 1318, as part of his campaign against the Spirituals, John XXII deliberately and forcefully targeted this apocalyptic commentary, commissioning eight masters of theology to scrutinize Olivi's teachings.[61] Dominican Pierre de la Palaude and Carmelite Guido Terreni examined a summary of Olivi's ideas written in Catalan by an anonymous Beguin, who included predictions about the destruction of the carnal Roman Church and the coming of a Sabbath age, when the Franciscan rule would bring about a time of renewal and apostolic living.[62] Another one of the investigators, Nicholas Alberti de Prato, commissioned a direct refutation of the *Lesson on the Apocalypse.* A fascinating—if prolix—document in its own right, this work provides a vivid example of how mainstream ecclesiastical authorities refuted forms of radical eschatology, including scenarios about the future conversion of the world's peoples.[63]

The author of this tract declared that Olivi's dangerous ideas were similar to those of the Eternal Gospel, condemned under Pope Alexander IV and burned in Paris. In particular, he denied that the carnal Latin Church would be superseded during the sixth and seventh ages, much like the Synagogue with the waning of the Old Testament. There would be no "emptying" of the New Testament, nor would the Latin Church be destroyed "temporally and eternally" as the Synagogue had been in the past.[64] The author also attacked Olivi's belief that the future would bring about the conversion of the world's peoples during the Sabbath age of spiritual perfection. Drawing upon the *Ordinary Gloss,* Augustine, and other patristic authorities, the author countered this radical scenario with a conservative vision of the end, including the conversion of the Gentiles before the coming of Antichrist, the conversion of the Jews with the arrival of Elijah and Enoch, and Final Judgment. For one thing, the author stressed, there simply was not enough time for all of these conversions to happen during the brief period of the Antichrist's persecution and the limited time afterwards. In fact, if the Gospel were to be preached to all the Gentiles before the coming of Antichrist (as Scripture said it would) but most of the faithful would lapse and become followers of Antichrist (again, as Scripture indicated), then there would need to be a *second* conversion of the Gentiles following the conversion of the Jews to fulfill Olivi's vision of a universal fold during the Sabbath age—something that was plainly impossible within the amount of time allowed and contrary to the authority of the Bible.[65]

Nor did the anonymous critic fail to pick up on Olivi's damning claim that the spiritual men, rejected by the "carnal Latin Church," would be received instead among schismatics, heretics, and unbelievers, such as "Greeks, Saracens, Tartars, and Jews." The so-called "spiritual men" from the Franciscan order were ill-suited to carry out the worldwide spread of the Gospel among the non-believers of the world. "It ought not to be believed," the author declared, "that this conversion to the true faith and catholic Church will come about more through such schismatics and infidels."[66] It was Elijah and Enoch, not heretical Franciscan preachers, who would preach against Antichrist and convert the Jews toward the end of time. Although the debate over poverty primarily fueled the condemnation of Olivi, his suspect predictions of eschatological conversion provided additional leverage against his vision of the future. Much like the opponents of the Eternal Gospel, those investigating Olivi preferred the safer, limited, and somewhat colorless apocalyptic scenario of traditional authorities to the wild imaginings of a world transformed beyond recognition.[67]

In 1319, and again after further scrutiny in 1325, the commission declared that Olivi's eschatology should be condemned, including his propositions about the "renovation of the evangelical life, the defeat of the anti-Christian sect, and the conversion of the Jews and Gentiles."[68] In particular, the commission noted two problems with his vision of that evangelical conversion. First, the Gospel made it clear that the pseudo-preachers of Antichrist, not any sort of spiritual men, would hold sway during the end-times. After all, the commission asked, who would be present to listen to the latter, since so many of the faithful would have turned away from the Church at that time, seduced or intimidated by Antichrist? Second, reiterating a point made by the lengthy condemnation of Olivi's *Lesson on the Apocalypse,* they asserted that the universal spread of the Gospel to the Gentiles would be carried out *before* Antichrist, followed by the conversion of the Jews and the end of history. Did Olivi mean that there would be two conversions of the world, before and after Antichrist? Would the "fullness of the Gentiles" enter the Church twice? Would the second conversion of the Gentiles occur after the conversion of the Jews (plainly impossible, since the world would end after the Jews converted)? The commission reasserted the traditional apocalyptic scenario—the Gospel would spread to all the Gentiles, the Jews would convert at the behest of Elijah and Enoch (not some group of supposedly spiritual men), and the world would end.[69]

In 1326, John XXII formally condemned Olivi's apocalyptic commentary. In some cases, the ripples of this conflict washed up on distant shores. In 1333 Dominican authorities in Tabriz accused seven local Franciscans of heresy because of their belief that the pope was Antichrist and his followers were damned. According to the report of their investigation, one of the Franciscans, George of Adria, openly preached to the Genoese merchants living in the community "many things about Gospel and about the Apocalypse, making mention of future events that would come before Judgment Day, and also things that pertained to Antichrist."[70] George not only preached against John XXII as Antichrist but also spoke about the "poverty of Christ and his apostles." Many of the merchants became outraged, although the Dominican author of the report, Raynier of Vercelli, had difficulty convincing one of them about the error of George's beliefs (but the merchant, Raynier noted, being a good man, ultimately rejected what he had heard from Friar George). Another one of the Franciscans, Hugolino of Gubbio, told Raynier that he believed Pope John was Antichrist because of his attack on the poverty of Christ. "Does this mean," Raynier asked him, "that all the cardinals, bishops, and religious men who reckon that he is pope are damned, and you all alone are saved?" "Well," Hugolino responded, implying the affirmative, "the cardinals are certainly aware that he is a heretic and do not dare to say anything against him, because they fear him."[71]

According to a number of surviving letters connected with the same circle of Spiritual Franciscans at Tabriz, many of their ideas about evangelical poverty, Antichrist, and the end of the world drew upon the writings of Peter John Olivi. Raynier of Florence, another one of the "Tabriz seven," possessed at least two of Olivi's works, his *Commentary on Matthew* and his *Lesson on the Apocalypse,* which he apparently shared with other friars in the region.[72] His fellow Franciscans, convinced that the "final days" were close at hand, looked to him and his companions for advice and information about the future. As one wrote to Raynier:

> According to Peter John, in this year the final conversion both of schismatics and also Saracens ought to begin through our brothers minor, and more so through the preachers that will emerge from among us. Yet, if Antichrist will hold sway over the world in those times, why is it that the Gentiles are converting now? Will they be entangled in their errors again for a brief time? I ask, therefore, that you write about these things insofar as you are able.[73]

Much like Peter Olivi's enemies, these friars saw problems with his timetable for the conversion of the world and wanted clarification.

In 1334, prosecutors presented evidence against George, Hugolino, Raynier of Florence, and the others before the papal curia at Avignon, although the death of John XXII later that same year stalled any definitive action against them. Yet again, the "timely" demise of a pope saved apocalyptic critics of the papacy from imprisonment or something worse. Nevertheless, the investigation against the friars at Tabriz provides another marker for the changing religious and political climate of the fourteenth century. For generations, reformers had pointed to the "hypocrites" in their midst as a threat to the true liberty and spiritual health of the Roman Church. For these Franciscans living on the front lines of missionary territory, wondering and hopeful about the eschatological expansion of their faith, the worst enemies of God were no longer the outside threat of Jews, pagans, or infidels—they were the false Christians of the Roman Church.[74]

Eschatology Incarcerated

One of the last important apocalyptic innovators of the Middle Ages, John of Rupescissa, was painfully aware of the consequences of radical speculation about the future of Christendom.[75] Ten years after he joined the Franciscans in 1332, John began to experience a series of visions about the spiritual meaning of the Bible. Educated in Toulouse, he became a suspect character, perhaps because of his involvement with local Beguines or his opinions about the role of poverty in the Franciscan order. For reasons that are not entirely clear, Franciscan authorities imprisoned John at Figeac in 1344. Tried for heresy at Toulouse in 1346 and again at Avignon in 1349, he escaped outright condemnation but remained incarcerated. Later he presented these misfortunes, including imprisonment, a broken leg, and a case of the plague, as evidence that he was a prophesied messenger, charged with warning contemporaries about imminent apocalyptic trials. John would remain a prisoner in and around Avignon until he died in 1365.[76]

Despite the fact that ecclesiastical authorities targeted John as a threatening voice, they remained equally interested in what he had to say as long as his predictions were safely contained. He produced all of his major works, except for his commentary on the *Angelic Oracle of Saint Cyril* and its Joachite gloss, during his imprisonment at Avignon, allowed if not encouraged to keep writing for decades to come.[77] In 1349, he wrote his *Book of Secret Events* as part of his trial defense at the papal curia.[78] In 1353 he composed his *Book Showing that the Times are Rushing to an End*, followed in 1356 by his immensely popular *Pocket-Guide for the Tribulation*, literally an apocalyptic "vade mecum."[79] Judging by the impressive number of references to various works and authors in his writings, including the "pope prophecies," the *Book of Fiore*, Peter John Olivi, Arnold of Villanova, Hildegard of Bingen, and many more, John even had access to books during his confinement.[80] His "success" as a prophet contributed to his fame and popularity, perhaps lending him credibility and keeping him alive. John had predicted war between France and England. In 1337, the Hundred Years' War broke out between France and England. John had predicted plague. In 1348, the Black Death began to ravish Europe, afflicting John himself in prison. In a sense, the friar was fortunate that the "calamitous" fourteenth century favored his dire predictions.[81]

Throughout his considerable body of works, John produced a highly complicated, widely ranging, and not always consistent vision of historical events, present-day occurrences, and future developments. He offered relentless criticism of avarice and corruption in the contemporary Western Church. His unprecedented predictions of social upheaval assumed a violently populist edge; John foresaw popular uprisings by the humble against the lordly, including the plunder of ecclesiastical property and riches, intended by God to humble the greedy and corrupt clergy.[82] This time of upset, he claimed, was imminent. Using calculations borrowed in part from Arnold of Villanova, John declared that the time of Antichrist would begin 1290 years after the sack of the Jewish Temple by the Romans, meaning that the apocalyptic tribulations would start in earnest around 1365. He believed that there would be two Antichrists: a tyrant in the East ruling over Asia, and a wicked Roman emperor in the West, the final Antichrist who would rule over Europe. John literally believed in the figure of "the millennium." After the defeat of the final Antichrist, he claimed that a thousand-year period of spiritual perfection and peace would begin on earth until the final persecution of the faithful under Gog and Magog. Part of that future age, he insisted, would involve the fulfillment of evangelical poverty within the Church, a "renewal" or "renovation" of apostolic living.[83]

In his commentary on the *Angelic Oracle of Saint Cyril*, John showed a particular fascination with the deteriorating power of the Byzantine Empire, as well as the failed efforts in the past to restore unity between the Greeks and the Roman Church.[84] In one noteworthy passage, he observed that he could not entirely agree with Joachim's interpretation that the "serpent reentering the cavern" symbolized the deceptive return of the "kingdom of the Greeks" to the "unity of the Church." John described how the Greek ruler had sent a Franciscan envoy named Garcia Arnaldi to Pope John XXII in 1334 to negotiate an ecclesiastical union. This situation led Pope John to send another friar, Girald Odonis, with a contingent of clerics to meet with the Greeks. John's death that same year, however, prevented any further moves in that direction. A second delegation had arrived from Greece to inquire about establishing unity under Pope Clement VI (r. 1342–1352), who intended to dispatch another group of friars to the Greek people. For reasons not explained, Clement recalled them shortly before they sailed.[85]

For John, these events seemed to confirm that the time for a union with the Greeks was not at hand. Instead, the Greek Church was being "given over to the Gentiles" for trampling, as predicted by Joachim of Fiore and Peter John Olivi. "If, therefore, the schismatics are given over to the Gentiles," John queried, "how can they 'renter the cavern'"? Even if the Greeks had managed to return to the Roman Church at that point, he added, it would have been under false pretenses. The kingdom of the Greeks, he declared, would instead be "handed over to the Turks, Saracens, and Tartars for punishment until Antichrist comes and dies; then, they will perfectly return to the faith and enclose themselves with the fold of Christ."[86] In his *Book Showing that the Times are Rushing to an End*, John pursued a similar logic, arguing that the eastern Antichrist and his preachers would persecute and gather followers from the various communities of heretical and schismatic Christians, including Indians, Alans, Nestorians, Armenians, Georgians, Greeks, and others, before they finally rejoined the harmony of the "general Roman Church."[87]

More vividly than his predecessors, John imagined the eschatological union of all peoples as part of his scenario for the Sabbath age. In his major works, the friar constantly elucidated this anticipated creation of a "single general fold" from "Jews, Saracens, Turks, Tartars, heretics, and schismatics."[88] In a shift away from earlier predictions of this process, he did not imagine this conversion to be entirely irenic. In his *Book of Secret Events,* John proposed that the Western imperial Antichrist, through an "incomprehensible" mystery, would actually do the Roman Church a great favor by destroying the power of the Saracens, Turks, Tartars, and others, subjecting them to his dominion.[89] This development would set the stage for their conversion, since when Antichrist's followers saw his defeat, they would turn to Christ as the victor in that eschatological struggle, much like the Jews in traditional apocalyptic scenarios. All of the false religious laws of the world, John proclaimed, would be gathered under a single head—a head that would be cut off with one stroke. At other times he referred to the destruction of the Saracens, as well as their conversion, seeming to imply they would be somehow defeated and their power broken before they converted to the Christian faith.[90]

The genuine hero of John's schemes, however, was an angelic pontiff, the "renovator of the world," who would emerge from among the Spiritual Franciscans during a time of schism within the papacy. In his *Book Showing that the Times are Rushing to an End,* John described this "religious man" as follows:

> . . . evangelical in profession, in life and habit a Friar Minor, a follower of the highest poverty, the reformer of the fallen world, the restorer of the Friars Minor who have lapsed from the highest perfection back to the path of their first most holy father, the illuminator of the blind world, the most powerful foe of Antichrist, the striker against the heretical Mammonists, the defender of the general Church, the consoler of the evangelical paupers, the converter of the blind Jews, the hammer of the Saracens, the restorer of schismatics, the expander of the general Church to the ends of the earth, the oppressor of tyrants, the peace of the world, the scourge of the wicked, and the performer of divine miracles.[91]

Under the auspices of this figure, John declared, "the four parts of the world, except the four corners where Gog and Magog lurk, will be converted to Christ and the overall 'single shepherd,' the Roman pontiff, will preside over all of Asia, Africa, and Europe . . . there will be 'one' in the world, that is 'one' most Christian 'fold' of Jews, Saracens, Turks, Tartars, heretics, and schismatics all converted to Jesus Christ."[92] Although the time of this Franciscan pope would be brief, perhaps as little as nine or ten years, it would set the stage for a thousand-year period of peace for all the converted peoples on earth.[93] As John put it: "The world will be converted and there will be 'one' catholic 'fold' of all nations, and the Roman pontiff, the general Vicar of Jesus Christ, the 'shepherd' of the Christian people, will reign over the entire world."[94]

It is easy to imagine how current popes measured up to this longed-for restorer of the world. Commenting on the collapse of a bridge at Avignon in 1346, John declared that this prophesied event symbolized the imminent troubles of the papal curia, including its persecution by the eastern and western Antichrists, and a schism between a "false pope" and the true pope, the Franciscan "renovator" of the world.[95] He also railed against the "Mammonists," members of the Franciscan order who rejected apostolic poverty and persecuted those who followed the mandates of evangelical living. At times the French friar explicitly tied the need for the renewal of evangelical poverty to the future conversion of the world. The restoration of apostolic living would make it possible for the "spiritual men" of his schemes to convert the infidels and other peoples.[96]

More vividly than anyone before him, John imagined a complete transformation of Christendom, effectively beyond recognition. Seizing upon a notion briefly raised by Peter John Olivi, he declared that "after Antichrist, Jerusalem will be made the see of the highest pontiff, so that the head of the world might be in that place, where the Christian faith began under Christ."[97] The center of the Christian world, transferred to Rome by Saint Peter, would be transferred once again back to Jerusalem, where it would remain for one thousand years. In other passages John declared that Jerusalem would also become the heart of a newly restored Roman Empire. Rather than pitting church and empire against each other, he allied the figure of the Last World Emperor (in this case a French ruler) with his angelic pope, creating a twin power to fight against the forces of evil in the end-times.[98] With an apocalyptic perspective reminiscent of Joachim and Olivi, John assigned a prominent role in his apocalypticism to the Jews—first as servants of Antichrist, but afterwards as agents of spiritual renewal following their conversion. In his commentary on the *Angelic Oracle of Saint Cyril,* he declared:

The seat of the general Church and Roman Empire will be transferred to Jerusalem. Rome will be given over to the desolation of the wasteland until the end of the world. The Jews will be made into the most holy and faithful Christians, and from among them, one will be elevated to the papacy, and one to govern the entire world.[99]

In this vision of Christendom, we find a converted Jew presiding over a flock of former pagans and infidels from his spiritual capital of Jerusalem after the destruction of the corrupt Western Church. No wonder ecclesiastical authorities remained fascinated by John's prophecies, allowed him to record them, and kept him safely locked in prison.

Much like his predictions of war and plague, John of Rupescissa's prophecies about a papal schism within the Roman Church proved remarkably prescient. Not long after the friar died, the so-called Great Schism (1378–1417) pitted two and eventually three rival claimants to the Apostolic See against each other. Monarchs across Europe lined up behind one side or the other, depending largely upon their political affiliations. Together with the Hundred Years' War, the Black Death, and the "Babylonian Captivity" at Avignon, the Great Schism left its pessimistic stamp on the religious and political landscape of the later Middle Ages, above all damaging the prestige and authority of the Roman Church. As they had for centuries, the purveyors of prophecy reacted to this divisive turn of events. Writing his *Little Book on the Knowledge of the World* in 1410, John, the Dominican bishop of Sulthanyek in Persia, described for his readers a number of predictions about the ultimate defeat of Islam by the "Franks."[100] According to John, the "Saracens" were well aware of these prophecies, but believed that the prevalence of sin among the Christians would postpone their divinely ordained victory. One Turkish leader, the Dominican prelate related, told his people that "since the Franks have two popes, I do not fear to make war against them; when there is one pope, however, it will behoove me to make peace with them."[101]

From this perspective, the dysfunctional papacy of the early fifteenth century formed an impediment to the prophesied triumph of Christianity. In the words of Norman Housely, medieval prophecy and politics formed part of a "dialectical process." When the papal monarchy lost its political currency, prophecies of world conversion began to move in new and different directions. Certainly, eschatological speculation about the future of the Roman Church did not end when John of Rupescissa died in 1365. An alternate and expanded version of the "pope prophecies," for example, enjoyed continued popularity in the late fourteenth and fifteenth centuries, especially around the time of the Council of Constance which resolved the Great Schism in 1417.[102] The stakes in such visions of the end, however, had changed considerably for members of the Roman Church. The dream of Christendom—meaning the "Gregorian" vision of churches, peoples, and kingdoms united under the sacerdotal authority of Rome— no longer held its electrifying charge, or at least, that current had begun to flow along other pathways.

In 1324, when the Italian political thinker Marsilius of Padua had methodically attacked the universal pretensions of the Roman papacy in his famous treatise on the prerogatives of secular governance, *The Defender of the Peace*, he specifically targeted its interpretation of John 10:16, Christ's promise that there would be "one fold, and one shepherd." Citing the authority of Pope Gregory I, Marsilius wrote: "Gregory did not say that it becomes one fold because all the faithful are subordinated to the Roman bishop, or to any other single individual except Christ." Jesus Christ, Marsilius declared, not the pope of Rome, was the true "head and foundation and prince of all shepherds."[103] In this famous work, Marsilius did not engage with apocalyptic speculations, but his words nevertheless held significance for prophecies of world order. Increasingly, the Christian inhabitants of Europe could imagine the expansion of their faith without the claims of the papal monarchy to universal dominion. At the close of the fifteenth century, when the Dominican prophet Savonarola predicted a coming age of spiritual renewal, he located the center of this new world order not in Rome or even in Jerusalem, but rather in the city-state of Florence, "decreed to receive the seed of this divine word in order to propagate it throughout the world."[104] One thing had not changed, however, from the earlier days of radical eschatology. In May 1498, when the Florentine civil and clerical elite tired of Savonarola and his unrealized prophecies, they hanged and burned him.

Epilogue

In 1539, on the feast of Corpus Christi, a group of Tlax-caltecas Indians in central Mexico performed an elaborate play with the oversight of the Franciscan missionaries living among them. The chronicler Torbio Motolinía transcribed a letter by one of those friars, who related how the natives decided to "stage the conquest of Jerusalem, a prediction which, we pray, God may fulfill in our day."[1] The participants erected a mock version of the holy city, with some of the natives inside playing the role of the Muslim sultan and his followers. Outside, the Tlaxcaltecas divided themselves into three armies: the first, representing the Spanish under Emperor Charles V (r. 1516–1556); the second, other European armies following the emperor's lead; and the third, a force of Tlaxcaltecas, likewise serving the Spanish ruler. The battle for Jerusalem was waged back and forth. When things looked grim, "Emperor Charles" sent a letter to his "Esteemed Father," the pope of Rome, who replied with prayers and words of encouragement. Angels and saints appeared, including the patron saint of New Spain, Hippolytus, who encouraged the faint-hearted Tlaxcaltecas warriors, new to the Christian faith but worthy of great deeds. Eventually, the "Moorish" sultan admitted defeat, proclaiming to Charles: "We have clearly seen how God had favored you and sent you help from heaven . . . I know that all the world must render obedience to God and to you who are His captain on earth."² Jerusalem was restored, and the defeated "Moors" were brought before the pope to be baptized. In reality, the letter states, these actors were "adult Indians, who had been designedly prepared for baptism," and they were "actually baptized."³

Sixteenth-century Franciscan friars baptizing Native Americans, who were pretending to be Muslims, after enacting the divinely ordained recovery of Jerusalem with the help of the newly converted peoples of New Spain—this episode reads like yet another iteration of the historical and eschatological imaginings examined throughout this book. Indeed, influenced in part by Joachim of Fiore, Franciscan missionaries in Mexico spun their own millennial dreams of a world transformed by the spread of the Gospel before the coming of the Apocalypse.⁴ Nor were those friars the first Europeans to view the spiritual conquest of the Americas in this prophetic light. Between his third and fourth voyages to the New World, none other than Christopher Columbus had spent time assembling his *Book of Prophecies.* As the dedicatory letter of the volume declared:

> This is the beginning of the book or collection of authorities, sayings, opinions, and prophecies concerning the need to recover the holy city and Mount Zion, and the discovery and conversion of the islands of the Indies and of all the peoples and nations, for Ferdinand and Isabella, our Spanish rulers.⁵

Among the "authorities" that Columbus cited were Augustine, Pseudo-Methodius, and Abbot Joachim of Fiore.⁶ Often envisioned as a "modern man" who turned his back on the narrow limits of the past, Columbus drew upon patristic and medieval sources to interpret his voyages as part of a divine mission to liberate Jerusalem and spread Christ's word around the world.

The belief that history was heading in the direction of Christianity's universal realization did not disappear with the waning of the medieval era. Many things had changed, however, with the closure of the Middle Ages and the beginning of the early modern era, the "discovery" of the Americas standing prominently among them. After a relative lull in their.

expansionary activities during the late fourteenth and early fifteenth centuries, Christian Europeans such as Columbus had begun to bring their faith to places that the wildest prophets of the preceding era could never have imagined. When members of the Roman Church encountered the indigenous inhabitants of places like the Canary Islands and the Americas, the papacy continued to project its notion of sacerdotal authority onto those newly discovered lands and peoples. More and more, however, those involved with acts of conquest and colonization could afford to disregard what the bishops of Rome had to say, unless it suited their purposes. When Columbus proclaimed that his overseas voyages marked the prophesied culmination of history in the conversion of unknown islands and peoples, he celebrated his position as a servant of the Spanish king and queen—not the pope of Rome.[7] Even during the "golden age" of papal supremacy from the eleventh to the fourteenth centuries, Rome had never possessed an exclusive monopoly on dreams of a unified Christian world. Empire, the papal monarchy's sometime partner and more often competitor, always remained as an uncomfortable presence with its counter-claims and universal aspirations. European theories of imperial power as a principle for Christian order acquired a new lease on life during the early modern age of overseas expansion in Africa, Asia, and the Americas. In the Corpus Christi play at Tlaxcallan, the pope played a notable role in the Christian victory and baptism of the Moors, but it was the character of Emperor Charles V—reprising the role of the Last World Emperor—who stood front and center in the eschatological drama.

As late as the seventeenth century, in his *Eleven Books on Antichrist,* the Jesuit thinker Thomas of Malvenda interpreted the spread of the Gospel among the American Indians as a sign of the world's approaching end.[8] Malvenda approached this task cautiously, well aware of those in the past who had overstepped their bounds by predicting a concrete date or scenario for the end, including Joachim of Fiore and Arnold of Villanova.[9] By Malvenda's day of the "Catholic Reformation," however, the anticipated historical figure of Antichrist was becoming more of an embarrassment for the Roman Church than anything else, a "medieval" superstition to be downplayed.[10] Later, in the eighteenth and nineteenth centuries, the eschatological drive to create "one fold" of the world's peoples before the consummation of history would effectively yield to the "civilizing mission" and other "enlightened" narratives of historical progress. The question is whether the religious impulse to unify the world entirely disappeared, or whether it somehow contributed to such secular ideologies. In his 1949 work on the relationship between Christian theology of history and modern philosophy of history, Karl Löwith wondered about precisely this sort of connection between apocalyptic eschatology and the Western impact on the globe:

> Is it perhaps Jewish Messianism and Christian eschatology, though in their secular transformations, that have developed those appalling energies of creative activity which changed the Christian Occident into a world-wide civilization? . . . Is it perhaps that the belief in being created in the image of a Creator-God, the hope in a future Kingdom of God, and the Christian command to spread the gospel to all the nations for the sake of salvation have turned into the secular presumption that we have to transform the world into a better world in the image of man and to save unregenerate nations by Westernization and re-education?[11]

The following year, Christopher Dawson offered a similar perspective, though with a much more sanguine appraisal of Christianity's role on the global stage. "Imperialistic aggression" and "economic exploitation," Dawson declared, were not sufficient to account for the Western conquest and transformation of the world in the modern era. Rather, there were "new spiritual forces driving Western man towards a new destiny."[12] For Dawson, the root of those forces lay with the Christian faith of antiquity and the medieval era. "Western culture," he writes,

> preserved a spiritual energy which was independent of political power or economic prosperity. Even in the darkest periods of the Middle Ages this dynamic principle continued to operate. For what distinguishes Western culture from the other world civilizations is its *missionary character*—its transmission from one people to another in a continuous series of spiritual movements.[13]

While their tone could not have been more different, both Löwith and Dawson recognized the unmistakable continuities that bridged the pre-modern and modern world view of the "Christian West," even if modern Westerners had largely secularized their narratives of global dominion.

Ironically, more than fifty years later, the religious framing of history and impulse to remake the world no longer seem content to rest beneath the surface of secular ideologies. Rather, we live at a time when secular and religious views of the future openly compete, overlap, and intertwine. "How Will the World Become One?" asks a recent issue of *Midnight Call*, an evangelical periodical that styles itself as the "international prophetic voice for the end times." In this case, the answer lies with democracy, which "has produced the greatest forms of peace and prosperity the world has ever known, and it will spread in a world-wide fashion under the Antichrist."[14] According to others, the same spread of liberal democracy and capitalism around the world holds the key to God's promise for the universal triumph of freedom. Nor do "Westerners" have a monopoly on such interpretations of history. Christian fundamentalists in the United States support the state of Israel as part of their apocalyptic scenario, still waiting for the "remnant" of the Jews to enter the Church after the Second Coming of Christ; their counterparts in the Islamic world denounce Israel and the United States as agents of evil, awaiting the arrival of the Madhī, the prophesied redeemer of the Shia tradition. Small but vocal minorities interpret war, pestilence, famine, and false prophets as signs of the end, when scores will be settled on a global scale. For the silent majority, universal peace and prosperity remain elusive, with or without the promise of eschatological justice.[15]

ABBREVIATIONS

NOTES

SELECT BIBLIOGRAPHY

ACKNOWLEDGMENTS

INDEX

Abbreviations

AM	*Annales minorum seu trium ordinum a S. Francisco institutorum.* Ed. Luke Wadding. 32 vols. Quarrachi, 1931–.
ASGL	*Acta et scripta quae de controversiis ecclesiae Graecae et Latinae saeculo undecimo composita extant.* Ed. Cornelius Will. Leipzig, 1861.
BF	*Bullarium Franciscanum Romanorum pontificum constitutiones, epistolas, ac diplomata continens.* Ed. J. H. Sbaralea. 8 vols. Rome, 1759.
BL	British Library, London.
BNF	Bibliothèque Nationale de France, Paris.
BBTSOF	*Biblioteca bio-bibliografica della Terra Santa e dell'oriente francescano.* Ed. Girolamo Golubovich. 5 vols. Quaracchi, 1906–1927.
CCCM	*Corpus Christianorum continuatio mediaevalis.* Turnhout, 1966–.
CCSL	*Corpus Christianorum series Latina.* Turnhout, 1953–.
CSEL	*Corpus scriptorum ecclesiasticorum Latinorum.* Vienna, 1866–.
EA	*The Encyclopedia of Apocalypticism: Apocalypticism in Western History and Culture.* 4 vols. Ed. Bernard McGinn. New York, 1998.
MANSI	*Sacrorum conciliorum nova et amplissima collectio.* Ed. J. D. Mansi. 31 vols. Paris, 1901–1927.
MEFRM	*Mélanges de l'École française de Rome: moyen age.*

MGH	*Monumenta Germaniae historica.* Hannover, 1826–.
Epp. Karol.	Epistolae Karolini Aevi
Epp. sel.	Epistolae selectae
Ldl	Libelli de lite imperatorem et pontificium seaculis XI et XIII conscripti
Fontes	Leges. Fontes iuris Germanici antique
QG	Quellen zur Geistesgeschichte des Mittelalters
SRG (in us. schol.)	Scriptores rerum Germanicarum (in usum scholarum)
SS	Scriptores
Staatsschriften	*Staatsschriften des späteren Mittelalters*
PL	*Patrologia cursus completes, series Latina.* Ed. J. P. Migne. 221 vols. Paris, 1841–1864.
RHC Occ	*Recueil des historiens des croisades, historiens occidentaux.* 5 vols. Paris, 1844–1895.
RS	*Rerum Britannicarum medii aevi scriptores.* London, 1858–1896.
RTAM	*Recherches de théologie ancienne et médiévale.*
SC	*Sources chrétiennes.* Paris, 1913–.

Notes

Introduction

1. Mt. 24:4–51, Mk. 13:5–37, and Lk. 21:6–36.

2. As noted by Bernard McGinn, "The Apocalyptic Imagination in the Middle Ages," in *Ende und Vollendung: Eschatologische Perspektiven im Mittelalter,* ed. Jan Aertsen and Martin Pickavé (Berlin, 2002), 79–94: "Apocalypticism has always been characterized by an intricate mixture of optimism and pessimism" (quotation from p. 84). Throughout this book, I follow scholars who distinguish between general *eschatology* (including any set of beliefs about the end of time, including the fate of the individual soul) and *apocalyptic eschatology* or *apocalypticism* (the belief that the end of history is imminent and will involve a series of crises, followed by the defeat of evil and the triumph of the elect). *Millenarianism* is a specific form of apocalyptic eschatology that anticipates a miraculous "thousand-year" reign of Christ on earth (based on Rev. 20:2), which will completely transform terrestrial institutions and bring collective salvation. *Prophecy* is a generic term, referring to any sort of divine revelation about the future, though commonly involving a reinterpretation of the past and present. See the introduction to Bernard McGinn, *Visions of the End: Apocalyptic Traditions in the Middle Ages* (1979; New York, 1998), 1–36; and Richard Landes, "Lest the Millennium Be Fulfilled: Apocalyptic Expectations and the Pattern of Western Chronography 100–

800," in *The Use and Abuse of Eschatology in the Middle Ages,* ed. Werner Verbeke, Daniel Verhelst, and Andries Welkenhuysen (Leuven, 1988), 137–211, especially pp. 205–208. On the development of the Antichrist tradition, see Bernard McGinn, *Antichrist: Two Thousand Years of the Human Fascination with Evil* (New York, 2000); and Kevin Hughes, *Constructing Antichrist: Paul, Biblical Commentary, and the Development of Doctrine in the Early Middle Ages* (Washington, 2005).

3. Jn. 10:16.

4. John Van Engen, "Faith as a Concept of Order," in *Belief in History: Innovative Approaches to European and American Religion,* ed. Thomas Kselman (Notre Dame, 1991), 19–67, quotation from p. 20. See also John Van Engen, "The Christian Middle Ages as an Historiographical Problem," *American Historical Review* 91 (1986): 519–552; and the introduction to *The Origins of Christendom in the West,* ed. Alan Kreider (Edinburgh, 2001), vii. On the Latin term for Christendom *(Christianitas),* see Jean Rupp, *L'idée de chrétienté dans la pensée pontificale des origins à Innocent III* (Paris, 1939), who points out that there are a number of "equivalent" Latin terms to *Christianitas* with the same fundamental meaning as the English word "Christendom," including "Christian people" *(Christiani, Christianorum gens, Christianus populus),* "Christian republic" *(Christiana republica),* and "Christian world" *(Christianus orbis).*

5. Bronisław Geremek, *The Common Roots of Europe,* trans. Jan Aleksandrowicz et al. (Cambridge, Mass., 1996), 70–131; Michael Mitterauer, *Warum Europa? Mittelalterliche Grundlagen eines Sonderwegs* (Munich, 2003), 152–198; Christopher Dawson, *Medieval Essays* (1954; Washington, D.C., 2002), 49–66; and Collin Morris, *The Papal Monarchy: The Western Church from 1050–1250* (Oxford, 1989), 2.

6. See Christopher Dawson, *The Making of Europe: An Introduction to the History of European Unity* (1932; New York, 1952), 188–282; Christopher Dawson, *The Formation of Christendom* (New York, 1967), 214–228; Denys Hay, *Europe: The Emergence of an Idea* (Edinburgh, 1957), 16–36; Timothy Reuter, "Medieval Ideas of Europe and Their Modern Historians," *History Workshop* 33 (1992): 176–180; Richard Balzaretti, "The Creation of Europe," *History Workshop* 33 (1992): 181–196; Karl Leyser, *Communications and Power in Medieval Europe,* ed. Timothy Reuter (London, 1994), 1–18; Heikki Mikkeli, *Europe as an Idea and an Identity* (New York, 1998); Anthony Pagden, "Europe: Conceptualizing a Continent," in *The Idea of Europe,* ed. Anthony Pagden (Cambridge, 2002), 33–54; William Chester Jordan, "'Europe' in the Middle Ages," in *The Idea of Europe,* 72–90; and Mary Anne Perkins, *Christendom and European Identity: The Legacy of a Grand Narrative since 1789,* Religion and Society 40 (Berlin, 2004).

7. The work of James Muldoon, exploring the importance of canon law for papal claims of authority over pagans and infidels, offers an important exception in this

regard. See James Muldoon, *Popes, Lawyers, and Infidels: The Church and the Non-Christian World, 1250–1550* (Philadelphia, 1979), and his essays collected in James Muldoon, *Canon Law, the Expansion of Europe, and World Order* (Aldershot, U.K., 1998).

8. Ernst Kantorowicz, "The Problem of Medieval World Unity," *Annual Report of the American Historical Association for 1942* 3 (1944): 31–37, quotation from p. 33. See also Bernard McGinn, "The End of the World and the Beginning of Christendom," in *Apocalypse Theory and the Ends of the World*, ed. Marcus Bull (Oxford, 1995), 58–89.

9. See Richard K. Emmerson and Ronald B. Herzman, *The Apocalyptic Imagination in Medieval Literature* (Philadelphia, 1992), 101: "To make a historical statement is to make an eschatological one, because historical events and patterns in the Middle Ages are always understood with the larger philosophy of Christian history that sees history as essentially teleological, to be judged by its ending, from the perspective of eschatology."

10. See my article "From Adam to the Apocalypse: Post-Classical Christianity and the Patterns of World History," *World History Association Bulletin* 23 (2007): 21–26.

11. Benedict Anderson, *Imagined Communities: Reflections on the Origin and Spread of Nationalism* (1983; London, 1991), 12–17, describes Christendom as a "religious community" that preceded the formation of modern nation-states. Anderson views the imagining of the nation as a modern phenomenon and declares that the "grandeur and power of the great religiously imagined communities, their *unselfconscious coherence* waned steadily after the late Middle Ages" (ibid., 16; emphasis in the original). Scholars have criticized Anderson for this presentation of Christendom in the Middle Ages as a monolithic entity with a static and unreflexive sense of history. See Kathleen Davis, "National Writing in the Ninth Century: A Reminder for Postcolonial Thinking about the Nation," *Journal of Medieval and Early Modern Studies* 28 (1998): 611–637, who argues that this vision of an undifferentiated Middle Ages reinforces the very notion of modernity that postcolonial theorists try to destabilize. See also the essays collected in *The Uses of the Past in the Early Middle Ages*, ed. Yitzhak Hen and Matthew Innes (Cambridge, 2000); and Jeffrey Jerome Cohen's introduction to *The Postcolonial Middle Ages*, ed. Jeffrey Jerome Cohen (New York, 2000), 1–17.

12. See Norman Housely, "The Eschatological Imperative: Messianism and Holy War in Europe, 1260–1556," in *Toward the Millennium: Messianic Expectations from the Bible to Waco*, ed. Peter Schäfer and Mark Cohen, Studies in the History of Religion 77 (Leiden, 1998), 123–150, quotation from p. 135; and Robert Lerner, "Medieval Prophecy and Politics," *Annali dell'Istituto storico italo-germanico in Trento* 15 (1999): 417–432.

13. See Robert Bartlett, *The Making of Europe: Conquest, Colonization, and Cultural Change, 950–1350* (Princeton, 1993); J. R. S. Philips, *The Medieval Expansion of Europe*, 2nd ed. (1988; Oxford, 1998); and John France, *The Crusades and the Expansion of Catholic Christendom 1000–1714* (London, 2005).

14. On the importance of "Others" for the formation of normative Christian identity in the Middle Ages, see Paul Freedman and Gabrielle Spiegel, "Medievalism Old and New: The Rediscovery of Alterity in North American Medieval Studies," *American Historical Review* 103 (1998): 677–704. Much of the work in this field responds to R. I. Moore, *Formation of a Persecuting Society: Power and Deviance in Western Europe, 950–1250* (Oxford, 1987), who argues that the eleventh through thirteenth centuries saw the development of a Christian clerical elite that secured its power through the labeling and oppression of marginal groups. He revisits this argument in R. I. Moore, *The First European Revolution* (Oxford, 2001). While acknowledging their debts to Moore, many scholars have questioned the totalizing nature of his thesis, including its tendency to overemphasize the homogeneity of the "oppressors" and to flatten out differences between "marginal groups." See the essays in *Christendom and Its Discontents: Exclusion, Persecution, and Rebellion: 1000–1500*, ed. Scott Waugh and Peter Diehl (Cambridge, 1996); the essays in John Laursen and Cary Nederman, eds., *Beyond the Persecuting Society: Religious Toleration before the Enlightenment* (Philadelphia, 1998); and Dominique Iogna-Prat, *Order and Exclusion: Cluny and Christendom Face Heresy, Judaism, and Islam (1000–1150)*, trans. Graham Robert Edwards (Ithaca, 2002). For a response to his critics, see the expanded edition of R. I. Moore, *Formation of a Persecuting Society: Power and Deviance in Western Europe, 950–1250*, 2nd ed. (Malden, Mass., 2007), 172–196.

15. Norman Cohn, *The Pursuit of the Millennium: Revolutionary Millenarians and Mystical Anarchists of the Middle Ages*, rev. ed. (1957; London, 1970). Cohn has been criticized on a number of points, including his tendency to overestimate the violent implications of apocalypticism and underestimate its conservative potential to reinforce institutions and sources of authority. For some contrasting views, see Bernard Töpfer, *Das kommende Reich des Friedens: zur Entwicklung chiliastischer Zukunftshoffungen im Hochmittelalter*, Forschungen zur Mittelalterlichen Geschichte 11 (Berlin, 1964); Robert Lerner, "Medieval Millenarianism and Violence," in *Pace e guerra nel basso medioevo: atti del XL convegno storico internazionale, Todi, 12–14 Ottobre 2003* (Spoleto, 2004), 37–52; Bernard McGinn, "Apocalypticism and Church Reform: 1100–1500," EA, 2: 74–109; and the conclusion by André Vauchez, *L'attente des temps nouveaux: eschatologie, millénarisme, et visions du future du Moyen Âge au XXe siècle* (Turnhout, 2000), 143–150.

16. On the importance of empire as a principle spanning both the medieval and

modern eras, see Anthony Pagden, *Lords of All the World: Ideologies of Empire in Spain, Britain, and France c. 1500–c. 1800* (New Haven, 1995); and James Muldoon, *Empire and Order: The Concept of Empire, 800–1800* (Houndmills, U.K., 1999).

1. Christendom and the Origins of Papal Monarchy

1. *Gerberti acta concilii Remensis,* ed. Georg Waitz, MGH SS 3 (Hannover, 1839), 658–686. Arnulf was the son of the former Carolingian ruler, Lothair IV (r. 954–986).
2. Ibid., 672–673 (compare with Dan. 9:27, Matt. 24:15, and 2 Thess. 2:4).
3. Ibid., 676. See Claude Carozzi, "Gerbert et le concile de St-Basle," in *Gerberto: scienza, storia e mito: atti del Gerberti symposium, Bobbio 25–27 luglio 1983* (Piacenza, 1985), 661–676.
4. *Leonis abbatis et legati ad Hugonem et Robertum epistola,* ed. Georg Waitz, MGH SS 3, 686–890. In 995, after further deliberations, Arnulf was reinstated and Gerbert removed from episcopal office until his election as the archbishop of Ravenna in 998.
5. There has been considerable debate over the precise intentions of Otto III and his "restoration ideology." See Carl Erdmann, "Das Ottonische Reich als Imperium Romanum," in *Ottonische Studien,* ed. Helmut Beumann (Darmstadt, 1968), 174–203, especially pp. 188–195 (published originally in *Deutsches Archiv für Erforschung der Mittelalters* 6 [1943]: 412–441); Percy Schramm, *Kaiser, Rom, und Renovatio,* 2 vols. (Berlin, 1929), especially 1: 87–187; Knut Görich, *Otto III: Romanus, Saxonicus, et Italicus,* Historisches Forschungen 18 (Sigmarigen, 1993), 187–209; and Gerd Althoff, *Otto III,* trans. Phyllis Jestice (Philadephia, 2003).
6. See Benjamin Arnold, "Eschatological Imagination and the Program of Roman Imperial and Ecclesiastical Renewal at the End of the Tenth Century," in *The Apocalyptic Year 1000,* ed. Richard Landes, Andrew Gow, and David van Meter (Oxford, 2003), 271–287. On apocalyptic eschatology and the year 1000, see Johannes Fried, "Awaiting the End of Time Around the Year 1000," in *The Apocalyptic Year 1000,* 17–63, published originally with footnotes as "Endzeiterwartung um die Jahrtausendwende," *Deutsches Archiv für Erforschung der Mittelalters* 45 (1989): 385–473.
7. Gregory VII to Hermann of Metz, 15 March 1081, *Das Register des Gregors VII,* ed. Erich Caspar, MGH Epp. sel. 2 (Berlin, 1955), 553 (hereafter Reg.). See H. E. J. Cowdrey, *Gregory VII, 1073–1085* (Oxford, 1998), especially pp. 495–583.
8. Gregory VII to all the faithful, 16 December 1074, Reg. 2:37, 172–173.
9. See H. E. J. Cowdrey, "Pope Gregory's 'Crusading' Plans of 1074," in *Outremer: Studies in the History of the Crusading Kingdom of Jerusalem Presented to Joshua Prawer,* ed. Benjamin Kedar et al. (Jerusalem, 1982), 27–40; and Cowdrey, "The

Gregorian Papacy, Byzantium and the First Crusade," *Byzantinische Forschungen* 13 (1988): 145–169.

10. On ideas of reform, see Giles Constable, "Renewal and Reform in Religious Life: Concepts and Realities," in *Renaissance and Renewal in the Twelfth Century,* ed. Robert Benson and Giles Constable (Cambridge, Mass., 1982), 37–67; and Gerhart Ladner, "Reform: Innovation and Tradition in Medieval Christendom," in *Images and Ideas in the Middle Ages: Selected Studies in History and Art,* 2 vols. (Rome, 1983), 2: 533–558.

11. On the eleventh-century reform in particular, see Augustin Fliche, *La réforme Grégorienne,* 3 vols. (Paris, 1924); Gerd Tellenbach, *Libertas: Kirche und Weltordnung im Zeitalter des Investiturstreites* (Leipzig, 1936), partial English translation, *Church, State, and Christian Society at the Time of the Investiture Contest,* trans. R. F. Bennett (1948; Toronto, 1991); Walter Ullmann, *The Growth of Papal Government in the Middle Ages: A Study in the Ideological Relation of Clerical to Lay Power* (1955; London, 1965), especially pp. 262–309; Ian Robinson, *Authority and Resistance in the Investiture Contest* (Manchester, U.K., 1978); Colin Morris, *The Papal Monarchy: The Western Church from 1050–1250* (Oxford, 1989), especially pp. 28–33, 79–108; U.-R. Blumenthal, *The Investiture Controversy: Church and Monarchy from the Ninth to the Twelfth Century,* 2nd ed. (Philadelphia, 1992); Gerd Tellenbach, *The Church in Western Europe from the Tenth to the Early Twelfth Century,* trans. Timothy Reuter (Cambridge, 1993); and Kathleen Cushing, *Reform and the Papacy in the Eleventh Century: Spirituality and Social Change* (Manchester, U.K., 2005).

12. Adso of Montier-en-Der, *De ortu et tempore antichristi,* ed. Daniel Verhelst, CCCM 45 (Turnholt, 1976), 26. See Richard K. Emmerson, "Antichrist as Anti-Saint: The Significance of Abbot Adso's *Libellus de Antichristo,*" *American Benedictine Review* 30 (1979): 175–190, and Daniel Verhelst, "Adso of Montier-en-Der and the Fear of the Year 1000," in *The Apocalyptic Year 1000,* 81–92.

13. Adso, *De ortu et tempore antichristi,* 25–29. In the Latin exegetical tradition, elements of this scenario can be traced back to the first extant commentary on the Book of Revelation (ca. 260) by Victorinus of Pettau, *Sur l'Apocalypse suivi du fragment chronologique et de la construction du monde,* ed. Martine Dulaey, SC 423 (Paris, 1997). See also the eighth-century work of Bede, *De temporum ratione liber,* in *Opera: opera didascalia,* ed. C. W. Jones, CCSL 123B, 6/2 (Turnhout, 1977), 538–539.

14. Typically, this period of rest was "forty-five days," based on the difference between the numbers 1290 and 1335 found in the Book of Daniel (Dan. 12:11–12). See Robert Lerner, "Refreshment of the Saints: The Time after Antichrist as a Station for Earthly Progress in Medieval Thought," *Traditio* 32 (1976): 97–144.

15. Adso, *De ortu et tempore antichristi,* 26.

16. Ibid., 26. On the tradition of the Last World Emperor, see Hannes Möhring, *Der*

Weltkaiser der Endzeit: Entstehung, Wandel und Wirkung einer tausendjährigen Weissagung (Stuttgart, 2000).

17. See the third-century commentary on the Book of Daniel by Hippolytus, *Commentaire sur Daniel*, ed. Maurice Lefèvre, SC 14 (Paris, 1947), 171–174.

18. In fact, Christian thinkers such as Origen and Tertullian had expressed similar (if more reserved) sentiments about Roman imperial power even before Constantine's conversion. See Wolfram Kinzig, "The Idea of Progress in the Early Church until the Age of Constantine," *Studia Patristica* 24 (1993): 119–134; Martin Haeusler, *Das Ende der Geschichte in der mittelalterlichen Weltchronistik*, Beihefte zum Archiv für Kulturgeschichte 13 (Cologne, 1980), 6–32; and Michael Allen, "Universal History 300–1000: Origins and Western Developments," in *Historiography in the Middle Ages*, ed. Deborah Mauskopf Deliyannis, Orbis mediaevalis 1 (Leiden, 2003), 17–42.

19. See Robert Markus, *Saeculum: History and Society in the Theology of St. Augustine* (Cambridge, 1989); and Alfred Schindler, "Augustine and the History of the Roman Empire," *Studia Patristica* 22 (1989): 326–336.

20. For Augustine's famous denunciation of millenarianism in *The City of God*, see *Sancti Aurelii Augustini de civitate dei*, CCSL 48, 14/2 (Turnhout, 1955), 708–712; on the coming of Antichrist, ibid., 730–733. See also Paula Fredriksen, "Tyconius and Augustine on the Apocalypse," in *The Apocalypse in the Middle Ages*, ed. Richard K. Emmerson and Bernard McGinn (Ithaca, 1992), 20–37.

21. See Augustine's famous letter (ca. 418) to Hesychius, bishop of Salona, no. 199, ed. Alois Goldbacher, CSEL 57/4 (1911; London, 1961), 285–289, along with Jacques Chocheyras, "Fin des terres et fin des temps d'Hésychius (Ve siècle) à Béatus (VIIIe siècle)," in *The Use and Abuse of Eschatology in the Middle Ages*, ed. Werner Verbeke, Daniel Verhelst, and Andries Welkenhuysen (Leuven, 1988), 72–81.

22. Prosper of Aquitaine, *De vocatione omnium gentium*, PL 51, 704.

23. Ibid., 664.

24. Jerome, *Commentariorum in Danielem libri III<IV>*, ed. Francis Glorie, CCSL 75A (Turnhout, 1964), 793–795.

25. Jerome, *Commentaire sur S. Matthieu*, ed. and trans. Émile Bonnard, SC 259 (Paris, 1979), 190–191.

26. Critical edition of the Greek and Latin versions in *Die Apokalypse des Pseudo-Methodius: die ältesten griechischen und lateinischen Übersetzungen*, ed. J. A. Aerts and G. A. A. Kortekaas, 2 vols., Corpus Scriptorum Christianorum Orientalium 569–570 (Subsidia 97–98) (Leuven, 1998). On the Pseudo-Methodius, see Paul Alexander, *The Byzantine Apocalyptic Tradition* (Berkeley, 1985), 13–51; and David Olster, "Byzantine Apocalypses," EA, 2: 48–73.

27. *Die Apokalypse des Pseudo-Methodius*, 1: 177–189.

28. On the role of Islam in early Christian apocalypticism, see John V. Tolan, *Saracens: Islam in the Medieval European Imagination* (New York, 2002), 3–20; and Jean Flori, *L'islam et la fin des temps: l'interprétation prophétique des invasions musulmanes dans la chrétienté médiévale* (Paris, 2007), 111–147.

29. Ibid., 133–141, 182–187; see also Hannes Möhring, "Karl der Grosse und die Endkaiser-Weissagung: Der Sieger über Islam Kommt aus dem Westen," in *Montjoie: Studies in Crusade History in Honour of Hans Eberhard Mayer,* ed. Benjamin Kedar, Jonathan Riley-Smith, and Rudolf Hiestand (Aldershot, U.K., 1997), 1–19. On the "translation of empire," see Werner Goez, *Translatio Imperii: ein Betrag zur Geschichte des Geschichtsdenkens und der politischen Theorien im Mittelalter und in der frühen Neuzeit* (Tubingen, 1958).

30. Charlemagne to Pope Leo III, no. 93, ed. Ernst Dümmler, MGH Epp. Karol. 2 (Berlin, 1895), 137–138.

31. See the letters of Alcuin of York, nos. 41, 100, and 136, MGH Epp. Karol. 2, 84–85, 156–159, 205–210. See also Mary Garrison, "The Franks as the New Israel? Education for an Identity from Pippin to Charlemagne," in *The Uses of the Past in the Early Middle Ages,* ed. Yitzhak Hen and Matthew Innes (Cambridge, 2000), 114–161. On Carolingian apocalyptic exegesis, see E. Ann Matter, "Exegesis of the Apocalypse in the Early Middle Ages," in *The Year 1000: Religious and Social Response to the Turning of the First Millennium,* ed. Michael Frassetto (New York, 2002), 29–40.

32. Charlemagne to Byzantine Emperor Michael I, no. 37, MGH Epp. Karol. 2, 555–556.

33. E.g., the *Annales regni Francorum,* ed. G. H. Pertz, MGH SRG (in us. schol.) 6 (Hannover, 1985), 112; *Chronicon Moissiacense,* ed. G. H. Pertz, MGH SS 1 (Hannover, 1896), 305; and Anskarius, *Vita sancti Willehadi,* ed. G. H. Pertz, MGH SS 2 (Hannover, 1829), 38.

34. Anastasius Bibliothecarius, no. 5, *Epistolae sive praefationes,* ed. Ernst Perels and Gerhard Laehr, MGH Epp. Karol. 5 (Berlin, 1928), 411–412.

35. Louis II, *Epistola ad Basilium I. imperatorem Constantinopolitanum missa,* ed. Walter Henze, MGH Epp. Karol. 5, 385–394.

36. Liudprand of Cremona, *Relatio de legatione Constantinopolitana,* ed. Paolo Chiesa, CCCM 156 (Turnholt, 1998), 204–205. On the "Visions of Daniel," see Alexander, *Byzantine Apocalyptic Tradition,* 96–122.

37. *Das Constitutum Constantini (Konstantinische Schenkung) Text,* ed. Horst Furhmann, MGH Fontes 10 (Hannover, 1968). See also the *Decretales Pseudo-Isidorianae et capitula Angilramni,* ed. Paul Hinschius (1863; Leipzig, 1963), 249–254, and the analysis of Horst Fuhrmann, "Konstantinische Schenkung und abendländisches Kaisertum," *Deutsches Archiv für Erforschung des Mittelalters* 22 (1966): 63–178.

38. *Constitutum Constantini*, 94–95.

39. Liudprand of Cremona, *Relatio*, 194–195. On Otto III and the *Donation of Constantine*, see Kurt Zeillinger, "Otto III. und die Konstantinische Schenkung: Ein Beitrag zur Interpretation des Diploms Kaiser Otto III. für Papst Silvester II (DO III.389)," in *Fälschungen im Mittelalter: Gefälschte Rechtstexte: der bestrafte Fälscher*, MGH Schriften 33/2 (Hannover, 1988), 509–536.

40. Sylvester II to King Stephen of Hungary, 27 March 1000, no. 382, *Papsturkunden 896–1046*, ed. Harald Zimmermann, Österreichische Akademie der Wissenschaften: philosophische-historische Klasse 117/2 (Vienna, 1985), 737–740. On Sylvester's attitude toward the empire's eastern frontier, see Aleksander Gieysztor, "Sylvestre et les églises de Pologne et Hongrie," in *Gerberto: scienza, storia e mito*, 733–746.

41. Sylvester II, *Papsturkunden 896–1046*, 739.

42. Pierre Riché, *Gerbert d'Aurillac: le pape de l'an mil* (Paris, 1987).

43. For a discussion of this problem, see Richard Landes, "The Fear of an Apocalyptic Year 1000: Augustinian Historiography, Medieval and Modern," *Speculum 75* (2000): 97–145; and Edward Peters, "Mutations, Adjustments, Terrors, Historians, and the Year 1000," in *The Year 1000*, 9–28. There remain "hyper-skeptics" about the apocalyptic year 1000. See Sylvain Gouguenheim, *Les fausses terreurs de l'an mil: attente de la fin des temps ou approfondissement de la foi?* (Paris, 1999).

44. R. B. C. Huygens, "Un témoin de la crainte de l'an 1000: la lettre sur les Hongrois," *Latomus 15* (1956): 225–239, includes (pp. 229–235) the text of a letter on the Hungarian invasions commonly attributed to Remi of Auxerre (Huygens argues against his authorship). Responding to an earlier inquiry on the subject, the author of this letter (in good Augustinian fashion) tries to refute the apparently widespread notion that the Hungarians were Gog and Magog of biblical infamy.

45. Rodulfus Glaber, *Historiarum libri quinque (The Five Books of the Histories)*, ed. and trans. John France (Oxford, 1989), 38; see also Glaber, *Histories*, 97. There is a considerable bibliography on Rodulfus Glaber and his chronicle. In particular, see the observations of John France, "War and Christendom in the Thought of Rodulfus Glaber," *Studia Monastica 30* (1988): 105–109.

46. Glaber, *Histories*, trans. France, 93. For examples of the various portents listed above, see ibid., 81–83, 89, 185–189, 191–193, 211. Glaber's contemporary, Ademar of Chabannes, provides another important source of testimony to the "apocalyptic" moods around the year 1000. See Richard Landes, *Relics, Apocalypse, and the Deceits of History: Ademar of Chabannes, 989–1034* (Cambridge, Mass., 1995); and Michael Frassetto, "Heretics, Antichrists, and the Year 1000: Apocalyptic Expectations in the Writings of Ademar of Chabannes," in *The Year 1000*, 73–84.

47. Glaber, *Histories,* trans. France, 205.

48. Ibid., 117.

49. Ibid., 43.

50. Ibid., 173–177. Since at least the fourth century, popes and patriarchs had periodi-
cally traded barbs over the question of their relative status in the "pentarchy"
(the five major sees of the ancient Church: Rome, Constantinople, Alexandria,
Antioch, and Jerusalem). At the First Council of Constantinople (381), the patriarchs of the "New Rome" on the Bosporus had claimed second place for themselves and asserted their own ecclesiastical prerogatives as the patriarchs of the
current imperial capital. The Roman Church refused to recognize this "innovation." See Francis Dvornik, *Byzantium and the Roman Primacy* (New York, 1964);
John Meyendorff, "Rome and Constantinople," in *Rome, Constantinople, Moscow:
Historical and Theological Studies* (Crestwood, N.Y., 1996), 7–26; and Judith Herrin, "The Pentarchy: Theory and Reality in the Ninth Century," in *Cristianità
d'occidente e Cristianità d'oriente (secoli VI–XI),* Settimane di studio della fondazi-
one centro italiano di studi sull'alto medioevo 51 (Spoleto, 2004), 591–626.

51. Glaber, *Histories,* trans. France, 175.

52. Ibid., 251–253.

53. At the Synod of Sutri (1046), Henry III deposed Gregory VI and a number of
other papal claimants, electing Clement II, who is sometimes seen as the first (if
modest) papal reformer. See Cushing, *Reform and the Papacy,* 63–64.

54. The links between the earlier stages of monastic reform and the later papal reform have been a subject of considerable debate. See H. E. J. Cowdrey, *The Cluniacs and the Gregorian Reform* (Oxford, 1970), xiii–xxvii.

55. See the contemporary life of Leo IX, *La vie du Pape Léon IX (Brunon, évêque de
Toul),* ed. Michel Parisse, trans. Monique Goulet (Paris, 1997), 88–91; and Cushing, *Reform and the Papacy,* 49, 125–128.

56. *Epistola Leonis Achridiani ad Ioannem Tranensem ab Humberto in Latinum sermonem
translata,* ASGL, 61–64. See my observations on the azymes controversy in Brett
Whalen, "Rethinking the Schism of 1054: Heresy, Authority, and the Latin Rite,"
Traditio 62 (2007): 1–24, along with M. H. Smith III, *And Taking Bread: Cerularius
and the Azymes Controversy of 1054* (Paris, 1978); John Erickson, "Leavened and
Unleavened: Some Theological Implications of the Schism of 1054," *Saint Vladi-
mir's Theological Quarterly* 14 (1970): 155–176; Tia Kolbaba, *The Byzantine Lists:
Errors of the Latins* (Chicago, 2000); and Tia Kolbaba, "Byzantine Perceptions of
Latin Religious 'Errors': Themes and Changes from 850 to 1300," in *The Crusades
from the Perspective of Byzantium and the Muslim World,* ed. Angeliki Laiou and Roy
Parviz Mottahedeh (Washington, D.C., 2001), 117–143.

57. Both the polemical letter and the closure of churches were apparently fueled by

the forced "Latinization" of Greek religious houses in southern Italy by the Normans. See Richard Mayne, "East and West in 1054," *Cambridge Historical Journal* 11 (1954): 133–148.

58. ASGL, 150–154.

59. See Louis Bréhier, *Le schisme oriental du XIe siècle* (New York, 1899); Walter Norden, *Das Papsttum und Byzanz: Die Trennung der beiden Mächte und das Problem ihrer Wiedervereinigung* (New York, 1903); George Every, *The Byzantine Patriarchate, 451–1204* (1947; London, 1962); Steven Runciman, *The Eastern Schism: A Study of the Papacy and the Eastern Churches during the XI and XII Centuries* (Oxford, 1955), who borrowed generously from Every's earlier work; and Axel Bayer, *Spaltung der Christenheit: Das sogennante Morgenländische Schisma von 1054* (Cologne, 2002). At this point, there is a general consensus among scholars that a state of political, religious, and cultural "estrangement" developed between Latins and Greeks over the long term, meaning that the schism cannot be dated to a single event or cause. See Yves Congar, *After Nine Hundred Years: The Background of the Schism between the Eastern and Western Churches,* trans. Paul Mailleux (1954; New York, 1959); Timothy Ware, *The Orthodox Church,* 2nd ed. (1963; London, 1997), 43–72; Paul Lemerle, "L'orthodoxie byzantine et l'oecuménisme médiéval: les origines du 'schisme' des églises," *Bulletin de l'association Guillaume Budé* 2 (1965): 228–246; and Henry Chadwick, *East and West: The Making of a Rift in the Church from Apostolic Times until the Council of Florence* (Oxford, 2003).

60. Historians have not always appreciated the real importance of the "schism" for the general development of the reform movement. For example, Cushing, *Reform and the Papacy,* makes no mention of the events in 1054; Blumenthal, *Investiture Controversy,* 81, covers them in a paragraph; and Tellenbach, *Church, State, and Christian Society,* 140, makes only the curious statement that the "historic conflict with Byzantium" (presumably a reference to 1054) actually "weakened" the position of the papal reforms.

61. Leo IX to Michael, patriarch of Constantinople, September 1053, ASGL, 83. Scholars sometimes call this letter Pope Leo's "Little Book," although others attribute its authorship to Humbert of Silva Candida. In general, there has been a misleading tendency in the past to ascribe all the key sources from the schism of 1054 solely to Humbert. By contrast, Margit Dischner, *Humbert von Silva Candida: Werk und Wirkung des lothringischen Reformmönches* (Neuried, 1996), convincingly argues that the body of texts related to the schism were a group effort, reflecting input by Pope Leo, Humbert, and others in their immediate circle.

62. ASGL, 68–69, 72–74.

63. Leo IX to Emperor Constantine Monomachus, January 1054, ASGL, 88.

64. ASGL, 87.

65. For an early exposition of Petrine primacy, see the sermons of Pope Leo I (r. 440–461), in *Sancti Leonis magni: Romani pontificis tractatus septem et nonaginta*, ed. Anthony Chausse, CCSL 40 (Turnhout, 1973), 16–21. See also Ulmann, *Papal Government*, 2–14.

66. See (ca. 1070) the anonymous canon law collection *Diversorum patrum sententie sive Collectio in LXXIV titulos digesta*, ed. John Gilchrist, Monumenta iuris canonici series B: Corpus collectionum (Vatican City, 1973), 21, 32. See also the analysis of John Gilchrist, "Canon Law Aspects of the Eleventh-Century Gregorian Reform Programme," *Journal of Ecclesiastical History* 12 (1961): 21–38.

67. See the text *De sancta Romana ecclesia*, in *Kaiser, Rom und Renovatio*, 2: 121–136. See also J. Joseph Ryan, "Cardinal Humbert *De s. Romana ecclesia*: Relics of Roman-Byzantine Relations," *Mediaeval Studies* 20 (1958): 205–238.

68. ASGL, 68–76. See also the *Dialogi*, ASGL, 93–126, a fictive debate between representatives of Rome and Constantinople that was composed before or during the legates' stay at Constantinople.

69. ASGL, 67.

70. Ibid., 78.

71. For example, Tellenbach, *Church in Western Europe*, 191–192, expresses his astonishment that Leo IX allowed a "secondary question of ritual" to spoil his attempts at a political alliance with the Byzantine emperor against the Norman invaders of southern Italy. Bayer, *Spaltung der Christenheit*, 214–221, deals with the azymes dispute in an appendix to his main work.

72. *La vie du Pape Léon*, 106.

73. See Anton Michel, "Der Berichte des Pantaleo von Amalfi über den kirchlichen Bruch zu Byzanz im Jahre 1054 und seine angebliche Sammlung der Aktenstücke," in *Amalfi und Jerusalem im Griechischen Kirchgenstreit (1054–1090)*, Orientalia Christiana Analecta 121 (Rome, 1936), 53.

74. *Fragmentum disputationis adversus Graecos*, ASGL, 256.

75. See, however, J. R. Geiselmann, *Die Abendmahlslehre an der Wende der christlichen Spätantike zum Frühmittelalter* (Munich, 1933), 21–72, who suggests that the two controversies might have mutually reinforced a Roman concern over the proper definition of the Eucharist. He is followed in this point by Gary Macy, *The Theologies of the Eucharist in the Early Scholastic Period: A Study of the Salvific Function of the Sacrament according to the Theologians c. 1080–1220* (Oxford, 1984), 35–43.

76. See Brian Stock, *The Implications of Literacy: Written Language and Models of Interpretation in the Eleventh and Twelfth Centuries* (Princeton, 1987), 231–345; Jean de Montclos, *Lafranc et Bérenger: La controverse eucharistique du XIe siècle* (Louvain, 1971); H. E. J. Cowdrey, "The Papacy and the Berengarian Controversy," in *Auctoritas et Ratio: Studien zu Berengar von Tours*, ed. Peter Ganz (Wiesbaden, 1990),

109–138; and Charles Radding and Francis Newton, *Theology, Rhetoric, and Politics in the Eucharistic Controversy, 1078–1079: Alberic of Monte Cassino Against Berengar of Tours* (New York, 2003).

77. See the anonymous *Epistola de sacramentis haereticorum*, ed. Ernst Sackur, MGH Ldl 3 (Hannover, 1897), 14. On the theme of heretical sacraments as a source of pollution in the community, see R. I. Moore, "Family, Community and Cult on the Eve of the Gregorian Reform," *Transactions of the Royal Historical Society* 5th series, 30 (1980): 49–69; and Amy Remensnyder, "Pollution, Purity, and Peace: An Aspect of Social Reform between the Late Tenth Century and 1076," in *The Peace of God*, 280–307.

78. Humbert, *Libri III adversus simoniacos*, ed. Friedrich Thaner, MGH Ldl 1 (Hannover, 1891), 116, 174, 188, 194–195.

79. Ibid., 206–207.

80. On the historical memory of 1054 in the Greek Church, see Aristeides Papdakis, "Byzantine Perceptions of the Latin West," *Greek Orthodox Theological Review* 36 (1991): 231–242; and Tia Kolbaba, "The Legacy of Humbert and Cerularius: The Tradition of the 'Schism of 1054' in Byzantine Texts and Manuscripts," in *Porphyrogenita: Essays in the History and Literature of Byzantium and the Latin East in Honour of Julian Chrysostomides,* ed. Judith Herrin (Burlington, Vt., 2003), 47–62.

81. Gregory VII to all the faithful, 30 June 1073, Reg. 1:15, 24; to the judges of Sardinia, 14 October 1073, 1:29, 46; and to the rulers of Spain, 28 June 1077, 4:28, 343.

82. Gregory VII to Sven II, king of Sweden, 17 April 1075, Reg. 2:75, 237–238.

83. Gregory VII to Laon, 3 March 1075, Reg. 2:55, 201–208.

84. See Gregory's letter to the judges of Sardinia, Reg. 1:29, 46–47; and to Archbishop Roffred of Benevento, in 1080, Reg. 7:28, 509–510.

85. Gregory VII, 6 June 1080, Reg. 8:1, 510–514. See Georg Hofmann, "Papst Gregor VII. und der christliche Osten," *Studi Gregoriani* (1947): 169–181; and Cowdrey, *Gregory VII,* 481–494.

86. Gregory VII to Michael VII, 9 July 1073, Reg. 1:18, 29–30.

87. See Carl Erdmann, *Die Entstehung des Kreuzzugsgedankens* (Stuttgart, 1935); *The Origin of the Idea of the Crusade,* trans. Marshall Baldwin and Walter Goffart (Princeton, 1977), 148–228. The precise nature of the "Peace and Truce of God" movement remains a subject of debate among historians. See Frederick Paxton, "History, Historians, and the Peace of God," in *The Peace of God: Social Violence and Religious Response in France around the Year 1000,* ed. Thomas Head and Richard Landes (Ithaca, 1992), 21–40. See also Philippe Buc, "La vengeance de Dieu: de l'exégèse patristique à la reforme ecclésiastique et à la première croisade," *Collection de l'École française de Rome* 357 (2006): 451–486, who highlights the com-

plexity of clerical attitudes toward violence in preexisting patristic exegesis before the "shift" identified by Erdmann and others. My thanks to Igor Gorevich for this reference.

88. In addition to the works cited above, see John Gilchrist, "The Papacy and War against the 'Saracens' 795–1216," *International History Review* 10 (1988): 173–197; Tomaž Mastnak, *Crusading Peace: Christendom, the Muslim World, and Western Political Order* (Berkeley, 2002), 1–24; Jean Flori, *La guerre sainte: la formation de l'idée de croisade dans l'occident chrétien* (Paris, 2002), 159–172; and Cushing, *Reform and the Papacy,* 39–54.

89. *La vie du Pape Léon,* 110–115. See also Erdmann, *Idea of the Crusade,* 120–125; and Norman Housely, "Crusades against Christians: Their Origins and Early Development, c. 1000–1216," in *Crusade and Settlement,* ed. Peter Edbury (Cardiff, 1985), 17–36.

90. Erdmann, *Idea of the Crusade,* 118–147; Flori, *La guerre sainte,* 190–205.

91. Alexander II (1063), *Epistolae pontificum Romanorum ineditae,* ed. Samuel Loewenfeld (Graz, 1959), 43.

92. Fliche, *La réforme Grégorienne,* 52. See also Flori, *La guerre sainte,* 213–217. An early letter of unclear dating by Pope Nicholas II, PL 143, 1337–1339, suggested that it was the pope's duty to defend churches liberated from Muslims by Christian warriors.

93. Erdmann, *Idea of the Crusade,* 148–181.

94. Gregory VII to Sancho II of Aragon, 20 March 1074, Reg. 1:63, 91–92; and to Alfonso VI of Leon and Sancho of IV of Navarre, 19 March 1074, Reg. 1:64, 92–94. On Gregory's "Spanish policy," see Cowdrey, *Gregory VII,* 468–480.

95. See Alexander II, 18 October 1071, PL 146, 1362–1363, announcing the need for his legate Hugh Candidus to restore the proper (i.e., Roman) worship in regions where the "discipline" of the Spanish church had lapsed.

96. Gregory VII to the Spanish kings and nobles, 28 June 1077, Reg. 4:28, 343–347; and to the bishop of Jaca in 1084, no. 215, *Quellen und Forschungen zum Urkunden- und Kanzleiwesen Papst Gregors VII,* ed. Leo Santifaller, Biblioteca Vaticana studi e testi 190 (Vatican City, 1957), 258–260.

97. Gregory VII, 30 April 1073, Reg. 1:7, 11–12. See Flori, *La guerre sainte,* 217–219.

98. Gregory VII, 18 January 1074, no. 61, *Quellen,* 40–41.

99. Gregory VII, 16 April 1083, no. 212, *Quellen,* 252–254.

100. See Gregory's letter to William of Burgundy, 2 February 1074, Reg. 1:46, 69–71; to all the faithful, 1 March 1074, Reg. 1:49, 75–76; to Henry IV, 7 December 1074, Reg. 2:31, 165–168; and to all the faithful, Reg. 2:37, 172–173. See also his letter to Countess Matilda of Tuscany, no. 5, *The Epistolae Vagantes of Gregory VII,* ed. and trans. H. E. J. Cowdrey (Oxford, 1971), 10–13.

101. On the polemics of the reform era, see Robinson, *Authority and Resistance,* 19–47; and Cushing, *Reform and Papacy,* 111–138.

102. *Dicta cuiusdam de discordia papae et regis,* ed. Kuno Francke, MGH Ldl 1, 454–460 (especially pp. 455–456).

103. *De unitate ecclesiae conservanda,* ed. Wilhelm Schwenkenbecker, MGH Ldl 2 (Hannover, 1892), 185–186.

104. See McGinn, *Antichrist,* 120–121, who defines "Antichrist language" as "a weapon to smear opponents," used by those "paying no attention to the general course of salvation history," while "Antichrist application" involves a "conscious and concerted effort" to interpret historical events as "part of an apocalyptic view of history."

105. See Karl Josef Benz, "Eschatologie und Politik bei Gregor VII," *Studi Gregoriani* 14 (1991): 1–20; and Christian Schneider, *Prophetisches Sacerdotium und Heilsgeschichtliches Regnum im Dialog, 1073–1077: zur Geschichte Gregors VII. und Heinrichs IV* (Munich, 1972). For references to Antichrist in Gregory's letters, see Gregory VII to the faithful in the kingdom of Henry IV, 25 July 1076, Reg. 4:1, 289; to Hermann of Metz, 25 August 1076, Reg. 4:2, 295; and to the bishops in Apulia and Calabria, 21 July 1080, Reg. 8:5, 522.

106. On the renewal of interest in such prophecies, see Robert Lerner, "Millennialism," EA, 2: 326–360 (especially pp. 329–335).

107. The Sibylline oracle is edited in *Sibyllinische Texte und Forschungen: Pseudomethodius, Adso und Tiburtinische Sibylle,* ed. Ernst Sackur (1898; Turin, 1963), 114–187. See also Bernard McGinn, "*Teste David cum Sibylla:* The Significance of the Sibylline Tradition in the Middle Ages," in *Women of the Medieval World,* ed. Julius Kirschner and Suzanne Wemple (Oxford, 1985), 7–35; and Anke Holdenried, *The Sibyl and Her Scribes: Manuscripts and Interpretation of the Latin Sibylla Tiburtina c. 1050–1500* (Aldershot, U.K., 2006). Holdenried, in fact, downplays the "political uses" of the Tiburtine tradition and emphasizes its other attractions for contemporaries.

108. *Sibyllinische Texte,* 185 (Isa. 11:10).

109. See Benzo of Alba, *Sieben Bücher an Kaiser Heinrich IV. (ad Heinricum IV. imperatorem libri VII),* ed. Hans Seyffert, MGH SRG (in us. schol.) 65 (Hannover, 1996), 224–228; and Carl Erdmann, "Endkaiserglaube und Kreuzzugsgedanke im 11. Jahrhundert," *Zeitschrift für Kirchengeschichte* 51 (1932): 384–414, which includes excerpts from Benzo of Alba, along with sections of a redacted eleventh-century version of the Tiburtine Sibyl. It has even been suggested that Pope Gregory VII was directly responding to the politically charged prophecy of the Last World Emperor with his famous "crusade plan" of 1074. See Paul Magdalino, "Church, Empire and Christendom in c. 600 and c. 1075: The View from the Registers of

Popes Gregory I and Gregory VII," in *Cristianità d'occidente e Cristianità d'oriente*, 1–30 (especially pp. 29–30).

110. Text in Erdmann, "Endkaiserglaube und Kreuzzugsgedanke," 386–394.

2. The Chosen People and the Enemies of God

1. Raymond d'Aguilers, *Le 'Liber' de Raymond d'Aguilers*, ed. John Hugh and Laurita Hill, Documents relatifs à l'histoire des croisades 9 (Paris, 1969), 150–151.

2. The expression "clash of civilizations" was coined by Samuel Huntington, "A Clash of Civilizations," *Foreign Affairs* 72 (1993): 22–44.

3. There is a vast literature on the crusading movement. For some reflections on the state of the field, see Jonathan Riley-Smith, "The Crusading Movement and Historians," in *The Oxford History of the Crusades*, ed. Jonathan Riley-Smith (Oxford, 1999), 1–14; Giles Constable, "The Historiography of the Crusades," in *The Crusades from the Perspective of Byzantium and the Muslim World*, ed. Angeliki Laiou and Roy Mottahedeh (Washington, D.C., 2001), 2–22; and Norman Housley, *Contesting the Crusades* (Malden, Mass., 2006), 24–38. Much of the debate on the origins of the crusade centers on the groundbreaking study of Carl Erdmann, *Die Entstehung des Kreuzzugsgedankens* (Stuttgart, 1935), English translation in *The Origin of the Idea of the Crusade*, trans. Marshall Baldwin and Walter Goffart (Princeton, 1977). Erdmann emphasized continuities between the First Crusade and notions of holy war that had developed during the ecclesiastical reform movement of the earlier eleventh century. Critics of Erdmann stress the centrality of Jerusalem to the call for the First Crusade and the nature of crusading as a penitential act of pilgrimage. For various positions on this problem, see Hans E. Mayer, *The Crusades*, trans. John Gillingham, 2nd ed. (1965; Oxford, 1988), 9–40; E.-D. von Hehl, "Was ist Eigentlich ein Kreuzzug?" *Historische Zeitschrift* 259 (1994): 297–336; John France, "Les origines de la première croisade: un nouvel examen," in *Autour de la première croisade,* ed. Michel Balard (Paris, 1996), 43–56; Marcus Bull, "Origins," in *The Oxford History of the Crusades*, 15–34; Jean Flori, *La guerre sainte: la formation de l'idée de croisade dans l'occident chrétien* (Paris, 2001); and Jonathan Riley-Smith, *What Were the Crusades?*, 3rd ed. (New York, 2002).

4. See Paul Rousset, "La notion de Chrétienté aux XIe et XIIe siècles," *Le moyen age* 69 (1963): 191–203, quotation from p. 191. See also Jean Rupp, *L'idée de chrétienté dans la pensée pontificale des origins à Innocent III* (Paris, 1939), 73–83.

5. Denys Hay, *Europe: The Emergence of an Idea* (Edinburgh, 1957), 34.

6. Tomaž Mastnak, *Crusading Peace: Christendom, the Muslim World, and Western Political Order* (Berkeley, 2002), 91–152, quotation from p. 91.

7. Christopher Tyerman, *God's War: A New History of the Crusades* (Cambridge,

Mass., 2006), xiii. In this book, Tyerman steps back somewhat from his controversial claim in his work *The Invention of the Crusades* (London, 1998), that the
identifiable and legally sanctioned phenomenon of "crusading" did not exist as
such until the late twelfth and thirteenth centuries.

8. As noted by Kurt Lehtonen in *Medieval History Writing and Crusading Ideology*, ed.
Tuomas M. S. Lehtonen and Kurt Villads Jensen, Studia Fennica Historica 9 (Hel-
sinki, 2005), 16, historical interpretation of the First Crusade "must have begun
in Jerusalem on the late Sunday afternoon of the 17th July when the fighting had
ceased and the city was completely in control of the Christians."

9. See David Blanks and Michael Frassetto, eds., *Western Views of Islam in Medieval
and Early Modern Europe: Perception of Other* (London, 1999), 3; and Joseph Fon-
tana, *The Distorted Past: A Reinterpretation of Europe* (Cambridge, 1995), 54.

10. On the crusades and Western "images" of Islam, see Dana C. Munro, "The Western Attitude Toward Islam during the Period of the Crusades," *Speculum* 6 (1931):
329–343; Norman Daniel, *Islam and the West: The Making of an Image* (Edinburgh,
1960); Richard Southern, *Western Views of Islam in the Middle Ages* (Cambridge,
Mass., 1962); Raoul Manselli, "La res publica Christiana e l'Islam," in *L'occidente e
Islam nell'alto medioevo* 1 (Spoleto, 1965), 115–147; Bernard Hamilton, "Knowing
the Enemy: Western Understandings of Islam at the Times of the Crusades,"
Journal of the Royal Asiatic Society, 3rd series, vol. 7 (1997): 373–387; the essays in
Medieval Christian Perceptions of Islam, ed. John V. Tolan (New York, 1996); Franco
Cardini, *Europe and Islam*, trans. Caroline Beamish (Oxford, 2001); and John V.
Tolan, *Saracens: Islam in the Medieval European Imagination* (New York, 2002).
Many efforts in this field are (directly or indirectly) indebted to Edward Said, *Ori-
entalism* (New York, 1978).

11. See Riley-Smith, *What Were the Crusades?*, 1–8.

12. Heikki Mikkeli, *Europe as an Idea and an Identity* (New York, 1998), 20–21.

13. See Giles Constable, "The Place of the Crusader in Medieval Society," *Viator* 29
(1998): 377–403.

14. On the place of the crusades in theology of history, see the groundbreaking
work of Paul Rousset, *Les origines et les caractères de la première croisade* (Neuchâ-
tel, 1945); Paul Rousset, "La croyance en la justice immanente à l'époque
féodale," *Le Moyen Age* 55 (1948): 225–248; and Paul Alphandéry, *La chrétienté et
l'idée de croisade*, ed. Alfons Dupront, 2 vols. (Paris, 1954–1959). More recently,
see Jonathan Riley-Smith, *The First Crusade and the Idea of Crusading* (London,
1986); James Powell, "Myth, Legend, Propaganda, and History: The First Crusade, 1140–ca. 1300," in *Autour de la première croisade*, ed. Michel Balard (Paris,
1996), 127–141; and Henri Bresc, "Les historiens de la croisade: guerre sainte,
justice et paix," MEFRM 115 (2003): 727–753.

15. BNF Lat. 1706, fols. 23r–23v. Based on paleographic evidence, this manuscript dates to the late tenth or early eleventh century. See the "Inventaire sommaire des manuscrits relatifs à l'histoire et à la géographie de l'orient latin," *Archives d'Orient latin* 2 (1884): 131–204, especially p. 134.

16. BNF Lat. 1706, fol. 23v: *O bone rex et multarum proviciarum et gentium potentissime princeps! Si hunc de quo loquimur Constantinum augustum cultorem dei et Christianissimum imperatorem imitatus fueris, regnum terrenum diu cum honore et felicitate tenebis et in aeternum cum Christo et eius sanctis regnabis.*

17. See Philippe Buc, "La vengeance de Dieu: de l'exégèse patristique à la reforme ecclésiastique et à la première croisade," *Collection de l'École française de Rome* 357 (2006): 451–486, especially pp. 459–467; and Colin Morris, *The Sepulcher of Christ and the Medieval West* (Oxford, 2005).

18. Among numerous examples, see the early twelfth-century work by Honorius Augustodunensis, *Speculum ecclesiae*, PL 172, 946–948, 1004–1006. See also Jan Williams Drijvers, *Helena Augusta: The Mother of Constantine and the Legend of her Finding of the True Cross* (Leiden, 1992).

19. See Jean Flori, *L'islam et la fin des temps: l'interprétation prophétique des invasions musulmanes dans la chrétienté médiévale* (Paris, 2007), 111–147.

20. Rodulfus Glaber, *Historiarum libri quinque (The Five Books of the Histories)*, ed. and trans. John France (Oxford, 1989), 199–205.

21. Glaber, *Histories*, trans. France, 133–137. On this famous episode, see Richard Landes, "The Massacres of 1010: On the Origins of Popular Anti-Jewish Violence in Western Europe," in *From Witness to Witchcraft: Jews and Judaism in Medieval Christian Thought*, ed. Jeremy Cohen (Wiesbaden, 1996), 79–112. This "plot" was also reported in detail by Ademar of Chabannes, who dates the destruction of the Holy Sepulcher to 1010. See Daniel Callahan, "The Cross, the Jews, and the Destruction of the Church of the Holy Sepulcher in the Writings of Ademar of Chabannes," in *Christian Attitudes toward the Jews in the Middle Ages: A Casebook*, ed. Michael Frassetto (New York, 2007), 15–23.

22. See Einar Joranson, "The Great German Pilgrimage of 1064–1065," in *The Crusades and Other Historical Essays Presented to Dana C. Munro by His Former Students*, ed. Louis Paetow (New York, 1928), 3–43.

23. The Latin tradition of Charlemagne's legendary journey is commonly referred to by its incipit, *Descriptio qualiter Karolus Magnus*. For an edition of the text, see *Die Legende Karls des Grossen im 11. und 12. Jahrhundert*, ed. Gerhard Rauschen (Leipzig, 1890), 103–125. See also Matthew Gabriele, "The Provenance of the *Descriptio qualiter Karolus Magnus*: Remembering the Carolingians in the Entourage of King Philip I (1060–1108) before the First Crusade," *Viator* 39 (2008), 93–117.

24. Text in *Die Briefsammlung Gerberts von Reims,* ed. Fritz Weigle (Berlin, 1966), 50–52. On the debated provenance of this letter, see Paul Riant, "Inventaire critique des lettres historiques des croisades," *Archives d'Orient latin* 1 (1881): 1–224; pp. 31–38.

25. See Alexander Gieysztor, "The Genesis of the Crusades: The Encyclical of Sergius IV (1009–1012)," *Medievalia et Humanistica* 6 (1950): 3–34; text pp. 33–34. In this article, and its preceding part in *Medievalia et Humanistica* 5 (1948): 3–23, Gieysztor argues that the bull is a forgery from the time of Urban II's crusade-preaching tour in 1095. See also Riant, "Inventaire," 40–50. For a contrary view that the bull is genuine, see Hans Martin Schaller, "Zur Kreuzzugsenzyklika Papst Sergius IV," in *Papsttum, Kirche und Recht im Mittelalter: Festschrift für Horst Fuhrmann zum 65 Geburtstag,* ed. Humbert Mordek (Tübingen, 1991), 135–152.

26. On the long-term development of the "crusading-ideal" before and during the eleventh century, in addition to Erdmann, *Idea of the Crusade,* see Étienne Delaruelle, *L'idée de croisade au moyen âge* (Turin, 1980); and Paul Rousset, *Histoire d'une idéologie: la croisade* (Lausanne, 1983), especially pp. 13–40.

27. See Urban to Bernhard, archbishop of Toledo, 15 October 1088, PL 151, 288–289; to Berengar, archbishop of Tarragona, 17 November 1091, PL 151, 331–333; and to Roger, bishop of Syracuse, 17 November 1093, PL 151, 370–372. On the development of Urban's "biblical *translatio*-theory," see Alfons Becker, *Papst Urban II. (1088–1099): Der Papst, die griechische Christenheit und der Kreuzzug,* vol. 2 (Stuttgart, 1988), 333–376; and I. H. Ringel, "*Ipse transfert regna et mutat tempora:* Beobachtungen zur Herkunft von Dan. 2, 21 bei Urban II," in *Deus qui mutat tempora: Menschen und Institutionen im Wandel des Mittelalters,* ed. E.-D. Hehl (Simarigen, 1987), 137–156. See also Hehl, "Was ist Eigentlich ein Kreuzzug," 301, who refers to Urban's placement of the crusade in a "geschichtstheologie schema."

28. Urban II, 15 October 1088, PL 151, 289–299; and PL 151, 370–372.

29. For a positivist view, see Dana C. Munro, "The Speech of Pope Urban II at Clermont, 1095," *American Historical Review* 2 (1906): 231–242. More critically, see H. E. J. Cowdrey, "Pope Urban II's Preaching of the First Crusade," *History* (1970): 178–188; H. E. J. Cowdrey, "Pope Urban II and the Idea of Crusade," *Studi Medievali* 36 (1995): 721–742; and H. E. J. Cowdrey, "The Reform Papacy and the Origin of the Crusades," in *Le Concile de Clermont de 1095 et l'appel à la croisade* (Rome, 1997), 65–83.

30. In addition to *Le 'Liber' de Raymond d'Aguilers,* ed. Hugh and Hill, see the anonymous *The Deeds of the Franks and Other Pilgrims to Jerusalem (Gesta Francorum et aliorum Hierosolymitanorum),* ed. and trans. Rosalind Hill (1962; Oxford, 1972); Fulcher of Chartres, *Historia Hierosolymitana,* ed. Heinrich Hagenmeyer (Heidel-

berg, 1913); Peter Tudebode, *Historia de Hierosolymitano itinere,* RHC Occ 3, 9–117; Robert the Monk, *Historia Hierosolimitana,* RHC Occ 3, 717–882; Baldric of Dol, *Historia Jerosolimitana,* RHC Occ 4, 1–111; and Guibert of Nogent, *Dei gesta per Francos et cinq autre texts,* ed. R. C. B. Huygens, CCCM 127A (Turnhout, 1996). On the relationship between these "first" and "second" generation chronicles, see Riley-Smith, *The First Crusade and the Idea of Crusading,* 135–152, along with the criticisms of Bresc, "Les historiens de la croisade," 739, 744, who feels that the "first" generation of crusade chronicles show far more theological sophistication than Riley-Smith gives them credit for. Specifically on the use of the *Gesta Francorum* by later crusade-historians, see John France, "The Uses of the Anonymous Gesta Francorum in the Early Twelfth-Century Sources for the First Crusade," in *From Clermont to Jerusalem: The Crusades and Crusader Societies 1095–1500,* ed. Alan Murray (Turnhout, 1998), 29–42.

31. See Penny Cole, *The Preaching of the Crusades to the Holy Land, 1095–1270* (Cambridge, Mass., 1991), 1–36; and Flori, *L'islam et la fin des temps,* 276.

32. Cole, *Preaching of the Crusades,* 32.

33. Fulcher of Chartres, *Historia Hierosolymitana,* 130–138; Robert the Monk, *Historia Hierosolimitana,* 727–730; Baldric of Dol, *Historia Jerosolimitana,* 12–15; and Guibert of Nogent, *Dei gesta per Francos,* 137–140.

34. Baldric of Dol, *Historia Jerosolimitana,* 14–15.

35. See Geoffry of Malaterra, *De rebus gestis Rogerii comitis,* ed. L. A. Muratori, Rereum Italicarum scriptores 5 (Bologna, 1902–1925), 92–93. For Greek primary sources relating to these negotiations, see Walter Holtzmann, "Die Unionsverhandlungen zwischen Kaiser Alexius I. und Papst Urban II. im Jahre 1089," *Byzantiniche Zeitschrift* 28 (1928): 38–67; and the observations of Becker, *Papst Urban II.,* 215–222.

36. See Bernold of Constance, *Chronicon,* ed. G. H. Pertz, MGH SS 5 (Hannover, 1844), 462; see also the analysis of Dana C. Munro, "Did the Emperor Alexius I Ask for Aid to the Council of Placenza, 1095?" *American Historical Review* 27 (1922): 731–733.

37. The famous English theologian Anselm of Canterbury was included among the council's more notable participants, attending at Urban's personal request. See the report of Eadmer, *The Life of St Anselm Archbishop of Canterbury by Eadmer,* ed. and trans. Richard Southern (London, 1962), 72–73, 112–113.

38. See A. C. Krey, "Urban's Crusade—Success or Failure?," *American Historical Review* 53 (1948): 234–250; J. H. Hill, "Raymond of Saint Gilles in Urban's Plan of Greek and Latin Friendship," *Speculum* 26 (1951): 265–276; James Brundage, "Adhemar of Puy: The Bishop and His Critics," *Speculum* 34 (1959): 201–212; Peter

Charanis, "Byzantium, the West and the Origin of the First Crusade," *Byzantion* 19 (1949): 17–36; and Charanis, "Aims of the Medieval Crusades and How They Were Viewed by Byzantines," *Church History* 21 (1952): 123–134.

39. See Penny Cole, "The Theme of Religious Pollution in Crusade Documents, 1095–1188," in *Crusaders and Muslims in Twelfth-Century Syria,* ed. Maya Shatzmiller (Leiden, 1993), 84–111.

40. Urban to the faithful in Flanders, December 1095, no. 2, *Epistulae et chartae ad historiam primi belli sacri spectantes: Die Kreuzzugsbriefe aus dem Jahren 1088–1100,* ed. Heinrich Hagenmeyer (1901; Hildesheim, 1973), 136–137.

41. Robert the Monk, *Historia Hierosolimitana,* 723.

42. Baldric of Dol, *Historia Jerosolimitana,* 9.

43. Robert the Monk, *Historia Hierosolimitana,* 723, 727–729, 732.

44. See Fulcher of Chartres, *Historia Hierosolymitana,* 101–102; Robert the Monk, *Historia Hierosolimitana,* 739; and the universal chronicle of Sigerbert of Gembloux, *Sigberti Gemblacensis chronica cum continuationibus,* ed. D. L. Bethmann, MGH SS 6 (Hannover, 1844), 367–368. See also Rousset, *La première croisade,* 102–104; and Marcus Bull, "Overlapping and Competing Identities in the Frankish First Crusade," in *Le concile de Clermont,* 195–211.

45. Fulcher of Chartres, *Historia Hierosolymitana,* 118.

46. Guibert of Nogent, *Dei gesta per Francos,* 115–116.

47. Ibid., 113–117. On Guibert's version of the sermon at Clermont, see Jay Rubenstein, *Guibert of Nogent: Portrait of a Medieval Mind* (New York, 2002), 95–101.

48. On the role of eschatological expectation in the formation of the crusade, in addition to Alphandéry, *La chrétienté et l'idée de croisade,* 43–135, and Bresc, "Les historiens de la croisade," 727–732, see Norman Cohn, *The Pursuit of the Millennium: Revolutionary Millenarians and Mystical Anarchists of the Middle Ages,* rev. ed. (1957; London, 1970), 61–70; André Vauchez, "Les composantes eschatologique de l'idée de croisade," in *Le concile de Clermont,* 233–243; Flori, *L'islam et la fin des temps,* 250–281; and Jay Rubenstein, "How, or How Much, to Reevaluate Peter the Hermit," in *The Medieval Crusade,* ed. Susan Ridyard (Woodbridge, U.K., 2004), 53–69. For a contrasting opinion, see Bernard McGinn, "*Iter sancti Sepulchri:* The Piety of the First Crusaders," in *The Walter Prescott Webb Memorial Lectures: Essays on Medieval Civilization,* ed. Bede Lackner and Kenneth Philip (Austin, 1978), 33–71.

49. Rubenstein, "Peter the Hermit," 62; Flori, *L'islam et la fin des temps,* 276–281.

50. Albert of Aachen, *Historia Ierosolimitana: History of the Journey to Jerusalem,* ed. and trans. Susan B. Edgington (Oxford, 2007), 2–9. On Albert's work and authorship, which Edginton dates to the decades immediately after the First Crusade (earlier than many previous scholars), see ibid., xxi–xxxvii.

51. Caffaro, *De liberatione civitatum orientis liber,* RHC Occ 5, 47–49.

52. See the comments of Rubenstein, "Peter the Hermit," 69.

53. On the different "waves" of First Crusaders, see Jonathan Riley-Smith, *The Crusades: A Short History* (New Haven, 1987), 18–36.

54. Robert the Monk, *Historia Hierosolimitana,* 739–740, 880, 882; and Guibert of Nogent, *Dei gesta per Francos,* 237–243.

55. Baldric of Dol, *Historia Hierosolimitana,* 23.

56. For a discussion of Islam's place in medieval Christian missionary theory, see Benjamin Kedar, *Crusade and Mission* (Princeton, 1994).

57. One of the lengthier Latin accounts of the pogroms is given by Albert of Aachen, *Historia Ierosolimitana,* 50–53. See also Robert Chazan, *European Jewry and the First Crusade* (Berkeley, 1987), especially pp. 223–297.

58. There is a vast bibliography on this topic. See Jonathan Riley-Smith, "The First Crusade and the Persecution of the Jews," *Studies in Church History* 21 (1984): 51–52; Benjamin Kedar, "Crusade Historians and the Massacres of 1096," *Jewish History* 12 (1998): 11–31; Robert Chazan, *God, Humanity, and History: The Hebrew First Crusade Narratives* (Berkeley, 2000); and David Malkiel, "Jewish-Christian Relations in Europe, 840–1096," *Journal of Medieval History* 29 (2003): 55–83.

59. It had even been suggested that Count Emicho played upon the tradition of the Last World Emperor, presenting himself in the role of the apocalyptic leader who would (among other things) convert the Jews. On the role of eschatological expectation in these pogroms, see Jean Flori, *La première croisade: l'occident chrétien contre l'Islam* (Paris, 1992), 53–54; Flori, *Pierre l'Ermite et la première croisade* (Paris, 1999), 276–281; and Rubenstein, "Peter the Hermit," 55. See also Kenneth Stow, "Conversion, Apostasy, and Apprehensiveness: Emicho of Flonheim and the Fear of the Jews in the Twelfth Century," *Speculum* 76 (2001): 911–933, who downplays the impact of eschatology in the attacks. The historiography of this problem is examined by Matthew Gabriele, "Against the Enemies of Christ: The Role of Count Emicho in the Anti-Jewish Violence of the First Crusade," in *Christian Attitudes toward the Jews,* 84–111, who reaffirms the role that apocalyptic expectations played in the pogroms.

60. Augustine, *Sancti Aurelii Augustini de civitate dei,* CCSL 48, 14/2 (Turnhout 1955), 644–645; see also the analysis of Jeremy Cohen, *Living Letters of the Law: Ideas of the Jew in Medieval Christianity* (Berkeley, 1999), 23–65.

61. Alexander II to the bishops of Spain (1063), PL 146, 1386–1387. See also Alexander's letters of that same year to Viscount Berengar and Archbishop Wifred of Narbonne, PL 146, 1387, praising them for their protection of the Jews from such outbreaks of violence.

62. On this earlier development, see Michael Frassetto, "Heretics and Jews in the

Early Eleventh Century: The Writings of Rodulfus Glaber and Ademar of Chabannes," in *Christian Attitudes toward the Jews*, 43–59.

63. Albert of Aachen, *Historia Ierosolimitana*, 56–59.

64. Steven Runciman, *The Eastern Schism: A Study of the Papacy and the Eastern Churches during the XI and XII Centuries* (Oxford, 1955), 101. For similar evaluations, see Timothy Ware, *The Orthodox Church*, 2nd ed. (1963; London, 1997), 59; and Aristeides Papadakis, *The Christian East and the Rise of the Papacy*, The Church in History 4 (Crestwood, N.Y., 1994), 89. On the installment of Latin clergy in Greek religious sites, see Bernard Hamilton, *The Latin Church in the Crusader States* (London, 1980).

65. For an early statement of this position, see William Daly, "Christian Fraternity, the Crusaders, and the Security of Constantinople, 1097–1204: The Precarious Survival of an Ideal," *Medieval Studies* 22 (1960): 43–91. Recent studies argue that the crusaders and native Eastern Christians viewed cooperation or grudging tolerance rather than conflict as the normative mode for their relations. See, for example, Andrew Jotischky, "The Frankish Encounter with the Greek Orthodox in the Crusader States: The Case of Gerard of Nazareth and Mary Magdalene," in *Tolerance and Intolerance: Social Conflict in the Age of the Crusades*, ed. Michel Gervers and James Powell (Syracuse, N.Y., 2001), 100–114; and Christopher MacEvitt, *The Crusades and the Christian World of the East: Rough Tolerance* (Philadelphia, 2008), 1–26.

66. See A. C. Krey, "A Neglected Passage in the *Gesta* and Its Bearing on the Literature of the First Crusade," in *The Crusades and Other Historical Essays*, 57–78; and William McQueen, "Relations between the Normans and Byzantium 1071–1112," *Byzantion* 56 (1986): 427–476.

67. See Einar Joranson, "The Problem of the Spurious Letter of Emperor Alexius to the Court of Flanders," *American Historical Review* 55 (1950): 811–832; see also the *Epistola Alexii I Komneni ad Robertum I comitem Flandrensem*, no. 1, *Epistulae et chartae*, 129–136.

68. For such negative appraisals of Alexius, see the *Gesta Francorum*, 10; Robert the Monk, *Historia Hierosolimitana*, 742–743, 749–750; and Baldric of Dol, *Historia Hierosolimitana*, 22, 30–31; along with the contrasting opinions of Albert of Aachen, *Historia Hierosolymitana*, 28–33, 76–77, 108–111.

69. Letter to Urban II, September 1098, no. 16, *Epistulae et chartae*, 164. Some historians have speculated that the hand of Bohemond was behind this letter, already laying the groundwork for his post-crusade, anti-Byzantine campaigns. The same letter, ibid., 165, asked Urban to free the crusade leaders from their obligations toward the "unjust" Byzantine emperor, who "promised us a great many things, but did not carry through."

70. There are numerous portrayals of such cooperative prayer and liturgical proces-

sions in the chronicles and crusader correspondence, e.g., the *Gesta francorum*, 94; Fulcher of Chartres, *Historia Hierosolymitana*, 368; and the letter of Anselm of Ribodimonte to Manasses, the archbishop of Reims, November 1097, no. 8, *Epistulae et chartae*, 144–146.

71. On Eastern reactions to the crusaders, see Bresc, "Les historiens de la croisade," 727–753, and MacEvitt, 50–73. For a subtle treatment of crusader reactions to Byzantine Christians, see Annetta Ilieva and Mitko Delev, "La conscience des croisés et l'altérité chrétienne: essai typologique sur les conflits pendant la Prèmiere Croisade," in *Autour de la première croisade*, 109–118.

72. Guibert of Nogent, *Dei gesta per Francos*, 94–95.

73. Ibid., 266.

74. Anselm of Ribodimonte, no. 8, *Epistulae et chartae*, 145–146.

75. On the place of relics in crusader piety, see Riley-Smith, *The First Crusade*, 91–119.

76. The episode of the Holy Lance was widely reported in the chronicles and in crusader correspondence, e.g., the *Gesta Francorum*, 59–66; Fulcher of Chartres, *Historia Hierosolymitana*, 235–241; Robert the Monk, *Historia Hierosolimitana*, 822–823; and the letter of the crusader leaders at Antioch to Urban II, no. 16, *Epistulae et chartae*, 161–165. See Colin Morris, "Policy and Visions: The Case of the Holy Lance at Antioch," in *War and Government in the Middle Ages*, ed. John Gillingham and J. C. Holt (Cambridge, 1984), 33–45.

77. Raymond d'Aguilers, *Le 'Liber' de Raymond d'Aguilers*, 154. On the discovery of the True Cross, see also Fulcher of Chartres, *Historia Hierosolymitana*, 309–310; and Albert of Aachen, *Historia Ierosolimitana*, 450–453.

78. On relic-related hagiographical sources, see Patrick Geary, *Furta Sacra: Thefts of Relics in the Central Middle Ages* (1978; Princeton, 1990); and Peter Brown, *The Cult of Saints: Its Rise and Function in Latin Christianity* (Chicago, 1981).

79. *De translatione Nicholai*, RHC Occ 5, 260–261.

80. Cerbanus Cerbani, *Translatio mirifici martyris Isidori*, RHC Occ 5, 327.

81. *Tractatus de inventione sanctorum patriarcharum Abraham, Ysaac et Jacob*, RHC Occ 5, 302–314; critical edition in R. B. C. Huygens, "Inventio Patriarcharum," *Crusades* 4 (2005): 131–155. See also Kaspar Elm, "Nec minori celebritate a catholicis cultoribus observatur et colitur: Zwei Berichte über die 1119/20 erfolgte Auffindung und Erhebung der Gebeine der Patriarchen Abraham, Isaak und Jacob," *Zeitschrift für Religions und Geistesgeschichte* 49 (1997): 318–344; and Brett Whalen, "*The Discovery of the Holy Patriarchs*: Relics, Ecclesiastical Politics and Sacred History in Twelfth-Century Crusader Palestine," *Historical Reflections/Réflexions Historiques* 27 (2001): 139–176.

82. *De inventione sanctorum patriarcharum*, RHC Occ 5, 308. The author also claims

that Hebron was an episcopal see during the fifth century, an assertion made in support of the city's controversial elevation to episcopal status in the Latin Church of Jerusalem in 1168. See Whalen, *"Discovery of the Patriarchs,"* 143–145.

83. On this "théologie de la libération," see Bresc, "Les historiens de la croisade," 734; and Jean Flori, *Guerre sainte, jihad, croisade: violence et religion dans la christianisme et l'islam* (Paris, 2002), 190–192.

84. *Gesta Francorum,* 22.

85. Albert of Aachen, *Historia Hierosolymitana,* 338–339, 398–401, 452–453.

86. Ibid., 401. My translation.

87. On the establishment of Latin canons at the Holy Sepulcher, see Albert of Aachen, *Historia Hierosolymitana,* 454–455.

88. See Manasses of Reims, November-December 1099, no. 20, *Epistulae et chartae,* 175–176; and Paschal II, 28 April 1100, no. 4, *Papsturkunden für Kirchen im Heiligen Lande,* ed. Rudolf Hiestand, Abhandlungen der Akademie Wissenschaften in Göttingen: Philologisch-Historiche Klasse 136 (Göttingen, 1985), 90–92.

89. Manasses of Reims, no. 20, *Epistulae et chartae,* 176.

90. For some accounts of the Easter fire miracle, see Fulcher of Chartres, *Historia Hierosolymitana,* ed. Hagenmeyer, 395–396; the chronicle of Bartolf Nangis, *Gesta Francorum Iherusalem expugnatium,* RHC Occ 3, 524–526; Ekkehard of Aura, *Hierosolymita,* ed. Heinrich Hagenmeyer (Tübingen, 1877), 276–283; and Caffaro, *De liberatione civitatum orientis liber,* 61–62. See also MacEvitt, 115–120.

91. On this expedition, sometimes called the "third wave" of the First Crusade, see Riley-Smith, *First Crusade,* 120–134; and Tyerman, *God's War,* 170–175.

92. Ekkehard, *Hierosolymita,* 237.

93. See Orderic Vitalis, *The Ecclesiastical History of Orderic Vitalis,* ed. and trans. Marjorie Chibnall, 6 vols. (Oxford, 1980), 5: 330–333, 338–341; and Albert of Aachen, *Historia Hierosolymitana,* 563–564, 584.

94. For efforts to "reform" the sinful crusader camp during such setbacks, see, for example, Guibert of Nogent, *Dei gesta per Francos,* 196, 276–277.

95. Important works on this topic include Ralph Yewdale, *Bohemond I, Prince of Antioch* (Princeton, 1924), 106–134; J. G. Rowe, "Paschal II, Bohemond of Antioch and the Byzantine Empire," *Bulletin of the John Rylands Library* 49 (1966–1967): 165–202; Gerhard Rösch, "Der 'Kreuzzug' Bohemonds gegen Dyrrhacion 1107/1108 in der lateinische Tradition des 12. Jahrhunderts," *Römische Historische Mitteilungen* 26 (1984): 181–190; and Luigi Russo, "Il viaggio di Boemondo d'Altavilla in Francia (1106): un riesame," *Archivo storico Italiano* 163 (2005): 3–42.

96. *Narratio Floriacensis,* RHC Occ 5, 361; and Albert of Aachen, *Historia Hierosolymitana,* 620.

97. Bartolf Nangis, *Gesta Francorum,* 538.

98. See Yewdale, *Bohemond*, 115; Steven Runciman, *A History of the Crusades*, 3 vols. (Cambridge, 1952–1954), 1: 48; and Rowe, "Pachal II," 167–182.

99. There are signs that Bohemond tried to play on Paschal's sympathies by highlighting the need to resolve religious disagreements between the church of Rome and the Greeks. See his letter to Paschal in 1107, no. 7, *Papsturkunden für Kirchen im Heiligen Lande*, 102–104, also published with commentary by Walter Holtmann, "Zur Geschichte des Investiturestreites 2. Bohemund von Antiochen und Alexios I," *Neues archiv der Gesellschaft für ältere deutsche Geschichtskunde* 50 (1957): 270–282. Nevertheless, years later in 1115, Paschal was still willing to address Alexius in respectful terms about the need for increased harmony between the Latin and Greek Churches (PL 163, 388–389).

100. *Narratio Floriacensis*, 362; the *Historia peregrinorum euntium Jerusolymam seu Tudebodus imitatus et continuatus*, RHC Occ 3, 229; and Albert of Aachen, *Historia Hierosolymitana*, 652.

101. Orderic Vitalis, *The Ecclesiastical History*, trans. Chibnall, 6: 102–105.

102. Paschal II, 4 December 1107, PL 163, 230–232.

103. For the canons of Nablus and analysis, see Benjamin Kedar, "On the Origins of the Earliest Laws of Frankish Jerusalem: The Canons of the Council of Nablus," *Speculum* 74 (1999): 310–335, with the prologue to the canons, pp. 331–332.

104. See Sylvia Schein, *Gateway to the Heavenly City: Crusader Jerusalem and the Catholic West (1099–1187)* (Aldershot, U.K., 2005).

3. Reformist Apocalypticism and the Battlefield of History

1. Pope Eugene III to King Louis VII of France, 1 December 1145, PL 180, 1063–1066, quotation from col. 1064. See also the contemporary account of the German chronicler Otto of Freising, *Gesta Frederici*, ed. Franz-Josef Schmale, Ausgewählte Quellen zur deutschen Geschichte des Mittelalters 17 (Darmstadt, 1965), 200–206. On the development and impact of the Second Crusade, see the essays in Michael Gervers, ed., *The Second Crusade and the Cistercians* (New York, 1992); the essays in Jonathan Phillips and Martin Hoch, eds., *The Second Crusade: Scope and Consequences* (Manchester, U.K., 2001); Christopher Tyerman, *God's War: A New History of the Crusades* (Cambridge, Mass., 2006), 268–338; and Jonathan Phillips, *The Second Crusade: Extending the Frontiers of Christendom* (New Haven, 2007).

2. Pope Eugene III, 11 April 1147, PL 180, 1202–1204. Eugene's former abbot, the famous Cistercian monk Bernard of Clairvaux, emerged as one of the most outspoken advocates for the new campaign. See, for example, Bernard of Clairvaux, no. 457, *Sancti Bernardi opera: tractatus et opuscula*, ed. Jean Leclerq and H. M. Rochais, 8 vols. (Rome, 1963), 8: 432–433.

3. Bernard of Clairvaux addressed the failure of the crusade in his well-known tract addressed to Pope Eugene III, *De consideratione*, in *Sancti Bernardi opera*, 3: 410–413. On reactions to the outcome of the expedition, see Giles Constable, "The Second Crusade as seen by Contemporaries," *Traditio* 9 (1953): 213–279; H.-D. Kahl, "Crusade Eschatology as Seen by St. Bernard in the Years 1146–1148," in Gervers, ed., *The Second Crusade and the Cistercians*, 35–47; and Graham Loud, "Some Reflections on the Failure of the Second Crusade," *Crusades* 4 (2004): 1–14.

4. Gerhoh of Reichersberg, *Commentarius in Psalmos*, ed. Ernst Sackur, MGH Ldl 3 (Hannover, 1897), 436. Bernard McGinn, *Antichrist: Two Thousand Years of the Human Fascination with Evil* (New York, 2000), 122, describes Gerhoh as "one of the major historical theorists of his time." See also Damien Van den Eynde, *L'oeuvre littéraire de Gerhoh de Reichersberg*, Spicilegium Pontificii Athenai Antoniani 11 (Rome, 1957); Eric Meutheun, *Kirche und Heilsgeschichte bei Gerhoh von Reichersberg* (Leiden, 1959); and Peter Classen, *Gerhoch von Reichersberg* (Wiesbaden, 1960).

5. Gerhoh of Reichersberg, *De investigatione Antichristi liber I*, ed. Ernst Sackur, MGH Ldl 3 (Hannover, 1897), 331; and Gerhoh, *Libellus de ordine donorum sancti spiritus*, in *Gerhohi praepositi Reichersbergensis opera inedita*, ed. Damien Van den Eynde et al., 2 vols. (Rome, 1955), 1: 84–85.

6. Marie-Dominique Chenu, "Theology and the New Awareness of History," in *Nature, Man and Society in the Twelfth Century*, trans. Jerome Taylor and Lester Little (Chicago, 1968), 162–201, quotation from p. 162.

7. Amos Funkenstein, *Theology and the Scientific Imagination* (Princeton, 1986), 243–271, quotation from p. 263. For similar evaluations, see Richard Southern, "Aspects of the European Tradition of Historical Writings," *Transactions of the Royal Historical Society*, 5th series (London, 1971), 21: 159–179; 22: 159–180; Guntram Bischoff, "Early Premonstratensian Eschatology: The Apocalyptic Myth," in *The Spirituality of Western Christendom*, ed. E. Rozanne Elder (Kalamazoo, 1976), 41–71; and Peter Classen, "*Res Gestae*, Universal History, Apocalypse: Visions of Past and Future," in *Renaissance and Renewal in the Twelfth Century*, ed. Robert Benson and Giles Constable (Cambridge, Mass., 1982), 387–417.

8. Alois Dempf, *Sacrum Imperium: Geschichts- und Staatsphilosophie des Mittelalters und der politischen Renaissance* (1929; Darmstadt, 1962), 229–268, coined the label of "German symbolism" (*der deutsche Symbolismus*) to describe the works of Rupert of Deutz, Honorius Augustodunensis, Anselm of Havelberg, and Gerhoh of Reicherberg. Dempf also included Hugh of Saint Victor, Otto of Freising, and Hildegard of Bingen in his discussion of this phenomenon. Various scholars have followed Dempf in identifying roughly this same group of thinkers as sharing a common style of biblical interpretation and view of salvation history. See, for

example, Horst Dieter Rauh, *Das Bild des Antichrist im Mittelalter: von Tyconius zum deutschen Symbolismus,* Beiträge zur Geschichte der Philosophie und Theologie des Mittelalters, Neue Folge 9 (Münster, 1973); and Wolfgang Beinert, *Die Kirche—Gottes Heil in der Welt: die Lehre von der Kirche nach den Schriften des Rupert von Deutz, Honorius Augustodunensis und Gerhoh von Reichersberg,* Beiträge zur Geschichte der Philosophie und Theologie des Mittelalters, Neue Folge 13 (Münster, 1973). Labeling this cluster of thinkers "German" has been criticized as overly restrictive, especially considering the fact that the greatest "symbolic" exegete of the twelfth century, Joachim of Fiore, was from Calabria. See the review of Rauh by Bernard McGinn in *Church History* 45 (1976): 247–248.

9. This label, coined by Kathryn Kerby-Fulton, *Reformist Apocalypticism and Piers Plowman* (Cambridge, 1990), has been adopted by Bernard McGinn, "Apocalypticism and Church Reform: 1100–1500," EA, 2: 81–86; Roberto Rusconi, "Antichrist and Antichrists," EA, 2: 294–300; and E. Randolph Daniel, "Reformist Apocalypticism and the Friars Minor," in *That Others May Know and Love: Essays in Honor of Zachary Hayes,* ed. Michael Cusato and F. Edward Coughlin (New York, 1997), 237–253.

10. See Giles Constable, *The Reformation of the Twelfth Century* (Cambridge, U.K., 1996); Constable, "Renewal and Reform in Religious Life: Concepts and Realities," in *Renaissance and Renewal,* 37–67; John Van Engen, "The Crisis of Cenobitism Reconsidered: Benedictine Monasticism," *Speculum* 61 (1982): 269–304; Christopher Holdsworth, "The Past and Monastic Debate in the Time of Bernard of Clairvaux," *Studies in Church History* 33 (1997): 91–114; and Caroline Walker Bynum, "Did the Twelfth Century Discover the Individual?" in *Jesus as Mother: Studies in the Spirituality of the High Middle Ages* (Berkeley, 1982), 82–109.

11. On the relationship between these earlier twelfth-century thinkers and Joachim of Fiore, see Marjorie Reeves, "The Originality and Influence of Joachim of Fiore," *Traditio* 36 (1980): 296–316; and Bernard McGinn, "*Ratio* and *Visio*: Reflections on Joachim of Fiore's Place in Twelfth-Century Theology," in *Gioacchino da Fiore tra Bernardo di Clairvaux e Innocenzo III,* ed. Robert Rusconi (Rome, 2001), 27–46.

12. On the seven ages of history, see Augustine, *De Genesi contra Manichaeos,* ed. Dorothy Weber, CSEL 91 (Vienna, 1998), 104–110. The seven ages ran as follows: (1) from Adam to Noah; (2) from Noah to Abraham; (3) from Abraham to Moses; (4) from Moses to David; (5) from David to the Babylonian Captivity; (6) from the captivity to Christ; and (7) from Christ until the end of time. See Auguste Luneau, *Histoire du salut chez les pères de l'église: la doctrine des âges du monde,* Théologie historique 9 (Paris, 1964); and Roderich Schmidt, "*Aetates mundi:* Die Weltalter als Gliederungsprinzip der Geschichte," *Zeitschrift für Kirchengeschichte* 67 (1955–1956): 287–317.

13. As noted by Robert Markus, *Saeculum: History and Society in the Theology of St. Augustine* (Cambridge, 1970), 20: "Augustine's thought moved with increasing certainty towards the rejection of any attempt to introduce any division derived from sacred history into the history of the age after Christ."

14. On the "ten persecutions" of the pre-Constantinian Church, see Orosius, *Historiarum adversum paganos (libri VII)*, ed. Charles Zangemeister, CSEL 5 (Vienna, 1882), 494–500. For Augustine's condemnation of the scheme, see Augustine, *Sancti Aurelii Augustini de civitate dei*, CCSL 48, 14/2 (Turnhout 1955), 650–652. For an example of this scheme's enduring popularity, see BNF Lat. 5018, fols. 88r–92r, an anonymous twelfth-century universal chronicle that includes marginal notations for each numbered persecution (*persecutio*) from Nero to Diocletian.

15. See Sigebert of Gembloux, *Chronica*, ed. D. L. Bethmann, MGH SS 6 (Hannover, 1844), 300–302; and Otto of Freising, *Chronica sive historia de duabus civitatibus*, ed. Adolf Hofmeister, MGH SS (in us. schol.) 45 (Hannover, 1912), 5, 9, 134. See also the analysis of Mireille Chazan, *L'empire et l'histoire universelle* (Paris, 1999).

16. On this "seven-seals" scheme, see Wilhelm Kamlah, *Apokalypse und Geschichtstheologie: Die mittelalterliche Auslegung der Apokalypse vor Joachim von Fiore* (1935; Vaduz, 1965).

17. *Biblia Latina cum glossa ordinaria: Facsimile Reprint of the* editio princeps *Adolph Rusch of Strassburg 1480/81* (Turnhout, 1992), fols. 556, 559, 573. On the development of "scholastic" biblical exegesis, see Beryl Smalley, *The Study of the Bible in the Middle Ages* (1952; Oxford, 1984); Henri de Lubac, *Exégèse médiévale*, 2 vols. (Paris, 1961); Marie-Dominique Chenu, "The Old Testament in Twelfth-Century Theology," in *Nature, Man and Society*, 146–161; Philippe Buc, *L'ambiguïté du livre: prince, pouvoir, et peuple dans les commentaires de la Bible au moyen age* (Paris, 1994); and Gilbert Dahan, *L'exégèse chrétienne de la Bible en Occident médiéval (XIIe–XIVe siècle)* (Paris, 1999).

18. McGinn, *Antichrist*, 122. On Rupert's life and career, see John Van Engen, *Rupert of Deutz* (Berkeley, 1983). On his theology of history, see also the comments of Classen, "*Res Gestae,*" 404–407; Beinert, *Die Kirche*, 29–37, 322–326; Wanda Cizewski, "A Theological Feast: The Commentary by Rupert of Deutz on Trinity Sunday," RTAM 55 (1988): 41–52; and Maria Arduini, *Rupert von Deutz (1076–1129) und der 'Status Christianitatis' seiner Zeit* (Böhlau, 1987).

19. Rupert of Deutz, *Liber de divinis officiis*, ed. Rhabanus Haacke, CCCM 7 (Turnhout, 1967), 104, 109, 112–120.

20. Ibid., 366–368. See also Beinert, *Die Kirches-Gotte*, 327.

21. *De divinis officiis*, 417–418.

22. Rupert of Deutz, *Commentaria in Apocalypsim*, PL 169, 1043–1045; and *De victoria verbi dei*, ed. Hrabanus Haacke, MGH QG 5 (Hannover, 1970), 11–12.

23. *Commentaria in Apocalypsim,* PL 169, 1066–1067.

24. See Valerie Flint, "The Chronology of the Works of Honorius Augustodunensis," *Revue Bénédictine* 82 (1972): 215–242; and Flint, "The Place and Purpose of the Works of Honorius Augustondunesis," *Revue Bénédictine* 87 (1977): 97–118. On Honorius's historical thinking and ecclesiology, in addition to Beinert, *Die Kirche,* 328–331, see Maria Arduini, "'Rerum mutabilitas': Welt, Zeit, Menschenbild und 'Corpus Ecclesiae-Christianae' bei Honorius von Regensburg (Augustodunensis)," RTAM 52 (1985): 78–108.

25. Honorius Augustodunensis, *Gemma animae,* PL 172, 541–738; and the *Expositio in cantica canticorum,* PL 172, 347–496. For a critical edition of Honorius's world chronicle, see Valerie Flint, "Honorius Augustodunensis: Imago Mundi," *Archives d'histoire doctrinale et littéraire du moyen age* 49 (1982): 7–153. See also her observations in Flint, "World History in the Early Twelfth Century: The 'Imago Mundi' of Honorius Augustodunensis," in *The Writing of History in the Middle Ages,* ed. R. H. C. Davis (Oxford, 1981), 211–238.

26. Honorius Augustodunensis, *Summa gloria,* ed. Ernst Sackur, MGH Ldl 3, 63–80 (especially pp. 71–72, 77–79).

27. *Expositio in Cantica Canticorum,* PL 172, 452.

28. *Gemma animae,* PL 172, 724–727.

29. Bernard of Clairvaux, *De consideratione,* 433–434.

30. On the dispute over azymes, see Anselm of Canterbury, *Epistola de sacrificio azimi et fermentati,* in *Anselm: opera omnia,* ed. F. S. Schmidt, 6 vols. (Stuttgart, 1968), 2: 223–232; on *filioque,* see Anselm, *De processione spiritus sancti,* in *opera omnia,* 2: 177–219.

31. See Anna Sapir Abulafia, "St Anselm and Those Outside the Church," in *Faith and Identity: Christian Political Experience,* ed. D. M. Loades and Katherine Walsh (Oxford, 1990), 11–38; and Gilbert Dahan, "Saint Anselme, les juifs, le judaïsme," in *Les mutations socio-culturelles au tournant des XIe–XIIe siècles,* ed. Jean Pouilloux (Paris, 1984), 521–534.

32. Odo of Deuil, *De profectione Ludovici VII in orientem (The Journey of Louis VII to the East),* ed. and trans. Virginia Berry (New York, 1948), 55–56, 69–71. In recent years, scholars have begun to temper the idea that the outcome of the Second Crusade generated widespread "anti-Greek" sentiments in the Western Church. See Timothy Reuter, "The 'Non-Crusade' of 1149–50," in Phillips and Hoch, eds., *The Second Crusade: Scope and Consequences,* 150–163; and Jonathan Phillips, "Odo of Deuil's *De profectione Ludovici VII in Orientem* as a Source for the Second Crusade," in *The Crusading Experience,* ed. Marcus Bull and Norman Housely (Cambridge, 2003), 80–95.

33. Rupert, *De divinis officiis,* 53.

34. Rupert of Deutz, *De sancta trinitate et operibus eius,* ed. Hrabanus Haacke, CCCM 21, 22, 24 (Turnhout, 1971–1972), 21: 279–280, 22: 635, 1193, and 24: 1860–1861. Rupert's exaltation of the Holy Spirit, a central theme in *De sancta trinitate,* continued in one of his final works (ca. 1128), *De glorificatione trinitatis et processione Sancti Spiritus,* PL 169, 13–202.

35. Rupert of Deutz, *Commentaria in evangelium sancti Iohannis,* ed. Hrabanus Haacke, CCCM 9 (Turnhout, 1969), 671, 773; and *De glorificatione trinitatis,* PL 69, 29.

36. In addition to Gerhoh's works cited earlier, see the *Opusculum de edificio dei,* ed. Ernst Sackur, MGH Ldl 3, 136–202; *Libri III de investigatione Antichristi, unacum tractatu adversus Graecos,* ed. Friederic Scheibelberger, Gerhohi Reicherbergensis praepositi opera hactenus inedita 1 (Linz, 1975); and *De quarta vigilia noctis,* ed. Ernst Sackur, MGH Ldl 3, 503–525.

37. *De ordine donorum sancti spiritus,* 91–132.

38. *De investigatione antichristi,* ed. Scheibelberger, 250–251.

39. Ibid., 343–362, quotation from p. 362. Gerhoh openly borrowed the Greek arguments from a letter that was sent to "our emperor" by a learned Greek scholar, who thereby tried to ensnare "our people" in his errors. Apparently, Gerhoh had already written a tract against the Greeks (no longer extant). See Van den Eynde, *L'oeuvre littéraire de Gerhoh de Reichersberg,* 115–121.

40. Anselm of Havelberg, *Dialogi,* PL 188, 1139–1248. The first book is published with Latin text and French translation: *Anselme de Havelberg: Dialogues, livre 1,* ed. and trans. Gaston Salet, SC 118 (Paris, 1966). References are to the PL, with Salet in parentheses when applicable.

41. On Anselm, his writings, and his position in the debates over religious life, see Jay T. Lees, *Anselm of Havelberg: Deeds into Words in the Twelfth Century* (Leiden, 1998); and Lees, "Charity and Enmity in the Writings of Anselm of Havelberg," *Viator* 25 (1994): 53–62. On Anselm's theology of history see Classen, *"Res Gestae,"* 407–409; Chenu, "Theology," 174–184; Kamlah, *Apokalypse und Geschichtstheologie,* 64–70 (who includes a chart of Anselm's schemes); K. F. Morrison, "Anselm of Havelberg: Play and the Dilemma of Historical Progress," in *Religion, Culture, and Society in the Early Middle Ages: Studies in Honor of Richard Sullivan,* ed. T. F. X. Noble and J. J. Contreni (Kalamazoo, Mich., 1987), 229–256; and Carol Neel, "Philip of Harvengt and Anselm of Havelberg: The Premonstratensian Vision of Time," *Church History* 62 (1993): 483–493.

42. Anselm, *Dialogi,* PL 188, 1145–1147 (Salet, *Dialogues,* 46–52).

43. Ibid., 1148–1156 (Salet, *Dialogues,* 68–104).

44. Ibid., 1156 (Salet, *Dialogues,* 100).

45. Lees, *Anselm of Havelberg,* 164–281, convincingly demonstrates that Anselm's account of the debates is better thought of as a carefully worded thought-piece,

packaged in the form of an exchange between two nominal opponents, rather than a verbatim transcript of the actual words delivered at Constantinople. In addition to Lees, *Anselm of Havelberg*, see Jay T. Lees, "Confronting the Otherness of the Greeks: Anselm of Havelberg and the Division between Greeks and Latins," *Analecta Praemonstratensia* 68 (1992): 224–240. For examples of scholarship that take debates at Constantinople literally, see Gillian Evans, "Anselm of Canterbury and Anselm of Havelberg: The Controversy with the Greeks," *Analecta Praemonstratensia* 53 (1977): 158–175; Theodore Russell, "Anselm of Havelberg and the Union of the Churches," *Sobornost* 1:2 (1979): 19–41; 2:1 (1980): 29–41; and Henry Chadwick, *East and West: The Making of a Rift in the Church from Apostolic Times until the Council of Florence* (Oxford, 2003), 228.

46. Anselm, *Dialogi*, PL 188, 1101–1102, 1163–1210, 1215–1217, 1233.

47. Ibid., 1181–1183, 1218–1224, 1231.

48. Ibid., 1248.

49. Hugh of Saint Victor, *De sacramentis Christianae fidei*, PL 176, 173–618. As noted by Chenu, "New Awareness of History," 168: "Scholasticism detached itself from sacred history." See the similar evaluation of Richard Southern, "Tradition of Historical Writing," 21: 163, who observes that twelfth-century scholasticism was "favorable to systematization, and this was achieved by a method which was hostile to historical speculation." Both Chenu and Southern, however, recognize Hugh of Saint Victor as somewhat of an exception to this general trend.

50. *De sacramentis Christianae fidei*, PL 176, 597–598. See also Stephen Benin, "Jews and Christian History: Hugh of St. Victor, Anselm of Havelberg and William of Auvergne," in *From Witness to Witchcraft: Jews and Judaism in Medieval Christian Thought*, ed. Jeremy Cohen (Wiesbaden, 1996), 203–219.

51. Otto of Freising, *Chronica*, 390–399.

52. Ibid., 395; and Hugh of Saint Victor, *In epistolam II ad Thessalonicenses*, PL 175, 591.

53. For an introduction and English translation of this text, see John Wright, *The Play of Antichrist* (Toronto, 1967); Latin text in *Der Antichrist: Der staufische Ludus de Antichristo*, ed. Gerhard Günther (Hamburg, 1970), 89–156 (with facing German translation). See also Hannes Möhring, *Der Weltkaiser der Endzeit: Entstehung, Wandel und Wirkung einer tausendjährigen Weissagung* (Stuttgart, 2000), 176–184.

54. *Der Antichrist*, ed. Günther, 154.

55. As noted by McGinn, *Antichrist*, 128–132, Hildegard was a somewhat anomalous figure who did not precisely fit with the other "Gregorian" apocalyptic thinkers of her day because of her lack of direct support for the reform-era papacy.

56. See Hildegard of Bingen, *Scivias*, ed. Adelgundis Führkötter and Angela Carlevaris, CCCM 43A/3 (Turnhout, 1978), 574–603; and Hildegard, *Liber divinorum ope-*

rum, ed. Albert Derolez and Peter Dronke, CCCM 92 (Turnhout, 1996), 405–464.

57. See the foundational piece by Robert Lerner, "Refreshment of the Saints: The Time after Antichrist as a Station for Earthly Progress in Medieval Thought," *Traditio* 32 (1976): 97–144; and Lerner, "The Medieval Return to the Thousand-Year Sabbath," in *The Apocalypse in the Middle Ages,* ed. Richard Emmerson and Bernard McGinn (Ithaca, 1992), 51–71

58. BNF Lat. 16300, fols. 1r, 28r–31r, 36r–36v, 65v.

59. Rupert of Deutz, *De sancta trinitate,* 24: 1994.

60. Ibid., 2095–2097. For some early thoughts on the conversion of the Jews, see also Rupert, *De divinis officiis,* 364–365. Rupert also examined the relationship between Jews and Christians in his tract *Anulus sive dialogus inter Christianum et Judaeum,* PL 170, 559–610. On Rupert's place in the history of anti-Judaism, see Anna S. Abulafia, "The Ideology of Reform and Changing Ideas concerning Jews in the Works of Rupert of Deutz and Hermannus Quondam Iudeus," *Jewish History* 7 (1993): 43–63; and David Timmer, "Biblical Exegesis and the Jewish-Christian Controversy in the Early Twelfth Century," *Church History* 58 (1989): 309–321.

61. Honorius, *Gemma animae,* PL 172, 627; and *Sacramentarium,* PL 172, 768.

62. Honorius, *Expositio in cantica canticorum,* PL 172, 359, 379–382, 387, 415. In another passage of this work, he connected the "five praises" given to the brides with the five stages of the Church: the Primitive Church; the church of the Gentiles; the church of Martyrs; the church of the imperfect in an era of peace (i.e., the mixture of true and false Christians in his own day); and, finally, the "church of the Synagogue converted to the faith" at the end of time.

63. *Expositio in cantica canticorum,* PL 172, 455, 468–472, 478–480.

64. Jeremy Cohen, "*Synagoga conversa:* Honorius Augustodunensis, the Song of Songs, and Christianity's 'Eschatological Jew,'" *Speculum* 79 (2004): 309–340, quotation from pp. 318–319.

65. On this twelfth-century shift, see Gavin Langmuir, *Toward a Definition of Anti-Semitism* (Berkeley, 1990); Gilbert Dahan, *Les intellectuels chrétiens et les juifs au moyen age* (Paris, 1990); Anna S. Abulafia, *Christians and Jews in the Twelfth-Century Renaissance* (London, 1995); Robert Chazan, "The Deteriorating Image of the Jews—Twelfth and Thirteenth Centuries," in *Christendom and Its Discontents,* ed. Scott Waugh and Peter Diehl (Cambridge, 1996), 220–233; and Jeremy Cohen, *Living Letters of the Law: Ideas of the Jew in Medieval Christianity* (Berkeley, 1999), 147–166.

66. Cohen, "*Synagoga conversa,*" 325.

67. Gerhoh of Reichersberg, *In psalmum LXIIII,* ed. Ernst Sackur, MGH Ldl 3, 439–

492. See the comments of Classen, *Gerhoh von Reichersberg*, 141–149. Generally on Gerhoh's theology of history, see Beinert, *Die Kirche-Gottes*, 50–68; and Classen, *"Res Gestae*, Universal History, Apocalypse," 409–411.

68. *In psalmum LXIIII*, 448–451.

69. Gerhoh of Reichersberg, *De quarta vigilia noctis*, 503–525 (especially pp. 508–509). For similar sentiments about the struggles of the reform-era Roman Church, see also Gerhoh of Reichersberg, *Opusculum de edificio dei*, 150–152; *De investigatione antichristi*, ed. Sackur, 322–329; and *De ordine donorum sancti spiritus*, 73–74.

70. Gerhoh followed Rupert of Deutz's lead in this regard, positing a full conversion of both Gentiles and Jews, who would receive "counsel" from among the seven gifts of the Holy Spirit (e.g., *De ordine donorum*, 127–128).

71. *De quarta vigilia noctis*, 508–509.

72. *De investigatione Antichristi*, ed. Sackur, 352.

4. Joachim of Fiore and the Sabbath Age

1. Important studies on the abbot include Herbert Grundmann, *Studien über Joachim von Fiore* (1927; repr. Darmstadt, 1966); the essays in Herbert Grundmann, *Ausgewählte Aufsätze*, Schriften der Monumenta Germaniae Historica 25/2 (Stuttgart, 1977); Marjorie Reeves, *Joachim of Fiore and the Prophetic Future* (1976; repr. Stroud, U.K., 1999); Marjorie Reeves, *The Influence of Prophecy in the Later Middle Ages* (1969; repr. Notre Dame, 1993); Ernesto Buonaiuti, *Gioacchino da Fiore: i tempi—la vita—il messaggio* (1931; repr. Cosenza, 1984); Bernard McGinn, *The Calabrian Abbot: Joachim of Fiore in the History of Western Thought* (New York, 1985); and Gian Luca Potestà, *Il tempo dell'apocalisse: vita di Gioacchino da Fiore* (Rome, 2004). On the long-term reception of Joachim's ideas, see Marjorie Reeves and Gould Warwick, *Joachim of Fiore and the Myth of the Eternal Evangel in the Nineteenth Century* (Oxford, 1987), and Matthias Riedl, *Joachim von Fiore: Denker der vollendeten Menschheit* (Würzburg, 2004).

2. Joachim of Fiore, *Liber de concordia novi et veteris testamenti*, ed. E. Randolph Daniel, American Philosophy Society 73 (Philadelphia, 1983), 403.

3. There has been a great deal of debate about Joachim's immediate and long-term influence. In addition to Reeves, *The Influence of Prophecy*, see Morton Bloomfield and Marjorie Reeves, "The Penetration of Joachimism into Northern Europe," *Speculum* 29 (1954): 772–793; Henri de Lubac, *La postérité spirituelle de Joachim de Flore* (Paris, 1978); Marjorie Reeves, "The Originality and Influence of Joachim of Fiore," *Traditio* 36 (1980): 296–316; and Bernard McGinn, "Influence and Importance in Evaluating Joachim of Fiore," in *Il profetismo gioachimita tra quattrocento e cinquecento*, ed. Gian Luca Potestà (Genoa, 1991), 15–36.

4. Two near-contemporary *vitae* provide the main source of information for Joachim's life. See Herbert Grundmann, "Zur Biographie Joachims von Fiore und Raniers von Ponza," *Deutsches Archiv für Erforschung des Mittelalters* 16 (1960): 437–546. The first *vita* (pp. 528–539) is anonymous, and the second (pp. 539–544) is attributed to Luke of Cosenza (d. 1224), a monk at Casamari around the time of Joachim's stay in 1183–1184. See also *Gioacchino da Fiore: vitae e opera*, ed. Gian Luca Potestà, Opere di Gioacchino da Fiore: testi e strumenti 8 (Rome, 1997).

5. On Joachim's spiritual insights and experiences, see two important articles by Robert Lerner, "Joachim of Fiore's Breakthrough to Chiliasm," *Cristianesimo nella storia* 6 (1985): 489–512; and Lerner, "Ecstatic Dissent," *Speculum* 67 (1992): 33–57.

6. See Grundmann, "Biographie," 532–533.

7. In addition to the two *vitae* cited above, see Robert of Auxerre, *Chronicon*, ed. Oswald Holder-Egger, MGH SS 26 (Hannover, 1882), 248–249, who reports that Joachim later met with Pope Urban III around 1186, and a letter urging Joachim to continue his works by Pope Clement III, included as a preface to the *Liber de concordia*, 3.

8. In recent years, Joachim's treatment of the Jews has attracted growing attention. See Robert Lerner, *The Feast of St. Abraham: Medieval Millenarians and the Jews* (Philadelphia, 2002); Anna S. Abulafia, "The Conquest of Jerusalem: Joachim of Fiore and the Jews," in *The Experience of Crusading*, ed. Marcus Bull and Norman Housely (Cambridge, 2003), 127–146; and E. Randolph Daniel, "Abbot Joachim of Fiore and the Conversion of the Jews," in *Friars and Jews in the Middle Ages and Renaissance*, ed. Steven McMichael and Susan Myers (Leiden, 2004), 1–22. For earlier observations, see Beatrice Hirsch-Reich, "Joachim von Fiore und das Judentum," in *Judentum im Mittelalter: Beiträge zum christlich-jüdischen Gespräch*, ed. Paul Wilpert (Berlin, 1966), 228–263.

9. Generally speaking, the place of the Greek Church in Joachim's schemes has been understudied. See, however, my article "Joachim of Fiore and the Division of Christendom," *Viator* 98 (2003): 89–108, along with A.-D. von Den Brincken, *Die "Nationes Christianorum Orientalium" im Verständnis der lateinischen Historiographie* (Cologne, 1973), 32–34; Gert Wendelborn, *Gott und Geschichte: Joachim von Fiore und die Hoffnung der Christenheit* (Vienna, 1974), 142–148; and Felicitas Schmieder, "Two Unequal Brothers Split and Reunited—the Greeks in Latin Eschatological Perceptions of Politics and History before and after 1204," in *Quarta crociata: Venezia—Bisanzio—impero Latino*, ed. Gherardo Ortalli et al. (Venice, 2006), 633–651.

10. Richard Southern, "Aspects of the European Tradition of Historical Writings," *Transactions of the Royal Historical Society*, 5th series, 22 (London, 1971): 159–180,

observes that "Joachim was doing for prophetic history what scholastic thinkers were doing for the general structure of theology: bringing order into thought by a stricter application of the methods and interpretations of the past and by giving a clear and logical arrangement to the results" (quotation from p. 175). See also Marjorie Reeves, "The Development of Apocalyptic Thought: Medieval Attitudes," in *The Apocalypse in English Renaissance Thought and Literature,* ed. C. A. Patrides and Joseph Wittreich (Manchester, U.K., 1984), 40–72.

11. In this regard, I agree with E. Randolph Daniel, "Abbot Joachim of Fiore: A Reformist Apocalyptic," in *Fearful Hope: Approaching the New Millennium,* ed. Christopher Kleinhenz and Fannie LeMoine (Madison, 1999), 207–210.

12. The first four books of the *Book of Concordance* are available in Daniel, *Joachim of Fiore: Liber de concordia novi et veteris testamenti.* For book five, see the early modern Venetian edition, *Concordia novi et veteri testamento* (1519; Frankfurt, 1964). I would like to thank Julia Wannenmacher for making available a typescript of book five by Herbert Grundmann. There is no critical edition of Joachim's *Expositio in Apocalypsim* (1527; Frankfurt, 1964), although the abbot's introduction to this work is published as the *Introduzione all'Apocalisse,* ed. Kurt-Victor Selge, trans. Gian Luca Potestà, Opera di Gioacchino da Fiore: testi e strumenti 6 (Rome, 1995). See also the *Enchiridion super Apocalypsim,* ed. Edward K. Burger, Pontifical Institute of Mediaeval Studies: Studies and Texts 78 (Toronto, 1986), which offers a longer, independent version of the introduction to the *Expositio.* There is no critical edition of the *Psalterium decem chordarum* (1527; Frankfurt, 1964), but see the Italian translation of the *Psalterium* based on a forthcoming critical edition, *Psalterium, il salterio a dieci corde,* ed. Kurt-Victor Selge, Opere di Gioacchino da Fiore: testi e strumenti 16 (Rome, 2004).

13. Joachim of Fiore, *Tractatus super quatuor evangelia,* ed. Francesco Santi, Fonti per la storia dell'Italia medievale: antiquitates 17 (Rome, 2002); *Exhortatorium Iudeorum,* ed. Alexander Patschovsky, Fonti per la storia dell'Italia medievale: antiquitates 26 (Rome, 2006); and Cipriano Baraut, "Un tratado inédito de Joaquín de Fiore: *De vita sancti Benedicti et de officio divino secundum eius doctrinam,*" *Analecta sacra Tarraconensia* 24 (1951): 33–122.

14. *Gioacchino da Fiore: Il libro delle figure,* ed. Leone Tondelli (Turin, 1953). See also the commentary of Marjorie Reeves and Beatrice Hirsch-Reich, *The Figurae of Joachim of Fiore* (Oxford, 1972); and Marco Rainini, *Disegni dei tempi: il "Liber Figurarum" e la teologia figurative di Gioacchino da Fiore,* Opera di Gioacchino da Fiore: testi e strumenti 18 (Rome, 2006).

15. See Gian Luca Potestà, "Die Genealogia: ein frühes Werk Joachims von Fiore und die Anfänge seines Geschichtsbildes," *Deutsches Archiv für Erforschung des Mittelalters* 56 (2000): 55–101; *De prophetia ignota: eine frühe Schrift Joachims von Fiore,*

ed. Matthias Kaup, MGH Studien und Texte 19 (Hannover, 1998); Julia Wannenmacher, *Hermeneutik der Heilsgeschichte: De septem sigillis und die sieben Siegel im
Werk Joachims von Fiore*, Studies in the History of Christian Traditions 118 (Leiden, 2005), 336–355; and *Ioachim abbas Florensis sermones*, ed. Valeria de Fraja,
Fonti per la storia dell'Italia medievale: antiquitates 18 (Rome, 2004).

16. *De prophetia ignota*, 184.

17. Ibid., 184–190. For a concise definition of concordance, see Joachim of Fiore,
Liber de concordia, ed. Daniel, 62: *Concordiam proprie esse dicimus similitudinem eque
proportionis novi et veteris testamenti, eque, dico quo ad numerum non quo ad digni-
tatem; cum videlicet persona et persona, ordo et ordo, bellum et bellum ex parilitate qua-
dam mutuis se uultibus intuentur.* Joachim labeled this correspondence between the
Old and New Testaments the *secunda diffinitio*. See Reeves, *Joachim of Fiore*, 1–28;
E. Randolph Daniel, "Joachim of Fiore: Patterns of History in the Apocalypse,"
in *The Apocalypse in the Middle Ages*, ed. Richard K. Emmerson and Bernard
McGinn (Ithaca, N.Y., 1992), 72–88; and E. Randolph Daniel, "A New Understanding of Joachim: The Concords, the Exile, and the Exodus," in *Gioacchino da
Fiore tra Bernardo di Clairvaux e Innocenzo III*, ed. Robert Riusconi (Rome, 2001),
209–222.

18. *Genealogia*, 95–96. On the identification of the *Genealogia* as Joachim's first extant
work, see Stephen Wessley, "A New Writing of Joachim of Fiore: Preliminary
Observations," in *Prophecy and Eschatology*, ed. Michael Wilks, Studies in Church
History: Subsidia 10 (Oxford, 1994), 15–28.

19. *De prophetia ignota*, 192.

20. *Liber de concordia*, ed. Daniel, 81; and *Genealogia*, 94. For some other notable examples, see the *Liber de concordia*, ed. Daniel, 45–48; *De septem sigillis*, 336–355;
and *Enchiridion super Apocalypsim*, 32–33. In *De vita sancti Benedicti*, 42–44, 52–53,
Joachim argued that the daily twelve psalms prescribed in divine offices of the
Benedictine rule represented two sets of "six spiritual wars" fought first by the
Hebrews (against the Egyptians; Philistines; Syrians; Assyrians; Chaldaeans; and
the Hellenistic Greeks under Antiochus) and second by the Church (fought by
the apostles; martyrs; doctors; confessors; virgins; and monks). Joachim revisited
this scheme of two sets of seven persecutions in another minor work (ca. 1190),
the *Praephatio super Apocalypsim*, in Kurt-Victor Selge, "Eine Einführung Joachims
von Fiore in die Johannesapokalypse," *Deutsches Archiv für Erforschung des Mittelalters* 46 (1990): 85–131.

21. Some manuscripts of the *Book of Concordance* included generational charts that
traced the genealogy of biblical figures in the time of the Old Testament and the
corresponding generations in the time of the New Testament. See Gian Luca
Potestà, "Geschichte als Ordnung in der Diagrammatik Joachims von Fiore," in

Die Bildwelt der Diagramme Joachims von Fiore, ed. Alexander Patschovsky (Ostfildern, 2003), 115–146.

22. For the most part Joachim resisted making any precise predictions about dates, since the number of years in each generation (both biblical and post-biblical) varied. He was unequivocal, however, in saying that he was living in the fortieth generation after Christ, leaving only two more generations before the opening of the sixth seal. Among other passages, see the *Liber de concordia,* ed. Daniel, 400 (where Joachim predicts that the forty-first generation will begin in the year 1201), and 402 (where he adds the qualification that God alone knows when the forty-second generation will start). See also *Genealogia,* 92, where the abbot declared that the opening of the sixth seal would be in sixty years. In order to make room for the seventh age of history (the earthly Sabbath) *after* the seventh persecution, Joachim argued that the sixth and seventh persecutions would in fact be a "double" *(duplex)* development during the sixth seal at the close of the sixth age. The two persecutions of the Church aligned with the double persecution of the Hebrews recorded in the Books of Judith and Esther. The abbot explained this development with reference to Exodus 16:22, where the Hebrews were instructed to collect two *gomor* of manna on the sixth day of the week in preparation for the Sabbath on the seventh day (see the *Genealogia,* 95; *Praephatio super Apocalypsim,* 111; and *Liber de concordia,* ed. Daniel, 402, where Joachim places the sixth "tribulation" during the imminent forty-first generation, followed by the seventh during the forty-second generation).

23. See Reeves, *Influence of Prophecy,* 16–27, 126–132. Joachim's Trinitarian vision did not displace the notion of the two Testaments with Christ at their center. To use his labels, the *prima diffinitio* (i.e., his tertiary model of history) and the *secunda diffinitio* (his binary model of concordance) were complementary. Joachim argued that the "spiritual understanding" which revealed the mysteries of the Trinity in history emerged from the careful concordance of the two Testaments. Specifically, the time of the Old Testament pertained principally to the *status* of the Father, and the time of the New Testament to both the *status* of the Son and the *status* of the Holy Spirit. The third *status* was contiguous with the seventh seal in the time of the New Testament (that is, the third *status* and the seventh "little age" were one and the same era of peace on earth).

24. Among numerous examples, see the *Liber de concordia,* ed. Daniel, 66–67, 405; *Liber de concordia,* bk. 5, fol. 65va; and *Psalterium decem cordarum,* fols. 249va-b.

25. Joachim revisited this theme of the "spiritual men" frequently. See the *Liber de concordia,* ed. Daniel, 75; *De vita sancti Benedicti,* 24–26; *Psalterium decem cordarum,* fol. 153va; and *Quatuor evangelia,* 192–193.

26. Among numerous passages, see the *Liber de concordia,* ed. Daniel, 66–77, 144,

405–406; *Enchiridion super Apocalypsim*, 23; and *Psalterium decem cordarum*, fols. 249va-b, 253va. See also Joachim's sermon *De mistico intellectu Helisabeth et Marie* in *Ioachim abbas Florensis sermones*, 128. On the theology of *filioque* in Joachim's schemes, see E. Randolph Daniel, "The Double Procession of the Holy Spirit in Joachim of Fiore's Understanding of History," *Speculum* 55 (1983): 469–483.

27. *Exhortatorium Iudeorum*, 276–277.

28. Ibid., 282–283; and *Quatuor evangelia*, 19–36.

29. *Liber de concordia*, bk. 5, fol. 114va.

30. *De septem sigillis*, 337; *Quatuor evangelia*, 29.

31. *De septem sigillis*, 337, 339, 341; *Liber de concordia*, ed. Daniel, 290–291, 335; and *Quatuor evangelia*, 116, 140–141.

32. This basic argument appears constantly in Joachim's writings. See the *Liber de concordia*, ed. Daniel, 292; *De septem sigillis*, 343; *Enchiridion super Apocalypsim*, 73; and *Quatuor evangelia*, 287–288. In the *Liber de concordia*, ed. Daniel, 337, Joachim refers to the schism as occurring during the fourteenth generation after Christ at the first Council of Constantinople (381).

33. *Quatuor evangelia*, 187–193, 291. On the general charge that the Greek Church was overly carnal and guilty of Judaizing, see the *Enchiridion super Apocalypsim*, 22, 49 (on the Greek failure to fast on Saturdays); and the *Liber de concordia*, bk. 5, fol. 82va (on the Greek habit of wearing beards), fol. 83ra (on clerical marriage), and fols. 100rb–100va (on the Greek disparaging of azymes).

34. *Quatuor evangelia*, 13.

35. On this transferal from the Greeks to the Latins, see the *Quatuor evangelia*, 13–14, 150, 229; and *Enchiridion super Apocalypsim*, 22.

36. *De prophetia ignota*, 186; and *Liber de concordia*, ed. Daniel, 296–297. This attack against the Greeks under the fourth seal was twofold: first, by the Persians, matching the Syrian assault on Israel, followed by the Saracens.

37. *Liber de concordia*, ed. Daniel, 297, 300.

38. This exegesis appears frequently in Joachim's works. See *Expositio in Apocalypsim*, fol. 142v–145r; and *Enchiridion super Apocalypsim*, 36.

39. On the barbarian invasions of the third seal, see *De prophetia ignota*, 186; *De septem sigillis*, 343; and the *Liber de concordia*, ed. Daniel, 294.

40. *Liber de concordia*, ed. Daniel, 136–137; *De septem sigillis*, 343; and *Enchiridion super Apocalypsim*, 35.

41. *Quatuor evangelia*, 228–229.

42. As Daniel, "Double Procession," 474, notes: "For Joachim, historical fact confirmed the Latin position on the *filioque* against the Greeks. He accepted the double initiation of the monastic order. This could only be possible if the Holy Spirit proceeded from both the Father and the Son."

43. *Liber de concordia*, ed. Daniel, 351. See also the *Liber de concordia*, bk. 5, fol. 98vb; *Quatuor evangelia*, 192–193; and *De vita sancti Benedicti*, 25–26; along with the observations of Wessley, *Joachim of Fiore*, 1–27, and Stephen Wessley, "'Bonum est Benedicto mutare locum': The Role of the 'Life of Saint Benedict' in Joachim of Fiore's Monastic Reform," *Revue Bénédictine* 90 (1980): 314–328. See also Otto of Freising, *Chronica sive historia de duabus civitatibus*, ed. Adolf Hofmeister, MGH SS (in us. schol.) 45 (Hannover, 1912), 372.

44. *Liber de concordia*, ed. Daniel, 296.

45. *Genealogia*, 92; and *De prophetia ignota*, 186. In his introduction to *De prophetia ignota*, 32–38, Kaup makes a convincing argument that because of Joachim's generational concordance, this "Charles" refers to Charles Martel, not Charlemagne as often assumed. On the transferal of empire from the Greeks to the Franks and God's promise of protection for the Latin Church, see also the *Liber de concordia*, ed. Daniel, 366–367.

46. *Intelligentia super calathis*, in *Gioacchino da Fiore: aspetti inediti della vita e delle opera*, ed. Pietro de Leo (Soveria Manelli, 1988), 135–148. For analysis of this text, see Herbert Grundmann, "Kirchenfreiheit und Kaisermacht um 1190 in der Sicht Joachims von Fiore," *Deutsches Archiv für Erforschung des Mittelalters* 19 (1963): 353–396.

47. *Intelligentia super calathis*, 138–139. On this shift from the imperial patronage of Rome by the early Frankish emperors to the later persecution by the German emperors, see the *Liber de concordia*, ed. Daniel, 368–369, 376–377.

48. *Liber de concordia*, ed. Daniel, 378–379, 383; *Liber de concordia*, bk. 5, fol. 125va; and *Intelligentia super calathis*, 143.

49. For a discussion of Joachim's attitude toward the crusades, see E. Randolph Daniel, "Apocalyptic Conversion: The Joachite Alternative to Crusade," *Traditio* 25 (1969): 127–154. Daniel argues that Joachim was generally not sympathetic toward the crusading movement. This general conclusion is followed by Benjamin Kedar, *Crusade and Mission* (Princeton, 1994), 112–116. For a contrasting view, see Richard Southern, *Western Views of Islam in the Middle Ages* (Cambridge, Mass., 1962), 40–41. More recently, see Jean Flori, *L'islam et la fin des temps: l'interprétation prophétique des invasions musulmanes dans la chrétienté médiévale* (Paris, 2007), 307–312, 317–326.

50. *Liber de concordia*, bk. 5, fol. 127ra-va. Joachim offered a similar interpretation of Daniel in his tract *Exhortatorium Iudeorum*, 194–195.

51. *Liber de concordia*, bk. 5, fols. 127vb–128ra; and *De vita Benedicti*, 52–53.

52. *Il libro delle figure*, ed. Tondelli, table 14. In other instances, Joachim associated the fifth head of the dragon with Emperor Henry IV. See, for example, his exegesis

of the dragon in his *Ioachim abbas Florensis sermones*, 59, along with the observations of Alexander Patschovsky, "The Holy Emperor Henry 'the First' As One of the Dragon's Heads of Apocalypse: On the Image of the Holy Roman Empire under German Rule in the Tradition of Joachim of Fiore," *Viator* 29 (1998): 291–322. Joachim's association of the imminent seventh head of the dragon with the "great Antichrist" also required him to posit the coming of a "final" Antichrist, after the third *status* and just before the end of time (represented by the dragon's tail). See Robert Lerner, "Antichrists and Antichrist in Joachim of Fiore," *Speculum* 60 (1985): 553–570.

53. *De vita Benedicti*, 53.

54. For the earlier account of this meeting, see the *Gesta Richardi I*, RS 49/2 (London, 1867), 151–155; for the later recension, see Roger of Hoveden, *Chronica*, RS 51/3 (London, 1867), 75–77. On the authorship of both chronicles, see Antonia Gransden, *Historical Writing in England c. 550 to 1307* (Ithaca, N.Y., 1974), 222–230.

55. Roger of Hovedon, *Chronica*, 75–77.

56. Ibid., 77.

57. Ibid., 255.

58. *De prophetia ignota*, 200.

59. To the best of my knowledge, Joachim's earliest explicit reference to the reunion of the Latin and Greek Churches as preceding the conversion of the Jews comes in the *Liber de concordia*, ed. Daniel, 137.

60. Ibid., 413–417; and *De vita Benedicti*, 20–28. See also Bernard McGinn, "*Alter Moyses*: The Role of Bernard of Clairvaux in the Thought of Joachim of Fiore," in *Bernardus Magister: Papers Presented at the Nonacentenary Celebration of the Birth of Saint Bernard of Clairvaux*, ed. John Sommerfeldt (Kalamazoo, 1990), 429–448.

61. *Quatuor evangelia*, 97–101; and *Liber de concordia*, ed. Daniel, 402. I would like to thank Bernard McGinn for sharing a draft of his essay in preparation, "Joachim of Fiore and the Twelfth-Century Papacy," which helped to clarify my views on Joachim's sentiments toward the Roman papacy. See also Reeves, *Influence of Poverty*, 395–400.

62. *Liber de concordia*, bk. 5, fol. 117ra.

63. *Exhortatorium Iudeorum*, 276–283. For additional passages on the conversion of the Jews, see the *Liber de concordia*, ed. Daniel, 158–160; *Quatuor evangelia*, 26, 108, 117; and *De vita Benedicti*, 82–83. There is an emerging consensus among scholars of anti-Judaism that Joachim's predictions of a future union between Christians and Jews seems to mitigate some of the more extreme expressions of anti-Semitism that are found among some of his contemporaries. See Abulafia,

"Conquest of Jerusalem," 146, who declares that Joachim's writings have "made it possible for us to see clearly the continuing existence of the built-in ambiguities of Christian teaching about Jews at the end of the twelfth century." See the similar comments of Lerner, *Feast of Saint Abraham*, 121; and Daniel, "Abbot Joachim," 21.

64. Among numerous examples, see the *Liber de concordia*, bk. 5, fols. 82ra–85ra; *Quatuor evangelia*, 109; and *De vita Benedicti*, 24.

65. *Expositio in Apocalypsim*, fols. 142va–145vb; *Quatuor evangelia*, 150, 288–89, 308; and *Ioachim abbas Florensis sermones*, 81.

66. *Exhortatorium Iudeorum*, 271.

67. *Liber de concordia*, bk. 5, fols. 95va, 104va; and *Quatuor evangelia*, 111–112, 152, 353. For disagreement on Joachim's timetable, see Lerner, "Antichrist and Antichrists," 566–569; and Daniel, "Conversion of the Jews," 12.

68. *Exhortatorium Iudeorum*, 122; and *Quatuor evangelia*, 105, 160. Recently, Gian Luca Potestà, *Il tempo dell'apocalisse*, 338–349, 360–364, and also in Potestà, *Trattati sui quattro vangeli*, xix–xx, has drawn attention to these passages referring to negotiations between Rome and the Armenian Church that sought to unite formally the two Christian peoples. This was apparently around the year 1198. There is evidence that Joachim modified a later recension of the *Psalterium decem cordarum* to emphasize his eschatological vision of Latin and Greek harmony. Variations between the earliest extant manuscripts of the text, attributed to the abbot himself, indicate his growing fascination with the reunion of Christendom. These variants are published in the endnotes to Potestà, *Il tempo dell'apocalisse*, 439–440, n. 5. An earlier version of the *Psalterium* reads: *In Iudeis et gentibus, manentibus ad tempus divisi ob diversitatem morum atque consuetudinem, procedent de cetero due linee, sed una erit gens et unus populus creatus ad laudem Dei, cognoscens optime Deum suum a minimo usque ad maiorem.* A later version was modified to read: *In Grecis et Latinis procedent de cetero due linee, sed una erit gens et unus populus creatus ad laudem Dei, cognoscens optime Deum suum a minimo usque ad maiorem.* This variant reading of the *Psalterium* first came to my attention in the endnotes to Lerner, *Feast of Saint Abraham*, 137, n. 58. Lerner, who describes the insertion of "Greeks and Latins" in the passage as "forced," sees it as an indication that Joachim was "backing away from philo-Semitism" in response to his critics. That may have been a factor, but we should also note Joachim's growing interest in the reunion of the Latins and Greeks as another possible reason for these substitutions.

69. Roger of Hoveden, *Chronica*, 153–154; and Ralph of Coggeshall, *Chronicon Anglicanum*, RS 66 (London, 1875), 67–70. On the emergence of Antichrist in the Western Church, see Joachim, *De vita Benedicti*, 58–62. At other points, Joachim

implies that Antichrist will arise in the Eastern Church (e.g., *Quatuor evangelia,* 113).

70. *Liber de concordia,* bk. 5, fol. 133ra.

5. The Shepherd of the World

1. Matthew of Rievaulx, BNF lat. 15157, fols. 124v–125r: *Primo quidem, favente deo, revocavit Christi vicarius ad sinum universalis ecclesie schismaticos orientales, scilicet Constantinopolim cum finibus suis, quod est pars maxima Christianitatis, que ab annis trecentis erroris sui excecata tenebris, omnino recalcitravit, detractans obedire summo pontifici.* Although the title "vicar of Christ" (rather than Saint Peter) dated back to the papacy of Eugene III, Innocent III was the first to employ it regularly.

2. Matthew of Rievaulx, BNF lat. 15157, fol. 125r. On Innocent's crusading activities and relations with Byzantium, see Alfred J. Andrea, "Pope Innocent III as Crusader and Canonist: His Relations with the Greeks of Constantinople, 1198–1216" (Ph.D. diss., Cornell, 1969); Helmut Roscher, *Papst Innocenz III. und die Kreuzzüge* (Göttingen, 1969); Joseph Gill, "Innocent III and the Greeks: Aggressor or Apostle?" in *Relations between East and West in the Middle Ages,* ed. Derek Baker (Edinburgh, 1973), 95–108; John C. Moore, *Pope Innocent III (1160/61–1216): To Root Up and to Plant* (Leiden, 2003), 102–134; and Christopher Tyerman, *God's War: A New History of the Crusades* (Cambridge, Mass., 2006), 479–500. For some insightful (and sometimes cutting) comments on crusading violence in Innocent's broader theology, see John Gilchrist, "The Lord's War as the Proving Ground of Faith: Pope Innocent III and the Propagation of Violence (1198–1216)," in *Crusaders and Muslims in Twelfth-Century Syria,* ed. Maya Shatzmiller (Leiden, 1993), 65–83. On Innocent's view of the "wider world," see also Jane Sayers, *Innocent III: Leader of Europe 1198–1216* (London, 1994), 164–188.

3. Several ground-breaking essays on Pope Innocent are assembled and excerpted in James Powell, ed., *Innocent III: Vicar of Christ or Lord of the World?* 2nd ed. (1963; Washington, D.C., 1994). For debate about Innocent's legal training and his education as a theologian, see Kenneth Pennington, "The Legal Education of Pope Innocent III," *Bulletin of Medieval Canon Law* 4 (1974): 70–77; Pennington, "Innocent III and the Divine Authority of the Pope," in *Popes and Bishops: The Papal Monarchy in the Twelfth and Thirteenth Centuries* (Philadelphia, 1984), 13–42; Christopher Egger, "Papst Innocenz III. als Theologe: Beiträge zur Kenntnis seines Denkens im Rahmen der Frühscholastik," *Archivum Historiae Pontificiae* 30 (1992): 55–123; Egger, "A Theologian at Work: Remarks on Methods and Sources in In-

nocent III's Writings," in *Pope Innocent and His World*, ed. John C. Moore (Aldershot, U.K., 1999), 25–49; Joseph Canning, "Power and Pastor: A Reassessment of Innocent III's Contribution to Political Ideas," in *Pope Innocent and His World*, 245–255; and Brenda Bolton, "Signposts from the Past: Reflections on Innocent III's Providential Path," in *Innocenzo III: Urbs et Orbis (atti del congresso internationale Roma, 9–15 settembre 1998)*, ed. Andrea Sommerlechner, 2 vols. (Rome, 2003), 1: 21–55.

4. Innocent III, no. 18, *Regestum Innocentii papae super negotio Romani imperii*, ed. Friedrich Kempf, Miscellenea historiae pontificae 12 (Rome, 1947), 48.

5. On Innocent's apocalyptic views of the Fourth Crusade, see Alfred J. Andrea, "Innocent III, the Fourth Crusade, and the Coming Apocalypse," in *The Medieval Crusade*, ed. Susan Ridyard (Woodbridge, U.K., 2004), 97–106; Gilchrist, "The Lord's War," 76, 80; and Jean Flori, *L'islam et la fin des temps: l'interprétation prophétique des invasions musulmanes dans la chrétienté médiévale* (Paris, 2007), 326–331.

6. *Emonis chronicon*, ed. Louis Weiland, MGH SS 23 (Hannover, 1874), 474–475.

7. My analysis of Latin historical perspectives on the Fourth Crusade is greatly indebted to Alfred J. Andrea. Among other works, see Alfred J. Andrea and Paul I. Rachlin, "Holy War, Holy Relics, Holy Theft: The Anonymous of Soissons's *De terra Iherosolimitana*, An Analysis, Edition, and Translation," *Historical Relections/Réflexions Historiques* 18 (1992): 157–175; Andrea, "Conrad of Krosigk, Bishop of Halberstadt, Crusader and Monk of Sittichenbach: His Ecclesiastical Career, 1184–1225," *Analecta Cisterciensia* 43 (1987): 11–91; and Andrea, *The Capture of Constantinople: The* Hystoria Constantinopolitana *of Gunther of Pairis* (Philadelphia, 1997).

8. See Ernle Bradford, *The Great Betrayal: Constantinople 1204* (London, 1967); John Godfrey, *1204: The Unholy Crusade* (Oxford, 1980); and W. B. Bartlett, *An Ungodly War: The Sack of Constantinople and the Fourth Crusade* (Thrupp, U.K., 2000).

9. Innocent III, *Sermo XXII*, PL 217, 555–558, quotation from col. 556. See also PL 217, 547–555, 649–672.

10. For an insightful discussion of Innocent's sermons on Saints Peter and Paul, along with a number of his famous papal predecessors, see John Doran, "In Whose Footsteps? The Role Models of Innocent III," in *Innocenzo III: Urbs et Orbis*, 1: 56–73.

11. On the "transferal of empire" from Greece to the Franks, see Innocent III, nos. 29, 30, 33, 62, *Regestum Innocentii*, 75, 92, 97, 102, and 168.

12. Innocent III, no. 2, *Regestum Innocentii*, 6–9. In this letter Innocent invoked the well-known trope of the "two swords" (Lk. 22:38), symbolizing the (subordinate) secular and (superior) spiritual spheres. For some similar statements about the proper relationship between the Roman Empire and the Apostolic See, see also

Innocent's letter to envoys of the French king, late 1199 or early 1200, Innocent III, no. 18, *Regestum Innocentii*, 45–52, and also his letter to the secular and ecclesiastical magnates of Germany, 5 January 1201, no. 31, *Regestum Innocentii*, 95–97. See also Pennington, "Innocent III and the Divine Authority of the Pope," 13; and John A. Watt, "The Theory of Papal Monarchy in the Thirteenth Century: The Contribution of the Canonists," *Traditio* 20 (1964): 179–317.

13. Gregory VIII to all the Christian faithful, 29 October 1187, no. 4, PL 202, 1539–1542 *(De audita tremendi)*. See also Tyerman, *God's War*, 366–399.

14. *Libellus de expugnatione Terrae Sanctae per Saladinum*, RS 66 (London, 1875), 227, 250. See also Roger of Wendover, *Flores historiarum*, RS 84/1 (London, 1886–1889), 140–142; Berter of Orléans, RS 51/2 (London, 1870), 300–332; and Matthew of Rievaulx, BNF lat. 15157, fols. 106v–108v *(De captione sanctae crucis)*. On the crusader True Cross, see Alan Murray, "'Mighty against the Enemies of Christ': The Relic of the True Cross in the Armies of the Kingdom of Jerusalem," in *The Crusades and Their Sources*, ed. John France and William Zajac (Aldershot, U.K.), 217–238.

15. Innocent III to Haimo of Jerusalem, February 1198, 1:11, *Die Register Innocenz' III.*, ed. Othman Hageneder et al. (Graz-Cologne, 1964–), 18–20 (hereafter Reg.).

16. See Innocent III to Laurence, bishop of Syracuse, and Luke, abbot of Sambucina, June 1198, Reg. 1:302, 430–433, quotation from p. 431.

17. Innocent III to the bishop of Lydda, 30 August 1198, Reg. 1:343, 512–514. On Luke's connections to Joachim, see Herbert Grundmann, "Zur Biographie Joachims von Fiore und Raniers von Ponza," *Deutsches Archiv für Erforschung des Mittelalters* 16 (1960): 437–546, including the *vita* attributed to Luke, pp. 539–544.

18. Innocent III to Fulk of Neuilly, 5 November 1198, Reg. 1:398, 597. See Milton Gutsch, "A Twelfth-Century Preacher—Fulk of Neuilly," in *The Crusades and Other Historical Essays*, ed. Louis Paetow (New York, 1928), 183–206.

19. Innocent III to the diocese of Narbonne, 15 August 1198, Reg. 1:336, 498–505; and to the diocese of Magdeburg, 31 December 1199, Reg. 2:258, 490–497. These bulls are translated with introductions and substantial annotation in Alfred J. Andrea, *Contemporary Sources for the Fourth Crusade* (Leiden, 2000), 9–21, 24–32.

20. See Gerd Hagedorn, "Papst Innozenz III. und Byzanz am Vorabend des Vierten Kreuzzugs (1198–1203)," *Ostkirchliche Studien* 23 (1974): 3–20, 105–136; and James Powell, "Innocent III and Alexius III: A Crusade Plan that Failed," in *The Crusading Experience*, ed. Marcus Bull and Norman Housely (Cambridge, U.K., 2003), 96–102; and Tyerman, *God's War*, 479–500.

21. Innocent III to Alexius III, August-September 1198, Reg. 1:353, 525–528.

22. Emil Friedberg, ed., *Corpus iuris canonici* (I.23.6), 2 vols. (1879; Graz, 1955), 2: 196–198.

23. Innocent III, August-September 1198, Reg. 1:354, 528–530. On the recipient of the letter, see Alfred J. Andrea, "Latin Evidence for the Accession Date of John X Camaterus, Patriarch of Constantinople," *Byzantinische Zeitschrift* 66 (1973): 354–358.

24. Reg. 1:354, 529.

25. Innocent III to John X Camaterus, February 1199, Reg. 2:200, 382–389; for the Latin version of Camaterus's initial letter, see Reg. 2:199, 379–382. For the original Greek version (sent in February 1199), along with an accompanying letter sent the following year to the pope, see Aristeides Papadakis and Alice M. Talbot, "John X Camaterus Confronts Innocent III: An Unpublished Correspondence," *Byzantinoslavica* 33 (1972): 26–41; see also Jannis Spiteris, *La critica bizantintina del primato Romano nel secolo XII* (Rome, 1979).

26. Reg. 2:200, 384.

27. Reg. 2:200, 385–388.

28. Innocent III to Kalojan, December 1199 or January 1200, Reg. 2:255, 485–486; and to Kalojan, 22 November 1202, Reg. 5:115, 226–239.

29. Gregory of Armenia to Pope Innocent, Reg. 2:208, 404–406, quotation from pp. 404–405; and Innocent's response, 23 November 1199, Reg. 2:209, 406–408.

30. King Leo of Armenia to Pope Innocent, 23 May 1199, Reg. 210, 408–409; and Innocent's response, 24 November 1199, Reg. 2:111, 409–411.

31. Innocent to King Leo of Armenia, 17 December 1199, Reg. 2:245, 469–470.

32. Gilchrist, "The Lord's War," 75.

33. For a survey of trends in the historiography of the Fourth Crusade, see Donald Queller and Susan Stratton, "A Century of Controversy on the Fourth Crusade," *Studies in Medieval and Renaissance History* 6 (1969): 233–277; and Thomas Madden, "Outside and Inside the Fourth Crusade," *International History Review* 17 (1995): 726–743. See also Donald Queller and Thomas Madden, *The Fourth Crusade: The Conquest of Constantinople,* 2nd ed. (1977; Philadelphia, 1997); Michael Angold, *The Fourth Crusade: Event and Context* (Harlow, U.K., 2003), who additionally covers the state of the Latin Church in crusader Greece after 1204; Jonathan Phillips, *The Fourth Crusade and the Sack of Constantinople* (London, 2004); and Tyerman, *God's War,* 524–560. For a Byzantine perspective, see Charles Brand, *Byzantium Confronts the West, 1180–1204* (Cambridge, Mass., 1968). The two major crusader eyewitness sources for the narrative of the expedition, Geoffrey of Villehardouin and Robert of Clari, are available in multiple editions and translations. See Geoffrey of Villehardouin, *La conquête de Constantinople,* ed. Edmond Faral (Paris, 1938–1939); and Robert of Clari, *La conquête de Constantinople par Robert de Clari,* trans. Alexandre Micha (Paris, 1991). The two accounts are published together in Geoffroy de Villehardouin, *Un chevalier à la croisade: l'histoire de*

la conquête de Constantinople, ed. Jean Longnon (Paris, 1981). There are numerous minor reports about the crusade by other participants and near-contemporaries. See the essay on primary sources and bibliography by Alfred J. Andrea in Queller and Madden, *The Fourth Crusade,* 299–318.

34. When he met Prince Alexius, Innocent was already involved in his diplomatic negotiations with Emperor Alexius III, who had deposed Isaac and temporarily imprisoned the young Alexius. See Innocent's later mention of this meeting in a letter to Alexius, dated February 1204, Reg. 6:212, 386–387.

35. On this dissension in the crusader ranks, see William Daly, "Christian Fraternity, the Crusaders, and the Security of Constantinople, 1097–1204: The Precarious Survival of an Ideal," *Medieval Studies* 22 (1960): 43–91; Donald Queller, Thomas Compton, and Donald Campbell, "The Fourth Crusade: The Neglected Majority," *Speculum* 49 (1974): 441–465; and Raymond Schmandt, "The Fourth Crusade and the Just-War Theory," *Catholic Historical Review* 61 (1975): 191–221.

36. Thomas Madden, "Vows and Contracts in the Fourth Crusade: The Treaty of Zara and the Attack on Constantinople in 1204," *International History Review* 15 (1993): 441–468.

37. For a detailed analysis of Innocent's reactions to the constantly shifting course of the crusading expedition, see Alfred J. Andrea and John C. Moore, "A Question of Character: Two Views on Innocent III and the Fourth Crusade," in *Innocenzo III: Urbs et Orbis,* 1: 525–585.

38. Innocent III to Boniface of Montferrat and Baldwin of Flanders, June 1230, Reg. 6:101, 163–165.

39. Alexius IV to Innocent III, 25 August 1204, Reg. 6:209, 355–358 (reminding Innocent of their early meeting in 1202 and promising again to recognize the rights and dignities of the Roman Church); Innocent III to Alexius IV, February 1204, Reg. 6:228, 386–387; and Innocent III to the crusade leaders, February 1204, Reg. 6:231, 388–389.

40. Reg. 6:231, 390; translation in Andrea, *Fourth Crusade,* 90–92.

41. See the reports of Geoffrey of Villehardouin and Robert of Clari, *Un chevalier à la croisade,* 96, 235–236.

42. *Gesta Treverorum continuatio IV,* ed. Hermann Cardauns, MGH SS 24 (Hannover, 1879), 392. As observed by Queller and Madden, *Fourth Crusade,* 174: "From the crusaders' point of view, Jerusalem was now on the Bosporus."

43. Baldwin to Innocent III, after 16 May 1204, Reg. 7:152, 253–260; translation in Andrea, *Fourth Crusade,* 98–112. For a contemporary chronicle that included excerpts of a variation of this letter, see Robert of Auxerre, *Chronicon,* ed. Oswald Holder-Egger, MGH SS 26 (Hannover, 1882), 267–269.

44. Innocent III, 13 November 1204, Reg. 7:154, 264; translation in Andrea, *Fourth*

Crusade, 115–126. Innocent had already invoked this "transferal of empire" in a letter to Baldwin of Flanders, 7 November 1204, Reg. 7:153, 263.

45. Reg. 7:154, 265. Compare with Joachim of Fiore, *Expositio in Apocalypsim* (1527; Frankfurt, 1964), fols. 142va–145vb. This borrowing was first recognized by Christopher Egger. Among other places, see Egger, "Joachim von Fiore, Rainer von Ponza und die römische Kurie," in *Gioacchino da Fiore tra Bernardo di Clairvaux e Innocenzo III,* ed. Robert Rusconi (Rome, 2001), 129–162.

46. Reg. 7:154, 268.

47. Ibid., 268.

48. Ibid., 268.

49. On Innocent's connections to Joachim through Rainer of Ponza, in addition to Egger, "Joachim von Fiore, Rainer von Ponza und die römische Kurie," and Egger, "Papst Innocenz III. als Theologe," see Fiona Robb, "Did Innocent III Personally Condemn Joachim of Fiore?" *Florensia* 7 (1993): 77–91; and Robb, "Joachimist Exegesis in the Theology of Innocent III and Rainer of Ponza," *Florensia* 11 (1997): 137–152.

50. Innocent III, 21 January 1205, Reg. 7:203, 354–359; translation in Andrea, *Fourth Crusade,* 131–139. See also the comments of Moore, *Pope Innocent III,* 133–134.

51. Reg. 7:203, 354.

52. Ibid., 355.

53. Ibid., 355–356.

54. Innocent frequently stressed the idea that the capture of Constantinople would provide an opportunity to recover Jerusalem. See, for example, his letter to the crusading army in Constantinople, late April or early May 1205, Reg. 8:64, 108–109.

55. Innocent III to Thomas Morosini, 30 March 1205, Reg. 8:19, 32–33; and the pope's announcement of his new papal legate, 25 April 1205, Reg. 8:57, 98–99.

56. Innocent III to Baldwin, 15 May 1205, Reg. 8:56, 96–98.

57. Innocent III to Guido of Reims, 12 May 1205, Reg. 8:70, 126–129, quotation from p. 126.

58. Reg. 8:70, 127.

59. Innocent III to the prelates of France, 25 May 1205, Reg. 8:71, 129–130, quotation from p. 130.

60. Peter Vaux-de-Cernay, *Petri Vallium Sarnii monachi hystoria Albigensis,* ed. Pascal Guébin and Ernest Lyon, 3 vols. (Paris, 1926–1930), 1: 108–110.

61. For the text and translation, see Alfred J. Andrea, "The *Devastatio Constantinopolitana,* A Special Perspective on the Fourth Crusade: An Analysis, New Edition, and Translation," *Historical Reflections/Réflexions Historiques* 19 (1993): 107–149; translation also in Andrea, *Fourth Crusade,* 205–221.

62. Arnold of Lübeck, *Chronica Slavorum*, ed. Georg Pertz, MGH SRG (in us. schol.) 14 (Hannover, 1868), 240.

63. *Chronicon Montis Sereni*, ed. Ernest Ehrenfeuchter, MGH SS 23 (Hannover, 1874), 171.

64. *Annales Colonienses maximi*, ed. Charles Pertz, MGH SS 17 (Hannover, 1861), 810; and Robert of Auxerre, *Chronicon*, 265. Robert also included excerpts from Baldwin of Flanders' letter to the West explaining the reasons for the sack.

65. See Alberic of Trois-Fontaines, *Chronica*, ed. Paul Scheffer-Boichorst, MGH SS 23, 876–884; and Ralph of Coggeshall, *Chronicon Anglicanum*, 129–130, 142–143, 149–151; see my translation of both sections in Andrea, *Fourth Crusade*, 277–309. For some general observations on Cistercian historiography of the crusade, see Alfred J. Andrea, "Cistercian Accounts of the Fourth Crusade: Were They Anti-Venetian?" *Analecta Cisterciensia* 41 (1985): 3–41. On the Cistercian presence in crusader Greece, see E. A. R. Brown, "The Cistercians in the Latin Empire of Constantinople and Greece, 1204–1276," *Traditio* 14 (1958): 63–120.

66. Alberic of Trois-Fontaines, *Chronicon*, 886.

67. See the Anonymous of Halberstadt, *Gesta episcoporum Halberstadensium*, ed. Louis Weiland, MGH SS 23 (Hannover, 1874), 73–123; for the sections on the Fourth Crusade, pp. 116–121. For a translation with analysis, see Alfred J. Andrea, "The Anonymous Chronicler of Halberstadt's Account of the Fourth Crusade: Popular Religiosity in the Early Thirteenth Century," *Historical Relections/Réflexions Historiques* 22 (1996): 447–477; translation also in Andrea, *Fourth Crusade*, 239–264.

68. See Rostang of Cluny, "Narratio exceptionis apud Cluniacum capitis beati Clementis, ex ore Dalmacii de Serciaco, militis, excepta," in *Exuviae sacrae Constantinopolitanae*, ed. Paul Riant, 2 vols. (Geneva, 1878), 1: 127–140; Gunther of Pairis, *Hystoria Constantinopolitana*, ed. Peter Orth (Hildesheim, 1994), with English translation in Andrea, *The Capture of Constantinople*, 63–131; and Andrea and Rachlin, "Holy War, Holy Relics, Holy Theft," 157–163, which provides a critical edition of the anonymous of Soissons with English translation.

69. The anonymous of Soissons is contained in a single manuscript, BNF lat. 8898, fols. 211r–213v. Not included in the Andrea and Rachlin edition is a series of liturgical instructions for celebrating feast days associated with the relics from Greece. The first is fol. 214r: *Incipit ordo servitii tenendus in festivitatibus sancte crucis et sanctorum quorum reliquie adlate sunt ab urbe Constantinopolitana ad Suessionensem ecclesiam;* the last is fol. 124r: *cum aliis pluribus sanctorum reliquias quas dominus Nivelo episcopus anno incarnationis verbi M CC V ab urbe Constantinopolitana ad suam et sibi subiectas Suess. diocesis detulit ecclesias.*

70. Rostang of Cluny, "Narratio," in *Exuviae sacrae Constantinopolitanae*, 1: 129–132.

71. *Translatio corporis beatissimi Pauli martyris de Constantinopoli Venetias*, in *Exuviae sacrae Constantinopolitanae*, 1: 141.

72. See the account of Constantinople's plundering by Constantine Stilbès in Jean Darrouzés, "Le mémoire de Constantin Stilbès contre les Latins," *Revue des études Byzantines* 21 (1963): 50–100, especially pp. 81–86.

73. Innocent III to Boniface of Montferrat, August-September 1205, Reg. 8: 134, 247; translation in Andrea, *Fourth Crusade*, 171–176.

74. On Innocent's policies toward the Greeks, see Angold, *Fourth Crusade*, 163–192; and Alfred J. Andrea, "Innocent III and the Byzantine Rite," in *Urbs Capta: The Fourth Crusade and Its Consequences/La IVᵉ Croisade et ses conséquences*, ed. Angeliki Laiou, Réalités Byzantine 10 (Paris, 2005), 111–122.

75. Innocent III to Theodore Lascaris, 17 March 1208, PL 215, 1372–1375, quotation from col. 1373.

76. Innocent III to King Philip II of France, 17 November 1207, PL 215, 1246–1247. See also Roscher, *Papst Innocenz III,* 214–241; and Tyerman, *God's War,* 563–605.

77. See Roscher, *Papst Innocenz III,* 192–207; Tina Kala, "The Incorporation of the Northern Baltic Lands into the Western Christian World," in *Crusade and Conversion on the Baltic Frontier,* ed. Alan Murray (Aldershot, U.K., 2001), 3–20; and Tyerman, *God's War,* 674–712.

78. Innocent III, PL 216, 699. See also Roscher, *Papst Innocenz III,* 170–191.

79. Innocent III, PL 216, 699–704. See also Tyerman, *God's War,* 664–673.

80. Innocent III, 19–29 April 1213, PL 216, 817–822; especially col. 818. See also Flori, *L'islam et la fin des temps,* 335–337; James Powell, *Anatomy of a Crusade 1213–1221* (Philadelphia, 1986), 18–19; and Tyerman, *God's War,* 612–617.

81. Ralph of Coggeshall, *Chronicon Anglicanum,* 68.

82. Ibid., 68–70.

83. *Annales sancti Iacobi Leodiensis,* ed. G. H. Pertz, MGH SS 16 (Hannover, 1863), 667.

84. Innocent III, PL 216, 823–827. See Alberto Melloni, *"Vineam Domini*—10 April 1213: New Efforts and Traditional *Topoi*—Summoning Lateran IV," in *Pope Innocent and His World, 63–73.*

85. Innocent III, 26 April 1213, no. 3, *Die Beziehungen der Päpste zu islamischen und mongolischen Herrschern im 13. Jahrhundert anhand ihres Briefwechsels,* ed. Karl-Ernst Lupprian, Studi e testi 291 (Vatican City, 1981), 110–114; especially p. 113. For commentary, see Moore, *Innocent III,* 208.

86. Antonio García y García, ed., *Constitutiones concilii quarti Lateranensis una cum commentariis glossatorum,* Series A: monumenta iuris canonici (Vatican City, 1981), 51–52. On the connections between reform, Christian unity, and crusading at the Fourth Lateran Council, see also the comments of Powell, *Fifth Crusade,* 4; and

John France, *The Crusades and the Expansion of Catholic Christendom 1000–1714* (London, 2005), 160.

87. Innocent III, *Sermo VI: In concilio generali Lateranesis habitus*, PL 217, 673–680, especially cols. 674–675. See also Doran, "Role Models of Innocent III," 72–73.

88. Sayer, *Innocent III*, 186. See also Stephen Kuttner and Antonio García y García, "A New Eye-Witness Account of the Fourth Lateran Council," *Traditio* 20 (1964): 115–178.

89. Oliver Scholasticus, *Die Schriften des kölner Domscholasters, späteren Bishofs von Paderborn und Kardinalbishofs von S. Sabina*, ed. Hermann Hoogeweg, Bibliotek des Litterarischen Vereins in Stuttgart 202 (Tübingen, 1894), 156–157.

6. Crusaders, Missionaries, and Prophets

1. James of Vitry to Honorius III, 18 April 1221, *Lettres de Jacques de Vitry*, ed. R. B. C. Huygens (Leiden, 1960), 134–153. On the development and course of the Fifth Crusade, see James Powell, *Anatomy of a Crusade 1213–1221* (Philadelphia, 1996); and Christopher Tyerman, *God's War: A New History of the Crusades* (Cambridge, Mass., 2006), 606–649.

2. James of Vitry, *Lettres*, 150–153. There are variant versions of these prophecies in Latin and Old French: see *Prophetiae cuiusdam Arabicae in Latinorum castris ante Damiatam vulgatae versio quadruplex*, in *Quinti belli sacri scriptores minores*, ed. Reinhold Röhricht, Société de l'Orient Latin: série historique 2 (Geneva, 1879), 204–228. See also John V. Tolan, *Saracens: Islam in the Medieval European Imagination* (New York, 2002), 194–213; and Jean Flori, *L'islam et la fin des temps: l'interprétation prophétique des invasions musulmanes dans la chrétienté médiévale* (Paris, 2007), 338–347.

3. See Joseph Gill, *Byzantium and the Papacy, 1198–1400* (New Brunswick, N.J., 1979); and Kenneth Setton, *The Papacy and the Levant (1204–1571): The Thirteenth and Fourteenth Centuries*, vol. 1 (Philadelphia, 1976).

4. For an overview, see J. R. S Philips, *The Medieval Expansion of Europe* (1988; Oxford, 1998), 55–95; and Felicitas Schmieder, *Europa und die Fremden: die Mongolen im Urteil des Abendlandes vom 13. bis das 15. Jahrhundert* (Sigmaringen, 1994).

5. See Berthold Altaner, *Die Dominikanermissionen des 13. Jahrhunderts: Forschungen zur Geschichte der kirchliche Unionen und der Mohammedaner- und Heidenmission des Mittelalters* (Habelschwerdt, 1924); and Odulphus Van der Vat, *Die Anfänge der Franziskanermissionen* (Werl im Westf., 1934). See also E. Randolph Daniel, *The Franciscan Concept of Mission in the High Middle Ages* (Lexington, 1975).

6. For this thirteenth-century shift in European attitudes toward mission, see Tolan, *Saracens*, 214–255; Jean Richard, *La papauté et les missions d'orient au moyen*

âge, Collection de l'École française de Rome 33 (Rome, 1977); James Muldoon, *Popes, Lawyers, and Infidels: The Church and the Non-Christian World, 1250–1550* (Philadelphia, 1979); and Benjamin Kedar, *Crusade and Mission* (Princeton, 1994). For some similar observations about Spain and northern Africa, see R. I. Burns, "Christian-Islamic Confrontation in the West: The Thirteenth-Century Dream of Conversion," *American Historical Review* 76 (1971): 1386–1434.

7. See James of Vitry, *Libri duo, quorum prior Orientalis sive Hierosolymitanae alter Occidentalis historiae nomine inscribitur* (1597; Farnborough, 1971); along with *La traduction de l'Historia orientalis de James de Vitry,* ed. Claude Buridant, Bibliothèque Française et Romane 19 (Paris, 1986); and *The Historia Occidentalis of Jacques de Vitry,* ed. John Hinnebusch (Fribourg, 1972). For background on James and his works, see the introductions to Buridant, *La traduction de l'Historia orientalis,* 9–13; and Hinnebuch, *Historia Occidentalis,* 3–15.

8. For Oliver of Paderborn's corpus of writings (the *Descriptio Terre sancta,* the *Historia de ortu Jerusalem et eius variis eventibus,* the *Historia regum Terre sancte,* and the *Historia Damiatina*), see Oliver Scholasticus, *Die Schriften des kölner Domscholasters, späteren Bishofs von Paderborn und Kardinalbishofs von S. Sabina,* ed. Hermann Hoogeweg, Bibliotek des litterarischen Vereins in Stuttgart 202 (Tübingen, 1894).

9. James of Vitry, *Historia Orientalis,* 1–54, 85, 123; and *Lettres,* 112–113, 123–224.

10. *Historia Occidentalis,* ed. Hinnebusch, 73–74.

11. Oliver of Paderborn, *Schriften,* 156–157.

12. James of Vitry, *Lettres,* 79–97. For a similar compendium of information on Eastern Christians, with an emphasis on their rites and habits, see the *Historia Damiatina* in Oliver Scholasticus, *Schriften,* 264–267, where Oliver describes "Ethiopians" and "Nubians," "Georgians," "Maronites," "Armenians," "Nestorians," "Syrians," "Jacobites" and "Russians."

13. Oliver Scholasticus, *Schriften,* 232.

14. Ibid., 232–233.

15. A number of important articles and key primary sources for the legend of Prester John have been assembled and reprinted in *Prester John, the Mongols, and the Ten Lost Tribes,* ed. Charles Beckingham and Bernard Hamilton (Aldershot, U.K., 1996). In particular, see Charles Beckingham, "The Achievements of Prester John," in *Prester John,* 1–22.

16. See the anonymous *De adventu patriarchae Indorum ad urbem sub Calisto papa II,* in *Prester John,* 29–35; and the letter (ca. 1130) by eyewitness Odo of Reims, *Epistola ad Thomam comitem de quodam miraculo S. Thomae Apostoli,* in *Prester John,* 37–38.

17. Otto of Freising, *Chronica sive historia de duabus civitatibus,* ed. Adolf Hofmeister, MGH SS (in us. schol.) 45 (Hannover, 1912), 365–366.

18. See Friedrich Zarncke, "Prester John's Letter to the Byzantine Emperor Emanuel," in *Prester John,* 40–102; for Alexander's letter, 27 September 1177, see Zarncke, "Alexander III's Letter to Prester John," in *Prester John,* 103–112.

19. James of Vitry, *Lettres,* 141.

20. Ibid., 102–103; see also pp. 83, 89, 91–92, 95–97.

21. Ibid., 112–113, 123–124, 128.

22. On this shifting attitude toward crusading and missionary activities, see Kedar, *Crusade and Mission,* 116–135; Richard, *La papauté et les missions d'orient,* 34–37; Flori, *L'islam et la fin des temps,* 347–351; and Elizabeth Siberry, *Criticism of Crusading 1095–1274* (Oxford, 1985).

23. Oliver Scholasticus, *Schriften,* 299–300. See also Kedar, *Crusade and Mission,* 131.

24. James of Vitry, *Lettres,* 96–97.

25. For a general survey, see John Moorman, *A History of the Franciscan Order from Its Origins to the Year 1517* (Oxford, 1968), 3–80.

26. See Francis's sermon before the expedition to Morocco in Wadding, AM, 1:353–354; and section XII of the Franciscan rule in 1221 and 1223 (*De euntibus inter saracenos et alios infideles*), in *Opuscula sancti patris Francisci,* Biblioteca Franciscana ascetica medii aevi 1 (Quaracchi, 1904), 43–46, 73–74. A similar provision was made in the subsequent version of the rule, formally approved in 1223 by Pope Honorius III. See also Moorman, *History of the Franciscan Order,* 226–239, and James Powell, "St. Francis of Assisi's Way of Peace," *Medieval Encounters* 13 (2007): 271–280.

27. James of Vitry, *Lettres,* 132–133.

28. Thomas Celano, *Vita prima s. Francisci Assisiensis et eiusdem legenda,* Analecta Franciscana 10 (Quaracchi, 1926), 58–62; and *Vita secunda s. Francisci Assisiensis et eiusdem legenda,* Analecta Franciscana 10 (Quaracchi, 1927), 36–37. See also the testimonies excerpted in Golubovich, BBTSOF, 1: 1–41.

29. Alberic of Trois-Fontaines, *Chronicon,* ed. Paul Scheffer-Boichorst, MGH SS 23 (Hannover, 1874), 910.

30. Ibid., 911–912.

31. On the Talmud trials, see Benjamin Kedar, "Canon Law and the Burning of the Talmud," *Bulletin of Medieval Canon Law,* n.s. 9 (1979): 79–82; and Joel Rembaum, "The Talmud and the Popes: Reflections on the Talmud Trials of the 1240s," *Viator* 13 (1982): 203–223.

32. See Daniel, *Franciscan Concept of Mission,* 26–36; E. Randolph Daniel, "Reformist Apocalypticism and the Friars Minor," in *That Others May Know and Love: Essays*

in Honor of Zachary Hayes, ed. Michael Cusato and F. Edward Coughlin (New York, 1997), 237–253; and Marco Rainini, "I predicatori dei tempi ultimi: la rielaborazione di un tema escatologico nel costituirsi dell'identità profetica dell'Ordine domenicano," *Cristianesimo nella storia* 23 (2002): 307–343.

33. See Robert Lerner and Christine Morerod, "The Vision of 'John, Hermit of the Asturias': Lucas of Tuy, Apostolic Religion, and Eschatological Expectation," *Traditio* 61 (2006): 195–225, with critical edition of the prophecy, pp. 218–225.

34. Ibid., 225.

35. There is evidence that the Franciscans were active in Constantinople as early as 1220. See Golubovich, BBTSOF, 1: 128–129; and Robert Lee Wolff, "The Latin Empire of Constantinople and the Franciscans," *Traditio* 2 (1944): 213–237.

36. For an official account of the delegation to Nympha (probably written by Rodulph of Reims), see the *Disputatio Latinorum et Graecorum seu relatio apocrisariorum Gregorii IX de gestis Nicaeae in Bythnia et Nymphaeae in Lydia,* ed. Girolamo Golubovich, *Archivum Franciscanum Historicum* 12 (1919): 418–470. See also Golubovich, BBTSOF, 1: 161–162, 163–170; and (with caveats about his confessional-sounding conclusions) John Doran, "Rites and Wrongs: The Latin Mission to Nicaea, 1234," in *Unity and Diversity in the Church,* ed. R. N. Swanson, Studies in Church History 32 (Oxford, 1996), 131–144.

37. For this correspondence between Rome and the Greek patriarch, see Wadding, AM, 2: 333–342, 362–367; and the chronicle of Matthew Paris, *Chronica Majora,* RS 57/3 (London, 1872–83), 448–469.

38. Certainly, Gregory's curia was no stranger to Joachite apocalyptic sensibilities and eschatology. During this contemporary conflict with Frederick II, the pope drew upon such language to attack the emperor as Antichrist. See Hans Martin Schaller, "Endzeit-Erwartung und Antichrist-Vorstellungen in der Politk des 13. Jahrhunderts," in *Festschrift für Hermann Heimpel zum 70. Geburtstag am 19. September 1971* (Göttingen, 1972), 924–947.

39. *Disputatio Latinorum et Graecorum,* 450–451.

40. On this proposed crusade to support the Latin Empire of Constantinople, see Richard Spence, "Gregory IX's Attempted Expeditions to the Latin Empire of Constantinople: The Crusade for the Union of the Latin and Greek Churches," *Journal of Medieval History* 5 (1979): 163–176; and Michael Lower, *The Baron's Crusade: A Call to Arms and Its Consequences* (Philadelphia, 2005).

41. Matthew Paris, *Chronica Majora,* RS 57/3, 396–397.

42. Ibid., 396–398, 447–469; and Alberic of Trois-Fontaines, *Chronicon,* 935.

43. See BF, 1: 269–270; and *Les registres de Grégoire IX,* ed. Lucien Auvray, Bibliotèque des Écoles françaises d'Athènes et de Rome, second series 1 (Paris, 1896–1955), 1267–1268. For discussion of this bull, see Muldoon, *Popes, Lawyers, and Infidels,*

36; and Felicitas Schmieder, "*Cum hora undecima:* The Incorporation of Asia into the *Orbis Christianus*," in *Christianizing Peoples and Converting Individuals*, ed. Guyda Armstrong and Ian Wood (Turnhout, 2000), 259–265.

44. Daniel, *Franciscan Concept of Mission*, 12.

45. Ibid., 55–75.

46. Matthew Paris, *Chronica Majora*, RS 57/3, 489.

47. Ibid., RS 57/4, 109.

48. Ibid., 131–133, 109–119, 386–390.

49. See Innocent IV, 21 July 1243, no. 2, MGH Epp. sel. 2 (Berlin, 1887), 3–4; and Livarius Oliger, "Exhortatio Henrici episcopi Constantiensis ad Fratres Minores, ut crucem contra Tartaros praedicent a. 1241," *Archivum Franciscanum Historicum* 11 (1918): 556–557, quotation from p. 557. See also Peter Jackson, "The Crusade against the Mongols (1241)," *Journal of Ecclesiastical History* 42 (1991): 1–18.

50. Louis Weiland, ed., *Relatio de concilio Lugdunensi*, MGH Constitutiones 2 (Hannover, 1896), 514; and Matthew Paris, *Chronica Majora*, RS 57/4, 434–435.

51. Joseph Alberigo, ed., *Bulla depositionis Friderici II imperatoris*, in *Conciliorum oecumenicorum decreta*, 3rd ed. (Bologna, 1973), 278–283. On Frederick's crusade, see Tyerman, *God's War*, 739–755.

52. *Conciliorum oecumenicorum decreta*, 295–301.

53. On Innocent's concept of papal dominion over infidels, see the insights of Muldoon, *Popes, Lawyers, and Infidels*, 29–48; and Kedar, *Crusade and Mission*, 159–169. See also James Muldoon, "*Extra ecclesiam non est imperium:* The Canonists and the Legitimacy of Secular Power," *Studia Gratiana* 9 (1966): 553–580; and Benjamin Kedar, "De Iudeis et Sarracenis: On the Categorization of Muslims and Jews in Medieval Canon Law," in *Studia in Honorem Eminentissimi Cardinalis Alphonsi M. Stickler*, ed. Rosalio José Castillo Lara (Rome, 1992), 207–213.

54. For the juridical status of heretics and schismatics in the *Decretum*, see Emil Friedberg, ed., *Corpus iuris canonici*, 2 vols. (Graz, 1955), 1: 72–76; on Jews, Saracens, and heretics, vol. 2: 771–778, 778–779. See also John Watt, "Jews and Christians in the Gregorian Decretals," in *Christianity and Judaism*, ed. Diana Wood (Cambridge, Mass., 1992), 93–105.

55. Innocent IV, *Commentaria doctissima in quinque libros decretalium* (Venice, 1610), fols. 605b–607a. To the best of my knowledge, the schismatic status of the Greek Church was addressed in canon law for the first time in the late-twelfth century. See Gerard Fransen, ed., *Summa 'Elegantius in iure divino' seu Coloniensis*, Monumenta iuris canonici, series A: corpus glossatorum 1 (Vatican City, 1986), 235–237.

56. Innocent IV, *Acta Innocentii PP. IV (1243–1254)*, ed. Theodosius Haluščynskyl and Meletius Voinar, Pontificia commissio ad redigendum codicem iuris canonici orientalis, fontes, 3rd series, 1 (Rome, 1962), 11–15.

57. Ibid., 36–42.

58. See John of Plano Carpini, *Ystoria Mongalorum,* in *Sinica Francicscana: Itinera et relationes fratrum minorum saeculi XII et XIV,* ed. Anastasius Van den Wyngaert, 5 vols. (Quaracchi, 1929), 1: 3–130; and the account of his companion, Benedict the Pole, *Relatio Fr. Benedicti Poloni,* in *Sinica Francicscana,* 1: 133–143. For an overview of the Mongol missions with a helpful bibliography of primary sources, see Gregory Guzman, "European Clerical Envoys to the Mongols: Reports of Western Merchants in Eastern Europe and Central Asia, 1231–1255," *Journal of Medieval History* 22 (1996): 53–67.

59. For the letter from Göjük, see *Sinica Francicscana,* 1: 142–143.

60. See the account of Dominican Simon de Saint Quetin, *Histoire des Tartares,* ed. Jean Richard, Documents relatifs a l'histoire des croisades 8 (Paris, 1965).

61. See Heinrich Dörrie, "Drei Texte zur Geschichte der Ungarn und Mongolen: Die Missionsreisen des Fr. Iulianus O.P. ins Ural-Gebiet (1234/5) und nach Russland (1237) und der Bericht des Erzbischofs Peter über die Tartaren," *Nachrichten der Akademie der Wissenschaften in Göttigen aus dem Jahre 1956: Philologische-Historische Klasse* 6 (1956): 125–202.

62. Ibid., 160–161.

63. See Joinville, *Vie de Saint Louis,* ed. and trans. Jacques Monfrin (Paris, 1995), 67, 233; and Tyerman, *God's War,* 784–786.

64. William of Rubruck, *Itinerarium,* in *Sinica Francicscana,* 1: 164–332.

65. See Robert Lerner, *The Powers of Prophecy: The Cedar of Lebanon Vision from the Mongol Onslaught to the Dawn of the Enlightenment* (Berkeley, 1983); and Felicitas Schmieder, "*Nota sectam maometicam atterendam a tartaris et christianis:* The Mongols as Non-Believing Apocalyptic Friends around the Year 1260," *Journal of Millennial Studies* 1 (1998): 1–11.

66. Flori, *L'islam et la fin des temps,* 357–359.

67. Salimbene of Adam, *Cronica,* ed. Guiseppe Scalia, CCCM 125/125A (Turnhout, 1998), 311–321.

68. See D. C. West, "The Education of Fra Salimbene of Parma: The Joachite Influence," in *Prophecy and Millenarianism: Essays in Honour of Marjorie Reeves,* ed. Ann Williams (Harlow, U.K., 1980), 191–216.

69. On the development of Joachite thought in the thirteenth century, see Marjorie Reeves, *The Influence of Prophecy in the Later Middle Ages* (1969; Notre Dame, 1993), 45–58, 145–160; and Morton Bloomfield and Marjorie Reeves, "The Penetration of Joachimism into Northern Europe," *Speculum* 29 (1954): 772–793.

70. Antonio García y García, ed., *Constitutiones concilii quarti Lateranensis una cum commentariis glossatorum,* Series A: monumenta iuris canonici (Vatican City, 1981),

46–47. See Fiona Robb, "The Fourth Lateran Council's Definition of Trinitarian Orthodoxy," *Journal of Ecclesiastical History* 48 (1997): 22–43.

71. On the development of Joachite thought among the Franciscans, see Reeves, *Influence of Prophecy*, 175–190; E. Randolph Daniel, "A Re-Examination of the Origins of Franciscan Joachitism," *Speculum* 43 (1968): 671–676; Bernard McGinn, "Apocalyptic Traditions and Spiritual Identity in Thirteenth-Century Religious Life," in *The Roots of the Modern Christian Tradition,* ed. E. Rozanne Elder, 1–26; and Robert Lerner, *The Feast of St. Abraham: Medieval Millenarians and the Jews* (Philadelphia, 2002), 38–43.

72. Salimbene, *Cronica,* 351, 356–357. See Jacques Paul, "Le Joachimisme et les Joachimites au milieu du XIIIe siècle d'après le témoignage de Fra Salimbene," in *1274 Année charnière: mutations et continuités* (Paris, 1977), 797–813.

73. For the commentary on Jeremiah, see *Abbatis Joachim divina prorsus in Jeremiam prophetam interpretatio* (Cologne, 1577). On the authorship of the commentary, see Robert Moynihan, "The Development of the 'Pseudo-Joachim' Commentary 'Super Hieremiam': New Manuscript Evidence," MEFRM 98 (1986): 109–142. Moynihan posits two manuscript traditions: an earlier "short" version, perhaps drafted by Joachim himself, and a later "long version" with additional materials added. For the commentary on Isaiah, see *Super Esaiam prophetam Abbatis Joachimi Florensis scripta* (Venice, 1516), which includes a marginal gloss that accompanied early manuscripts of the text (e.g., Vat. lat. 4959 and BL Cot.Tib.B.V Pt. II) along with a series of figures called the *Praemissiones,* fols. vi recto–viii verso. For two thirteenth-century compilations of genuine and pseudo-Joachite works, see the *Exceptiones,* BNF lat. 16397, fols. 61r–194v, and Vat. lat. 3822.

74. *Expositio Iezechielis prophete,* BNF lat. 16397, fols. 136r–138v (selections only); *Prophetia de tribus statibus sanctae ecclesiae transmissa Henrico imperatori Alemannie,* BNF Lat. 2599, fols. 244v–249r; *Liber de oneribus prophetarum editus ab abbate Ioachim,* in Oswald Holder-Egger, "Italienische Prophetieen des 13. Jahrhunderts. III," *Neues Archiv der Gesellschaft für ältere deutsche Geschichtskunde* 33 (1908): 139–187; *De oneribus provinciarum,* BL 11439 (add.), fols. f. 103v–123r (also published together with the commentary on Isaiah in *Super Esaiam prophetam,* Venice 1516, fols. 11r–27v); and *De decem plagis,* BNF lat. 3319, fols. 26v–28r.

75. For the Erythrean Sibyl and Merlin prophecies, see Oswald Holder-Egger, "Italienische Prophetieen des 13. Jahrhunderts. I," *Neues Archiv der Gesellschaft für ältere deutsche Geschichtskunde* 15 (1890): 151–177. See also Matthias Kaup, "Merlin, ein politischer Prophet: Genese, Funktion und Auslegung merlinischer Prophetie im Spiegel zweier unedierter Kommentare des 12. und 13. Jahrhunderts," *Cristianesimo nella storia* 20 (1999): 545–578; and Christian Jostmann, *Sibilia Erithea Babi-*

lonica: Papsttum und Prophetie im 13. Jahrhundert, MGH Schriften 54 (Hannover, 2006), including (pp. 377–527) a catalogue of manuscripts and critical editions of variant versions of the thirteenth-century Sibylline prophecies. For the Joachite commentary on the Sibyl and Merlin, see the *Expositio Abbatis Joachim super Sibillis et Merlino*, BNF lat. 3319, fols. 9v–24r (edition in Jostmann, *Sibilia Erithea*, 117–122).

76. On the "two orders," see *In Jeremiam prophetam*, 67–68, 77–80; *Prophetia de tribus statibus*, fol. 245v; and the Erythrean Sibyl in Oswald Holder-Egger, "Italienische Prophetieen I," 162–163, 165, 172.

77. For a Joachite presentation of history as a series of persecutions, see *In Jeremiam prophetam*, 85–95, 143, 236–237; the *Praemissiones* in *Super Esaiam prophetam*, fol. vii verso (the Joachite image of the seven-headed dragon); the *Expositio Iezechielis prophete*, BNF lat. 16397, fol. 136vb; the *Expositio Abbatis Joachim super Sibillis et Merlino*, BNF lat. 3319, fol. 13v; and *De decem plagis*, BNF 3319, fols. 26v–28r.

78. On the schism between the Latins and Greeks, as well as the predictions of its eschatological resolution, see *In Jeremiam prophetam*, 65–68, 321.

79. *Super Esaiam prophetam*, fols. 6r–8r; *Super Sibillis et Merlino*, BNF lat. 3319, fol. 11v.

80. *In Jeremiam prophetam*, 65.

81. For predictions of this worldwide union, see *In Jeremiam prophetam*, 68, 321, 359; *Super Sibillis et Merlino*, BNF lat. 3319, fol. 11v; *Prophetia de tribus statibus*, fol. 245r; the Erythrean Sibyl in Oswald Holder-Egger, "Italienische Prophetieen I," 163; and the short, anonymous prophecy in Oswald Holder-Egger, "Italienische Prophetieen des 13. Jahrhunderts. II," *Neues Archiv der Gesellschaft für ältere deutsche Geschichtskunde* 30 (1905): 323–386.

82. On the apocalyptic tribulations, see *In Jeremiam prophetam*, 85–86, 127, 258, 285; *Prophetia de tribus statibus*, fols. 244v–245r (lists the German empire, corrupt clergy, and the Saracens as three apocalyptic trials for the Roman Church); and the Erythrean Sibyl in Oswald Holder-Egger, "Italienische Prophetieen I," 170–172.

83. Wadding, AM, 1: 429–432.

7. Contesting the End of Days

1. Salimbene of Adam, *Cronica*, ed. Guiseppe Scalia, CCCM 125/125A (Turnhout, 1998), 356–357, 688–691. For an overview of the Scandal of the Eternal Gospel, see Marjorie Reeves, *The Influence of Prophecy in the Later Middle Ages* (1969; Notre Dame, 1993), 59–69; Henri de Lubac, *La postérité spirituelle de Joachim de Flore*, 2 vols. (Paris, 1978), 1: 80–84; and David Burr, *Olivi's Peaceable Kingdom: A Reading*

of the Apocalypse Commentary (Philadelphia, 1993), 1–25. See also Jean Flori, *L'islam et la fin des temps: l'interprétation prophétique des invasions musulmanes dans la chrétienté médiévale* (Paris, 2007), 367–371.

2. On the contested climate of apocalyptic thought, see Reeves, *Influence of Prophecy*, 146–189; and Michel-Marie Dufeil, "Trois 'sens de l'histoire' affrontés vers 1250–60," in *1274 Année charnière: mutations et continuités,* Colloques internationaux du centre national de la recherché 558 (Paris, 1977), 815–848.

3. See Burr, *Olivi's Peaceable Kingdom,* 26–72. See also Robert Lerner, "Poverty, Preaching, and Eschatology in the Commentaries of 'Hugh of St Cher,'" in *The Bible in the Medieval World: Essays in Memory of Beryl Smalley,* ed. Katherine Walsh and Diana Wood, Studies in Church History: Subsidia 4 (Oxford, 1985), 157–189; David Burr, "Antichrist and Islam in Medieval Franciscan Exegesis," in *Medieval Perceptions of Islam,* ed. John V. Tolan (New York, 1996), 131–152; and David Burr, "The Antichrist and the Jews in Four Thirteenth Century Apocalypse Commentaries," in *Friars and Jews in the Middle Ages and Renaissance,* ed. Steven McMichael and Susan Myers, The Medieval Franciscans 2 (Leiden, 2004), 23–38.

4. See Burkhard Roberg, *Die Union zwischen der griechischen und der lateinischen Kirche auf dem II. Konzil von Lyon (1274),* Bonner Historische Forschungen 24 (Bonn, 1964); Joseph Gill, *Byzantium and the Papacy, 1198–1400* (New Brunswick, N.J., 1979), 120–141; and Kenneth Setton, *The Papacy and the Levant (1204–1571): The Thirteenth and Fourteenth Centuries,* 4 vols. (Philadelphia, 1976), 1: 110–120.

5. Salimbene, *Cronica,* 687.

6. Ibid., 358.

7. See Penn Szittya, *The Antifraternal Tradition in Medieval Literature* (Princeton, 1986).

8. Salimbene, *Cronica,* 458–459. On William of Saint Amour's role in this conflict, see Szittya, *Antifraternal Tradition,* 11–31.

9. For these excerpts, see Ernst Benz, "Joachim Studien II: Die Exerptsätze der Pariser Professoren aus dem Evangelium Aeternum," *Zeitschrift für Kirchengeschichte* 51 (1932): 415–455; no. 243, *Chartularium universitatis Parisiensis,* ed. Heinrich Denifle and Émile Chatelain, 4 vols. (Paris, 1889), 1: 272–276; and the *additimenta,* a collection of documents appended to Matthew Paris, *Chronica majora,* RS 57/6 (London, 1872–1883), 335–339. See also BNF lat. 12971, fol. 73r-v, a manuscript with minor variations not used by Benz in his edition. For the findings of the commission at Anagni, see Heinrich Denifle, "Das Evangelium aeternum und die Commission zu Anagni," *Archiv für Litteratur- und Kirchengeschichte des Mittelalters* 1 (1885): 49–142. The manuscript of the proceedings at Anagni, BNF lat. 16397, fol. 139r–154v, is preceded by a series of excerpts from Joachim's genuine and spurious works (*Exceptiones,* ibid., fols. 61r–139r). The excerpts, which

label Joachim "venerable" and "most learned," were initially compiled by an admirer of the abbot but were subsequently bound together with the condemnation from Anagni by Peter of Limoges, a contemporary with an interest in both Joachim and his detractors. See Nicole Bériou, "Pierre de Limoges et la fin des temps," MEFRM 98 (1986): 65–107.

10. Benz, "Die Exzerptsätze," 416–417; and Denifle, "Das Evangelium aeternum," 99–101.

11. Benz, "Die Exzerptsätze," 417–418, 422–423; and Denifle, "Das Evangelium aeternum," 101, 115–116. Following Joachim's generational model, the end of the clerical order was projected for the end of the forty-second generation from Christ.

12. Denifle, "Das Evangelium aeternum," 105, 109.

13. Benz, "Die Exzerptsätze," 418–420. On the "philo-Judaism" of the Eternal Gospel, see Robert Lerner, *The Feast of St. Abraham: Medieval Millenarians and the Jews* (Philadelphia, 2000), 43–48, who comments about Gerard that "even more than Joachim, he was opposing the entrenched hatreds of this time."

14. Benz, "Die Exzerptsätze," 417. The number 1260 was the equivalent of "three and a half years" or "forty-two months" of thirty days each (cf. Rev. 11:3).

15. Nos. 257–258, *Chartularium universitatis Parisiensis*, 297–298.

16. William of Saint Amour, *De periculis novissimorum temporum*, in Orwin Gratius, *Fasciculum rerum expetendarum*, ed. Edward Brown, 2 vols. (London, 1690), 2: 18–54. For background, see Szittya, *Antifraternal Tradition*, 17–31.

17. William, *De periculis*, 21–22, 27–29.

18. *De antichristo et ejus ministries*, in *Veterum scriptorum et monumentorum historicorum, dogmaticorum, moralium, amplissima collectio*, ed. Edmund Martène and Ursin Durand, 9 vols. (Paris, 1724–1733), 9: 1273–1446. There has been debate over the authorship of this tract, attributed both to William of Saint Amour and to his student Nicholas of Lisieux. See Andrew Taver, "The *Liber de Antichristo* and the Failure of Joachite Expectations," *Florensia* 15 (2001): 87–98, who convincingly comes down on the side of William's authorship or at least direct involvement.

19. *Liber de antichristo*, 1283–1294.

20. Ibid., 1322–1323.

21. Ibid., 1333–1334, 1393–1428.

22. See Edmond Faral, "Les 'responsiones' de Guillaume de Saint-Amour," *Archives d'histoire doctrinale et littéraire du moyen âge* 18 (1950–1951): 337–394, especially pp. 346–347. Dominican detractors made this charge against William at Rome in 1256. William denied saying this precisely. Instead, he claimed to have said that it would be difficult to investigate Joachim's works properly because they were so voluminous, because the papal curia was occupied with other business, and finally, because Joachim's books did have some defenders at Rome.

23. Nos. 288–289, 314–315, *Chartularium universitatis Parisiensis*, 331–334, 362–363.

24. Salimbene, *Cronica*, 462. Later versions of the excerpts taken from the Eternal Gospel by the Paris masters attribute the work to John of Parma, indicating just how closely his reputation became associated with the scandal. See Benz, "Die Exerptsätze," 415.

25. Salimbene, *Cronica*, 705.

26. *Concilium Arelatense*, MANSI, 23: 1001–1004. The bishop of Arles, Florentius, had already approached the commission at Anagni in 1255 with complaints about Joachite teachings. See Denifle, "Das Evangelium aeternum," 102.

27. See Bernard McGinn, "The Abbot and the Doctors: Scholastic Reactions to the Radical Eschatology of Joachim of Fiore," *Church History* 40 (1971): 30–47; and Bernard Guillemain, "Le sens de l'histoire au XIIIe siècle," in *1274 Année charnière*, 881–886.

28. See Thomas Aquinas, *Opera omnia*, 25 vols. (New York, 1948–1950), *Summa theologica*, 2: 416–419; *Commentum in quattuor libros sententiarum*, 7/2: 1062–1065; and *Contra impugnantes dei cultum et religionem*, 15: 65–75. For analysis, in addition to McGinn, "The Abbot and the Doctors," 37–41, see Peter Meinhold, "Thomas von Aquin und Joachim von Fiore und ihre Deutung der Geschichte," *Saeculum: Jahrbuch für Universalgeschichte* 27 (1976): 66–76; and Rudi Te Velde, "Christian Eschatology and the End of Time according to Thomas of Aquinas (Summa contra Gentiles IV, c. 97)," in *Ende und Vollendung: Eschatologische Perspektiven im Mittelalter*, ed. Jan Aertsen and Martin Pickavé (Berlin, 2002), 595–604.

29. Aquinas, *Contra impugnantes dei cultum*, 70–71; and *Commentum in quattuor libros sententiarum*, 1064–1065. As noted above, forty-two months of thirty days equals 1260.

30. Aquinas, *Commentum in quattuor libros sententiarum*, 1062–1063.

31. *Summa theologica*, 419.

32. *Contra impugnantes dei cultum*, 72.

33. *Summa theologica*, 418–419.

34. See the ground-breaking work of Joseph Ratzinger, *The Theology of History in St. Bonaventure*, trans. Zachary Hayes (Chicago, 1971); Bernard McGinn, "The Significance of Bonaventure's Theology of History," *The Journal of Religion: Supplement* 58 (1978): 64–81; E. Randolph Daniel, "St. Bonaventure's Debt to Joachim," *Medievalia et Humanistica* 2 (1982): 61–75; David Burr, "Bonaventure, Olivi and Franciscan Eschatology," *Collectanea Franciscana* 53 (1983): 23–40; and Ilia Delio, "From Prophecy to Mysticism: Bonaventure's Theology in Light of Joachim of Fiore," *Traditio* 52 (1997): 153–177. There has been some debate about Bonaventure's use of Joachim. Ratzinger argues that Bonaventure drew from the abbot's model of the three *status*, damping down its radical implications; Daniel, by contrast, effectively shows that Bonaventure drew upon Joachim's "principle of con-

cordance" between the Old and New Testaments, thereby avoiding the problem of the third *status*.

35. Bonaventure, *In hexaëmeron collationes*, in *Opera omnia*, 10 vols. (Quaracchi, 1882–1889), 5: 329–449.

36. Ibid., 403–408.

37. Ibid., 407. To the best of my knowledge, scholars engaged with the question of Bonaventure's borrowings from Joachim have not drawn attention to these passages on the Latin and Greek Churches.

38. Ibid., 408.

39. Ibid., 440–441. See Burr, "Franciscan Eschatology," 32–35; and Delio, "From Prophecy to Mysticism," 163–169.

40. See E. Randolph Daniel, *The Franciscan Concept of Mission in the High Middle Ages* (Lexington, 1975), 55–66; Bernard McGinn, "Angel Pope and Papal Antichrist," *Church History* 47 (1978): 161; and Flori, *L'islam et la fin des temps*, 375–380.

41. See Roger Bacon, *The "Opus Majus" of Roger Bacon*, ed. J. H. Bridges, 3 vols. (Oxford, 1897; Frankfurt, 1964); *Opus tertium*, RS 15/1 (London, 1859), 3–310 (portions also reproduced in *Part of the Opus Tertium of Roger Bacon including a Fragment now Printed for the First Time*, ed. A. G. Little [Aberdeen, 1912]); *Opus minus*, RS 15/1, 311–390; and *Compendium studii philosophiae*, RS 15/1, 391–519.

42. Bacon, *Opus majus*, 1: 253–269, 2: 366–404; and *Opus Tertium*, ed. Little, 9–13.

43. *Opus majus*, 3: 120–122, quotation from p. 121.

44. *Opus Tertium*, ed. Little, 11; see also the *Opus majus*, 1: 92–96 (where Bacon specified the need to learn the languages of "schismatic" Christians who live under Latin dominion), and pp. 301–302 (where he stressed that missionaries need to know the "rites" and "conditions" of the people among whom they plan to proselytize).

45. *Opus majus*, 1: 399–403.

46. Ibid., 50–51, 59–61, 268–269.

47. Ibid., 402.

48. Ibid., 266 (where Bacon specifically noted the infidels' loss of their "caliph, who was just like their pope").

49. Ibid., 253, 268, 399–403; *Opus majus*, 2: 389; see also *Opus tertium*, ed. Little, 65.

50. *Opus majus*, 2: 234–235. Bacon drew attention to a long-standing tradition that Alexander the Great had enclosed the nations of "Gog and Magog" (Rev. 20:7) behind the "Caspian Gates" to the East, where they waited to burst forth and serve as Antichrist's armies. On William of Rubruck, the Tartars, and their link to Gog and Magog, see also Bacon, *Opus majus*, 1: 268–269, 302–304.

51. Daniel, *Franciscan Concept of Mission*, 57.

52. McGinn, "Angel Pope," 155–173; and Reeves, *Influence of Prophecy*, 401–415.

53. Bacon, *Opus tertium*, RS 15/1, 86.

54. Bacon, *Compendium studii*, RS 15/1, 402. Years earlier Adam Marsh, *Epistolae*, RS 4/1 (London, 1858), 426–428, had offered some similar sentiments. In language that foreshadowed Bacon's own encouragement for Pope Clement IV, Marsh celebrated Innocent IV's efforts at the First Council of Lyons to bring about the conversion of the Tartars, the crushing of the Saracens, the humbling of the Greeks, and the suppression of papal opponents within the Latin Church.

55. Bacon, *Compendium studii*, RS 15/1, 403. Bacon linked this same process of "purgation" to tribulations through Antichrist, the "discord of Christian princes," or an invasion by the Tartars, Saracens, and other "kings of the East." See also McGinn, "Angel Pope," 157, who notes that by "giving the papacy a position of true leadership in the religious consciousness of Latin Christianity," the ecclesiastical reform movement of the eleventh and twelfth centuries "provided the necessary, if not quite sufficient, cause for the apocalyptic role of the successors of Peter."

56. See Wadding, AM, 4: 197–199.

57. Alexander IV to Theodore Lascaris, 1256, no. 28b, *Acta Alexandri P.P. IV (1254–1261)*, ed. Theodosius Haluščynskyl, Pontificia commissio ad redigendum codicem iuris canonici orientalis, fontes series 3, vol. 4/2 (Vatican City, 1966), 48–52.

58. Indicating their support for Franciscan proselytizing, both Alexander IV and Urban IV reissued *Cum hora undecima* during their papacies. See Alexander IV, 19 April 1258, no. 38, *Acta Alexandri IV*, 73–74; and Urban IV, 28 July 1263, no. 7, *Acta Urbani IV, Clementis IV, Gregorii X (1261–1276)*, ed. A. L. Tàuta, Pontificia commissio ad redigendum codicem iuris canonici orientalis, fontes series 3, vol. 5/1 (Vatican City, 1953), 26–28.

59. Urban IV, BF, 2: 486–493; and *Acta Urbani IV*, 14–26, 31–37.

60. See the correspondence appended to Roberg, *Konzil von Lyon*, 223–247; and Donald Nicol, "The Greeks and the Union of the Churches: The Preliminaries to the Second Council of Lyons, 1261–1274," in *Medieval Studies Presented to Aubrey Gwynn*, ed. John A. Watt (Dublin, 1961), 454–480.

61. Gregory X, no. 32, *Acta Gregorii X*, 91–100, quotation from p. 92; and Wadding, AM, 4: 383–471.

62. Gilbert of Tournai, "Collectio de scandalis ecclesiae," *Archivum Franciscanum Historicum* 24 (1931): 33–62.

63. Ibid., 38–39.

64. William of Tripoli, *Tractatus de statu Saracenorum et de Mahomete pseudo-propheta et eorum lege et fide*, in *Kulturgeschichte der Kreuzzüge*, ed. Hans Prutz (1883; Hildesheim, 1964), 578–598. As noted by Flori, *L'islam et la fin des temps*, 381, and John V. Tolan, *Saracens: Islam in the Medieval European Imagination* (New York,

2002), 204, some question has emerged over the attribution of this tract to William of Tripoli; *De statu* might be the work of an anonymous author, who based his account on William's earlier tract *Notitia de Machometo*. See Peter Engels, ed., *Notitia de Machometo; De statu Saracenorum* (Würzburg, 1992).

65. William of Tripoli, *De statu Saracenorum,* 589–590, 597–598.

66. There is no extant manuscript of the complete text of the *Opusculum tripartitum.* Excerpts are published in Martène and Durand, *Veterum scriptorum et monumentorum,* 7: 174–198; reprinted in MANSI, 24: 109–132 (also in Brown, *Fasciculum rerum expetendarum et fugiendarum,* 2: 185–229, with additional passages). Herein, I have cited Martène and Durand. See also Edward Brett, *Humbert of Romans: His Life and Views of Thirteenth-Century Society* (Toronto, 1984), 175–194; Claude Carozzi, "Humbert de Romans et l'union avec les Grecs," in *1274 Année charnière,* 491–494; and Carozzi, "Humbert de Romans et l'histoire," in *1274 Année charnière,* 849–862.

67. Humbert of Romans, *Opusculum tripartitum,* 174..

68. *In Jeremiam prophetam,* BNF lat. 15637, fol. 211va.

69. *Opusculum tripartitum,* 175. Humbert listed among Christendom's enemies Jews, idolaters, pagan philosophers, heretics, pre-Constantinian emperors, and barbarians such as the Goths and the Saracens, who continued to pollute the holy places.

70. Ibid., 178. See Elizabeth Siberry, *Criticism of Crusading 1095–1274* (Oxford, 1985), 190–216; and Brett, *Humbert of Romans,* 177–186.

71. *Opusculum tripartitum,* 183–184.

72. Ibid., 190–195.

73. Ibid., 193–194.

74. For the acts of the council, see Joseph Alberigo, ed., *Conciliorum oecumenicorum decreta,* 3rd ed. (Bologna, 1973), 303–331, quotation from p. 309. See also the contemporary report (*Ordinatio concilii generalis Lugdunensis*) in Antonio Franchi, *Il concilio II di Lione (1274),* Studi e testi Francescani 33 (Rome, 1965), 67–100, especially pp. 72–73.

75. Franchi, *Il concilio,* 79–84.

76. For notices about the council in contemporary Latin chronicles, see Bernard of Limoges, *Chronicon,* ed. Oswald Holder-Egger, MGH SS 26 (Hannover, 1882), 437; the continuation of Obertus Stanconus, *Annales Italicae,* ed. G. H. Pertz, MGH SS 18 (Hannover, 1863), 282; *Annales breves Wormatienses,* ed. Louis Bethman, MGH SS 17 (Hannover, 1861), 77; and *Annales Heinrici Heimburgi,* ed. Wilhelm Wattenbach, MGH SS 17, 715. See also Donald Nicol, "The Byzantine Reaction to the Second Council of Lyons, 1274," in *Councils and Assemblies,* ed. G. J. Cuming and Derek Baker, Studies in Church History 7 (Cambridge, 1971), 113–146.

77. Vat. Lat. 3822, fol. 2r-v. Edited in Jeanne Bignami Odier, "Notes sur deux manuscrits de la bibliothèque de Vatican contenant des traités inédits de Joachim de Flore," *Mélanges d'archéologie et d'histoire* 4 (1937): 211–241, quotation from p. 219.

78. BL R8C.IV., fol. 66r. Edited in Reeves, *Influence of Prophecy,* 50.

79. Salimbene, *Cronica,* 744–749.

80. Flori, *L'islam et la fin des temps,* 383–386.

81. Salimbene, *Cronica,* 750–751.

82. Richard Southern, *Western Society and the Church in the Middle Ages* (Harmondsworth, U.K., 1970), 78.

83. For early examples of this new genre, see Charles Kohler, "Deux projets de croisade en Terre-Sainte composés a la fin du XIIIe siècle et au début de XIVe," *Revue de l'Orient latin* 10 (1904): 406–457; and Fidenzio of Padua, BBTSOF, 2: 1–60. See also Antony Leopold, *How to Recover the Holy Land: The Crusade Proposals of the Late Thirteenth and Early Fourteenth Centuries* (Aldershot, U.K., 2000), especially pp. 8–51; Sylvia Schein, *Fideles Crucis: The Papacy, the West, and the Recovery of the Holy Land (1274–1314)* (Oxford, 1991); Felicitas Schmieder, "Enemy, Obstacle, Ally? The Greek in Western Crusade Proposals (1274–1311)," in *The Man of Many Devices, Who Wandered Full Many Ways: Festschrift in Honor of János M. Bak,* ed. Balázs Nagy and Marcell Sebők (Budapest, 1999), 357–371; and Aryeh Grabois, "The Cyclical Views of History in Late Thirteenth-Century Acre," in *From Clermont to Jerusalem: The Crusades and Crusader Societies 1095–1500,* ed. Alan Murray (Turnhout, 1998), 131–139.

84. Leopold, *How to Recover the Holy Land,* 14.

85. Nicholas IV to Arghun Khan, 1288 and 1291, BF, 4: 6–8, 281–283. In 1291, Nicholas reissued *Cum hora undecima,* BF, 4: 278–280.

86. Key sources for this period are assembled in Golubovich, BBTSOF, vol. 3, covering Franciscan activities in Asia ca. 1300–1322. See also the three letters (in 1293, 1305, and 1306) from "Cathy" to Rome by John of Monte Corvino, appointed archbishop of China in 1307, in *Itinera et relationes fratrum minorum saeculi XIII et XIV,* Anastasius Van den Wyngaert, Sinica Franciscana, 5 vols. (Quaracchi, 1929), 1: 335–355.

87. Alexander of Roes, *Notitia saeculi,* in *Alexander von Roes Schriften,* ed. Herbert Grundmann and Hermann Heimpel, MGH Staatsschriften 1 (Stuttgart, 1958), 149–171.

88. Ibid., 154.

89. Ibid., 152–154, 162–164, 166–170.

90. Raymund Llull, *Quomodo Terra Sancta recuperari potest,* ed. Blanca Garí and Fernando Domínguez Reboiras, CCCM 28 (Turnhout, 1959), 257–331; and Llull, *Tractatus de modo convertendi infideles,* CCCM 28, 333–353. See also Leopold, *How*

to Recover the Holy Land, 20–21; Daniel, *Franciscan Concept of Mission,* 66–74; and Tolan, *Saracens,* 256–274.

91. In particular, see Golubovich, BBTSOF, 2: 373–375; and Raymund Llull, *De fine,* ed. Aloisius Madre, CCCM 25 (Turnhout, 1959), 233–291.

92. Llull, *Quomodo Terra Sancta recuperari potest,* 328–329; *De modo convertendi infideles,* 340–342; *De fine,* 252–269; and BBTSOF, 2: 373.

93. Llull, *De modo convertendi infideles,* 337–338; and BBTSOF, 2: 374.

94. Llull, *De modo convertendi infideles,* 345; *De fine,* 268; and BBTSOF, 2: 373.

8. The New Jerusalem and the Transfiguration of Christendom

1. Peter John Olivi, *De usu paupere: the Quaestio and the Tractatus,* ed. David Burr, Italian Medieval and Renaissance Studies: The University of Western Australia 4 (Florence, 1992), 30. This tract was written ca. 1279–1283. See David Burr, *Olivi and Franciscan Poverty: The Origins of Usus Pauper Controversy* (Philadelphia, 1989).

2. Peter John Olivi, *Postilla in Apocalypsim,* BNF lat. 713, fol. 107. There is no critical edition of Olivi's apocalypse commentary, commonly called the *Lectura super Apocalypsim.* One is forthcoming by Warren Lewis that will supersede the version in his dissertation, "Peter John Olivi: Prophet of the Year 2000" (Ph.D. diss., Tübingen, 1972). My thanks to Dr. Lewis for sharing a version of this forthcoming edition. See also David Burr, *Olivi's Peaceable Kingdom: A Reading of the Apocalypse Commentary* (Philadelphia, 1993); and Burr, *The Spiritual Franciscans: From Protest to Persecution in the Century after Saint Francis* (University Park, Penn., 2000), 75–88.

3. See Sylvain Piron, "Censures et condemnation de Pierre de Jean Olivi: Enquête dans les marges du Vatican," MEFRM 118/2 (2006): 313–373.

4. See Nicholas III, 14 August 1279, BF, 3: 404–416 (*Exiit qui seminat*). Indicative of his importance in this debate, Olivi sat on the papal commission charged with formulating this bull. See John Moorman, *A History of the Franciscan Order from Its Origins to the Year 1517* (Oxford, 1968), 179.

5. Piron, "Censures et condemnation," 316–336; and Burr, *Spiritual Franciscans,* 88–89.

6. In addition to Burr, *Spiritual Franciscans,* 43–65, see Marjorie Reeves, *The Influence of Prophecy in the Later Middle Ages* (1969; Notre Dame, 1993), 191–228; Harold Lee, Marjorie Reeves, and Giulio Silano, *Western Mediterranean Prophecy: The School of Joachim of Fiore and the Fourteenth-Century Breviloquium,* Studies and Texts 88 (Toronto, 1988), 3–16; Gian Luca Potestà, "Radical Apocalyptic Movements in the Late Middle Ages," EA, 2: 110–142; and Robert Lerner, "Millennialism," EA, 2: 326–360.

7. Burr, *Spiritual Franciscans*, 69–75.

8. See Peter John Olivi, *Questiones de Romano pontifice*, ed. Marco Bartoli, Collectio Olivinana 4 (Rome, 2002), especially 121–170 (on whether the pope can dispense with vows), and 171–180 (on whether the pope has "the most universal power"); and Livarius Oliger, "Petri Iohhanis Olivi *De renuntiatione Papae Coelstini V: questio et epistola*," *Archivum Franciscanum Historicum* 11 (1918): 309–373. For analysis, see Marco Bartoli, "Olivi et le pouvoir du pape," in *Pierre de Jean Olivi (1248–1298): pensée scolastique, dissidence spirituelle et société*, ed. Alain Boureau et Sylvain Piron, Études de philosophie médiévale 79 (1999): 173–191; Burr, *Olivi and Franciscan Poverty*, 166–169; and Burr, *Spiritual Franciscans*, 69–75.

9. Gary Dickson, "The Crowd at the Feet of Pope Boniface VIII: Pilgrimage, Crusade, and the First Roman Jubilee (1300)," *Journal of Medieval History* 25 (1999): 279–307.

10. Emil Frieberg, ed., *Corpus iuris canonici* (I.8.1), 2 vols. (Graz, 1955), 2: 1245–1246.

11. See Burr, *Spiritual Franciscans*, 137–158 (on the Clementine settlement with the bull *Exivi de paradiso*), and 159–177 (on the resolutions' subsequent collapse).

12. Moorman, *Franciscan Order*, 309–311; and Burr, *Spiritual Franciscans*, 191–206.

13. Peter Olivi, BNF 713, fol. 115va–b.

14. On the "foreign policy" of the Avignon papacy, see James Muldoon, *Popes, Lawyers, and Infidels: The Church and the Non-Christian World, 1250–1550* (Philadelphia, 1979); and Muldoon, "The Avignon Papacy and the Frontiers of Christendom: The Evidence of Vatican Register 62," *Archivium Historiae Pontificae* 17 (1979): 125–195.

15. Text in Peter John Olivi, *Peter Olivi's Rule Commentary: Edition and Presentation*, ed. David Flood (Wiesbaden, 1997).

16. *Olivi's Rule Commentary*, 192–194 (Rev. 6:12; 9:13; 7:12).

17. Ibid., 194–196, quotation from p. 195.

18. See Burr, *Olivi's Peaceable Kingdom*, 78–82; Henri de Lubac, *La postérité spirituelle de Joachim de Flore* (Paris, 1978), 93–104; and Lee, Reeves, and Silano, *Western Mediterranean Prophecy*, 17–26.

19. See David Burr, "Bonaventure, Olivi, and Franciscan Eschatology," *Collectanea Franciscana* 53 (1983): 23–40.

20. BNF 713, fols. 2va–b, 20rb–20vb, 128vb (citing Joachim on the "seven-headed dragon"); and fols. 142vb–143ra (citing Joachim on the "beast from the sea").

21. BNF 713, fol. 100ra–b. On Olivi's views of Islam, see Jean Flori, *L'islam et la fin des temps: l'interprétation prophétique des invasions musulmanes dans la chrétienté médiévale* (Paris, 2007), 388–391.

22. BNF 713, fols. 5vb–6ra, 19vb, 79vb–80ra, 118vb–119ra, 141rb–141va.

23. Ibid., fols. 2vb, 79va–b, 78va.

24. Ibid., fols. 20va–b, 135va–b.

25. Ibid., fol. 119va.

26. Ibid., fols. 4ra, 133rb–133va, 146va–b. On Olivi's theory of a double Antichrist, see Burr, *Olivi's Spiritual Kingdom,* 132–165; and Bernard McGinn, *Antichrist: Two Thousand Years of the Human Fascination with Evil* (New York, 2000), 159–162.

27. BNF 713, fols. 19vb–20ra.

28. Ibid., fol. 11vb.

29. For example, in his commentary on Rev. 11:2, Olivi, BNF 713, fol. 119ra, suggests that the "court" outside of the Temple does not refer to the "Greeks" (as indicated by Joachim of Fiore) but rather to the carnal Latin Church, as the Greeks were in a state of schism and already cut off from the Latins since the beginning of the fifth seal. On the "inward shift" of Olivi's exegesis, see Robert Lerner, *The Feast of St. Abraham: Medieval Millenarians and the Jews* (Philadelphia, 2002), 61.

30. BNF 713, fol. 2vb.

31. Ibid., fols. 2va, 6rb, 12ra–vb, 48vb–49ra, 88va, 93va, 115ra–115vb, 133rb–va.

32. Ibid., fol. 118ra–b.

33. Ibid., fol. 93vb.

34. Ibid., fols. 6rb, 12ra–b, 133rb–va. Recently, Olivi's ideas about the conversion of the Jews have received considerable attention. See David Burr, "The Antichrist and the Jews in Four Thirteenth-Century Apocalypse Commentaries," in *Friars and Jews in the Middle Ages and Renaissance,* ed. Seven McMichael and Susan Myers, The Medieval Franciscans 2 (Leiden, 2004), 23–38; Lerner, *Feast of St. Abraham,* 54–72; and Lerner, "Peter Olivi on the Conversion of the Jews," in *Pierre de Jean Olivi,* 207–216.

35. BNF 713, fol. 153vb: *Nec mirum si locus nostre redemptionis super omnia loca terre tunc temporis exaltetur, et maxime quia ad conversionem totius orbis et ad gubernationem totius iam converse ille locus erit congruentior summis rectoribus orbis tanquam centrale medium terre habitabilis.* See also Burr, *Spiritual Franciscans,* 87; and Lerner, *Feast of Saint Abraham,* 66.

36. On Arnold's life and apocalypticism, in addition to Lubac, *La postérité spirituelle,* 110–114, and Lee, Reeves, and Silano, *Western Mediterranean Prophecy,* 27–46, see Robert Lerner, "The Pope and the Doctor," *The Yale Review* 78 (1988–1989): 62–79; and Lerner, "Ecstatic Dissent," *Speculum* 67 (1992): 33–57, especially pp. 42–46.

37. There has been some confusion in the past about whether Arnold visited Paris twice (in 1299 and 1300) or once (in 1300) to address the university masters, cleared up in favor of the latter position by Michael McVaugh, "Arnaud de Vilanova and Paris: One Embassy or Two?" *Archives d'histoire doctrinale et littéraire du moyen âge* 73 (2006): 29–42.

38. Arnold of Villanova, *Tractatus de tempore de adventu antichrist*, in *Aus den Tagen Bonifaz VIII: Funde und Forschungen*, ed. Heinrich Finke (Münster, 1902), cxxix–clix.

39. Ibid., cxxxv.

40. Arnold of Villanova, *De mysterio cymbalorum d'Arnau de Vilanova*, ed. Joseph Perarnau i Espelt, Arxiu de Textos Catalans Antics 7–8 (Barcelona, 1988–1989), 7–169.

41. For Arnold's appeal to Rome, including an account of his intimidation by the Paris theologians, see no. 616, *Chartularium universitatis Parisiensis*, ed. Heinrich Denifle and Émile Chatelain, 4 vols. (Paris, 1889), 2: 87–90.

42. In 1306, as part of his ongoing effort to defend his views, Arnold produced a commentary on the Book of Revelation: Arnold of Villanova, *Expositio super Apocalypsim*, ed. Ioachim Carreras i Artau, Arnaldi de Villanova: Scripta Spiritualia 1 (Barcelona, 1971). On Arnold's time in Sicily, see Clifford Backman, "Arnau de Vilanova and the Franciscan Spirituals in Sicily," *Franciscan Studies* 50 (1990): 3–29

43. See Elizabeth A. R. Brown and Robert Lerner, "On the Origins and Import of the Columbinus Prophecy," *Traditio* 45 (1989): 219–256, quotation from p. 251.

44. Burr, *Spiritual Franciscans*, 111–112.

45. On the Beguines' apocalypticism, see Lerner, *Feast of Saint Abraham*, 66–72; Potestà, "Radical Apocalyptic Movements," 118–120; Lee, Reeves, and Silano, *Western Mediterranean Prophecy*, 47–74; and Burr, *Spiritual Franciscans*, 248–254.

46. The Italian "Apostolics" were founded in Parma by a layman, Gerardo Segarelli. When he was burned as a heretic in 1300, Dolcino assumed leadership of the group. See Potestà, "Radical Apocalyptic Movements," 111–114; and Arnaldo Segarizzi, ed., *Historia fratris Dulcini heresiarche*, Rerum Italicarum Scriptores 9/5 (Lapi, 1907).

47. *De secta illorum qui se dicunt de ordine Apostolorum*, in *Historia fratris Dulcini heresiarche*, 24–25.

48. *Historia fratris Dulcini heresiarche*, 8–9.

49. For analysis and a critical edition of the *Genus nequam* prophecy, see Martha Fleming, *The Late Medieval Pope Prophecies: The* Genus nequam *Group*, Medieval and Renaissance Texts and Studies 204 (Tempe, 1999). In his ground-breaking study on the subject, Herbert Grundmann, "Die Papstprophetien des Mittelalters," *Archiv für Kulturgeschichte* 19 (1929): 77–138 (also in *Ausgewahlte Aufsätze*, Schriften der Monumenta Germaniae Historica 25/2 [Stuttgart, 1977], 1–57), argued that the set of prophecies was compiled ca. 1304 by an Italian Spiritual Franciscan. Reopening this issue, Robert Lerner, "On the Origins of the Earliest Latin Prophecies: A Reconsideration," in *Fälschungen im Mittelalter: Internationaler Kongress der Monumenta Germaniae Historica München, 16.–19. September 1986*,

33/5 (Hannover, 1988), 611–635, argued based in part on the earliest manuscript evidence for an English origin, with portions circulating perhaps as early as 1277. Marjorie Reeves, "The *Vaticinia de Summis Pontificibus:* A Question of Authority," in *Intellectual Life in the Middle Ages: Essays Presented to Margaret Gibson,* ed. Lesley Smith and Benedicta Ward (London, 1992), 145–156, assigned the text a "Joachimist" Franciscan origin in southern France. Responding to recent scholarship and manuscript discoveries, Robert Lerner, "Recent Work on the Origins of the 'Genus nequam' Prophecies," *Florensia* 7 (1993): 141–157, disagreed with Reeves on the southern French, Spiritual Franciscan origin, retracted his argument for an English provenance, and settled on their creation in Italy, but *not* necessarily from within Spiritual Franciscan circles. Regardless of their precise origin, everyone would seem to agree with Fleming, *Pope Prophecies,* 1, that the prophecies were "linked historically with the fortunes of the Italian Spiritual Franciscans."

50. Critical edition in Fleming, *Pope Prophecies,* 147–187.

51. Konrad Burdach, ed., *Commentarius in S. Cyrilli Oraculum,* in *Vom Mittelalter zur Reformation,* vol. 2/4 (Berlin, 1912), 241–327, especially pp. 269–270.

52. Ibid., 280–283, 290–293, 298–303.

53. For a partial edition of the *Liber de flore,* see Herbert Grundmann, "Liber de flore: Eine Schrift der Franziskaner-Spiritualen aus dem Anfang des 14. Jahrhunderts," *Historisches Jahrbuch* 49 (1929): 33–91 (also in *Ausgewahlte Aufsätze,* 101–165).

54. See Gian Luca Potestà, *Angelo Clareno dai poveri eremeti ai Fraticelli,* Istituto storico italiano per il medio evo: nuovi studi storici 8 (Rome, 1990); and the introduction to Angelo Clareno, *Opera I: Epistole,* ed. Lydia von Auw, Istituto storico italiano per il medio evo: fonti per la storia d'Italia 103 (Rome, 1980), xxii–xxv.

55. Angelo Clareno, *Liber chronicarum, sive, tribulationum ordinis minorum,* ed. Giovanni Boccali, trans. Marino Bigaroni, Pubblicazioni della biblioteca francescana chiesa nuova 8 (Porziuncola, 1999). On Clareno and his work, see Reeves, *Influence of Prophecy,* 210–212; Lubac, *La postérité spirituelle,* 104–110; and Burr, *Spiritual Franciscans,* 95–96, 279–304. Clareno's fellow Spiritual Franciscan, Ubertino of Casale, pursued some similar themes in his *Arbor vitae crucifixae Jesu* (1485; Turin, 1961); and *De septem statibus ecclesie,* in *Abbatis Joachimi Florensis scripta* (Venice, 1516).

56. Angelo Clareno, *Liber chronicarum,* 771–784; see also Burr, *Spiritual Franciscans,* 183–190.

57. Angelo Clareno, *Liber chronicarum,* 412–416, 446–448.

58. Ibid., 470–476.

59. Ibid., 546–554, 572–594. See also Angelo Clareno, *Expositio super regulam fratrum minorum,* ed. Giovanni Boccali, trans. Marino Bigaroni, Pubblicazioni della biblioteca francescana chiesa nuova 7 (Porziuncola, 1995), 705–720. In his commen-

tary on the twelfth chapter of the rule, drawing upon Olivi, Clareno emphasized that Francis's preaching to the "infidel nations" represented an apocalyptic sign of the sixth seal.

60. In addition to Piron, "Censures et condemnation," 339–349, and Burr, *Spiritual Franciscans*, 179–212, see Malcolm Lambert, "The Franciscan Crisis under John XXII," *Franciscan Studies* 32 (1972): 123–143; and Thomas Turley, "John XXII and the Franciscans: A Reappraisal," in *Popes, Teachers, and Canon Law in the Middle Ages*, ed. James Ross Sweeney and Stanley Chodorow (Ithaca, N.Y., 1989), 74–88.

61. See Piron, "Censures et condemnation," 349–358; Leo Amorós, "Series condemnationem et processum contra doctrinam et sequaces Petri Ioannis Olivi," *Archivum Franciscanum Historicum* 24 (1931): 495–514; and Joseph Koch, "Der Prozess gegen die Postille Olivis zur Apokalypse," RTAM 5 (1933): 302–315.

62. For the Latin refutation of the (now lost) Catalan tract, see José Pou y Martí, *Visionarios, Beguinos y Fraticellos catalanes (siglos XIII–XIV)* (1930; Alicante, 1996), 661–697; see also Piron, "Censures et condemnation," 344–345, 351.

63. BNF lat. 3318A, fols. 1r–277v. On the production and contents of this work, perhaps written by the Dominican theologian William of Laudun, see Koch, "Der Prozess," 303–304; Turley, "John XXII," 83–85; Burr, "Antichrist and the Jews," 34–36; and Piron, "Censures et condemnation," 350–351.

64. BNF lat. 3318A, fols. 1r, 4r, 17v–22v, 137v.

65. Ibid., fols. 13r–15r, 25r, 33r-v. The anonymous critic's commitment to refuting the notion of a "second" conversion of the Gentiles led him to posit the unusual notion that the number of converted Jews would be much larger than the number of Gentiles who remained loyal to Christ during the tribulations of Antichrist. In fact, he argued that the ratio of Jews-to-Gentiles at the end of time would be opposite to the ratio of Gentiles-to-Jews during the initial period of apostolic conversion after Christ. See Burr, "Antichrist and the Jews," 34–36.

66. BNF lat. 3318A, fols.37v–38r, quotation from fol. 38r: *Item quod conversio ad veram fidem et ecclesiam catholicam magis fiat per tales schismaticos et infideles non est credendum.*

67. Ibid., fols. 165v–166v.

68. BNF lat. 4190, fols. 40r–49r, quotation from fol. 41r. These subsequent charges, *Alligationes super articulis tractatis per dominum papam de postilla quam composuit frater Iohannis super Apocalpsim,* date from around 1325. See Koch, "Der Prozess," 312–313, and Piron, "Censures et condemnation," 365–367.

69. BNF lat. 4190, fols. 48r–49r.

70. BBTSOF, 3: 424–452, quotation from pp. 442–443. On this episode at Tabriz, see Decima Douie, *The Nature and Effect of the Heresy of the Fraticelli* (Manchester, U.K., 1932), 186–190.

71. BBTSOF, 3: 444.

72. Ibid., 447–451.

73. Ibid., 450.

74. Ibid., 450–451.

75. See Jeanne Bignami-Odier, *Jean de Roquetaillade (Johannes de Rupescissa)*, Extraits de l'histoire littéraire de la France 41 (1952; Paris, 1981); Jean-Pierre Torrell, "La conception de la prophétie chez Jean de Roquetaillade," MEFRM 102 (1990): 557–576; the introduction to John of Rupescissa, *Liber secretorum eventorum*, ed. Robert Lerner and Christine Morerod-Fattebert, Spicilegium Friburgense: textes pour servir à l'histoire de la vie chrétienne 36 (Fribourg, Switz., 1994), 13–85; Lee, Reeves, and Silano, *Western Mediterranean Prophecy*, 75–88; and Lerner, *Feast of Saint Abraham*, 73–88.

76. See John of Rupescissa (Jean de Roquetaillade), *Liber ostensor quod adesse festinant tempora*, ed. Clémence Thévenaz Modestin and Christine Morerod-Fattebert, Sources et documents d'histoire du moyen âge publiées par l'École française de Rome 8 (Rome, 2005), 509–537.

77. John of Rupescissa, *Oraculum Cyrilli cum commentaries de ps. Ioachim et Iohannis de Rupecissa*, BNF 2599, fols. 1r–244v. This text was written ca. 1348.

78. John of Rupescissa, *Liber secretorum eventorum*, 89–218.

79. John of Rupescissa, *Vademecum in tribulatione*, in Orwin Gratius, *Fasciculus rerum expetendarum*, ed. Edward Brown, 2 vols. (London, 1690), 2: 497–498.

80. See the appendix to Modestin and Morerod-Fattebert, *Liber ostensor*, 865–956, for an exhaustive discussion of the prophetic sources used by John.

81. On war between France and England, see the letter of John of Rupescissa, *Vos misistis*, in *Fasciculus rerum expetendarum*, 2: 494 (also in the chronicle of William of Nangis and his continuators, *Chronique latine de Guillaume de Nangis de 1113 à 1300*, ed. Hercule Géraud, 2 vols. [Paris, 1863], 2: 234–237). On the plague, see Robert Lerner, "The Black Death and Western European Eschatological Mentalities," in *The Black Death: The Impact of the Fourteenth-Century Plague*, ed. Daniel Williman, Medieval and Renaissance Texts and Studies 13 (Binghamton, N.Y., 1982), 77–105.

82. John of Rupescissa, *Liber ostensor*, 175–178; and *Vademecum*, 499. See Reeves, *Influence of Prophecy*, 416–428; and Robert Lerner, "'Popular Justice': Rupescissa in Hussite Bohemia," in *Eschatologie und Hussitismus*, ed. Alexander Patschovsky and František Šmahel, Historica series nova suppl. 1 (Prague, 1996), 39–52.

83. John of Rupescissa, *Liber secretorum eventorum*, 141; and *Vademecum*, 498.

84. On John's general "views of the East," see Louis Boisset, "Vision d'orient chez Jean de Roquetaillade," MEFRM 102 (1990): 391–401.

85. John of Rupescissa, BNF lat. 2599, fol. 64r–65v. I would like to thank Marc Boilloux for sharing his transcription of these folios to aid my reading of the manuscript. On these negotiations between the pope and the Greek emperor, see the *Chronica generalium ministrorum ordinis fratrum minorum*, Analecta Franciscana 3 (Quarachi, 1897), 508.

86. John of Rupescissa, BNF lat. 2599, fol. 65r: *Futurum est enim ut regnum Grecorum tradatur Turcis, Sarracenis et Tartaris affligendum, donec venerit et mortuus fuerit Antichristus, et tunc perfecte ad fidem revenient et semetipsos in ovile Christi concludent.*

87. John of Rupescissa, *Liber ostensor*, 266–268.

88. John of Rupescissa, *Liber secretorum eventorum*, 192; *Liber ostensor*, 111, 129–130, 191; and *Vademecum*, 497, 502.

89. John of Rupescissa, *Liber secretorum eventorum*, 160, 188–189.

90. John of Rupescissa, *Liber ostensor*, 264–268, suggested that the Eastern Antichrist would perform a similar role by gathering schismatics and infidels under his banner, setting the stage for their ultimate conversion after his defeat.

91. Ibid., 191.

92. Ibid., 261.

93. Ibid., 253, 261.

94. John of Rupescissa, *Liber secretorum eventorum*, 194; and *Liber ostensor*, 297–298.

95. John of Rupescissa, *Liber ostensor*, 383–386.

96. Ibid., 229–230, 621–630; and *Vademecum*, 498.

97. John of Rupescissa, *Liber secretorum eventorum*, 197–198.

98. Ibid., 194; and *Vademecum*, 502. See Mark Dupuy, "The Unwilling Prophet and the New Maccabees: John de Roquetaillade and the Valois in the Fourteenth Century," *Florilegium* 17 (2000): 229–250.

99. BNF 2599, fol. 205v: *Et sedes generalis ecclesie et imperii Romani in Ierusalem transferetur. Et Roma dabitur in desolationes deserti usque ad finem mundi. Et efficientur Iudei fidelissimi et sanctissimi Christiani et ex eis assumeretur ad papatum et ad gubernaculam orbem terre.*

100. See Anton Kern, "Der 'Libellus de notitia orbis' Johannes III (de Galonifontibus?) O. P. Erzbishop von Sulthanyeh," *Archivum Fratrum Praedicatorum* 8 (1938): 82–123.

101. Ibid., 100.

102. Sometime around 1318–1340 (most likely ca. 1330), a second set of pope-prophecies appeared, the so-called *Ascende calve* group. In the early fifteenth century, around the time of the Council of Constance, the *Genus nequam* and *Ascende calve* prophecies were combined to form what became known as the *Vaticina de summis pontificibus*. For analysis and a critical edition of the *Ascende calve* group,

see Orit Schwartz and Robert Lerner, "Illuminated Propaganda: The Origins of the 'Ascende calve' Pope Prophecies," *Journal of Medieval History* 20 (1994): 157–191; see also Fleming, *Pope Prophecies*, 5.

103. Marsilius of Padua, *The Defensor Pacis of Marsilius of Padua*, ed. C. W. Previté-Orton (Cambridge, 1928), 447.

104. See Anne Borelli and Maria Pastore Passaro, trans. and eds., *Selected Writings of Girolamo Savonarola: Religion and Politics, 1490–1498* (New Haven, 2006), xv–xxxi, quotation from p. xxiii; see also Reeves, *Influence of Prophecy*, 429–504.

Epilogue

1. Torbio Motolinía, *Motolinía's History of the Indians of New Spain*, trans. Elizabeth Foster (Albuquerque, 1950), 159–167.

2. Ibid., 165.

3. Ibid., 166.

4. See John Phelan, *The Millennial Kingdom of the Franciscans in the New World* (1956; Berkley, 1970).

5. *The Book of Prophecies Edited by Christopher Columbus*, ed. Robert Rusconi, trans. Blair Sullivan, Repertorium Columbianum 3 (Berkeley, 1997), 59.

6. On the centrality of prophecy to Columbus's interpretation of his own explorations, see Pauline Moffit Watts, "Prophecy and Discovery: On the Spiritual Origins of Christopher Columbus's 'Enterprise of the Indies,'" *American Historical Review* 90 (1985): 73–102; D. C. West, "The Abbot and the Admiral: Joachite Influences in the Life and Writings of Christopher Columbus," in *Il profetismo gioachimita tra quattrocento e quinquecento: Atti del IIII congresso internazionale di studi gioachimiti*, ed. Gian Luca Potestà (Geneva, 1991), 461–473; Valerie I. J. Flint, *The Imaginative Landscape of Christopher Columbus* (Princeton, 1992); and Djelal Kadir, *Columbus and the Ends of the Earth: Europe's Prophetic Rhetoric as Conquering Ideology* (Berkeley, 1992).

7. See James Muldoon, "*Auctoritas, Potestas* and World Order," in *Plenitude of Power: The Doctrines and Exercises of Authority in the Middle Ages*, ed. Robert Figueira (Aldershot, U.K., 2006), 125–139.

8. Thomas of Malvenda, *De Antichristo libri undecim* (Rome, 1604).

9. Ibid., 54.

10. See Bernard McGinn, *Antichrist: Two Thousand Years of the Human Fascination with Evil* (New York, 2000), 229, 231–233.

11. Karl Löwith, *Meaning in History: The Theological Implications of the Philosophy of History* (Chicago, 1949), 202–203.

12. Christopher Dawson, *Religion and the Rise of Western Culture* (New York, 1950), 3–19, quotation from pp. 9–10.

13. Ibid., 12. The emphasis is Dawson's own. On the role of medieval Christian universalism in modern formulations of a "common humanity," see also John Headley, *The Europeanization of the World: On the Origins of Human Rights and Democracy* (Princeton, 2007), 66–102, who strikes an apologetic tone for the value of Western contributions to global political culture and notions of human rights.

14. Arno Froese, "How Will the World Become One?" *Midnight Call* (April 2008): 7–12.

15. For some perspectives on the American apocalyptic imagination, in addition to McGinn, *Antichrist*, 250–280, see Stephen Stein, "American Millennial Visions: Towards Construction of a New Architectonic of American Apocalypticism," in *Imagining the End: Visions of Apocalypse from the Ancient Middle East to Modern America,* ed. Abbas Amanat and Magnus Bernhardsson (London, 2001), 187–211; and Paul Boyer, "The Middle East in Modern American Popular Prophetic Belief," in *Imagining the End,* 312–335.

Select Bibliography

Manuscripts Consulted

British Library:
    Cot.Tib.B.V Part II
    Lat. 11439 (add.)
Bibliotèque Nationale de France:
    Lat. 713
    Lat. 1706
    Lat. 2599
    Lat. 3319
    Lat. 3381A
    Lat. 4190
    Lat. 5018
    Lat. 8898
    Lat. 12971
    Lat. 14778
    Lat. 15157
    Lat. 16300
    Lat. 16397
Vatican:
    Lat. 3822
    Lat. 4959
    Lat. Ross. 753

Primary Sources

Adso of Montier-en-Der. *De ortu et tempore antichristi necnon et tractatus qui ab eo de-pendunt.* Ed. Daniel Verhelst. CCCM 45. Turnholt, 1976.

Alberic of Trois-Fontaines. *Albrichi monachi Triumfontium chronicon.* Ed. Paul Scheffer-Boichorst. MGH SS 23. Hannover, 1874.

Alberigo, Joseph, ed. *Conciliorum oecumenicorum decreta.* 3rd ed. Bologna, 1973.

Albert of Aachen. *Historia Hierosolymitana,* 265–713. RHC Occ 4.

Alexander of Roes. *Notitia saeculi.* In *Alexander von Roes Schriften,* ed. Herbert Grund-mann and Hermann Heimpel, 149–171. Stuttgart, 1958.

Amorós, Leo. "Series condemnationem et processum contra doctrinam et sequaces Petri Ioannis Olivi." *Archivum Franciscanum Historicum* 24 (1931): 495–514.

Andrea, Alfred J. *The Capture of Constantinople: The* Hystoria Constantinopolitana *of Gunther of Pairis.* Philadelphia, 1997.

———. *Contemporary Sources for the Fourth Crusade.* The Medieval Mediterranean 29. Leiden, 2000.

Angelo Clareno. *Liber chronicarum, sive, tribulationum ordinis minorum.* Ed. Giovanni Boccali. Trans. Marino Bigaroni. Pubblicazioni della Biblioteca francescana Chiesa nuova 8. Porziuncola, 1999.

Anselm of Havelberg. *Dialogi,* 1139–1248. PL 188.

Arnold of Villanova. *Expositio super Apocalypsim.* Ed. Ioachim Carreras i Artau. Cor-pus philosophorum medii aevi: Arnaldi de Villanova scripta spiritualia 1. Barce-lona, 1971.

———. *Tractatus de tempore de adventu Antichristi.* In *Aus den Tagen Bonifaz VIII: Funde und Forschungen,* ed. Heinrich Finke, cxxix–clix. Münster, 1902.

Baldric of Dol. *Historia Jerosolimitana,* 1–111. RHC Occ 4.

Baraut, Cipriano. "Un tratado inédito de Joaquín de Fiore: 'De vita Sancti Benedicti et de officio divino secundum eius doctrinam.'" *Analecta Sacra Tarraconensia* 24 (1951): 33–122.

Benz, Ernst. "Joachim Studien II: Die Exzerptsätze der Pariser Professoren aus dem Evangelium Aeternum." *Zeitschrift für Kirchengeschichte* 51 (1932): 415–455.

Benzo of Alba. *Sieben Bücher an Kaiser Heinrich IV. (ad Heinricum IV. imperatorem libri VII).* Ed. Hans Seyffert. MGH scriptores rerum Germanicarum (in us. schol.) 65. Hannover, 1996.

Bonaventure. *In hexaëmeron collationes.* In *Opera omnia* 5, 329–449. Quaracchi, 1882–1889.

Brown, Elizabeth, and Robert Lerner, "On the Origins and Import of the Columbi-nus Prophecy," *Traditio* 45 (1989): 219–256.

Burdach, Konrad, ed. *Commentarius in S. Cyrilli oraculum.* In *Vom Mittelalter zur Refor-mation,* 241–327, vol. 2/4. Berlin, 1912.

Caffaro Caschifelone. *De liberatione civitatum orientis liber,* 41–73. RHC Occ 5.

Cerbanus Cerbanus. *Translatio mirifici martyris Isidori a Chio insula in civitatem Venetam,* 321–334. RHC Occ 5.

Christopher Columbus. *The Book of Prophecies Edited by Christopher Columbus.* Ed. Robert Rusconi. Trans. Blair Sullivan. *Repertorium Columbianum* 3. Berkeley, 1997.

Cowdrey, H. E. J. *The Epistolae Vagantes of Pope Gregory VII.* Oxford, 1972.

De unitate ecclesiae conservanda, ed. Ernst Sackur, 173–284. MGH Ldl 2.

Dörrie, Heinrich. "Drei Texte zur Geschichte der Ungarn und Mongolen: Die Missionsreisen des Fr. Iulianus O.P. ins Ural-Gebiet (1234/5) und nach Russland (1237) und der Bericht des Erzbishofs Peter über die Tartaren." *Nachrichten der Akademie der Wissenschaften in Göttigen aus dem Jahre 1956: Philologische-Historische Klasse* 6 (1956): 125–202.

Ekkehard of Aura. *Hierosolymita.* Ed. Heinrich Hagenmeyer. Tübingen, 1877.

Fleming, Martha H. *The Late Medieval Pope Prophecies: The* Genus Nequam *Group.* Medieval and Renaissance Texts and Studies 204. Tempe, 1999.

Fuhrmann, Horst, ed. *Das Constitutum Constantini (Konstantinische Schenkung) Text.* MGH fontes iuris Germanici antique 10. Hannover, 1968.

Fulcher of Chartres. *Historia Hierosolymitana.* Ed. Heinrich Hagenmeyer. Heidelberg, 1913.

García y García, Antonius, ed. *Constitutiones concilii quarti Lateranensis una cum commentariis glossatorum.* Series A: Monumenta iuris canonici 2. Vatican City, 1981.

Gerhoh of Reichersberg. *Commentarius in psalmos,* ed. Ernst Sackur, 411–502. MGH Ldl 3. Hannover, 1897.

———. *De investigatione Antichristi liber I,* ed. Ernst Sackur, 304–395. MGH Ldl 3. Hannover, 1897.

———. *De quarta vigila noctis,* ed. Ernst Sackur, 503–525. MGH Ldl 3. Hannover, 1897.

———. *Libellus de ordine donorum Sancti Spiritus.* Ed. Damien Van den Eynde and et al. Gerhohi Praepositi Reichersbergensis opera inedita 1. Rome, 1955.

———. *Libri III de investigatione Antichristi, unacum tractatu adversus Graecos.* Ed. Friederic Scheibelberger. Gerhohi Reicherbergensis Praepositi Opera Hactenus Inedita 1. Linz, 1875.

Gilbert of Tournai. "Collectio de scandalis ecclesiae." *Archivum Franciscanum Historicum* 24 (1931): 33–62.

Golubovich, Girolamo. *Biblioteca bio-bibliografica della terra santa e dell'oriente Francescano.* 5 vols. Quaracchi, 1906–1927.

———. "Disputatio Latinorum et Graecorum seu relatio apocrisariorum Gregorii IX de gestis Nicaeae in Bythnia et Nymphaeae in Lydia." *Archivum Franciscanum Historicum* 12 (1919): 418–470.

Gregory VII. *Das Register Gregors VII (Gregorii VII registrum lib. I-IV).* Ed. Erich Caspar. MGH epp. sel. in us. schol. 2. Berlin, 1955.

Grundmann, Herbert. "Zur Biographie Joachims von Fiore und Rainers von Ponza." *Deutsches Archiv für Erforschung des Mittelalters* 16 (1960): 437–546.

Guibert of Nogent. *Dei gesta per Francos et cinq autre texts.* Ed. R. C. B. Huygens. CCCM 127A. Turnhout, 1996.

Hagenmeyer, Heinrich, ed. *Epistulae et chartae ad historiam primi belli sacri spectantes: Die Kreuzzugsbriefe aus dem Jahren 1088–1100.* 1901; Hildesheim, 1973.

Hiestand, Rudolf, ed. *Papsturkunden für Kirchen im Heiligen Lande.* Abhandlungen der Akademie Wissenschaften in Göttingen 136. Göttingen, 1985.

Hill, Rosalind, ed. *The Deeds of the Franks and the Other Pilgrims to Jerusalem (Gesta Francorum et aliorum Hierosolymitanorum).* Oxford, 1972.

Holder-Egger, Oswald. "Italienische Prophetieen des 13. Jahrhunderts. I." *Neues Archiv der Gesellschaft für Ältere Deutsche Geschichtskunde* 15, 143–178. Hannover, 1890.

———. "Italienische Prophetieen des 13. Jahrhunderts. II." *Neues Archiv der Gesellschaft für Ältere Deutsche Geschichtskunde* 30, 323–386. Hannover, 1905.

———. "Italienische Prophetieen des 13. Jahrhunderts. III." *Neues Archiv der Gesellschaft für Ältere Deutsche Geschichtskunde* 33, 97–187. Hannover, 1908.

Honorius Augustodunesis. *Expositio in Cantica Canticorum,* 347–496. PL 172.

———. *Gemma animae,* 541–738. PL 172.

———. *Speculum ecclesiae,* 807–1108. PL 172.

———. *Summa Gloria,* ed. Ernst Sackur, 63–80. MGH Ldl 3. Hannover, 1897.

Humbert of Romans. *Opusculum tripartitum (excerpta de tractandis in concilio Lugdun.).* In *Veterum scriptorum et monumentorum,* ed. Edmund Martène and Ursin Durand, 174–198. Vol. 7. 1733; New York, 1968.

Humbert of Silva Candida. *Libri III adversus simoniacos,* ed. Friedrich Thaner, 95–253. MGH Ldl 1. Hannover, 1891.

Innocent III. *Regestum Innocentii III papae super negotio Romani imperii.* Ed. Friedrich Kempf. Miscellanea Historia Pontificae 12. Rome, 1947.

———. *Die Register Innocenz' III.* Ed. Othmar Hageneder et al. 8 vols. Graz-Cologne, 1964–.

James of Vitry. *The Historia Occidentalis of Jacques de Vitry: A Critical Edition.* Ed. John Hinnebusch. Fribourg, 1972.

———. *Lettres de Jacques de Vitry.* Ed. R. B. C. Huygens. Leiden, 1960.

———. *Libri duo, quorum prior orientalis sive Hierosolymitanae alter occidentalis historiae nomine inscribitur.* 1597; Farnborough, 1971.

Jerome. *Commentariorum in Danielem libri III<IV>.* Ed. Francis Glorie. CCSL 75A. Turnhout, 1964.

Joachim of Fiore. *Abbot Joachim of Fiore: Liber de concordia novi et veteris testamenti.* Ed. E. Randolph Daniel. American Philosophy Society 73. Philadelphia, 1983.

———. *Enchiridion super Apocalypsim.* Ed. Edward Kilian Burger. Studies and Texts 78. Toronto, 1986.

———. *Exhortatorium Iudeorum.* Ed. Alexander Patschovsky. Fonti per la storia dell'Italia medievale: antiquitates 26. Rome, 2006.

———. *Expositio in Apocalypsim.* 1527; Frankfurt, 1964.

———. *Intelligentia super calathis.* In *Gioacchino da Fiore: aspetti inediti della vita e delle opera,* ed. Pietro de Leo, 135–148. Rome, 1988.

————. *De prophetia ignota: eine frühe Schrift Joachims von Fiore.* Ed. Matthias Kaup. Monumenta Germaniae Historica Studien und Texte 19. Hannover, 1998.

————. *Psalterium decem cordarum.* 1527; Frankfurt, 1965.

————. *Tractatus super quatuor evangelia.* Ed. Francesco Santi. Fonti per la storia dell'Italia medievale 17. Rome, 2002.

Joachim of Fiore (Pseudo). *Abbatis Joachim divina prorsus in Jeremiam prophetam interpretatio.* Cologne, 1577.

————. *Super Esaiam prophetam, abbatis Joachimi Florensis scripta.* Venice, 1516.

John of Rupescissa (Jean de Roquetaillade). *Liber ostensor quod adesse festinant Tempora.* Ed. Clémence Thévenaz Modestin and Christine Morerod-Fattebert. Sources et documents d'histoire du moyen âge publiées par l'École française de Rome 8. Rome, 2005.

————. *Liber secretorum eventorum.* Ed. Robert Lerner and Christine Morerod-Fattebert. Spicilegium Friburgense: textes pour servir à l'histoire de la vie chrétienne 36. Fribourg, Switz., 1994.

———— *Vademecum in tribulation.* In Orwin Gratius, *Fasciculus rerum expetendarum,* ed. Edward Brown, 297–498. Vol. 2. London, 1690.

Kedar, Benjamin. "On the Origins of the Earliest Laws of Frankish Jerusalem: The Canons of the Council of Nablus." *Speculum* 74 (1999): 310–335.

Kohler, Charles. "Deux projets de croisade en terre-sainte composés a la fin du XIIe siècle et au début de XIVe." *Revue de l'Orient Latin* 10 (1904): 406–457.

Lupprian, Karl-Ernst, ed. *Die Beziehungen der Päpste zu islamischen und mongolischen Herrschern im 13. Jahrhundert anhand ihres Briefwechsels.* Studi e Testi 291. Vatican City, 1981.

Matthew Paris. *Chronica Majora.* 7 vols. RS 57.

Oliver Scholasticus. *Die Schriften des kölner Domscholasters, späteren Bishofs von Paderborn und Kardinalbishofs von S. Sabina.* Ed. Hermann Hoogeweg. Bibliotek des Litterarischen Vereins in Stuttgart 202. Tübingen, 1894.

Orderic Vitalis. *The Ecclesiastical History of Orderic Vitalis.* Ed. and trans. Marjorie Chibnall. 6 vols. Oxford, 1980.

Otto of Freising. *Chronica sive historia de duabus civitatibus.* Ed. Adolfus Hofmeister. MGH SS (in us. schol.) 45. Hannover, 1912.

Peter John Olivi. *De Usu Paupere: The Quaestio and the Tractatus.* Ed. David Burr. Italian Medieval and Renaissance Studies: The University of Western Australia 4. Perth, 1992.

————. *Peter Olivi's Rule Commentary: Edition and Presentation.* Ed. David Flood. Wiesbaden, 1972.

Peter Tudebode. *Historia de Hierosolymitano itinere.* Ed. John H. Hill and Laurita L. Hill. Memoirs of the American Philosophical Society 101. Philadelphia, 1974.

Potestà, Gian Luca. "Die Genealogia: ein frühes Werk Joachims von Fiore und die Anfänge seines Geschichtsbildes." *Deutsches Archiv für Erforschung des Mittelalters* 56 (2000): 55–101.

Prosper of Aquitaine. *De vocatione omnium gentium*, 647–722. PL 51.

Ralph of Coggeshall. *Chronicon Anglicanum*. RS 66.

Raymond d'Aguilers. *Le "Liber" de Raymond d'Aguilers*. Ed. John Hugh Hill and Laurita Hill. Documents relatifs à l'histoire des croisades 9. Paris, 1969.

Raymund Llull. *Quomodo Terra Sancta recuperari potest*. Ed. Blanca Garí and Fernando Domínguez Reboiras. CCCM 28. Turnhout, 1959.

Riant, Paul, ed. *Exuviae Sacrae Constantinopolitanae*. 2 vols. Geneva, 1878.

Robert of Auxerre. *Roberti canonici S. Mariani Autissiodorensis Chronicon*, ed. Oswald Holder-Egger, 216–276. MGH SS 26. Hannover, 1882.

Robert the Monk. *Historia Hierosolomitana*, 717–882. RHC Occ 3.

Roger Bacon. *Opus Tertium*, 3–310. RS 15/1.

———. *Opus Minus*, 311–390. RS 15/1.

———. *The 'Opus Majus' of Roger Bacon*. Ed. John Henry Bridges. 2 vols. 1897; Frankfurt, 1964.

Roger of Hoveden. *Chronica*. 4 vols. RS 51.

Rupert of Deutz. *Liber de divinis officiis*. Ed. Hrabanus Haacke. CCCM 7. Turnhout, 1967.

———. *De sancta trinitate et operibus eius*. Ed. Hrabanus Haacke. CCCM 21, 22, 24. Turnhout, 1971–1972.

———. *De victoria verbi dei*. Ed. Hrabanus Haacke. MGH QG 5. Hannover, 1970.

Sackur, Ernst, ed. *Sibyllinische Texte und Forschungen: Pseudomethodius, Adso und Tiburtinische Sibylle*. Turin, 1963.

Salimbene of Adam. *Cronica*. Ed. Guiseppe Scalia. CCCM 125/125A. Turnhout, 1998.

Santifaller, Leo, ed. *Quellen und Forschungen zum Urkunden- und Kanzleiwesen Papst Gregors VII*. Biblioteca Vaticana studi e testi 190. Vatican City, 1957.

Sbaralea, J. H., ed. *Bullarium Franciscanum Romanorum pontificum constitutiones, epistolas, ac diplomata continens*. 8 vols. Rome, 1759.

Selge, Kurt-Victor. "Eine Einführung Joachims von Fiore in die Johannesapokalypse." *Deutsches Archiv für Erforschung des Mittelalters* 46 (1990): 85–131.

Thomas Aquinas. *Commentum in quattuor libros sententiarum magistri Petri Lombardi*. In *Opera Omnia* 7/2. Parma, 1863.

———. *Contra impugnantes dei cultum et religionem*. In *Opera Omnia* 15. Parma, 1864.

———. *Summa theologica*. In *Opera Omnia* 2. Parma, 1853.

Thomas of Celano. *Vita prima S. Francisci Assisiensis et eiusdem legenda*. Analecta Franciscana 10. Quaracchi, 1926.

Tondelli, Leone, and Marjorie Reeves, eds. *Gioachino da Fiore: Il libro delle figure*. Turin, 1953.

Urban II. *Epistolae et privilegia*, 283–552. PL 151.

Van den Wyngaert, Anastasius. *Sinica Franciscana: itinera et relationes fratrum minorum saeculi XII et XIV*. Quaracchi, 1929.

Wannenmacher, Julie E. *Hermeneutik der Heilsgeschichte: De septem sigillis und die sie-*

ben Siegel im Werk Joachims von Fiore. Studies in the History of Christian Traditions 118. Leiden, 2005.

Will, Cornelius. *Acta et scripta quae de controversiis ecclesiae graecae et latinae saeculo undecimo composita extant.* Leipzig, 1861.

William of Tripoli. *Tractatus de statu Saracenorum et de Mahomete pseudo-propheta et eorum lege et fide.* In *Kulturgeschichte der Kreuzzüge,* ed. Hans Prutz, 575–598. Berlin, 1883.

Zimmermann, Harald, ed. *Papsturkunden 896–1046.* In *Österreichische Akademie der Wissenschaften philosophische-historische Klasse* 17/2. Vienna, 1985.

Acknowledgments

Although writing can make one feel like an anchorite, producing a book is a cenobitic experience. This particular book would not exist without Alfred J. Andrea, Emeritus Professor of History at the University of Vermont, who first introduced me to the historian's craft. He also read an early draft of this entire manuscript, greatly enhancing its quality. At the University of Vermont, I also thank Robert Rodgers and Denise Youngblood for helping to get me started. At Stanford University, my special thanks go to Philippe Buc, who challenged me to try new things, along with Brad Gregory (now at Notre Dame), Kathryn Miller, Richard Roberts, and Paula Findlen. Among my former peers at Stanford, my warm thanks to Alexander Bay, Emily Burrill, Holly Case, Shachar Link, and Jehangir Malegam. Since leaving Stanford, the circle of friends and colleagues who have helped me has constantly widened, including Jay Rubenstein and Matthew Gabriele, who read and commented on multiple chapters of this book. At the University of North Carolina, Chapel Hill, I would like to thank Chad Bryant, Melissa Bullard, Kathleen DuVal, John Headly, Lloyd Kramer, Michael McVaugh, and Richard Pfaff. My thanks also go to Adrian Lentz-Smith, Robert Lerner, Bernard McGinn, and Mattias Riedl, along with Marc Boilloux, George Dameron, Christopher

Egger, Matthias Kaup, Warren Lewis, Gui Lobrichon, Christine Morerod, David Perry, Paul Spaeth and Julia Wannenmacher. Finally, my thanks to Kathleen McDermott and Mary Ellen Geer at Harvard University Press, along with the Press's outside readers who critiqued an earlier version of this book. Whatever shortcomings remain, I claim as my own.

For financial support, I would like to thank the Stanford University Dean's Office, the Medieval Academy of America, and the UNC, Chapel Hill Research Council for travel funds. A Geballe Fellowship (2004–2005) at the Stanford Humanities Center provided me with an ideal situation to finish my early work on this project. At UNC, Chapel Hill, a semester of faculty leave along with a junior faculty development grant helped me to finish this project.

Beyond the academy, I owe debts of gratitude to so many friends and family that I cannot list them all. In no particular order, I would like especially to thank my brother Bradley Whalen, my father Thomas Whalen, my stepfather Paul S. Guare, the late Paul H. Guare, Bob, Diana, and Robert McLeod, Craig, Iva, and Vita Vezina, Isabelle and Arthur Baudiment, James T. Whitcomb, Seema Sohi and Andy Green, and Seth Marineau, along with Louis Marineau and Sons and the Kellogg-Hubbard Library. This is book is dedicated to my mother, Lynn, who encouraged my imagination and taught me the love of reading. Last, but certainly not least, my heartfelt thanks go to my wife, Malissa McLeod, who helps me to strike that difficult balance between the life of the mind and the life well lived. Going beyond the call of duty, she even read a draft of this entire manuscript—her own personal form of a medieval ordeal.

Index